A Brief History of Japanese Civilization

A Brief History of Japanese Civilization

Second Edition

Conrad Schirokauer
Senior Scholar, Columbia University

David Lurie
Columbia University

Suzanne Gay
Oberlin College

Australia • Brazil • Japan • Korea • Mexico • Singapore • Spain • United Kingdom • United States

A Brief History of Japanese Civilization, Second Edition
Conrad Schirokauer, Senior Scholar, Columbia University
David Lurie, Columbia University
Suzanne Gay, Oberlin College

Publisher: Clark Baxter

Assistant Editor: Paul Massicotte

Editorial Assistant: Lucinda Bingham

Technology Project Manager: David Lionetti

Marketing Manager: Lori Grebe Cook

Marketing Assistant: Teresa Jessen

Project Manager, Editorial Production: Katy German

Creative Director: Rob Hugel

Art Director: Maria Epes

Print Buyer: Judy Inouye

Permissions Editor: Kiely Sisk

Production Service: Graphic World Inc.

Text & Cover Designer: Andrew Ogus

Photo Researcher: Terri Wright

Copy Editor: Graphic World Inc.

Cover Image: Seikadō Bunko Art Museum, Tokyo

Library of Congress Control Number: 2005927855
ISBN-13: 978-0-618-91522-4
ISBN-10: 0-618-91522-2

Wadsworth
10 Davis Drive
Belmont, CA 94002-3098
USA

Printed in United States of America
3 4 5 6 7 12 11 10 09

Dedicated to our spouses: Lore, Hikari Hori, and James Dobbins

our children:

David & Oliver, Emily & Jeffrey

and representing the next generation:

Leo Kipton and Somiya

Contents

Preface

A revised edition such as this demands a new preface, because there is much about this book that is new. Most significantly, what was a solo has become a trio, extending our range and enriching our sound.

Before saying something about our collaboration, we need to affirm that some things said in earlier editions still apply. Certainly, the reasons for studying Japan are as urgent as ever and still can be subsumed under three broad headings: the richness of its long historical record, which forms an important part of the history of the human race and illuminates the nature of the human condition; the enduring value of its cultural achievements; and the contemporary importance of one of the world's strongest economies. Setting aside Japan's contemporary importance, surely some acquaintance with its civilization is required of one who would be an educated person, because to be educated means to be able to see beyond the narrow geographic, temporal, and cultural bounds of one's immediate neighborhood. Indeed, to be educated entails the ability to see oneself in a broader perspective, including that of history. In this day and age, that means not only the history of one's own tribe, state, or even civilization but also, ideally, the history of all humans—because it is all our history.

That history is woven of many strands, so we have economic and political history and the study of social structure, thought, and art. This text is based on the belief that an introduction to the history of a civilization requires consideration of all these facets of human activity—a general mapping out of the terrain so that the beginner may find his or her bearings and learn enough to consider in which direction to explore further, with some idea of the rewards to be gained for the effort. An introduction, then, is not a catalog (although it should contain basic data) or a personal synthesis or summation, nor is it the proper vehicle for extending the expanding frontiers of present knowledge. Instead, it should, among other things, introduce the reader to the conventions of a field of study and attempt to convey the state of our present understanding. The basic aim of this text, then, is to provide orientation. Thus, for example, where applicable, the standard framework provides the basic historical chronology. We have further decided to replace the B.C. and A.D. of previous editions with B.C.E. and C.E. (before and in the common era) because that seemed most appropriate for a twenty-first-century (C.E.!) book.

It also appears to have become standard—especially, but not exclusively—among students of the history of religion.

History is the study of change and continuity, and both elements are always present. Neither the people we study nor we ourselves begin with a blank slate, and our task is not to choose between change and continuity but the more challenging one of weighing the change within the continuity and the continuity within the change. Such a determination requires, in the final analysis, as much art as science, and no assessment is ever final. This is so not only because of the continual discovery of new evidence and new techniques (for example, in the dating of materials) but also because scholars' intellectual frameworks and analytic concepts change, and we all learn to ask new questions. Even if that was not the case, history would have to be rewritten at intervals, inasmuch as the ultimate significance of any individual historical episode depends, in the final analysis, on the whole story: as long as history is unfinished, so is its writing.

If this is true of all history, it seems especially so with the history of Japan and East Asia, about which we know a great deal more now than we did just a generation ago. Nevertheless, the areas of our ignorance continue to be enormous. Indeed, one of the continuing attractions of the field is that it offers great opportunities to the intellectually adventurous and hardy to work on major problems. Our hope is that the very inadequacies of a text such as this will spur some readers on to these endeavors. Thus, for this text to succeed, it must fail: readers must come away hungry, their appetites whetted but not satiated.

A broad survey such as this is by necessity based on the studies of many scholars (indeed, our pleasure in wide reading is matched only by our fear of inadvertent plagiarism). No attempt has been made to list all the works consulted. The suggested readings in the Appendix have been drawn up in the hope of meeting some readers' needs, not of acknowledging our indebtedness, although there is considerable overlap. It is also impossible to list all the individuals who contributed to this textbook by offering suggestions, criticism, and encouragement, or who helped by suggesting references, supplying a date or a translation for a term, and so forth. Similarly, we are unable to acknowledge individually the teachers, students, and colleagues who have influenced our thoughts about the broader problems of history, about Japan, past and present, and about the teaching of these subjects. As in the previous edition, however, the senior author, Conrad Schirokauer, wants to single out Professor Arthur F. Wright (1913–1976), scholar and humanist, whom he had the privilege of knowing as both teacher and friend. Similarly, David Lurie is grateful to Wayne Farris and Joan Piggott for the inspiration provided by their work and for the generosity with which they encouraged his explorations of early Japanese history. Suzanne Gay looks regularly to Japanese historians of the medieval period but also credits scholars in the West, such as Mary Elizabeth Berry, Hitomi Tonomura, and Andrew Goble, for extending the foundational work of John W. Hall.

In recent years scholarship has been so productive, as well as specialized, that it has become impossible for one person to keep up with it all, but we owe a debt to our colleagues at Columbia and Oberlin. Schirokauer wants to thank the members of the Department of East Asian Languages and Cultures, including fellow senior scholar Arthur Tiedemann, as well as Wm. Theodore de Bary, whose contributions and accomplishments are far too numerous to list here but include founding the Society for Senior Scholars. Also at Columbia, Lurie would like to thank his friends and comrades in teaching the Japanese history survey, Max Moerman and Greg Pflugfelder, for their advice, encouragement, and flexibility.

Although our interests remain broad, in the present edition there is a clear temporal division of responsibility. David Lurie is primarily responsible for Chapter 1 and Part II of Chapter 2, with an occasional assist from Schirokauer. Lurie also made revisions to Chapter 3 and suggested a few improvements to Chapter 4, which Suzanne Gay helped to bring up to date; she also made a major contribution to Chapter 5. Conrad Schirokauer is responsible for the remainder of the book but wants to point out that the "modern" (post-1600) chapters already appeared in *Modern East Asia: A Brief History*.

That we are different people is obvious at first sight: one of us is at the beginning of his career, charging up the tenure hill at full steam; another as a department chair may be said to be perched at the top of the hill; while the remaining author unabashedly claims senior discounts on trains and planes but not in his scholarly endeavors and hopes to demonstrate, to some at least, that he is not yet "over the hill." That we enjoyed our collaboration augurs well for the future. We have maintained our own voices and views even as we encourage our readers to develop their own.

Conrad Schirokauer
David Lurie
Suzanne Gay

Acknowledgments

We need to acknowledge those who contributed so much to the previous edition of this book and its precursors but will limit ourselves here to naming those directly involved in the present edition. These include Clark Baxter, Paul Massicotte, and the entire Wadsworth team as listed on the copyright page. We also want to thank the scholars whose critical reading of parts of the manuscript saved us from many an error of commission or omission, even though we did not always follow their advice. Several prefer to remain anonymous, but we can and do acknowledge Jeffrey Barlow, Wayne Farris, Fred G. Notehelfer, Margaret J. Pearson, and Marcia Yonemoto.

Among those at Columbia, special thanks are due the young scholars with whom Schirokauer has cotaught East Asian courses during the past few years, listed in chronological order: Jaret Weisfogel, Letty Chen, Naomi Fukumori, Katherine Rupp, Suzanne O'Brien, Nicole Cohen, Yasu Makimura, and Kerry Ross.

We also want to thank our students for fresh perspectives and ideas. Specifically, Lurie is grateful to the students in his Japan Civ. classes of Spring and Fall 2003 and especially to his teaching assistants: Adam Clulow, Michael Emmerich, Eric Han, Federico Marcon, and Leila Wice. He also thanks Adam Clulow and Steve Wills for reading parts of the manuscript and providing invaluable suggestions for their improvement.

Also deserving special mention are the staff of the Starr East Asian Library at Columbia for their help with books. For help in manuscript production and reproduction, we wish to thank Diana Nobile-Hernandez of the Heyman Center at Columbia.

Our greatest debt is to our families who have lived with this book and to whom it is dedicated. Lore, also known as Mrs. Schirokauer, not only helped in innumerable direct and indirect ways but also contributed greatly to the artwork, which includes a number of her own photographs.

Conrad Schirokauer
David Lurie
Suzanne Gay

About the Authors

Conrad Schirokauer currently serves as Senior Scholar and Adjunct Professor at Columbia University as well as Professor Emeritus at the City University of New York. In addition to *A Brief History of Chinese and Japanese Civilizations* (and its separate volumes on China and Japan), he has published articles on Song intellectual history and served as co-editor (with Robert Hymes) of *Ordering the World: Approaches to State and Society in Sung Dynasty China* and as translator of *China's Examination Hell,* by Miyazaki Ichisada.

David Lurie is an Assistant Professor in the Department of East Asian Languages and Cultures at Columbia University. His research concerns writing systems in Japan and, more broadly, in pre-modern East Asia; he also works on the cultural, intellectual, and literary history of Japan through the Heian Period. He is currently completing a manuscript titled *Realms of Literacy: Early Japan and the History of Writing.*

Suzanne Gay is a Professor of East Asian Studies at Oberlin College. Her research interests include the social and economic history of medieval Japan, with a particular emphasis on the role of commoners in history. Her monograph, *The Moneylenders of Late Medieval Kyoto,* was published by University of Hawaii Press in 2001.

KAZAKHSTAN
MONGOLIA
Lake Balkhash
Urumqi
KYRGYZSTAN
XINJIANG-UIGUR AUTONOMOUS REGION
Kashgar
Tarim R.
TARIM BASIN
Lake Lop
Lake Qinghai
G A N S U
NINGXIA-
HUI
A.R.
QINGHAI
Lanzhou
Wei R.
Qinling Mts.
PAKISTAN
TIBETAN AUTONOMOUS REGION
Tsangpo R.
Lhasa
SICHUAN
Yangzi R.
Chongqing
NEPAL
SIKKIM
BHUTAN
Kathmandu
Ganges R.
Brahmaputra R.
GUIZHOU
Kunming
Guiyang
YUNNAN
BANGLADESH
INDIA
Calcutta
GUANGXI
MYANMAR
Red R.
Hanoi
Irrawaddy R.
LAOS
VIETNAM
Mekong R.
Bay of Bengal
THAILAND

RUSSIA
SAKHALIN
Amur R.
HEILONGJIANG
KURILE ISLANDS (RUSSIA)
Harbin
Songhua R.
Ussuri R.
AUTONOMOUS REGION
JILIN
Vladivostok
Sapporo
HOKKAIDŌ
Shenyang
LIAONING
Yalu R.
Sea of Japan
BEIJING MUNICIPALITY
Beijing
NORTH KOREA
HONSHŪ
Tianjin
Lüda (Dalian)
P'yongyang
JAPAN
HEBEI
TIANJIN MUNICIPALITY
Seoul
Sendai
Yellow Sea
Jinan
Qingdao
SOUTH KOREA
Kyoto
Tokyo
Yellow R.
SHANDONG PENINSULA
Kobe
Pusan
Yokohama
Zhengzhou
Osaka
Nagoya
Huai R.
Grand Canal
JIANGSU
Nagasaki
SHIKOKU
Nanjing
ANHUI
Shanghai
KYŪSHŪ
SHANGHAI MUNICIPALITY
Hangzhou
Lake Poyang
ZHEJIANG
East China Sea
RYŪKYŪ ISLANDS
JIANGXI
Fuzhou
FUJIAN
Taipei
Pacific Ocean
TAIWAN
HONG KONG
PHILIPPINES
LUZON
China Sea
0 100 200 300 400 500 MILES
0 100 200 300 400 500 KILOMETERS

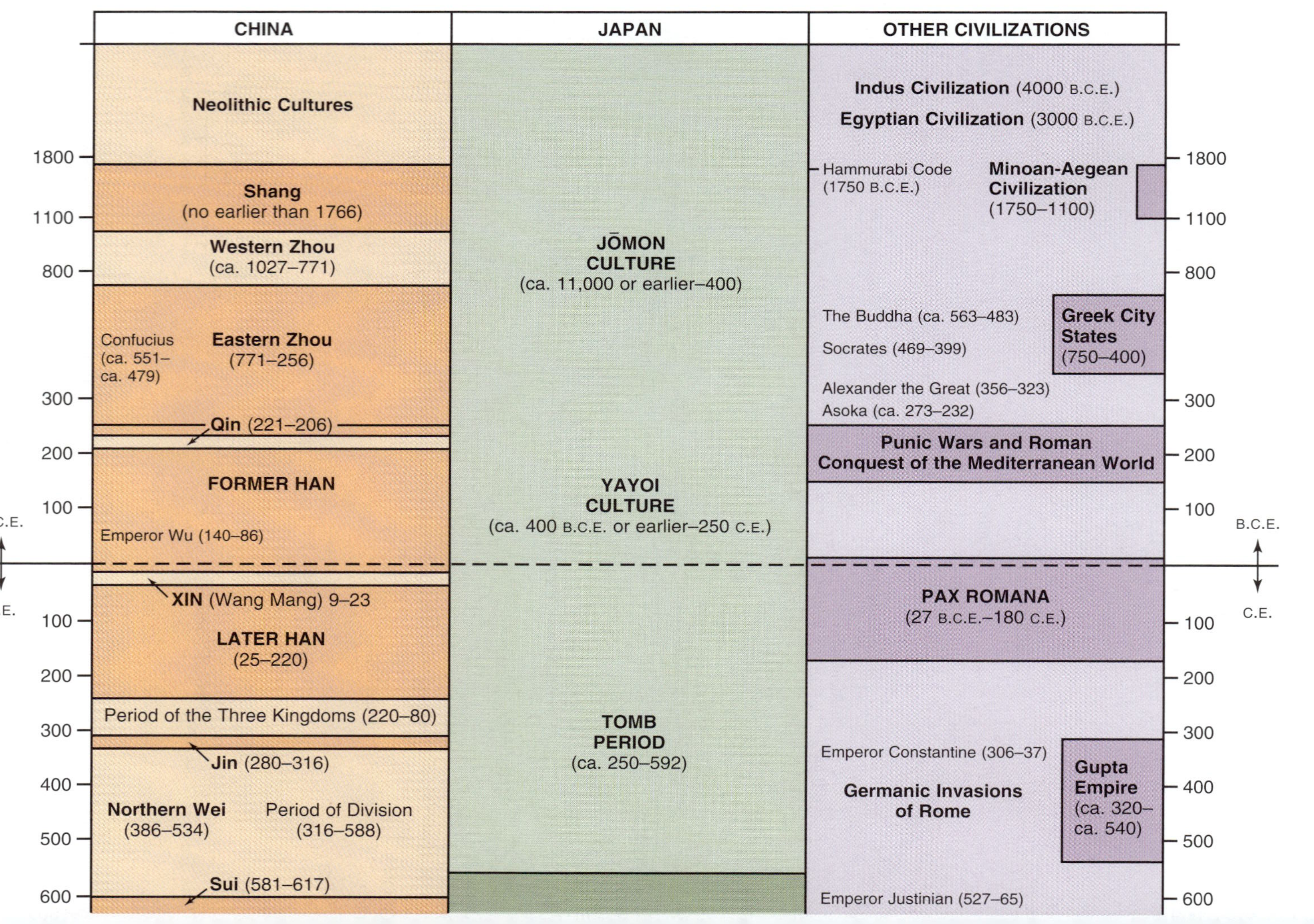
CHINA
JAPAN
OTHER CIVILIZATIONS
Neolithic Cultures
Shang
(no earlier than 1766)
Western Zhou
(ca. 1027–771)
Confucius
(ca. 551–
ca. 479)
Eastern Zhou
(771–256)
Qin (221–206)
FORMER HAN
Emperor Wu (140–86)
XIN (Wang Mang) 9–23
LATER HAN
(25–220)
Period of the Three Kingdoms (220–80)
Jin (280–316)
Northern Wei
(386–534)
Period of Division
(316–588)
Sui (581–617)
JŌMON
CULTURE
(ca. 11,000 or earlier–400)
YAYOI
CULTURE
(ca. 400 B.C.E. or earlier–250 C.E.)
TOMB
PERIOD
(ca. 250–592)
Indus Civilization (4000 B.C.E.)
Egyptian Civilization (3000 B.C.E.)
Hammurabi Code
(1750 B.C.E.)
Minoan-Aegean
Civilization
(1750–1100)
The Buddha (ca. 563–483)
Socrates (469–399)
Greek City
States
(750–400)
Alexander the Great (356–323)
Asoka (ca. 273–232)
Punic Wars and Roman
Conquest of the Mediterranean World
PAX ROMANA
(27 B.C.E.–180 C.E.)
Emperor Constantine (306–37)
Germanic Invasions
of Rome
Gupta
Empire
(ca. 320–
ca. 540)
Emperor Justinian (527–65)
1800
1100
800
300
200
100
B.C.E.
C.E.
100
200
300
400
500
600

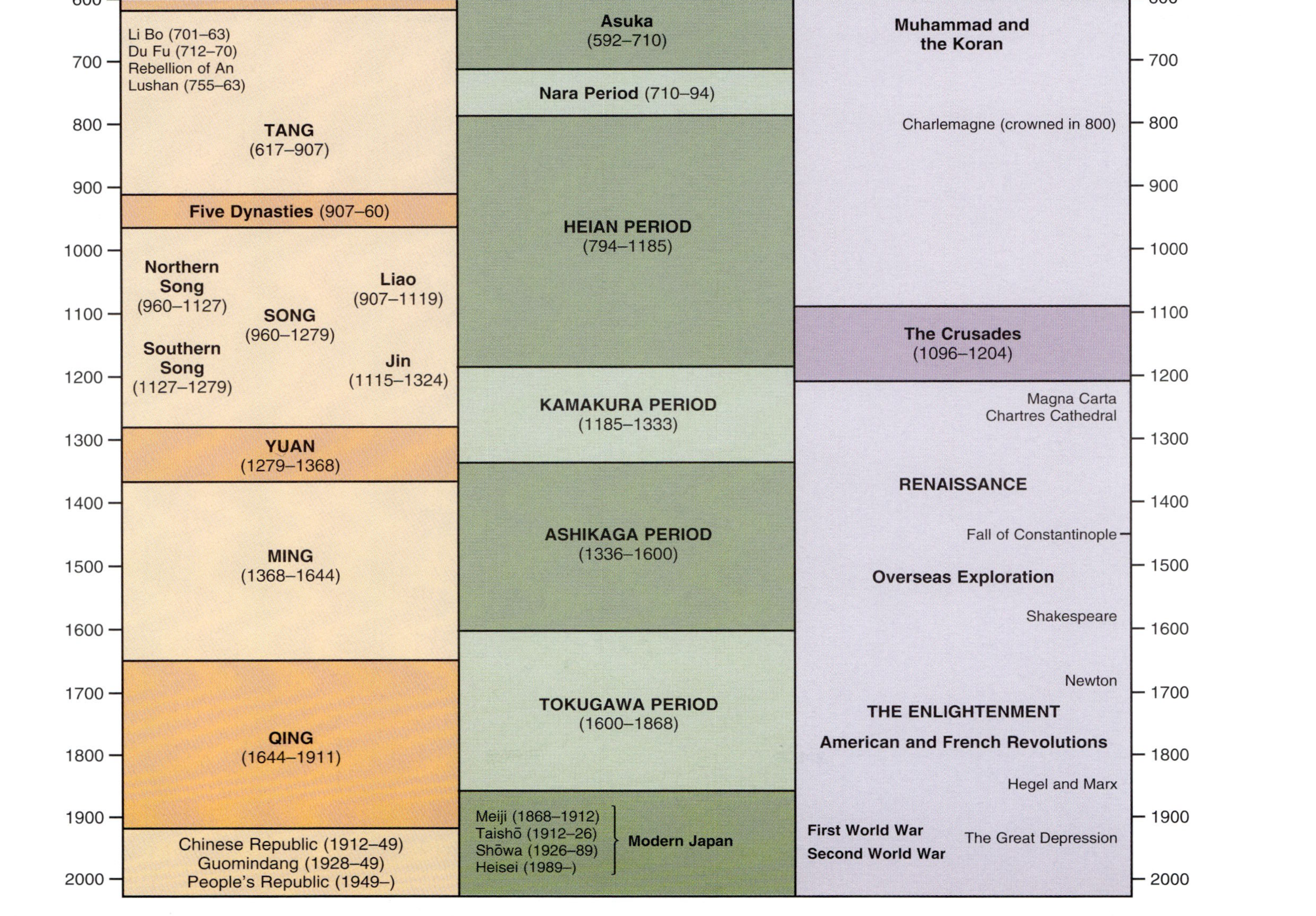

600
700
800
900
1000
1100
1200
1300
1400
1500
1600
1700
1800
1900
2000
Li Bo (701–63)
Du Fu (712–70)
Rebellion of An Lushan (755–63)
TANG (617–907)
Five Dynasties (907–60)
Northern Song (960–1127)
SONG (960–1279)
Liao (907–1119)
Southern Song (1127–1279)
Jin (1115–1324)
YUAN (1279–1368)
MING (1368–1644)
QING (1644–1911)
Chinese Republic (1912–49)
Guomindang (1928–49)
People's Republic (1949–)
Asuka (592–710)
Nara Period (710–94)
HEIAN PERIOD (794–1185)
KAMAKURA PERIOD (1185–1333)
ASHIKAGA PERIOD (1336–1600)
TOKUGAWA PERIOD (1600–1868)
Meiji (1868–1912)
Taishō (1912–26)
Shōwa (1926–89)
Heisei (1989–)
Modern Japan
Muhammad and the Koran
Charlemagne (crowned in 800)
The Crusades (1096–1204)
Magna Carta
Chartres Cathedral
RENAISSANCE
Fall of Constantinople
Overseas Exploration
Shakespeare
Newton
THE ENLIGHTENMENT
American and French Revolutions
Hegel and Marx
First World War
Second World War
The Great Depression

Part One

Beginnings and Foundations

In the chapters that form the first part of our book, we explore the seeds of what became Japan, the soil that nourished them, and the forces that stimulated their growth into a vibrant and complex civilization. A central part of our story is the growth of a center in a diverse environment where the very concept of centricity was molded under profound external influence. In these beginnings we can observe such interactive patterns as well as practices, achievements, and institutions that merit study in their own right, even as they set the stage for future developments of Japanese history.

Pair of Dancing *haniwa.* Ht. Left 22.3 in; right 25.2 in. Late Tomb Period. Konan site, Osato, Saitama Prefecture, Tokyo National Museum. Figures such as this, called *haniwa,* decorated the burial mounds that gave their name to the Tomb Period. They reveal much about life at the time—though it was by no means all song and dance! (TNM Image Archives, http://TNMArchives.jp)

1

The Prehistory of the Japanese Archipelago

Geography

Paleolithic Culture

Jōmon Culture

Yayoi Culture

Political and Social Developments

The Tomb Period

The Yamato Kings

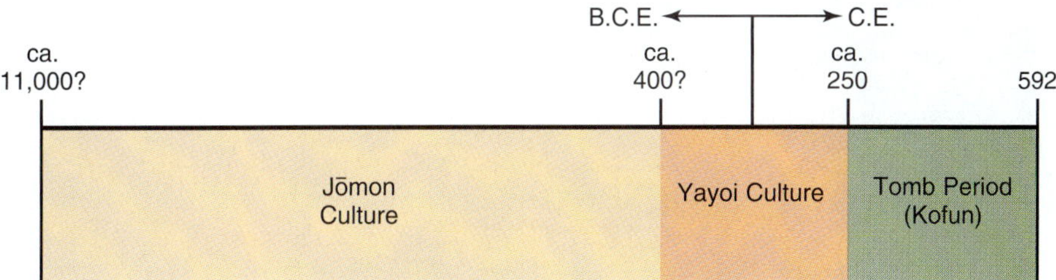

For many centuries before there were indigenous written records, people lived and cultures flourished in the Japanese archipelago. Gradually the groundwork was laid for what became the state and civilization known as "Japan." We begin by surveying the geography that shaped those developments, and go on to consider the Paleolithic, Jōmon, Yayoi, and Tomb Periods. These centuries are prehistory in that we must rely on archeological evidence supplemented by occasional accounts by outsiders. This is also prehistory in the sense that "Japan," the word and the concept, did not yet exist. In this sense we are dealing with Japan before there was a Japan.

Geography

If geography may be said to provide a stage for history, it is not only a revolving stage, following the rhythm of the seasons, but also an ever-changing one molded by natural and human energies. The modern nation we now know as Japan occupies the four main islands of Hokkaido, Honshu, Shikoku, and Kyushu (and dozens of smaller ones), stretching some 1500 miles from a latitude of forty-five degrees north (roughly that of Montreal) at the northern tip of Hokkaido to nearly twenty-four degrees north (parallel with the Bahamas) at the southernmost of the Ryukyu, or Okinawa, Islands (see Figure 1.1). With an area of about 146,000 square miles, Japan is much larger than Great Britain, slightly larger than Italy, and a bit smaller than California. Much is made of the supposed smallness of the country, but this is only in comparison to the largest nations, like China, the United States, or Russia.

In terms of physical geography, the modern political unit called Japan is part of a vast chain of islands separated from the eastern edge of the Asian continent

FIGURE 1.1 The Japanese archipelago.

by three bodies of water: the Sea of Okhotsk, the Sea of Japan, and the East China Sea. This island chain is part of a larger group of archipelagoes along the northwestern edges of the Pacific Ocean, including the Aleutian Islands to the north and the Philippines to the south. These archipelagos are homes to cultures that heavily depend on the ocean for food and transportation and are linked by straits and navigable seas to each other and to the Asian continent and its great Sinitic and Indic centers of civilization.

The Japanese archipelago, like its northern and southern neighbors, has been shaped by a confluence of powerful tectonic, climatic, and oceanic forces. It sits at the intersection of no fewer than four tectonic plates—the Pacific, North American, Eurasian, and Philippine Sea—and has therefore undergone a great deal of violent geologic upheaval. Even today, there are said to be as many as 1000 earthquakes and tremors per year and more than 40 active volcanoes. Because of this seismic activity, more than two-thirds of the archipelago consists of mountains, which are geologically young (about 5 million years old, in contrast to the American Rockies or Swiss Alps—formed tens of millions of years ago—or older mountain ranges like the Appalachians, which date back 500 million years) and therefore steep and rugged. Such steep mountain ranges produce fast-moving streams, rapid erosion, and attendant landslides and mudslides, preventing cultivation and extensive settlement. Hard to climb, they are also barriers to internal transportation and communication. This has helped preserve regional autonomy and diversity, but it has also resulted in widespread reliance on waterborne travel, especially along coastal routes connecting both adjacent and far-flung regions.

The sediment washed down from these steep slopes, as well as rich volcanic soil produced by numerous eruptions, collects in a few coastal plains, which make up only 13 percent of the archipelago's area but are tremendously fertile. A major factor in Japanese history has been this contrast between steep mountain ranges and the fertile plains they surround and isolate. The four most important plains are arranged in a rough line from west to east. The Tsukushi plain in northern Kyushu, close to advanced cultural centers on the Korean Peninsula and the Chinese continent, was an early center of social and technological development. On the main island of Honshu, at the head of Osaka Bay on the other end of the Inland Sea, the Kinai plain is the site of the famous former capitals at Nara and Kyoto. Further to the east are the Nobi plain, at the head of Ise Bay, and then the largest of them all, the great Kanto plain that surrounds modern Tokyo in eastern Honshu. This axis of fertile plains lies at the center of Japan's recorded history, and even today is the most heavily industrialized and urbanized part of the country.

The archipelago's steep mountains and coastal plains, in conjunction with its location between the Asian mainland and the Pacific Ocean, produce distinctive weather patterns. During the winter, prevailing winds blow across Asia, picking up moisture as they cross the Japan Sea, and then depositing it as snow on the northwestern sides of the mountains, but on the Pacific coast, winters are marked by dry winds and little precipitation. During the summer, warm moist air comes up from the south, making the climate in southern and central Japan warmer than its latitude would suggest. From the Ryukyu Islands to northeastern Honshu, early summer begins with a rainy season; in general, the archipelago has the largest amount of precipitation in the temperate zone. These differences in weather have affected the patterns of human settlement, as the areas along the Japan Sea are much less conducive to intensive agriculture than those on the Pacific side.

Ocean currents are another important environmental factor. Contributing to the warming of the Pacific side is the Kuroshio, or Japan Current, which flows up from the Philippines, through the Ryukyu Islands, and along the Pacific coast. In contrast, the Oyashio Current brings cold water along the Kuril Islands, around Hokkaido, and down both sides of northeastern Honshu. The Oyashio is rich in plankton and other marine nutrients.

The mixing of these warm and cold waters further contributes to the wealth of food, supporting many kinds of edible fish, shellfish, and seaweed in the waters surrounding the archipelago.

Except for the semitropical Ryukyu Islands in the south, the archipelago lies entirely in the temperate zone. However, its long north–south expanse, varied terrain, and differing weather patterns make for a variety of flora and fauna. Because of long periods of linkage by land bridges to the Asian continent, most of these are also found elsewhere in East Asia. Ample water and long, warm growing seasons create a paradise for plants and for dense forests of trees, many of which produce edible nuts or useful wood and fibers. Big mammals, such as mammoths, were wiped out by climate change and human predation, but monkeys, boar, bears, deer, and many other small animals remain, as do numerous water and land birds feasting on frogs, other amphibians, and all kinds of insects. Over the course of Japanese history, this varied repertoire of plants and animals has "offered humans a great variety of resources" and been capable of "many responses to human encroachment. Unquestionably that biological diversity has been critical to the archipelago's capacity to support a remarkably dense population for centuries on end."[1]

Paleolithic Culture

Until the end of the last Ice Age, about 12,000 years ago, land bridges periodically linked the Japanese archipelago to the Asian continent along the Sakhalin Peninsula in the north and the Korean Peninsula in the southwest. We may reasonably conjecture that early humans as well as plants and animals took these routes. However, while we have evidence that humans lived on the continent from at least 700,000 years ago, there is to date no undisputed evidence of a human presence in the Japanese archipelago before about 35,000 years ago.

It is likely that humans had arrived much earlier than that, but at any rate it is clear that by 30,000 years ago groups of them had spread throughout the archipelago, in what is known as the Late Paleolithic Period (Old Stone Age). It is thought that these Paleolithic peoples arrived over the southern land bridge. They were foragers who gathered plants, hunted, and fished, using stone blades and other tools similar to those found in sites elsewhere in Asia. Toward the end of the last Ice Age, there are indications of a cultural change of such magnitude that archeologists agree on the need to designate a new period.

Jōmon Culture

The Jōmon is both the first and the longest period of Japanese history: it lasted for more than 10,000 years. This period did not begin with a sudden departure from the preceding Paleolithic culture, but rather with the gradual appearance of several distinctive new features. These include bows and arrows and traps that enabled more hunting, more widespread gathering of foodstuffs, greater reliance on seafood, limited use of agriculture, larger communities, and the production of pottery. Indeed, it is its distinctive pottery that gives the period its name: Jōmon, literally "rope pattern," refers to characteristic markings imprinted on many pots by rolling knotted cords over the damp clay. In contrast to the Paleolithic, this period is often referred to as Neolithic ("New Stone Age"), although reliance on agriculture was less extensive than in most other prehistoric cultures given that label.

Subsuming 10,000-odd years of human life in diverse settings under a single designation should not obscure regional and temporal variety. Neolithic does not imply monolithic! It is best to see Jōmon as a "large, loosely integrated cultural complex."[2] The development of this complex seems to have been spurred by the arrival of new technologies and groups of people (especially from northeast Asia), as well as by responses to changes in climate and environment.

The warming that followed the end of the last Ice Age (12,000 years ago) separated the Japanese archipelago from the Asian mainland, leaving the closest point (in Kyushu) about 120 miles from the Korean Peninsula, near enough to be influenced by continental developments but far enough removed to develop its own ways. Within the archipelago the vegetation was transformed by the end of the Ice Age. In southwestern Honshu, Shikoku, and Kyushu, broadleaf evergreen trees dominated the forests, whereas broadleaf deciduous trees were common in northeastern Honshu and southern Hokkaido. The latter included many tree species, such as beeches and oaks, that produced edible nuts and acorns. These provided ready sources of food for Jōmon people to gather, store, transport, and consume, and to sustain the animals they hunted.

In the northeast, the plentiful marine life carried south by the Oyashio current, especially salmon, was an additional major source of food. Settlements along both the Sea of Japan and the Pacific Ocean subsisted on immense amounts of shellfish, leaving distinctive middens (mounds of discarded shells and other refuse) that are now prized sources of information for archeologists. Other sources of food meriting special mention include deer, yam-like tubers and other wild plants, and freshwater fish. Supported by the deciduous forests and an abundance of seafood, the population was concentrated in central and northern Honshu, but Jōmon sites range from Hokkaido to the Ryukyu Islands.

In addition to dietary evidence, these sites indicate the use of new technologies. There were spears and arrows with stone heads for hunting, pit traps for catching animals, and evidence of domesticated dogs (probably also used in hunting). Fishing equipment included nets, stone and bone hooks, harpoons, and weirs. Canoes could be used for fishing and transportation.

The Jōmon toolkit held other implements of wood and stone. There were shovels for unearthing roots and for digging pits and axes for felling trees to clear land for food-bearing plants and for cutting trees into lumber. More direct forms of cultivation appeared around 5000 B.C.E., but agriculture was never the primary means of sustenance. Foraging and hunting generally extracted enough food from the rich environment. There were mortars and pestles for grinding nuts and seeds,

FIGURE 1.2 Pots found in Jōmon sites are often strikingly creative in design, with surface decorations in regular patterns, and sometimes with a riot of abstract flame-like projections along the rims. (© The Cleveland Museum of Art, John L. Severance Fund, 1984.68)

drying mats for preserving food, and pits and aboveground structures for storage. Most notably, there was the famous pottery.

Jōmon pots are among the world's earliest. Recently discovered pottery has been dated as far back as 14,500 B.C.E., which would push back the beginning of the period considerably! Ceramics have been found in sites on the Asian mainland dated to the 15th millennium B.C.E., but it is possible that the world's first containers of baked clay were made in the Japanese archipelago. Many Jōmon vessels seem to have been used for storage and cooking, but the more elaborate pieces probably had ritual functions (see Figure 1.2). Other clay artifacts clearly had religious or magical significance, including figurines with bulging eyes, often found with one of the limbs broken off in what archeologists surmise may have been a fertility rite (see Figure 1.3). If the figure in our illustration concerns female fertility, the numerous stone rods identified as of the Jōmon Period are thought to have been phallic symbols.

Jōmon culture was marked by much regional variety, and temporal developments linked to changes in pottery styles lead archeologists to divide the period into several subperiods. Around the 7th millennium B.C.E., aboveground and semi-subterranean dwellings appear, and around 5000 B.C.E. characteristic living patterns developed. People now settled in stable communities, living mainly in pit dwellings with roofs of wood and thatch or earth. Villages often had larger, apparently communal wooden structures, which may have been storehouses. Subsequently, there were periods of thriving cultural activity in central Honshu between about 3000 and 2000 B.C.E., and then in the northeast from around 2000 B.C.E. through the first several centuries C.E. There is a tendency to think of hunter–gatherers as living lives of lack and scarcity, but Jōmon culture was surprisingly rich and complex, with sophisticated ceramic arts and extensive settled communities.

Yayoi Culture

FIGURE 1.3 Jōmon figurine, perhaps used in fertility rites. (© Scala/Art Resource, NY)

During the first millennium B.C.E., new living patterns and technologies began to appear. Archeologists see this as the beginning of a new period of prehistory, and call it Yayoi, after the part of Tokyo in which its distinctive pottery was first discovered (see Figure 1.4). Until recently, the Yayoi Period was thought to have begun around 400 B.C.E., but now carbon-dating results suggest that it may have to be pushed back as much as five centuries! At any rate, it is clear that during the last millennium B.C.E., a cluster of new technologies appeared in northern Kyushu and began to spread through much (though not all) of the archipelago. These include iron working, bronze-casting, glassmaking, weaving, and new techniques of woodworking. However, by far the most important new development was the cluster of food-producing technologies necessary for intensive agriculture.

In contrast to the limited role of agricultural products in the Jōmon diet, Yayoi people relied extensively on plant cultivation. The most notable method was wet rice agriculture, a laborious and time-consuming method of farming that yields more nourishment per unit of land than any other staple. Rice was initially grown in low-lying wetlands along rivers, but as earth-working techniques and organization improved, paddy fields were constructed and maintained on higher ground. Yayoi sites also show evidence of a wide range of other forms of agriculture, including dry cultivation, often in swidden (slash-and-burn) fields, of such crops as millet, barley, wheat, buckwheat, and beans. Several kinds of fruit trees contributed to a more varied diet, while people also continued to hunt and forage. As in Jōmon times and still today, the ocean yielded fish, shellfish, and seaweed, important foods alongside the newer farmed staples. Such continuities between Yayoi

FIGURE 1.4 Pottery jar excavated from Enda Site located in Zao-cho, Miyagi Prefecture, Japan, in the middle Yayoi Period. Small at the base and thin at the neck, the vessel is both functional and pleasing to the eye. It is similar to the form later developed to contain sake, but we do not know what it held originally. (© Tohoku University Archeology Laboratory)

and Jōmon are crucial to our understanding of the relationship between the two cultures.

The Jōmon-Yayoi transition did not occur all at once. New pottery types and other artifacts, as well as signs of widespread agriculture, first appeared in northern Kyushu, and then spread north and east, mainly along the Inland Sea and other waterways, over many centuries. The culture that spread through much of the archipelago in this way was neither unified nor homogenous. Individual regions were markedly different in their rates of change, patterns of community organization, and decorative and burial customs. In fact, there was no transition to Yayoi in northernmost Honshu and Hokkaido, where Jōmon culture persisted for many more centuries (archeologists refer to this northern continuation as Epi-Jōmon), or in the Ryukyus, where there are few signs of prehistoric agriculture and Jōmon is followed by a Shell Mound culture based on fishing and trading.

Vigorous debate about the nature of the transition between Jōmon and Yayoi continues. Given the Kyushu location of the earliest Yayoi sites and the similarities between their contents and those of contemporary sites on the Korean Peninsula, the overseas origins of the new technologies and subsistence patterns are clear. However, archeologists disagree about whether their spread through much of the Japanese archipelago was the result of the introduction and diffusion of new ideas or of the migration of large numbers of people. Anthropological and genetic studies of modern humans show similarities between the inhabitants of Korea and most of Japan, in a pattern consistent with the arrival of an immigrant population that spread out from Kyushu. Recent DNA testing of bones from Jōmon and Yayoi sites also suggests differences between their genetic makeup as well as genetic similarities between Yayoi and modern Japanese people. It seems safe to conclude that the transition to Yayoi culture was brought about by a complex process of migration and local adaptation, as people from the Korean Peninsula moved into northern Kyushu and then spread from there. (There also seems to have been mixing and intermarriage with pre-existing Jōmon populations along the way.) This hypothesis is further supported by the work of historical linguists examining the origins of the Japanese language.

Both the modern Japanese language and its earlier forms are very different from Chinese (itself a family of related languages, like the Romance tongues, rather than a single unified language). Japanese is often classified as an Altaic language, and as such would be related to Korean, Mongolian, and Turkish. In contrast to the Sinitic languages, these languages are agglutinative, which means that much of their expression of meaning involves the adding on (or "gluing" together) of words and word elements. Verbs and adjectives are highly inflected, with differences in tense, mood, level of formality, and so forth expressed by adding to the stem one element after another. There is no direct evidence of what languages were spoken by inhabitants of the archipelago during the Jōmon Period, or by the Yayoi migrants, but it is likely that the latter arrived speaking a language related to those spoken in the northeast of the Asian continent and the upper part of the Korean Peninsula. Such a Yayoi language (or languages), which probably absorbed elements of Jōmon tongues, is likely to have been the immediate ancestor of Japanese.[3]

Political and Social Developments

The emergence of extensive agriculture led to increased production of food, tools, weapons, clothing, and other artifacts, while a resulting rise in population intensified competition for resources, especially land and water. This competition, along with a need for greater organization created by the new forms of agriculture, contributed to the rise of communities with a clear division of labor and greater class stratification. There is no reason to think that relations among earlier groups of people were always peaceful, but now hostilities tended to accelerate into full-fledged warfare. This newly hierarchical and violent Yayoi order became the crucible in which more complex and powerful forms of social organization developed.

What happened is very clear archeologically. Life during the Jōmon Period was no picnic to begin with and apparently deteriorated over time. Skeletal remains show signs of disease and malnutrition, and a collapse of the food supply, perhaps brought on by climate change, is thought to have reduced the population dramatically in the centuries preceding the arrival of the Yayoi migrants. However, there are few signs of violent conflict in Jōmon sites, and though differences in dwelling structures and grave goods suggest a nascent social hierarchy, there does not seem to have been strong class differentiation. Yayoi communities, on the other hand, were frequently surrounded by moats and stockades, located on easily defended hilltops, and guarded by tall structures thought to have been watchtowers. Numerous weapons have been excavated from such sites, as have skeletal remains with such signs of violence as missing heads or embedded arrow points. Suggestions of an increasingly hierarchical society include large structures, thought to have been storehouses for surplus grain and other foods, and burials accompanied by valuable objects, often in elite areas separate from less lavish graves.

Underlying these developments was the emergence of small but growing political units, headed by chiefs who seem to have been in constant conflict with their neighbors. Some of these chiefs were in contact with authorities on the Korean Peninsula and beyond. They appear in Chinese records from the first century C.E. onward as "kings," in keeping with the Chinese court's diplomatic model of investiture. This was an idealized system according to which "barbarian" rulers on the periphery submitted to the central civilizing power of the Chinese emperor, and in return received official titles, ceremonial regalia, and valuable trade goods. As they fought amongst themselves and increased their domains and wealth, the "kings" of the "Wa" (the Chinese term for the inhabitants of the Japanese archipelago) relied on advanced technologies, raw materials (especially iron and bronze), and political legitimacy that could only be obtained through such interaction with the societies of the Korean Peninsula and, beyond it, the Chinese imperium.

The most extensive account of these circumstances is from the third-century Chinese history of the Wei Dynasty (220–265 C.E.). Chinese official histories contained sections describing peripheral cultures and their relations with Chinese states, and the history of the Wei is no exception. Its section on peripheral cultures includes a long description of life in the archipelago at the end of the late Yayoi Period. It portrays a society in constant warfare between small "kingdoms," temporarily united under a "queen" named Himiko (sometimes pronounced Pimiko), who used magical powers to rule a coalition of chiefdoms, assisted by her brother. Because the geographical directions provided by this account are garbled, the location of Himiko's kingdom of Yamatai remains a perennial topic of debate. The two leading candidates are northern Kyushu and the Kinai region. As mentioned previously, the earliest Yayoi sites are in northern Kyushu, which was the most technologically advanced part of the archipelago through at least the middle of the period. However, the subsequent center of political development was the Kinai area. Disagreement about the location of Yamatai concerns the extent of transregional authority during the Yayoi Period, and also the origins of the central kings who came to power in the following Tomb Period. There is no easy solution, but the weight of recent scholarly opinion favors the Kinai side.

The Tomb Period

The Tomb Period (mid-third century–late sixth century C.E.) is named for the great tombs (*kofun,* or "old burial mounds") that came to dominate the landscape in these centuries. These mounded tombs are the most ubiquitous and recognizable archeological feature of Japan: there are over 150,000 of them, spread throughout the three main islands of the archipelago (excluding Hokkaido). Usually overgrown with trees, and often treated as shrines by subsequent generations, the mounds can still be seen today, interrupting rice fields or looming over

FIGURE 1.5 Daisen Mound, Mozu, Sakai City, Osaka, from the Middle Tomb Period (Fifth Century). Its total length is approximately 892 yards. One theory about the square portion of the keyhole shape is that it originated in a platform for the performance of rituals for the deceased. (© Tomb of Emperor Nintoku, Mozu, Sakai City, Osaka)

residential areas (see Figure 1.5). An early type of these tombs first appeared in the Kinai area in the mid-third century. They continued to be built through the beginning of the seventh century, giving way eventually to Buddhist burial methods (in the remote northeast, the practice of building them continued for longer).

The increased status of elites in this period was symbolized by the size of the mounds and their isolation from settlements (though this changed in the sixth century). The largest mounds were surrounded by moats, and held one or more coffins within chambers that contained grave goods: protective or magical objects, such as mirrors and swords, as well as large numbers of valuable tools, ornaments, pieces of armor, saddles, and other horse trappings. The last items are emblematic of an important development: the arrival of horses, and horse-based methods of warfare, brought from the Korean Peninsula. The mounded tombs themselves had similar origins. They developed from the elite graves of the Yayoi Period, but they also seem to have been influenced by new Korean burial methods. The huge mounds were certainly dependent on imported technologies of surveying, earthmoving, and construction. The mounds came in many shapes and sizes, but the classic format was the keyhole shape, which joined together a square and a circular mound.

The tombs were sites for ceremonies performed on behalf of, or directed to, the dead. Offerings left outside included pottery dishes, which probably contained food, but the most characteristic items found on the surface of the tombs are low-fired clay statues called *haniwa.* Many of these are figurative, representing a wide variety of artifacts, animals, and people, including houses, weapons, musical instruments, boats, and agricultural tools; fish, pigs, birds, deer, monkeys, and especially horses; warriors, shamans, dancers, farmers, and servants. In some cases these figures seem to have been arranged to represent a procession, perhaps one honoring the occupant of the tomb.

Through around the beginning of the fifth century, mounds were often placed on slopes, or atop preexisting hills, which made them look larger. During the fifth century they began to be constructed in flat, open areas. The use of such arable land may have been a kind of conspicuous consumption. Being willing and able to take good food-producing land out of service showed a strong commitment to glorifying ones ancestors—or oneself, for the amount of time necessary to build the larger mounds suggests that rulers had theirs constructed while they were still alive. The fifth century features immense tombs, concentrated in Kinai (see Figure 1.5); the biggest are as long as 500 meters (almost a third of a mile), not counting the multiple moats that surrounded them. They are among the largest structures of the ancient world, rivaling the great pyramids of Egypt in volume (though not in height). In the sixth century, these massive mounds were abandoned, and tombs were constructed mainly on mountain slopes.

Changes in the size and location of the tombs were accompanied by changes in the style of coffins. Long wooden containers were replaced by huge chest-like stone sarcophagi, often quarried and shaped with great skill, and made from stone that had been transported long distances. Advanced techniques of stone-cutting and setting also produced another new feature of later tombs: the burial chamber. Early mounds were topped by shallow grave chambers, one for each burial, but later tombs were built on top of room-like chambers made of huge stones. These chambers, which could be reopened, may have had ritual functions, but they also allowed multiple interments.

These advanced techniques can be traced back to Chinese tomb-building practices, but it is clear that they were brought to the Japanese archipelago by stonemasons from the Korean Peninsula. This was another of the many ways in which "influence from the peninsula . . . played a crucial role in population growth, economic and cultural development, and the rise of a centralized Yamato state."[4]

The Yamato Kings

What was the source of the power of those buried in the immense tombs, and what kind of society supported them? As always, there was a relationship between wealth and power, with evidence suggesting that they grew in tandem. Especially from the fifth century, agricultural production grew spectacularly as new agricultural tools and techniques were brought from the Korean Peninsula. These included plows and new iron tools that facilitated clearing land and moving earth. Arable land was also expanded by building canals and improving irrigation, employing many of the skills necessary for constructing the giant mounds. There are also indications that fields were formally divided and allotted to farmers.

Trade grew. In the Kinai region, Osaka Bay in particular developed as a major port, leaving archeological evidence of large complexes of storehouses. Along with more local exchanges, there was trade through the Inland Sea to Kyushu and beyond it to the Korean Peninsula. Surplus production of food and other resources, monopolies over trade, and benefits derived from relationships with peninsular immigrant groups controlling advanced technologies made it possible for elites to muster the massive amounts of labor power necessary to build the huge tombs.

Many scholars have argued that the key to the political structure of this society lies in the way that the tombs themselves came to symbolize relationships of allegiance and fealty among the elites. The characteristic keyhole-shaped mound is thought to be a sign of allegiance to central chiefs in the Kinai region where they first emerged. After their initial appearance there, similar mound shapes came to be used elsewhere throughout the three main islands (Kyushu, Honshu, and Shikoku). Studies of bronze mirrors, one of the most common grave goods, also suggest a complex network of duplicate mirrors distributed from the Kinai region. This and other evidence suggests a developing hierarchy of regional chiefs with allegiances to a group of central rulers now known as the Yamato Kings, after an early term for the Kinai area that may be related to the name of Himiko's Yamatai. It is likely that these Yamato Kings controlled access to trade goods and advanced technologies, distributing them to regional leaders who were allies or subordinates. Such relationships were symbolized by tombs and mirrors, indicating a major religious component of power or, more likely, a fusion of what we think of as the religious and the secular. They provided for and honor the dead even as they reflected relations among the living.

Later written sources, very likely based on oral traditions, suggest that the fifth century also saw the development of a court centered on the emerging Yamato Kings. Associations of skilled craftsmen and technicians called *be* supplied the Yamato court with food, tools, weapons, clothing, and ornaments, and performed services, such as caring for horses or serving as scribes. Many of these *be* were composed of immigrants from the Korean Peninsula or their descendants. Another development at court was a system of hereditary kinship groups, or *uji* (sometimes translated as "clan"). These *uji* were corporations of households considered to constitute a kinship unit, inheriting a common name and common religious observances. Some *uji* monopolized ritual or military responsibilities, and others controlled particular *be* organizations. They were more political than familial groups, and certain lineages within them had additional hereditary titles that signified their rank within the putative kinship group and at court.

In the late-fifth and especially in the sixth century, the regional chiefs became less autonomous as they began to be incorporated into this system of kinship groups and titles, but they retained a great deal of independence. At court, high-ranking kinship groups, many of them of Korean origin, served the central kings, married into their families, and played a significant role in determining succession. At first the Yamato kings do not seem to have belonged to a single family, but in the sixth century a dominant lineage emerged. Even so, polygamy and loose principles of succession ensured there were always numerous candidates upon the death of a king, producing intense factional struggles between powerful kinship groups.

Despite power gained by the Yamato court over the course of the Tomb Period, the regional chiefs maintained considerable autonomy. The Yamato Kings reigned over a "segmented realm" with "fluid" connections to its periphery.[5] This realm did display many signs of nascent state formation, including high population concentrations in settled areas, an elite class supported by agricultural surpluses, payment of tribute, trade in luxury goods, construction of imposing structures, military power, craft and technical specialist groups, central kings with a court, and powerful noble families. However, several key developments had yet to come. There was no formal administrative structure, no laws or bureaucracy, and few signs of official ceremonies, taxation, or surveillance and control of outlying regions. The Yamato kings had no capital city and did not rule over an autonomous territory with clear borders. All of these things, however, were about to appear, as pressures from elsewhere in East Asia and internal developments led to the rapid emergence of the archipelago's first state over the course of the seventh century. This state both expressed and molded the emergent civilization of Japan.

Notes

1. Conrad Totman, *A History of Japan* (Oxford: Blackwell, 2000), p. 19.
2. Richard Pearson, *Ancient Japan* (New York: Arthur Sackler Gallery/George Braziller, 1992), p. 62.
3. On the Jōmon-Yayoi transition, see Mark Hudson, *Ruins of Identity: Ethnogenesis in the Japanese Islands* (Honolulu: Univ. of Hawaii Press, 1999).
4. Wayne Farris, *Sacred Texts and Buried Treasures: Issues in the Historical Archaeology of Ancient Japan* (Honolulu: Univ. of Hawaii Press, 1998), pp. 120–21.
5. Joan Piggott, *The Emergence of Japanese Kingship* (Stanford Univ. Press, 1997), p. 65.

2

The Early State: Chinese and Korean Influences

I. Chinese and Korean Backgrounds

Overview

Buddhism

Buddhism and the State

II. The Emergence of the Early Japanese State

The Late Tomb Period

The Seventh-Century Transition (the Asuka Period)

The Rise of the Soga

The 645 Coup d'Etat

The Defeat of 663

The Brief Civil War of 672

Nara as a Center and Symbol

Nara as a Religious Center

Documents and Structures

Writing and Literature

The Visual Arts

The End of the Nara Period

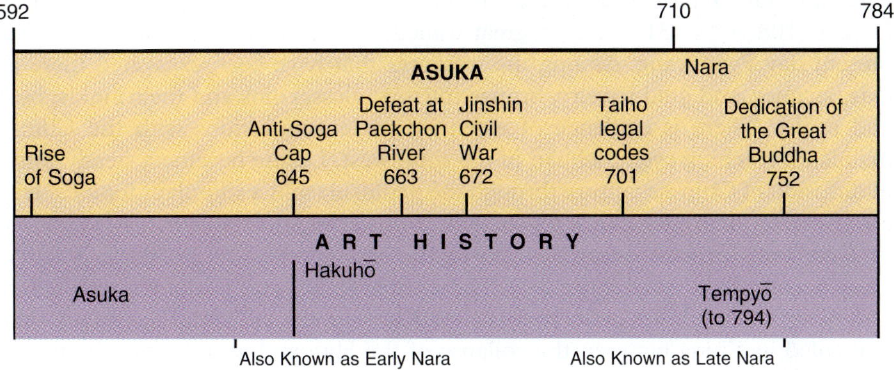

Beginning in the late Tomb Period, the interaction between events on the Korean Peninsula and the Chinese mainland became more intense and the flows of ideas, technologies, and techniques—as well as people—into the Japanese archipelago became ever more pronounced, paving the way for the development of the first Japanese state and new forms of elite culture. The changing entity called "Japan" had its roots in the Yayoi and Tomb Periods, but it is in the seventh century that it first comes clearly into view.

I. Chinese and Korean Backgrounds

For people in East Asia, China served as a model for governance, as a source of writing, and, above all, as a model of universally valid, time-tested principles, concepts, and patterns of doing things and organizing people. Buddhism originated in South Asia and began to flourish in China when the fall of the Han Dynasty (207 B.C.E.–220 C.E.) created a spiritual as well as political vacuum. Over the centuries, Buddhism simultaneously transformed and was transformed by Chinese civilization, until it came to pervade the cosmopolitan culture of Tang China and to serve as a carrier for an intensified spread of Chinese civilization to Korea and Japan. In the period considered in this chapter, the political, literary, cultural, and religious were deeply intertwined, but for the sake of analysis we will often consider them separately.

Overview

China was both the oldest and the most successful state in East Asia. In the first century B.C.E. people in what is now North Korea experienced this for themselves when the Han Dynasty established colonies there, the most successful of which was Lelang (108 B.C.E.–313 C.E.), a great walled city across the Taedong River from present-day Pyongyang. Among the treasures that have been excavated there are jade, lacquer, and gold jewelry, bronze mirrors, glass, coins and their molds, bells, and rattles. There is evidence of extensive trade connections with the Chinese mainland, reaching even Sichuan in the southwest. Lelang became a steady source of diffusion of Chinese culture through the peninsula and a stimulant for local leaders to create their own states, replacing less powerful and stable tribal federations. In Korea this process eventually led to the formation of three states: Koguryŏ, Paekche, and Silla (see Figure 2.1). These three states, and a southeastern federation of six small polities collectively called Kaya, interacted with the various states that ruled in China between the collapse of the Han and reunification by the Sui Dynasty (581–617), and also with the kingdoms of the Japanese archipelago.

The Sui and its more successful and magnificent Tang successor (618–907) became deeply embroiled in the Korean Peninsula (the Sui fatally so). Under the Tang, Chinese influence intensified as the country became the cultural and even religious capital of a Sinocentric world. In Korea a milestone was reached in 668 when the state of Silla prevailed over the last of its rivals and succeeded in creating a unified state. State building in both Korea and Japan depended on (Chinese) writing and the adoption of Chinese political titles, rituals, bureaucratic nomenclature, music, and dress, as well as, at least on paper, systems of taxation, conscription, and land allocation. Even so, these adoptions did not preclude the maintenance of many local institutions, practices, and beliefs, transformed though they were by their new contexts.

A significant aspect of Chinese influence was the importance placed on getting names and rites right—a theme found in the Confucian *Analects,* a text that retained its authority even when China and most of East Asia turned to Buddhism. The *Analects,* the purported conversations of Confucius (c. 551 B.C.E.–479 B.C.E.), is just one of the core texts that taught such basic values as humaneness and filiality, advocated paternalistic government, and stressed the importance of propriety and its rules. Other texts that became part of the Confucian tradition supplied historical models, negative as well as positive, and explained the functioning of the natural as well as human world. Ideas concerning the interaction of passivity and activity (Yin and Yang) and of the Five Phases (wood, fire, earth, metal, and water) had all the weight that science carries today. Much like modern science, such ideas were shared across cultural and political borders. They also resembled science in that they affected everyone's thinking, and most people had at least an inkling of what they were all about, but few plumbed their more subtle arguments or delved into the mysteries of cosmological theory, and no one

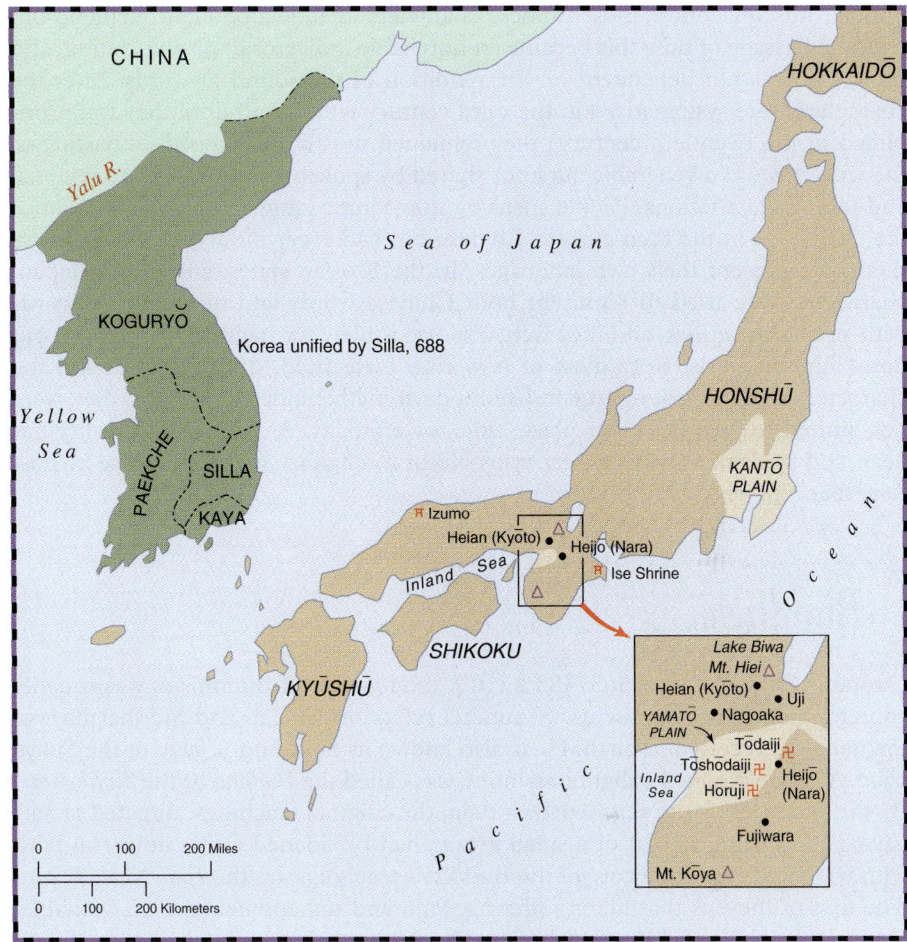

FIGURE 2.1 Map of Korea and Japan.

could attempt to master them all. Nevertheless, then as now, an awareness of the existence of such depths enhanced the respect evoked by the new teachings even among those not equipped for or inclined to concentrated study. Somewhat similarly, in introducing early Japan, we can only begin to suggest the richness of a continental civilization already then dating back a millennium; we hope that some of our readers will be stimulated to explore further on their own.

Most of the early East Asians exposed to these new ideas could not read, for literacy remained the monopoly of the elite even in China. Beyond China this literacy entailed learning a language fundamentally different in structure from those that were spoken. Everywhere literacy commanded great respect. Contrary to popular misconception, most Chinese characters include a phonetic element, but with the passage of time this became an unreliable indicator of pronunciation, and the script was not dependent on the rendition of the sound of words. After the characters were systematized in the third century B.C.E. (and until they were simplified in the twentieth century) they remained mostly unchanged, imparting to the written word a venerable aura not shared by spoken words subject to regional and temporal variations. People speaking non-Sinitic languages could pronounce the characters in the then current Chinese but had every inducement also to use them to represent their own languages. In the Korean states, and also in Japan, characters were used to represent both Chinese words and non-Chinese words with similar meanings, and they were also used solely for their sounds to spell out non-Chinese words. Regardless of how they were used, during this period the characters defined writing. Again like modern mathematics or science, they were not limited to any particular place, time, or ethnicity. A similar universality has been and is claimed by the great trans-cultural religions, and in the case of East Asia that religion was Buddhism.

Buddhism

Gautama Siddhartha (c. 563–483 B.C.E.), the founder of Buddhism, was roughly contemporary with Confucius. (Gautama refers to his clan and Siddhartha was the name he received at birth. He is also known as Sakyamuni, sage of the Sakya tribe. After he attained enlightenment he was called the *Buddha* or the *Tathagata.*) By the time Buddhism reached East Asia, the original teachings, directed at satisfying the spiritual quest of a small group, had broadened into a universal faith with wide appeal. At the core of the Buddha's teachings are the *Four Noble Truths.* The first of these is that life is suffering. Pain and unhappiness are unavoidable. Death is not the end: like other Indians, Buddhists believed that living beings are subject to reincarnation. According to the law of karma, for every action there is a moral reaction. A life of good deeds leads to reincarnation at a higher level; evil deeds lead in the opposite direction. But the ultimate goal is not rebirth as an emperor or billionaire: it is to achieve Nirvana and never be born again. Legend has it that the Buddha himself gained merit in many reincarnations before his final rebirth, and stories of his previous lives have provided rich subject matter for the artist (see Figure 2.2).

The second Truth explains the first. Human suffering has a cause that we can do something about: attachments that are produced by craving or desire. This leads to the third Truth: to stop the suffering, desire must be stopped. The cause of suffering must be completely understood and dissolved. The Fourth Truth proclaims the eightfold path to accomplish this: right views, right intention, right speech, right action, right livelihood, right effort, right mindfulness, and right concentration. Most schools understood the religious life as practiced by monks and

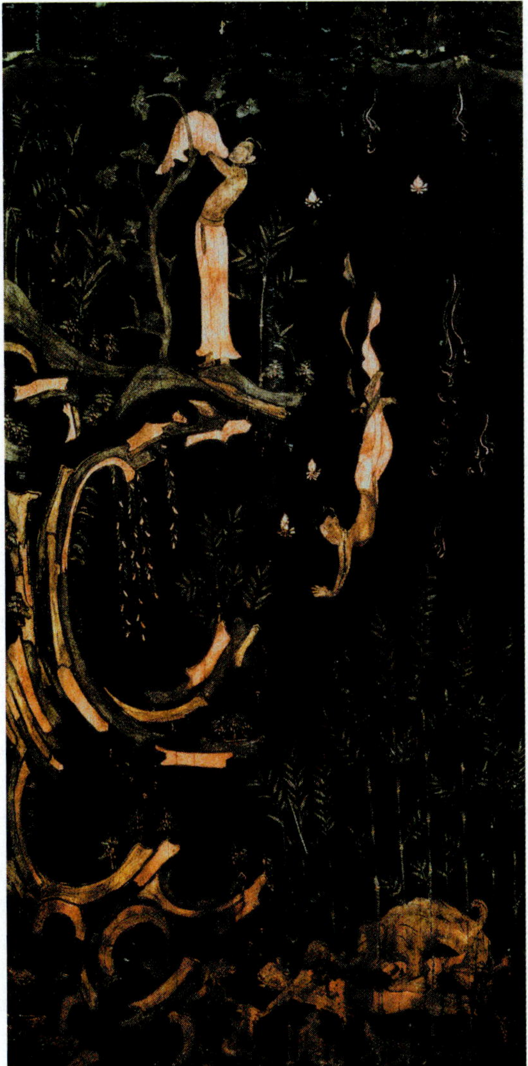

FIGURE 2.2 Tamamushi Shrine. Lacquer on wood, seventh century, 92 in high. Hōryūji, Nara Prefecture. The scene depicted here is from a famous story concerning an earlier incarnation of Sakyamuni. It shows the future Buddha sacrificing himself to feed a starving mother tiger unable to feed her young. The painting begins at the top where the future Buddha is shown hanging his clothes on a tree, and it ends at the bottom where the tigress is devouring him. (© Archivo Iconografico, S.A./Corbis)

nuns to entail vegetarianism, celibacy, and abstinence from alcohol as well as positive religious practices and meditation.

As Buddhism evolved and spread, the Buddha was transformed from a teacher of superlative wisdom, but a man nonetheless, into a deity whom people could worship and to whom they could pray. Statues of the Buddha appeared and inspired the faithful. As a Tang Period inscription puts it:

> The highest truth is without image. Yet if there were no image there would be no possibility for the truth to manifest itself. The highest principle is without words. Yet, if there were no words how could the principle be known?[1]

Ceremonies accompanied by musical chants and the burning of incense further served to spread and enrich the faith.

Many problems of doctrinal interpretation were left unanswered by the Buddha, for he was a religious teacher concerned with showing the way to salvation, not a philosopher interested in metaphysics for its own sake. As in other traditions, later commentators worked out the implications of the founder's teaching. The ultimate result was a rich variety of schools and sects, made possible by the absence of a universal Buddhist pope, by a body of scripture so vast that no one could master it all, and by the lack of a universal church language. Furthermore, through concepts of incarnation and emanation the Buddha could be identified with local deities, and the very influential *Lotus Sutra* taught the acceptability of unorthodox means to extend salvation to the greatest possible number of people.

Buddhism appealed to people in East Asia because it addressed itself to human suffering with a directness unmatched in the native traditions. It also provided a well-developed body of doctrine, art, magic and medicine, music and ritual, even heavens and hells, and a rich pantheon of deities. The historic Buddha was joined by other Buddhas: the Buddha of Medicine; Amitähba (Japanese, Amida), the Buddha who presides over the Western Paradise; Maitreya, the Buddha of the Future whose coming would usher in a new and perfect age; Vairocana, the cosmic Buddha. Most beloved among the recipients of worship were the bodhisattvas, beings who postponed their own salvation in order to help other living beings. Foremost among them was the embodiment of mercy, Avalokitesvara (Chinese, Guanyin; Japanese, Kannon. See Figure 2.3).

Avalokitesvara originally appeared as a male, but over the centuries this bodhisattva gradually came to be considered a woman. For those bewildered by the abstract concept of Nirvana, there were heavens and hells. Many people were comforted by the belief that one could earn merit, "the idea that there is an invisible moral order governing the universe, and that under this system one is rewarded in this life or the next for good deeds."[2] Such good deeds could include sponsoring statues and contributing to temples, but also acts of kindness such as releasing fish (frequently by ransoming those specially caught for this purpose), or building bridges.

Buddhism and the State

Early Buddhists relied on state tolerance and patronage; to credit later histories, even the introduction of Buddhism was accomplished by messages from Chinese states. The Tang capital of Chang'an became a great religious center. There, Buddhism enjoyed imperial patronage alongside Confucian scholarship and a third tradition known as religious Daoism, which venerated a deified Laozi, the purported author of the *Daodejing* ("The Way and Its Power") and a shadowy figure whose identity was very much in doubt even in Han times. Daoism was much favored by the Tang ruling house, which claimed descent from Laozi. But in terms of the number of its temples, the vitality of its institutions, and the pervasiveness of its influence (even on Daoism), Buddhism prevailed during this period.

In the wider East Asian setting, as had been the case when they first appeared in North China, Buddhist monks gained support by demonstrating the efficacy of the new religion and the power of their magic in protecting the state and its people. Buddhas and Bodhisattvas readily found their counterparts on the Korean Peninsula, and Maitreya, the Buddha of the future, discovered the southeastern Korean state of Silla as his native land. Charismatic monks offered ideological legitimacy and advice to kings and elites. For example, in Silla, the famous monk Wongwang gave the following five rules to the Silla military, intellectual, and artistic youth corps known as the Hwarang:

> Serve the king with loyalty
> Tend parents with filial piety
> Treat friends with sincerity
> Never retreat from the battlefield
> Be discriminate about the taking of life.[3]

The first three rules exemplify Buddhism as a carrier of Confucian teachings, and all five demonstrate Buddhist support for king and society and flexibility in the means used to propagate the faith. As was the case of Christianity in the West, Buddhism

FIGURE 2.3 Painted-wood Kudara Kannon. Asuka Period, 80.6 in high. Hōryūji, Nara Period. Kudara is Japanese for Paekche, and Kannon is Japanese for Guanyin (Avalokitesvara). The overall effect of this elongated figure is one of great elegance and grace. (© Askaen)

was also a cultural carrier in other vital areas, such as medicine, physiognomy, geomancy (divination of placement for graves and buildings), yin and yang theory, the calendar (necessary for determining when to plant, weed, and harvest), and history (accounts of the past essential for success in the present). State building went hand in hand with church building, in what we might call civilization building.

II. The Emergence of the Early Japanese State

The Late Tomb Period

The Seventh-Century Transition (the Asuka Period)

The Rise of the Soga

The 645 Coup d'Etat

The Defeat of 663

The Brief Civil War of 672

Nara as a Center and Symbol

Nara as a Religious Center

Documents and Structures

Writing and Literature

The Visual Arts

The End of the Nara Period

Among the most important components of a state are rulers legitimized by heredity, laws, histories, and literary works; a hierarchy of elites, supported by appropriation of products and services from the population; a central capital with ceremonial and administrative structures; and religious institutions enlisted in support of the rulers and their government. There were early signs of some of these during the Tomb Period, but all of them developed rapidly during twelve decades beginning in the late sixth century. This is the dynamic Asuka Period (592–710), named after the area within the Kinai region that was home to the court through many of these years. This seventh-century transition gave rise to immense new capital cities. For this chapter, the most important of these is Nara, which is the source of the name for the following Nara Period (710–794), renowned as a high point of the arts and literature. Because they served as the framework for subsequent developments in Japanese history, the formation of the first state and the accompanying emergence of a new elite culture merit careful attention.

The Late Tomb Period

The emerging states of the Korean Peninsula figured in the complex politics of the Japanese archipelago during the late Tomb Period, both through direct political and economic connections and indirectly by producing immigrants seeking a new home. Such people, longstanding residents as well as recent arrivals, were crucial transmitters of ideas and material culture. They brought powerful concepts of political legitimacy as well as trade goods, and introduced all kinds of advanced technologies, ranging from earthworking and construction to writing, and including weaving and metalworking. They were not all Albert Einsteins, but collectively they carried more powerful technologies and more sophisticated cultural practices than were then current locally.

Relations with the proto-Korean political entities were not always peaceful. From the late fourth century, in the middle of the Tomb Period, there is evidence that troops from the Japanese archipelago were involved in fighting on the Korean Peninsula. In the eighth century, the first official historians of Japan went to great lengths to portray this military activity in terms of conquest and subjugation, but these anachronistic and far-fetched depictions (which were resurrected during the twentieth-century Japanese colonization of Korea) cannot be taken seriously. Participation in peninsular conflicts was a form of payment for raw materials (especially iron), prestige goods, and advanced technologies that flowed from the states of the peninsula into the archipelago. This relationship bound the developing Yamato court to the state of Paekche and the small but well-situated Kaya federation, both in the southwestern part of the peninsula.

Fighting on the Korean Peninsula, which stimulated the flow of immigrant groups into the Japanese archipelago, intensified in the middle of the sixth century. When Silla conquered Kaya, it deprived the Yamato court of an important peninsular connection and weakened the position of Paekche. It is no coincidence that early Japanese histories record that around this time the king of Paekche formally transmitted Buddhism to the Yamato court. Such proselytizing was not unrelated to Buddhist ideals of compassion, but not unlike the transfer of technology today, it also had strong this-worldly dimensions. Buddhist ritual and magic were thought to protect states against military enemies and natural disasters. The transmission of such powerful practices at a time when Paekche was threatened by Silla and in need of military assistance from the Yamato court fits neatly into the overall pattern of early relations between the Korean Peninsula and the Japanese archipelago.

During the late Tomb Period, internal centralizing tendencies at home and the Yamato court's increasing involvement in the volatile situation on the Korean

Peninsula came together, leading to a dramatic transformation that began at the end of the sixth century and became irreversible in the seventh.

The Seventh-Century Transition (the Asuka Period)

The unification of China under the Sui in 589 sent shock waves throughout East Asia. It led eventually to the unification of the Korean Peninsula under the state of Silla, and also had a profound effect on the development of the early Japanese state. That development was shaped by four major events: upheaval in the Yamato court at the end of the sixth century, a coup d'etat in 645, the defeat of Wa forces by Silla and Tang in 663, and a brief civil war in 672. These events are each associated with particular political figures, whose names are known to us through late seventh and eighth century written sources.*

The Rise of the Soga

First came the seizure of power at court by the Soga, a kinship group that almost certainly had immigrant origins. They were closely associated with groups of artisans recently arrived from the Korean Peninsula, especially from Paekche, and were among the earliest patrons of Buddhism. Histories record that during the latter half of the sixth century, the Yamato court split into pro- and anti-Buddhist factions, with the former, led by the Soga, emerging victorious. Setting an influential precedent, the Soga secured their authority by marrying daughters into the royal family rather than attempting to replace it.

The head of the Soga in the late sixth century was Soga no Umako (?–626 C.E.),† two of whose sisters married the same king. Taking advantage of these connections, Umako managed to place a nephew on the throne in 587. From then until the middle of the seventh century, he and his descendants maintained power at court by continuing to marry daughters to kings and engineering the succession of the children. In some cases queens with royal blood also acceded to the throne after the death of their husband. The degree to which the royal family had a say in court decisions varied, but the Soga were the primary driving force, even to the point of engineering the assassination of an insufficiently pliable king in 592.

For the most part, however, the political dynamics were less a contest of Soga power versus royal power and more a matter of advancing the Soga by solidifying

---

*It is noteworthy that now for the first time it is possible to talk extensively about discrete, dated occurrences and about named individuals and their exploits. The third-century Queen Himiko of Yamatai and a king of the fifth century whose name appears on two sword inscriptions are exceptions, but in general it is not until the seventh century that the history of the Japanese archipelago takes on such personal dimensions.

†The convention for Japanese names is that family name precedes the given name. Moreover, the names of premodern elites often include the genitive particle "no," so that "Soga no Umako" literally translates as "Umako of the Soga." Prominent individuals were often referred to by their given rather than family names.

the power and authority of court and ruler. While continuing to sponsor Buddhism and patronize immigrant artisans and scribes, the Soga were associated with the creation of the new and stronger Asuka court characterized by an increase in the symbolic—and, to some extent, real—power of the Yamato Kings.

Eighth century state histories portray an age of enlightened rule by Umako's niece, Queen Suiko (554–628), and her famous nephew Prince Shotoku (574–622), incidentally also Umako's great-nephew. (Suiko's accession in 592 is treated as the beginning of the Asuka Period.) The extent to which this pair was involved in actual decision-making at court remains unclear, but an episode in the official dynastic history of the Sui reveals new royal confidence and spirit. It tells how the Wa sent an envoy to the Chinese emperor's court in 607, bringing a letter stating that the "son of heaven [i.e., emperor] in the land where the sun rises addresses a letter to the son of heaven in the land where the sun sets." This was a striking departure from the traditional Chinese model of diplomacy followed by earlier Wa rulers, in which kings of peripheral states took a supplicant, tribute-bearing posture in interactions with the Chinese throne. The Sui emperor "was displeased and told the chief official of foreign affairs that this letter from the barbarians was discourteous, and that such a letter should not again be brought to his attention."[4]

Some historians have argued that this breach of protocol was inadvertent, but it suggests a Soga-supported attempt to claim a newly prominent and independent position for the Yamato royal line at a time of parallel developments. These included the creation of a more elaborate palace compound to house the court and attempts to exert more control over trade with the peninsula and over the resources of outlying regions of the archipelago.

The 645 Coup d'Etat

After Umako's death, his son and grandson played prominent roles at court, but their increasing power eventually encountered a backlash. In 645 a dramatic coup d'etat was staged by Nakatomi no Kamatari (614–669), head of another powerful kinship group, and a young prince later known as Tenji, who was unrelated to the Soga. The leading Soga was summoned to court on a pretext and then assassinated in front of the horrified Queen, the prince's mother. After wiping out Soga supporters, Kamatari and Tenji began a program of strengthening the throne, creating formal structures of taxation and administration and constructing a more extensive palace surrounded by the beginnings of a capital city. Later historians exaggerated the scope of these measures, celebrating them as the Taika (Great Change) reforms, but Kamatari and Tenji do seem to have begun to move toward a more powerful centralized government. In doing so, they relied on the expertise of highly educated immigrants and on returned students and priests who had traveled to China to study Buddhism, statecraft, astronomy, and other practical pursuits. The new political developments stemmed partially from resentment of the great power accumulated by the Soga, but they were also inspired by an intensifying crisis on the Korean Peninsula.

In response to border disputes dating from the late sixth century, the Sui invaded the northern state of Koguryŏ three times, in 611, 613, and 614 C.E. The human, economic, and political cost of the failure of those expeditions contributed to the downfall of the Sui, but more fighting was to come after the Tang replaced the Sui in 618 C.E. After a period of jockeying among the competing states and the Tang superpower, the final stage of conflict began in 642 C.E., when Paekche captured territory from Silla and a minister at the Koguryŏ court carried out a bloody coup. Two years later, in 644 C.E., Tang began its own military campaign against Koguryŏ. As Kamatari and Tenji were overthrowing the Soga and embarking on a program of strengthening and centralizing the Yamato polity, the threat posed by this burgeoning crisis must have been foremost in their minds.

The Defeat of 663

The complex four-way interaction between Tang and the Korean states came to a head in a final configuration of alliances. Silla allied itself with Tang, and in 660 C.E. a unified Chinese–Sillan force gained the upper hand over Paekche. As remnants of its Paekche ally struggled to resurrect their state, the Yamato court was drawn into the conflict and sent a large expeditionary force of ships and troops to fight on the peninsula. The catastrophic defeat of that force by Tang and Silla at the Battle of Paekchon River in 663 C.E. was a key event in the unification of Korea. Five years later Koguryŏ fell, leaving Unified Silla in control of the entire peninsula.

Tenji and his advisors were now faced with a grave crisis. (Kamatari died in 669, by which time he had been given the surname Fujiwara, to become one of the most prominent noble kinship groups of premodern Japan). All too conscious of the continuing threat posed by ascendant Silla and its Tang ally, they fortified the potential invasion route, stationing guards and erecting beacons on islands in the straits separating Kyushu from the southern coast of the Korean Peninsula and constructed fortifications on the northern coast of Kyushu and along the Inland Sea. Most significantly, the Yamato court embarked on a crash program of institution building that included a bureaucracy based on written communication and formal taxation to pay for defense and to finance the construction of imposing capitals to project the central authority of the throne. Other major aspects of state formation included more direct control over outlying areas organized into administrative districts, attempts to create written laws, a census, and a draft system.

These changes seem to have happened quickly, an example of "foreign threat" inspiring "domestic reform."[5] The large number of refugees fleeing the conflicts of the 660s played a key role, because it seems that much of the literate manpower for the new administrative infrastructure was provided by immigrants, first from Paekche and then also from Koguryŏ.

The Brief Civil War of 672

Another leap forward in the process of state formation occurred after Tenji died in 671 C.E. Again there was a power struggle. One contender was Tenji's son, a pliable young man apparently favored by Tenji and backed by the majority of high-ranking kinship groups associated with the court. However, Tenji's brother, a powerful, determined man in his forties who was later known as Tenmu (631?–686), had strong support from middle-ranking nobles and military backing by some of the regional authorities. The tension over the succession erupted into violence in 672, a year after Tenji's death. In a brief civil war of less than two months, Tenmu's forces routed those of his nephew, who was driven to suicide. (This war is sometimes referred to as the "Jinshin Disturbance," after a traditional designation for the year in which it took place.) Although the overseas diplomatic and military crisis had somewhat abated, it remained in the background, and the victors in the civil war of 672 were now also faced with a need to unify the court and the country.

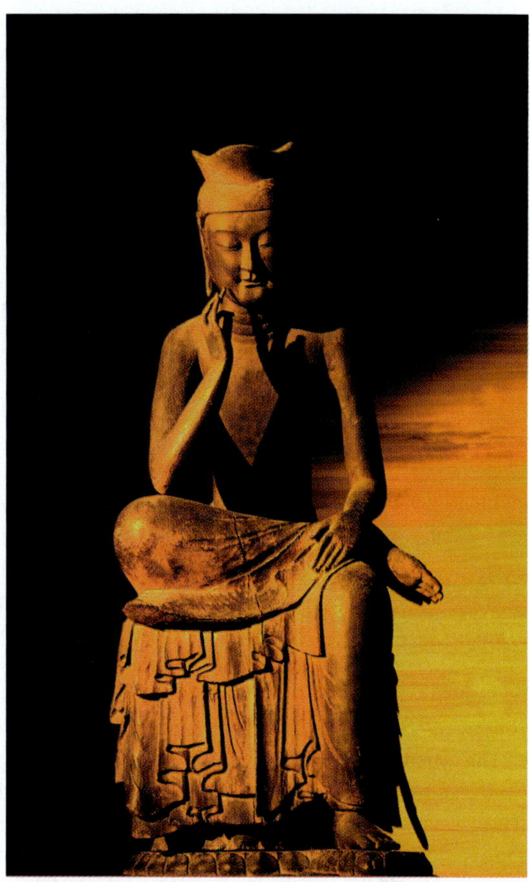

FIGURE 2.4 Pensive Buddha. Wood, Asuka Period, 48.6 in high. Kōryūji, Kyoto. Earlier identified as Maitreya, but at present we do not know which Buddha is represented in this remarkable fusion of piety and sensuousness. This rendering, which has clear Korean and Chinese antecedents, is an eloquent visual reminder of the spiritual and philosophical influence of Buddhism in linking cultures throughout East Asia. (© Chris Lisle/Corbis)

Tenmu and his consort Jitō (645–703), who ruled in her own right after his death, immediately began to consolidate their rule. They strengthened the bureaucracy, surveyed the population as a means of extracting taxes and military service, and worked to reduce the power of the pre-existing regional authorities, in part by enfolding them into an expanded provincial administrative structure. They also ordered the compilation of complete legal codes and official histories, the construction of large new palace compounds (and eventually of great capital cities), and the official sponsorship and control of religious institutions. These included Buddhist establishments, which had heretofore been largely spon-

DETAIL FIGURE 2.5 Detail of Pensive Buddha. Wood, Asuka Period. (© Chris Lisle/Corbis)

sored by prominent kinship groups. Over the course of the Asuka Period, Buddhism had maintained its this-worldly significance, but it was also the source of new forms of thought and artistic expression, represented here by a sculpture ranked as a foremost national treasure of modern Japan (see Figures 2.4 and 2.5).

In addition to Buddhist institutions, Tenmu and Jitō also exerted control over a variety of non-Buddhist cults of indigenous and imported deities (*kami*), which were later grouped under the rubric of "Shinto."

Among their most significant ideological innovations was the adoption of the title of Emperor (*Tennō*) and the country name of Japan (*Nihon* or *Nippon*). The exact dates are not entirely clear, but it is relatively certain that both were created during the reigns of Tenmu and Jitō, in an attempt to legitimize and strengthen the powers of the throne. *Tennō,* literally "heavenly sovereign," refers to the pole star, and is a Chinese term used for the emperor who sits at the center of the realm while everything revolves around him. For a brief period in the mid-seventh century, under Daoist influence, this term (C. *Tianhuang*) had been used as the official title for the Tang emperor, but the dominant Chinese term for emperor remained *Huangdi.* Both the Chinese and Japanese terms are usually translated "emperor," but they apply to the heads of very different political and ideological systems, even though they share some similar and related institutions. *Nihon* literally means base or origin of the sun, a concept that appears earlier, as in the 607 letter to the Sui court, but that now came into its own as a full-fledged term for the country.

Both the idea of a "heavenly sovereign" and the association of Japan with the sun were linked with religious beliefs, especially the notion of a sun deity who was claimed as the ultimate ancestor of the royal line. The intent was obvious: an absolute ruler, the Emperor, and a discrete realm for that Emperor to rule. This amounted to the assertion of an independent, sovereign empire within what had been the China-centered world of East Asia. In the late seventh century, this new realm was still limited to the three main islands of Kyushu, Shikoku, and Honshu, with parts of southern Kyushu and northeastern Honshu beyond its control. Even within those boundaries, a great deal of local autonomy and variety remained. The emergence of the new state was not a sudden transition to a fully centralized order, but an ongoing transformation that would continue, with many ups and downs, for centuries to come.

Nara as a Center and Symbol

Another project of Tenmu and Jitō was the establishment of a permanent capital city at the center of the new state. Previously, a new palace had been constructed for each new ruler. More extensive ceremonial spaces and structures came to accompany these palaces, especially after the coup of 645, but it was not until Jitō's reign that a full-fledged capital city was constructed, modeled on Chinese and Korean precedents. Known as the Fujiwara capital, it was located a few miles north of the old court sites in Asuka. It served as the capital only from 694 to 710, when the seat of government moved further north, to the huge new capital city of Nara, namesake of the Nara Period (710–794).

By the mid-eighth century, Nara was home to about 100,000 people, at a time when the population of the archipelago was around six million. Compared with the approximately one million inhabitants of the Tang capital of Chang'an, this is not impressive, but for early Japan it was unprecedented. The same applies to the city's dimensions. The great Suzaku Avenue, eighty-one yards wide, ran from the imposing city gatehouse to the entrance of the palace compound at the north end of the city. It bisected a grid of streets and avenues that was three miles from north to south and three and half from east to west.

Plots within the grid were allotted according to rank. As in Chang'an, there were two official markets. In addition to vegetables and crops grown within the city, many staples and supplies were available in these markets, which were connected by canals to rivers leading west to the port city of Naniwa and providing access to coastal routes linking Nara to economic centers throughout western Japan.

The markets provided the economic life of the city, but its priorities were clearly political. As in China, the palace was in the north so that the emperor faced south to receive the homage of his people. The closer one got to the palace compound, the higher the rank of the residents and the grander their dwellings. The most exalted of the nobility lived in compounds that took up entire blocks, with grand mansions surrounded by chapels, storehouses, kitchens, stables, and large pleasure gardens. From the even more elaborate palace compound, the emperor oversaw the city and could take pleasure in the laudatory words of an early Nara poet:

> The royal city,
> Nara of the blue-green earth,
> Like blossoming trees
> That shimmer into fragrant bloom,
> Is at the height of splendor now.[6]

The laborers who had built it, or the peasants whose hard-earned foodstuffs supported it, might have had different perspectives on the capital city, but it certainly made possible a glittering, refined lifestyle for the royal family and the nobles and officials who surrounded them at court.

The aesthetic richness of their lives is apparent in the precious articles preserved in the Shōsōin, a remarkable log-cabin-like storehouse still standing on pillars in the compound of the Tōdaiji temple. Inside this great repository are hundreds of objects and thousands of paper documents; its treasures include books; weapons; mirrors; screens; silks; musical instruments; medicines; fragrant woods; and objects of gold, lacquer, mother-of-pearl, and glass. Among them are items used in dedication ceremonies for the immense central Buddha image of the temple, as well as imported goods from China, Korea, India, Persia, Greece, and Rome. The music, art, and literature of the Nara court were a similarly sophisticated mixture of elements from Japan, Korea, China, and points beyond.

Nara as a Religious Center

Tenmu, Jitō, and their successors did not stop at creating the position of "Emperor" and the domain of "Japan"; they worked to construct elaborate ideological justifications of the legitimacy—even the divine necessity—of these political institutions and the norms they entailed. New religious developments supplied essential support. This came from two main sources: massive state sponsorship of, and control over, a variety of Buddhist institutions, and partial systematization of a variety of cults of local gods, or *kami,* into a complex hierarchy of shrines associated with divine narratives centered on the royal house. These religious institutions, with their solemn rites, revered texts, imposing buildings, lavish art, sacred music and dance, and charismatic practitioners, joined secular government institutions in asserting the legitimacy of the new state.

Buddhism was paramount in the city of Nara. Tōdaiji, the grandest temple of them all, was built in the middle of the eighth century on the eastern edge of the capital. Its name, "Great Eastern Temple," refers to its location in the capital, but perhaps also to Japan's status as the Buddhist country on the edge of the civilized world, out in the ocean to the east of China and India.

The Tōdaiji temple complex encompassed numerous halls, cloisters, service buildings, and belfries. It boasted two towering pagodas—at over 330 feet, among the highest structures in East Asia at the time. At the center was the Great Buddha Hall, over 280 feet wide and over 150 feet tall. Even today, in a rebuilt version smaller than the original, it is said to be the largest wooden structure in the world. The Great Buddha itself was a gargantuan gilt bronze statue of Vairocana, the cosmic Sun Buddha who was thought to sit at the center of all universes, projecting himself outward in the form of myriad Buddhas manifested in sundry times, places, and worlds. Over 50 feet tall and weighing more than a million pounds, this huge image was at the time the largest cast bronze statue in the world. Unfortunately, earthquakes, fires, and repeated warfare have taken their toll. The Buddha has been so much restored and rebuilt that the present version bears little resemblance to the original.

FIGURE 2.6 Izumo. Shrine building at the ancient sacred site of Izumo, in western Honshu. (© Lore Schirokauer)

The construction of the statue and the great hall that housed it was an immense undertaking, requiring massive state support and contributions and labor from hundreds of thousands of people. The dedication ceremony, in the spring of 752, involved 10,000 monks, 4000 musicians and dancers, and 7000 state officials. It centered on the painting in of the Buddha's eyes by Bodhisena (704–760), an Indian priest. This was surely one of the most magnificent spectacles of Japanese history, staged in a "vast cathedral of state religion," sitting at the center of the network of provincial temples, just as the emperor in his capital city sat at the center of the realm.[7]

Alongside this network was another of cults devoted to apparently indigenous gods (*kami*), worshipped in shrines that paralleled, in their own distinctive manner, the temples devoted to Buddhism (see Figure 2.6). In early histories, as in the system of official shrines that was laid out in legal codes and presided over by a Council of Shrine Affairs, these "native" cults were linked to the power, legitimacy, and putative divinity of the royal line. The worship of certain deities, often associated with sacred features of the landscape like mountains or rivers, must have had roots deep in the practices and beliefs of early inhabitants of the archipelago, but these cults also drew on an eclectic mixture of elements from overseas, including the Chinese religious practices often grouped under Daoism, gods and rituals of Korean immigrants, and ideas and practices developed under Buddhist influence. This conglomeration of beliefs and rituals eventually came to be grouped together under the term "Shinto" ("way of the gods"), but it is virtually impossible to sift out the indigenous from the imported and anachronistic to find a unified, "native" faith that pre-existed the importation of Buddhism. For that reason, we follow current scholarship in postponing the use of the term even though, when Shinto did appear, it incorporated earlier *kami,* sites, and practices.

Documents and Structures

If the capital, with its palaces and temples, reveals the body and something of the spirit of the late-seventh- and eighth-century state, writing was its lifeblood. There is evidence of written artifacts as early as the middle of the Yayoi Period, and we know that scribes from the Korean Peninsula were employed during the Tomb Period to produce diplomatic correspondence and ceremonial inscriptions, but not until the seventh century did government rely on writing as the primary means of communication and of information storage. The political transformation that followed the anti-Soga coup of 645 entailed an increase in the quantity and variety of writing. More texts appeared, as did people capable of reading and writing them, towards the end of the seventh century. The new state under Tenmu and Jitō relied on a wide range of texts, on institutions that produced and stored them, and on a staff that wrote them and was familiar with continental models, since, by century's end, many hailed from Paekche or Koguryŏ.

Impressed by the centrality of texts, historians designate this as the *Ritsuryō* state, referring to codes of penal (*ritsu*) and administrative (*ryō*) law at the heart of the system. Based largely on Tang models, they were modified to reflect Japanese circumstances. Whereas the penal code laid out classes of offenses and stipulated punishments, the administrative code specified the structure and conduct of the entire government, from the royal household at the top down to rules for operating provincial stables. Supplementing these laws were government orders spelling out how to carry out the administrative code in practice and official directives amending it.

The compilation of laws may go back to Tenji's reign, but the first reliably dated promulgation of a partial administrative code took place in 689, under Jitō, and the first full promulgation of penal and administrative codes (the Taihō codes) occurred at the beginning of the eighth century. Revisions were promulgated several decades later. Although these revisions were eventually supplanted in actual practice, they remained on the books as the nominal law of the land until the nineteenth century.

Of course, the mere promulgation of these codes did not change Japan overnight, but their vision of an ideal state and its institutions did correspond to some extent to late-seventh- and eighth-century governance, centered on a range of offices housed in the great palace compound that dominated Nara. As in China and Korea the codes provided for a vast bureaucracy, staffed by career officials and appointed, at least ostensibly, at the pleasure of the emperor. At the top, unlike China, there was the largely ceremonial Council of Shrine Affairs, but continental precedents were followed in the provision of a Council of State Affairs consisting of Ministers, Councilors, and Advisors who oversaw the workings of the government. Under the auspices of this Council were the Ministry of Military Affairs, the Ministry of the Treasury, the Ministry of Justice, and other ministries, each home to multiple levels of bureaucrats and offices.

An elaborate order of ranks ran alongside the complex structure of government offices, which had designated titles, responsibilities, and salaries. Particular offices were restricted to individuals of specified ranks. On the surface the system appeared meritocratic, with regular promotion a reward for exemplary service, but in practice the sons of high-ranking officials enjoyed a significant head-start in their initial appointments. The rank system was virtually restricted to elite capital residents and especially favored its upper echelons (a separate and unequal system was employed for provincial elites). Although the world of the capital was a small one, it was riven by political factionalism and rivalries. In this context rank was extremely important. In addition to determining eligibility for government offices, rank carried a great deal of social cachet and provided an official stipend that was often a significant source of income.

Several layers of government mediated between the central administration in the capital and the households that were actually farming the land, catching fish and game, making salt from seawater, and otherwise producing food and other necessities. The country was divided into around sixty provinces (*kuni*) (the precise number ranged from fifty-eight to sixty-six depending on the period), ruled by governors dispatched from the center. The governors and the senior staff that accompanied them resided in provincial capitals, overseeing a bureaucracy whose middle and lower ranks were staffed by local elites, often members of powerful kinship groups with local roots antedating the advent of the centralized state. Each province was divided into districts with their own chiefs and staffs drawing on similar local elites. Beneath the districts were "townships" (often paper-based administrative units rather than actual physical communities) and, at the bottom of the system, residential units of one to three dozen people living in close proximity to each other.

These residential units were exhaustively surveyed in comprehensive censuses, which provided the basis of a system of land distribution and taxation based on an "equal-field" system founded in Chinese theory and practice. Even in the Nara Period, this system was never established in full and began transforming into something else almost as soon as instituted. But, at least on paper, it stipulated public ownership of all land, which was then divided up and assigned to the people, who paid taxes in rice, other grains, other foodstuffs, textiles, and handicrafts. Men were also subject to labor service (corvée) in the capital and beyond, where they built and maintained roads, irrigation, and government structures. Furthermore, groups of districts were also responsible for supplying and equipping a fixed number of conscript soldiers for assignment to duty in the capital or to long, lonely tours guarding frontiers.

These exactions were a tremendous burden, especially on rural people vulnerable to epidemic disease, natural disasters, and failed harvests. Records abound in references to peasants absconding from the districts to which they were legally bound and descriptions of men starving by the side of the road as they attempted to return from military service or forced labor.

Clearly government had an impact, but it is also clear that it was not the fully centralized, top-down, code-based state depicted in official histories and in documents drafted by bureaucrats inclined, as we all are, to exaggerate their own importance. In practice, the reach of the state was limited in depth as well as in geographic extent. It took military campaigns in the early eighth century to bring Southern Kyushu into the fold, and the frontier in northeastern Honshu remained contested into the ninth century.

Even within the realm, different regions were under varying degrees of centralized control. Archeological finds of wooden labels from shipments of tax goods show that the vast majority came from western Honshu, Shikoku, and northern Kyushu, the area surrounding the Inland Sea that was traditionally the economic base for the Kinai region. At least in terms of its tax base, it is possible to argue that "the eighth-century state was truly a 'western Japanese' phenomenon."[8]

In sum, there was a great deal of local and regional variation in patterns of interaction among peripheral populations, their local elites, the officials dispatched from the capital, and the more or less distant offices of the central government. Even so, it is apparent from the vast public works projects of the eighth century that the early state succeeded, on an unprecedented scale, in mobilizing the labor of much of the population.

Writing and Literature

Writing was vital to the church and to the culture of the elite as well as to the government. Japanese priests made repeated trips to China in search of sacred texts, bringing back works that were copied, studied, and commented upon in the great monasteries of Nara. The state financed several sutra-copying projects to gain merit for the sponsoring royals and nobles and to protect the land from external and internal dangers. Many of the over 100,000 volumes of Buddhist works produced during the eighth century still survive, as do documents that present a vivid picture of the lives of the hard-working scribes who labored on them. One of them is a petition in which the scribes complain about poor working conditions and demand more vacation time, better rations, and regular distribution of rice wine!

The Nara Period also produced Japan's earliest extant historical and literary collections. Historical genres included officially sanctioned gazetteers (*fudoki*) detailing the history and geography of each province, but best known are the two earliest histories of Japan, the 712 *Kojiki* (*Record of Ancient Matters*), Japan's oldest extant literary work, and the 720 *Nihon shoki* (*Chronicles of Japan*).

By using some characters phonetically and others to render words directly, the compiler of the *Kojiki* created a text that can be read in Japanese. This work narrates the divine origins and the succession (always legitimate) of early "emperors." It features dramatic stories replete with magic, battles, and romance, and also contains 112 "songs" attributed to gods and legendary figures and including some compelling poetry. No doubt its compiler wanted to entertain, but this did not preclude him from grounding the legitimacy of the royal house and its dominion over the realm by providing genealogies of gods, emperors, their children, and their descendants. This served as a basis for the hierarchical ordering of noble kinship groups.

Like the *Kojiki,* the *Nihon shoki* starts with the origin of heaven and earth and narrates the divine ancestry of the royal house, but, in contrast to the earlier work, it does so in an explicitly Sinitic manner, borrowing extensively from Chinese cosmological and historical texts and generally modeling itself on the early Chinese dynastic histories. In the *Nihon shoki,* the legitimacy of the royal house is linked to its putative divine origins, but also to its adherence to classic Chinese moral and cultural models and, eventually, also to those of Buddhism. Although its earlier sections contain mythic and legendary material (much of which overlaps with the *Kojiki*), as it progresses it becomes more and more like a historical chronicle. Because it goes right up to the abdication of Jitō in 697, the *Nihon shoki* is the major source for seventh century history, even though it includes much that cannot be taken at face value. In the final analysis, it is a monumental work, containing an immense trove of detail and narrative incident, and should be appreciated as such, even though we cannot accept everything it tells us.

As in China, poetry was at the center of the literary culture of the Nara Period, leading to the compilation of major anthologies. One such, the *Kaifūsō* ("Patterned Sea-grasses of Cherished Style"), is a 751 collection of Chinese-style verse that provides a window into the elegant literary banquets of the time. Another, the *Man'yōshū* ("Collection of Ten Thousand Ages"), is a huge anthology of Japanese-style poetry compiled over the course of the eighth century. Though it is very much a product of the court, its over 4500 poems include a wide variety of literary forms, attributed to poets ranging from emperors to anonymous border guards. It is also the source of the poem about Nara quoted above.

Among its authors, the best known is the late-seventh-century court poet Kakinomoto no Hitomaro, whose rich body of work survives only in the *Man'yōshū*. He composed elegies to princes and propagandistic tributes to deified royal figures, but also moving laments such as the following, voiced by a man who has parted from his wife in the provinces to travel to the capital.

> . . . like the jeweled weed
> That slips and floats in the waves,
>   Riding in their embrace,
> Was she in soft and yielding sleep
>   Whom I have left behind,
> Helpless as a trace of dew or frost,
>   And come upon this road.
> At the fourscore bendings of the way
>   Ten thousand times
> I turn and look again,
>   But every time

Our village is yet further sunk away.
  And every mountain
Taller than the one I crossed before.
  Like summer grasses
She must droop, sorrowing in her heart,
  Yearning for her love,
The dear girl whose gates I long to see:
O mountains, I command you to bow down![9]

We can merely hint at the richness and variety of the poems collected in this splendid anthology. There is space for just one more excerpt to suggest something more of the range of themes and tones found in its pages. This was written by the great poet Yamanoue no Okura (660–730 C.E.), a cosmopolitan and deeply learned man who may have been born in Paekche. Even as it exemplifies Nara cultural achievements, it also evokes the lives of those whose labor made them possible. It appears that the village chief of the final lines is out to collect a tax payment from the unfortunate narrator:

  By my pillowside
My father and my mother crouch,
  And at my feet
My wife and children; thus am I
  Surrounded by grief
And hungry, piteous cries.
  But on the hearth
No kettle sends up clouds of steam,
  And in our pot
A spider spins its web.
  We have forgotten
The very way of cooking rice;
  Then where we huddle . . .
  There comes the voice
Of the village chief with his whip,
  Standing, shouting for me,
There outside the place we sleep.[10]

The Visual Arts

Much of the visual art that survives from this period is Buddhist, ranging from sculptures and ritual implements to banners and tapestries, and including carefully copied sutra texts that are masterpieces of calligraphy. This is partly because Buddhist temples, much like monasteries in the West, played an important role in preserving and maintaining works of art. But it also reflects the inspirational power of Buddhism and the role of art in conveying its message and meaning.

FIGURE 2.7 The Hōryūji, Nara Perfecture. This aerial photograph shows the nucleus of Hōryūji, a quadrangle enclosed by a cloistered walk. Equal emphasis is accorded the pagoda and the Golden Hall, balanced against each other along a rough east–west axis. This is one of a variety of temple compound layouts, based on Chinese and especially Korean prototypes, found in early Japanese temples. (© Askaen)

Temples, many of them in and around Nara, are treasure troves of seventh- and eighth-century art. Among the oldest surviving temples is Hōryūji, near Nara (see Figure 2.7). This temple is associated with Prince Shōtoku and is likely to have originated in a private establishment sponsored by him and members of his kinship group. A fire destroyed the early structures in 670 C.E. When the temple was reconstructed, links between Buddhist institutions and the nascent state were firmly woven into legends of Shōtoku's achievements.

Other buildings commonly found in temples included a lecture hall, usually located to the north or back, a sutra repository to store the scriptures, a belfry, a refectory, and buildings to house monks in their cells. The major buildings stood on stone bases and were roofed in clay tiles. Their heavy roofs were supported by an elaborate system of bracketing that, as on the continent, in itself contributed greatly to the aesthetics of the building. Large exterior wooden units were painted red; yellow paint covered the crosscut faces of the brackets, rafters, and so on; and other, intervening spaces were painted white. In their orientation, structure, and ornamentation, these buildings generally followed Chinese and Korean precedents.

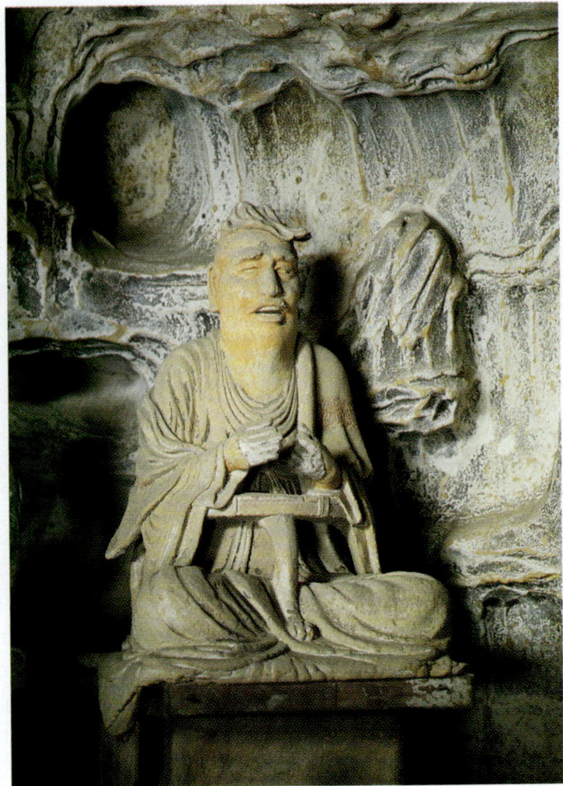

FIGURE 2.8 Vimalakirti. Clay, 17.8 in high. Pagoda of Hōryūji. Vimalakirti was a legendary Buddhist layman who became a model for Buddhist aristocrats. A wealthy man, he was renowned for his powerful intellect and pure and lofty personality. (© Askaen)

The art housed in these temples was also frequently the work of Chinese and Korean artists and craftsmen. Indeed, Nara Period temples in Japan are among our best sources for studying Chinese Buddhist art through the Tang in its temporal and regional variations. Hōryūji, like several other early temples, is a great treasure house of Buddhist art. One of the loveliest sculptures there is the Kudara Kannon (see Figure 2.3). Nara sculptors were also capable of striking realism, as in the miniature figure of Vimalakirti from the base of the Hōryūji pagoda (see Figure 2.8). Among the earliest paintings extant in Japan are those on the cabinet-sized Tamamushi (Jewel-Beetle) shrine, so named because it was decorated with iridescent beetle wings set into metal edging, a technique also practiced in Korea (see Figure 2.2).

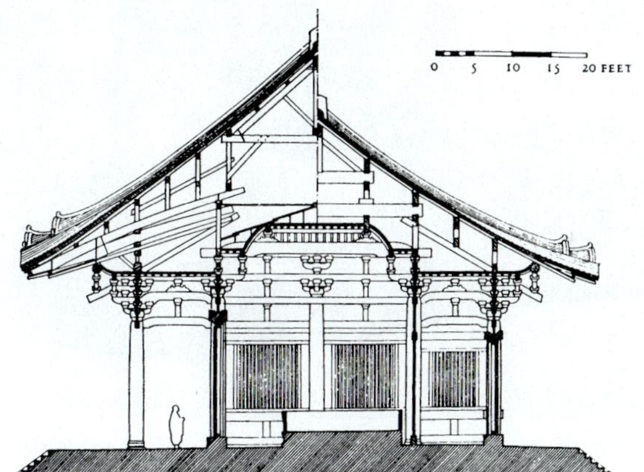

FIGURE 2.9 The golden hall of Tōshōdaiji, Nara. Although the original roof was more sloping and less steep than the present version, the illustration gives a good idea of the self-assured strength of Tang-style building at its best. (a: © Lore Schirokauer; b: From Robert Treat Paine & Alexander Soper, *The Art and Architecture of Japan* [Pelican History of Art, 2nd Edition. 1974], p. 186)

FIGURE 2.10 Portrait sculpture of the Chinese monk Ganjin (Jianzhen). Dry lacquer, mid-eighth century, 31.77 in high. Tōshōdaiji, Nara. (© Schirokauer Collection)

In seventh- and eighth-century East Asia, the art and architecture of Tang China was a transcultural idiom that projected elegance and power. The spirit of that architecture is well illustrated by the Golden Hall of Tōshōdaiji, an eighth-century temple in Nara (see Figure 2.9).

Tōshōdaiji was founded by the Chinese monk Ganjin (Jianzhen), who finally reached Japan on his sixth attempt, having earlier been frustrated by storms, pirates, shipwrecks, and once by the Chinese authorities. By the time he reached Japan, he had lost his sight. His portrait sculpture vividly invokes his blindness (see Figure 2.10). Like Bodhisena, the Indian priest who painted in the eyes of the

Great Buddha, the story of Ganjin is a reminder of the cosmopolitan Buddhist culture of the eighth century.

The End of the Nara Period

During the Nara Period there were no foreign crises as serious as the Korean conflict of the seventh century, and there was no full-blown civil war like that of 672. However, in addition to natural disasters (including famines and a horrible smallpox epidemic from 735 to 737), the court was repeatedly shaken by succession problems and power struggles that ended in the losers' exile or death. Frequently these involved the Fujiwara, whose descent from Kamatari, a planner of the anti-Soga coup of 645, did not prevent them from adopting the Soga strategy of gaining power through intermarriage with the royal line. Thus Emperor Shōmu (701–756, r. 724–749) who oversaw the expansion of the eighth-century state and the construction of the Great Buddha, had a Fujiwara mother and wife. Fuhito, the Fujiwara head at the time, was both his grandfather and his father-in-law.

In addition to such marriage politics, the Fujiwara also dominated by monopolizing, as much as possible, high-ranking positions on the Council of State, and by creating new offices. But after Shōmu's reign, the marriage politics backfired. His Fujiwara consort had no sons that survived infancy, so the royal couple's *daughter* was named crown prince and eventually placed on the throne. This daughter, Empress Kōken/Shōtoku (718–770), actually reigned twice, as she was forced to abdicate but later overthrew her successor and returned to the throne.

Kōken/Shōtoku had no offspring. Histories report that an unsuccessful attempt to pass the throne to Dōkyō, an influential Buddhist priest, excited great consternation at court. The relationship between the Empress and Dōkyō has been the subject of much unfounded speculation. With her patronage, he did obtain great political power, especially over Buddhist institutions, but he does not seem to have been the Rasputin-like figure he is often made out to be. The main sources of instability during Kōken/Shōtoku's rule were problems designating an heir to her throne and a growing preference for a "Chinese ideal of male-dominant gender hierarchy" in court politics and policy.[11] In her reigns, royal power was shaken by succession disputes, and also by struggles among powerful Buddhist institutions and ambitious kinship groups, especially the Fujiwara. Both would continue to play important political roles for centuries to come.

At any rate, in 781 a great-grandson of Tenji, Kanmu (737–806), acceded to the throne. Already middle-aged, he was a strong figure who set about reducing the influence of great temples and powerful kinship groups. Consistent with these goals, he decided to move the capital away from Nara in 784, selecting as the new site an area linked to his maternal relatives, Nagaoka (southwest of modern

Kyoto). Kanmu clearly intended to create a new center of power in an area removed from the temples and court families that loomed large in Nara. Other factors may have been the exhaustion of natural resources and taxable land in the area around Nara, and also the improved waterborne transportation available at the new site, which was linked by water to the port at Naniwa and, over Lake Biwa, to the coast along the Japan Sea. Problems encountered in building the capital at Nagaoka led to its abandonment after a mere decade, but the next capital site, that of modern Kyoto, was to remain the royal seat for eleven centuries.

Notes

1. Helmut Brinker, "Early Buddhist Art in China," in *Return of the Buddha: The Qingzhou Discovery* (London: Royal Academy of Arts, 2002), p. 20.
2. John Kieschnick, *The Impact of Buddhism on Chinese Material Culture* (Princeton: Princeton Univ. Press, 2003), p. 157.
3. Peter H. Lee and Wm. Theodore de Bary, eds., *Sources of Korean Tradition* (New York: Columbia Univ. Press, 1997), p. 54.
4. Ryusaku Tsunoda and L. Carrington Goodrich, *Japan in the Chinese Dynastic Histories,* 2nd edition (Kyoto: Perkins Oriental Books, 1968), pp. 40–41.
5. Bruce Batten, "Foreign Threat and Domestic Reform: The Emergence of the Ritsuryo State," *Monumenta Nipponica* 41:2 (Summer, 1986): 199–219.
6. Edwin Cranston, *A Waka Anthology Volume 1: The Gem-Glistening Cup* (Stanford: Stanford Univ. Press, 1993), p. 377.
7. William H. Coaldrake, *Architecture and Authority in Japan* (London: Routledge, 1996), p. 70.
8. Wayne Farris, *Sacred Texts and Buried Treasures: Issues in the Historical Archaeology of Early Japan* (Honolulu: Univ. of Hawai'i Press, 1998), p. 221.
9. Cranston, p. 205.
10. Cranston, pp. 362–63.
11. Joan Piggott, "The Last Classical Sovereign: Kōken-Shōtoku Tennō," in Dorothy Ko, JaHyun Kim Haboush, and Joan Piggott, eds., *Women and Confucian Culture in Premodern China, Korea, and Japan* (Berkeley: Univ. of California Press, 2003), p. 68.

Part Two

Aristocrats, Monks, and Samurai

The title of the second part of our book reflects the dominant elite players who occupied the center stage of the developing culture and institutions of Japan, though we do not mean to slight the contributions of commoners and nonaristocratic women. The court, religious institutions, and military groups coexisted as landholders and cultural authorities, though the samurai were ascendant by the end of this portion of Japan's history. For most of this age, aristocrats and warriors were mutually exclusive categories, whereas monks and nuns came from diverse backgrounds.

Pine Trees. Six-fold screen, ink, color, and gold on paper. Attributed to Tosa Mitsunobu, 1434–1522. Muromachi Period. Tokyo National Museum. Painted in the native style during the last period discussed in this part of our book, these pine trees decorate a screen suitable for a grand, aristocratic room. In Japan, as throughout East Asia, the pine that remains green even in bitter winter symbolizes steadfastness.

3

The Heian Period

The Fujiwara

The Estates

Government and Administration

The Warriors

Rule by Retired Emperors

Heian Buddhism: Tendai

Esoteric Buddhism: Shingon

Pietism

A World Permeated by Religion

Literature

Life of the Heian Aristocracy

The Visual Arts

Painting

The Phoenix Pavilion

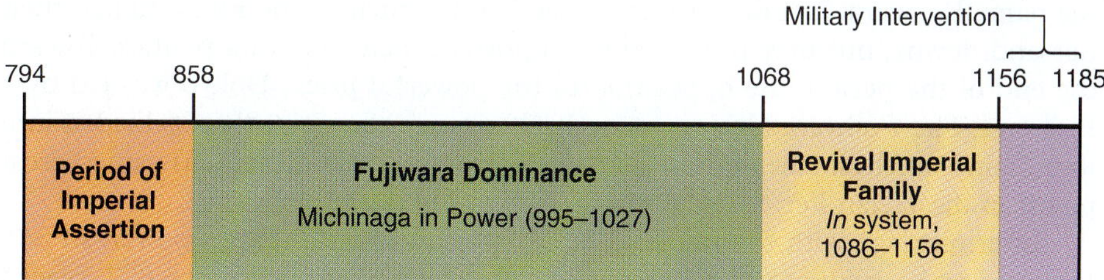

The Heian Period (794–1185) began with a vigorous assertion of imperial power under Emperor Kanmu, but that was not to last. The long-term trend favored an aristocracy that ruled at times with the emperor but more frequently in his stead, presiding over a refined culture that left a permanent mark on Japanese life and perceptions of the world. Although the four centuries of the Heian Period involved many innovations, disruptions, and departures from earlier practices, these changes grew from within the old order rather than challenging it from without. New forms of political power, extraction of resources, religious symbolism, and aesthetic expression arose within frameworks that were in place by the Nara Period.

By keeping the temples on the outskirts of the new capital of Kyoto and by patronizing new schools of Buddhism, which had their headquarters in the mountains, Emperor Kanmu was able to lessen the political influence of the old, city-based orders. Equally energetic and innovative in secular matters, he established new agencies to advise the throne and enforce its decisions, appointed inspectors to examine the books of retiring provincial governors, and replaced the ineffective conscript army with a militia system. In this way, he and his immediate successors were able, for almost half a century, to rule within the framework of the early state system.

This period of relative imperial assertion was followed by two centuries during which a particular lineage of the Fujiwara kinship group enjoyed political and economic ascendance. It ruled by using rather than seizing the throne, dominating the court without displacing the imperial house. This set a pattern for subsequent Japanese history. Emperors continued to function as titular heads of government, symbols of legitimacy, and objects of veneration based on the myth of their divine descent, their religious authority, and the court's preeminence in matters of high culture. Their extraordinary aura retained its radiance even when they had little actual political power.

The Fujiwara

The Fujiwara house, as already noted, was founded by Nakatomi no Kamatari (614–669), who was rewarded for his leading role in the coup of 645 by receiving the name Fujiwara, literally "wisteria plain." Subsequently, the Fujiwara had their ups and downs, but they remained an important factor in Nara politics. Toward the end of the period, the opposition to the powerful priest Dōkyō was led by a Fujiwara. The Fujiwara kinship group itself grew to the point that it divided into four main branches. One of these (the Northern, or "Hokke" branch) gained great power in the Heian Period.

Intermarriage with the imperial family was a key to Fujiwara power. In 858 Fujiwara no Yoshifusa (804–872), head of the Council of State since 857, placed his eight-year-old grandson on the throne and assumed the title of regent for a minor (*sesshō*). This was the first time anyone outside the imperial family had filled this position. Yoshifusa was succeeded by his nephew Mototsune (836–891), who was the first to continue as regent even after the emperor was no longer a minor, assuming for that purpose the new title of *kanpaku,* designating a regent for an adult emperor. This meant a claim to rule on behalf of the emperor as a general prerogative, not just as a temporary measure awaiting his majority. It was as regents that the Fujiwara institutionalized their power.

The ambitions of the house did not go uncontested. After Mototsune died in 891, there was an interlude without a Fujiwara regent until Tadahira (*sesshō,* 939–941; *kanpaku,* 941–949) resumed the tradition. The most famous of the opponents of the Fujiwara was Sugawara no Michizane (845–903). A noted scholar of Chinese studies and an accomplished poet, he enjoyed great influence for a time but could not withstand the Fujiwara machinations and was officially posted to Kyushu, a form of exile. There he died, but his ghost reputedly returned to punish his enemies, leading to a brilliant posthumous career. To put an end to a series of storms, floods, droughts, fires, and other calamities attributed to his angry spirit, he was promoted several times and finally became the patron god of letters and calligraphy, worshipped at shrines erected in his honor in the capital and elsewhere.

Other rivals of the Fujiwara were considerably less successful, and from 967 on the tradition of Fujiwara regents continued without interruption. A high point in Fujiwara power was reached under Michinaga (966–1027), who demonstrated great skill in the intrigue and political infighting necessary to succeed at court. He was especially skilled at marriage politics; he managed to marry four daughters to emperors, two of whom were also his grandsons. Emperors who were the sons of Fujiwara mothers and married to Fujiwara consorts were unlikely to resent the influence of the great family, let alone to resist it. Michinaga felt so secure that, although he briefly became a *sesshō,* he never assumed the title of *kanpaku,* preferring the reality to the trappings of power. His successors, however, resumed the title and continued to derive legitimacy and prestige from their close association with the imperial family. In the meantime, as the emperor's political power waned, his sacerdotal role grew even more important. Indeed, the ritual and ceremonial demands on the throne were so great that when the imperial family reasserted its power in the eleventh century, the lead was taken by abdicated emperors who, by resigning, had freed themselves from the burdensome routine of official observances.

The importance of marriage politics and control of the emperor should not be underestimated, but lasting political power usually is linked to some kind of economic power, and Heian Japan is no exception. In their heyday the Fujiwara were the wealthiest family in the land; their mansions outshone the imperial palace. To understand the source and nature of their wealth, it is necessary to examine changes in Japan's basic economic institutions, changes that had their origins in the Nara Period but reached their fruition in Heian times. At the heart of these changes was the development of estates (*shōen*).

The Estates

The estates or *shōen** were private landholdings essentially outside government control. Even after Japan officially adopted the Chinese "equal field" system, certain lands were exempt: (1) those held by the imperial family and certain aristocratic families, (2) those granted to great temples and shrines, and (3) newly developed fields, which after 743 could be retained in perpetuity. Furthermore, there was a natural tendency for all land assignments to become hereditary. This was true of lands assigned to accompany certain ranks and offices and of lands assigned to cultivators. It is unclear to what extent the system of public ownership and distribution of land was carried out, but the period from the mid-eighth century onward was marked by an increase in the amount of land officially declared private. Historians disagree about the reasons this happened. Some see the complicated system of land redistribution as unsuited to Japanese conditions; others attribute it to failure to adjust to economic growth; and still others, on the contrary, view it as a response to decline brought on by recurrent epidemics.

Whatever its causes, the growth of estates did not mean the sudden disappearance of public lands. Despite the reduction in the areas so designated, state-administered land remained economically and politically important until well after the end of the Heian Period. However, the development of private landholdings was accompanied by a growth of tax exemptions granted to influential aristocrats and temples. In time, these tax exemptions were broadened to include other privileges, such as immunity from inspection or interference by local provincial government officials, who were thus deprived of administrative authority over the estates. In many cases, they could not even enter them.

---

*To reduce the proliferation of technical terms, we will call them estates but ask the reader to keep in mind that there was nothing quite like them in Western history.

Landholdings of this type first appeared in the eighth century and grew thereafter largely by a process of commendation. Small landholders placed their fields under the protection of those powerful enough to enjoy tax exemption and immunities. Thus, a small, relatively powerless local landholder might assign his land to a richer and more influential family or religious institution, retaining the right to cultivate the land in exchange for a small rent, less than he would have had to pay to the tax collector. In this way, he secured an economic advantage and received protection from the exactions and pressures of the local officials. The new proprietor might in turn commend the land to one of the truly powerful houses, such as the Fujiwara, with high status at the capital. To obtain their protection, he would in turn cede certain rights.

Furthermore, because the proprietor was usually an absent landlord living in the capital area, he required the services of administrators, who also received certain rights to income from the land. These rights, called *shiki,* entitled the bearer to a certain portion or percentage of the income from the land. They could be divided, passed on to one's heirs, or even sold without affecting the integrity of the estate. As a result the system became very complicated: one person might hold different kinds of rights in one estate and/or hold rights in several estates. Women too could hold these rights, and the most fortunate were able to enjoy an independent source of income not unlike the modern owners of stocks and bonds.

It was a complicated system, but essentially four levels of people were associated with an individual estate in what Elizabeth Sato characterizes as a "hierarchy of tenures."[1] At the bottom of the scale were the cultivators (*shōmin*). Above them were the "resident managers" known variously as "local lords" or "proprietors" (*ryōshu*), members of influential families resident in the estate (*shoke*), or estate officials (*shōkan*). Still another step up were the "central proprietors" (*ryōke*), and at the top of the ladder were the patrons (*honke*) who frequently lived in the capital, as did many *ryōke.*

Government and Administration

The steady growth of large holdings outside government jurisdiction continued despite sporadic government efforts to halt the process by decree, for those profiting from the estates actually controlled the government. As a result, by the twelfth century more than half of Japan's rice land was incorporated into estates, and the government was faced with a decrease in revenue and a decline in power.

The rise of the estate system can be seen as a kind of privatization. Similarly, in the remaining areas of publicly administered land (*kokugaryō*), provincial governors gained a great deal of autonomy. Originally dispatched as administrators who oversaw the collection and transmission of taxes, they became virtual tax farmers, responsible for supplying a fixed amount annually for the entire province and allowed to keep whatever they could collect above that amount. Consequently, many governors became quite wealthy, and a class of current, former, and potential provincial governors formed a new mid-ranking noble elite. Ironically, many of the female authors whose vernacular accounts of life in the capital are masterpieces of Heian literature were from this class, and thus were economically dependent on the very hinterlands that they despised as remote and bumpkin-ridden.

The capital remained the arena in which the great families competed for status and its benefits, and there were still officials who took their duties seriously. However, public offices gradually became the hereditary prerogatives of particular noble kinship groups, which treated them as their own possessions. By the mid-Heian Period, deterioration in the public machinery of governance had affected even basic institutions for maintaining order. Pedigree, not ability, determined who was appointed chief of the Imperial Police. Established in the early ninth-century reassertion of imperial authority, in its heyday this organization exercised wide powers in the capital and even in the provinces. It was the only official source of armed support for the throne. But by the time of Michinaga, it lacked the strength even to secure the capital against internal disruptions and disorders. Already in 981, unruly priests from the great monastery on nearby Mt. Hiei encountered no effective resistance as they marched through the streets of the capital to press their demands. In 1040 robbers found their way into the imperial palace and made off with some of the emperor's clothes!

Clearly, the central government was no longer functioning as it had in Nara or during the period of vigorous imperial rule in Early Heian. The period of Fujiwara ascendancy has been discussed as a time of deterioration in government, a view consistent with economic growth produced by opening new lands, because not only in Japan have old political institutions often been undermined by economic development (nor is there any necessary correlation between political centralization and economic growth). However, to focus on the decline of certain institutions of the imperial government may blur the part played by nonofficial but legal institutions in the de facto government, now largely privatized.

What affected the lives of people on the estates were, mostly, not the decisions reached at court but rather those made by the aristocratic families or temples that served as the estate's patrons and by the administrators and overseers who reported to the patrons. To administer their estate holdings and, for aristocratic families, their household affairs, these patrons had a *mandokoro* or, as translated by G. Cameron Hurst, an "administrative council." Hurst describes the Fujiwara administrative council as consisting of the following:

A documents bureau (*fudono*) "for handling complaints and other types of correspondence"

A secretariat (*kurōdo-dokoro*)

A retainer's office (*samurai-dokoro*) "to coordinate the activities of the warriors in the service of the household"

A stable (*mimaya*)

An attendant's bureau (*zushin-dokoro*) "to control the attendants allotted by the court to high-ranking nobles"

An office of court dress (*gofuku-dokoro*)

A provisions bureau (*shinmotsu-dokoro*), which "handled the receipt and storage of rice and other grains, vegetables, fish, and other foods for the household's meals"

A cook's bureau (*zen-bu*) "in charge of the actual preparation of food"

There was also a judicial office (*monchūjo*) for administering justice in those estates where this right belonged to the patron.[2]

The Warriors

Heian aristocrats were civilians who preferred intrigue to war and often displayed a marked disdain for the military. However, no society seems able to dispense with military force entirely. Before the introduction of conscription and peasant armies, most fighting had been done by trained warriors affiliated with particular kinship groups. This class of fighters never disappeared. As less and less land was administered under the "equal field" system, raising conscript armies became less and less practical. In 792, two years before the move to Kyoto, the conscription system was abolished. The central government no longer had the means to raise armies—except as the emperor or his ministers raised fighting men in their own domains—and military power and responsibilities passed to provincial government officials and great families.

Because fighting involved costly equipment, such as horse and armor, and training in special techniques, such as archery and swordsmanship, it remained the profession of a rural elite established in both the political and the estate system. Some warrior leaders were originally provincial officials to whom the government had delegated military responsibilities. Others, rising within the estate system, were entrusted with defense responsibilities on the estates. The pace of the development of local warrior organizations and their size varied according to local conditions. They were especially prominent in the eastern part of the Kanto region, still a rough frontier area, where formidable warrior leagues grew and clashed.

It was fighting men of this type who kept order in the provinces, performing police and military functions and fighting for various patrons as they jockeyed for power. For example, such warrior organizations fought on both sides during a rebellion led in 935 by Taira no Masakado, a fifth-generation descendant of Emperor Kanmu. The practice was to keep the size of the imperial family within reasonable limits by cutting off collateral branches after a given number of generations. At that time, they were given a family name and endowed with rich official posts in the capital or the provinces, where their prestige, wealth, and political connections were great assets in attracting local warrior followers. Two of the greatest warrior associations were grouped around leaders who claimed such imperial antecedents: the Minamoto (also called Genji) and the Taira (or Heike). The Masakado Rebellion was put down only with great difficulty. Concurrently, there was trouble in the west: Fujiwara no Sumitomo (d. 941) had been sent to suppress piracy on the Inland Sea but instead turned outlaw himself. In the restoration of order, Minamoto no Tsunemoto (d. 961) played a leading role. Tsunemoto's son established an alliance between the Seiwa branch of the Minamoto (or Seiwa Genji) and the Fujiwara house.

During the eleventh century there was more fighting in the Kanto area, with wars from 1028 to 1031, smaller-scale fighting between 1051 and 1062, and another war from 1083 to 1087. These wars provided opportunities for building the strength of local warrior houses and of the Minamoto and Taira leagues. Although both leagues had adherents throughout the country, the Minamoto strength was centered in eastern and northern Honshu and the Taira developed a power base in the Inland Sea and capital areas.

Also in the second half of the eleventh century, the Fujiwara hold on the reins of power at court was challenged when a shortage of daughters hampered their marriage politics. Emperor Go-Sanjō (r. 1068–1072) came to the throne because his brother's Fujiwara empress was childless. Although he was opposed by the Fujiwara regent, he enjoyed the crucial support of another powerful Fujiwara noble. His success was to have far-reaching consequences for court politics.

Rule by Retired Emperors

A revival of the imperial family begun by Go-Sanjō was continued by his son Shirakawa, who became emperor in 1072. Shirakawa abdicated in 1086 but continued to exercise great power as retired emperor (*in*) until his death in 1129. Two more vigorous heads of the imperial line followed, Toba (r. 1107–1123; retired emperor, 1129–1156) and Go-Shirakawa (r. 1155–1158; retired emperor until 1192). The role of the retired emperor resembled that of the Fujiwara regent, with the emperor's paternal family replacing his maternal line. Like the Fujiwara, and despite the ambivalence of Shirakawa, the general policy of the retired emperors was to acquire for the imperial family the same type of assets enjoyed by the Fujiwara. As a result, the imperial house acquired a vast network of estates and was transformed into the country's largest landholder. This can be seen as another instance of the general trend towards a kind of privatization.

The political situation at this time could and did become complicated when there was more than one retired emperor on the scene. The ambitions and machinations of the courts, the Fujiwara, and the great temples (which had their own armed forces) contributed to political instability complicating the politics and the life of the capital. These complexities and instability provided an opening for the ambitions of the provincial warrior organizations serving the imperial and the Fujiwara families.

The retired emperor system came to an end under Go-Shirakawa. In 1156 military power was, for the first time, directly involved in a political dispute in the capital, and once the warriors had been called in, they could not readily be dismissed. By 1160, the Taira organization had gained an unprecedented degree of political power in the capital. This was still largely due to the sponsorship of Go-Shirakawa, but some historians see it as a kind of overture to subsequent developments, in which warrior organizations formed a parallel power system that ruled alongside the pre-existing state. Despite the rise of the warriors, however, for another 700 years (until 1869), the imperial family and the Fujiwara remained in Kyoto, and the Fujiwara provided the regents. Indeed, the Fujiwara house grew so large that men came to be called by the names of their branch families, and even in the twentieth century a member of one of these Fujiwara branches (Konoe) became a prime minister.

Heian Buddhism: Tendai

When Emperor Kanmu turned his back on Nara and moved his capital at the end of the eighth century, he curtailed the political power of the old schools, but Buddhism continued to grow and flourish. It also continued to enjoy imperial patronage. Kanmu himself supported the priest Saichō (767–822) who, dissatisfied with the worldliness of the Nara priesthood, had founded a small temple in 788 on Mt. Hiei northeast of Kyoto. In 804 Saichō traveled to China to advance his understanding of the faith, though surely he was also aware that for his temple to gain the high prestige enjoyed by the Nara temples, Chinese sanction was a must. The trip enhanced his standing at the court, with which he maintained a close relationship throughout his life.

Saichō originally moved to Mt. Hiei to escape the corrupt atmosphere of Nara, not because he disagreed with the teachings of Nara Buddhism. However, in China he studied the doctrines of the Tendai (Tiantai) school, which took its name from a mountain range in China. Its founder, Zhiyi (538–597), combined the scholarly tradition of south China with northern pietism and meditation. The complete truth was contained in the *Lotus Sutra,* believed to have been preached by the Buddha to 12,000 arhats (saints), 6000 nuns, 8000 Bodhisattvas, and 60,000 gods. The great god Brahma attended, accompanied by 12,000 dragons, and there were hundreds of thousands of other supernatural beings. As he talked, a ray of light emanated from the Buddha's forehead, revealing 18,000 worlds, in each of which a Buddha was preaching. This text was enormously influential in East Asia, and its imagery inspired many artistic representations.

Tiantai doctrine centered on a tripartite truth: (1) the truth that all phenomena are empty, products of causation without a nature of their own; (2) the truth that they do, however, exist temporarily; (3) the truth that encompasses but transcends emptiness and temporariness. These three truths all involve and require each other—throughout Tiantai the whole and the parts are one. A rich but unified cosmology is built on this basis: temporariness consists of 10 realms. Since each of these includes the other, a total of 1000 results. Each of these, in turn, has three aspects—that of living beings, of aggregates, and of space. The result is 3000 worlds interwoven so that all are present in each. Since, therefore, truth is immanent in everything, it follows that all beings contain the Buddha nature and can be saved. One eighth-century patriarch taught that this includes inanimate things, down to the tiniest grain of dust.

On his return from China, Saichō established this school in Japan, thereby removing himself both doctrinally and geographically from the Nara temples. The latter resented him bitterly, and when Emperor Kanmu died they fought back with some temporary success, such as when they disputed the new school's right to ordain priests, a right not granted to the Tendai temple on Mt. Hiei until 827, by which time Saichō was dead. The doctrinal content of Saichō's Tendai, like that of its Chinese parent, was grounded in the Lotus Sutra. In contrast to the proponents of some of the older schools, Saichō preached the universal possibility of enlightenment. Everyone could realize his Buddha nature through a life of true religious devotion. On Mt. Hiei, Saichō insisted on strict monastic regimen.

Saichō was more skilled as an organizer than as a theoretician. He laid solid foundations for the subsequent expansion of what he had built, and eventually his little temple grew to a vast complex of some 3000 buildings. It flourished on Mt. Hiei until it was destroyed in the sixteenth century for political reasons. In keeping with the syncretic nature of Tendai, the Buddhism propagated on Mt. Hiei was broad and accommodating, so much so that it remained the source of new developments in Japanese Buddhism even after the temple community had departed from the earnest religiosity of its founder.

After Saichō's death, a line of abbots succeeded him, among them Ennin, the famous traveler to China, whose diary is a major source of information about the Tang. Then late in the ninth century there developed a split between the followers of Ennin and those of his successor. This bitter rivalry, fueled as much by jealousy as by doctrinal differences, led to the introduction of force into religious politics and the appearance of temple militias ("evil monks," or *akusō*) who engaged in brawls and combat. The use of violence increased, and by the eleventh century prominent shrines and temples maintained large standing armies. Particularly troublesome was the monastery of Mt. Hiei, which kept several thousand troops. They repeatedly descended on the capital, terrorizing its inhabitants, to demand ecclesiastical positions, titles, and land rights. Ironically, the temple on Mt. Hiei, which was located on a mountain to the northeast partly to protect the capital from supernatural forces thought to approach from that direction, became in the Late Heian Period a major source of disturbances.

Esoteric Buddhism: Shingon

Contemporary with Saichō was Kūkai (774–835), founder of the other major school of Heian Buddhism, Shingon. He, too, studied in China and benefited from imperial patronage, although in his case it came not from Emperor Kanmu but from that emperor's successors. Like Saichō, he established his main monastery on a mountain, choosing Mt. Kōya on the Kii Peninsula, far removed from the capital. When Kūkai returned from China, Saichō befriended him and showed interest in the doctrines Kūkai brought back with him, but this cordial relationship did not last. A year after Saichō's death, Kūkai moved closer to the center of Heian life when he was appointed abbot of Tōji, the great temple at the main (southern) gateway to the capital.

In contrast to Tendai, which flourished in China as it did in Japan, the type of Buddhism introduced by Kūkai was never prominent in China and failed to survive the mid-Tang persecution of Buddhism. Shingon (*mantra,* in the original Sanskrit; *zhenyan,* in Chinese) literally means "true word," thus conveying the importance of mystic verbal formulae in this school and its insistence on a tradition of oral transmission of secret teachings from master to disciple. Because only the initiated were privy to the full truth, it is known as esoteric Buddhism. Transmitted in addition to the sacred teachings and verbal utterances were complicated ritual observances involving the *mudra* (hand positions of the Buddha but also used by Shingon priests) and the use of ritual instruments.

Central to Shingon teachings and observances is Dainichi (Vairocana), the cosmic Buddha whose absolute truth is all encompassing and true everywhere and forever. In his *Ten Stages of Religious Consciousness,* Kūkai ranked the various levels of spiritual life. At the lowest level he ranked animal life, lacking spiritual dimension. Confucianism he ranked as only the second step upward, with Daoism third. Then came various schools of Buddhism, including Tendai (eighth). At the top he placed Shingon. In this way, Shingon incorporated and found a place for other schools of Buddhism, although the Tendai monks were hardly pleased with their place in the Shingon hierarchy. No explicit provision was made in this schema for Japanese cults of local gods, but the name Dainichi (Great Sun) invited identification with the Sun Goddess claimed as ancestress by the imperial family, and Shingon proved hospitable to local deities through its concept of duality. This concept held that a single truth manifests itself under two aspects, the noumenal and the phenomenal, so Dainichi and the Sun Goddess could be considered as two forms of one identical truth.

The teachings of esoteric Buddhism were complex and difficult to understand, yet it was enormously popular during the Heian Period, even overshadowing Tendai until Ennin introduced esoteric practices into Tendai. One reason for the appeal of Shingon was the mystery of its rites. From the beginning, people in Japan had been drawn to Buddhism at least partly by the magical elements connected with Buddhist observances, such as incantations, divination, exorcism, and medicinal use of herbs. Now they were impressed by the mysterious elements in the secret rituals performed in the interior of Shingon temples, hidden from all but the most deeply initiated of the priests. The elites of Heian Japan, with their taste for pageantry, were also attracted by the richness of the colorful Shingon rites.

Much of the prosperity of Shingon can be attributed to the genius of Kūkai (also known by his posthumous name Kōbō Daishi, or Great Teacher Kōbō). He was an exceptional man, famed for his brilliance and learning, his artistic talents, and his calligraphy. He is so associated with writing that later hagiographers even

FIGURE 3.1 Mt. Kōya, Wakayama Prefecture. The path, almost two kilometers long, leading through a deep forest to Kūkai's resting place is lined with the tombstones, some grand and some humble, of those who will attain salvation when Kūkai rises up to meet Maitreya. (© Lore Schirokauer)

credited him with the invention of the *kana* syllabary that developed during the Early Heian Period. Kūkai is also credited with the introduction of tea to Japan and the building of bridges, and a cluster of miraculous stories grew up around his name. To this day, he lies in his grave on Mt. Kōya awaiting the coming of Maitreya (see Figure 3.1). One of Kūkai's most lasting contributions to Shingon, and a major source of its appeal, was his emphasis on the arts. A gifted artist himself, he saw art as the ideal vehicle for transmitting religious truth. Unlike Tendai, Shingon did not give birth to many new schools of Buddhist thought, but it did leave a rich artistic heritage.

Pietism

Later in the Heian Period, revulsion at the worldly (and military) success of the established temples, and hope of rescuing a world falling into increasing disorder, stimulated a pietistic movement. This movement was initiated by the priests Kūya

(903–972) and Genshin (942–1017) and centered around Amida (Amitabha, the Buddha of the Infinite Light, who presides over the Western Paradise). So disrupted was Japanese society that many people were convinced they were about to enter the last of the three Buddhist ages (*mappō*), the degenerate age of the decline of the Buddha's law. The pietists taught that only faith in Amida could provide salvation in such dire times, and a famous statue of Kūya shows him with little Amidas issuing from his mouth, symbolizing the power of chanted incantations calling on that Buddha (see Figure 4.4). In a spirit of evangelical zeal, he traveled throughout the countryside, bringing people his message of Buddhist salvation and leading them in dancing and chanting the name of Amida.

It is characteristic of the Heian Period that Genshin's teachings were propagated not only in writing but also in art. His work contains terrifying depictions of hell that inspired lurid scrolls illustrating all manner of posthumous torment, and he is associated with a genre of painting depicting *raigō,* that is, a descent by Amida mercifully coming down to a man's deathbed to gather his soul to paradise. One custom among the devout was for a dying person to hold a string attached to the figure of Amida in such a painting. For example, when Michinaga, the strong-minded Fujiwara who was de facto ruler of Japan, lay dying, he repeated the *nenbutsu,* invoking Amida and holding such a cord, while a chorus of monks chanted the Lotus Sutra. This practice became as widespread as the *raigō* depictions themselves.

Another deity worthy of mention is Jizō, who began as a bodhisattva who saved souls in hell but became popular as the embodiment of Amida's compassion. Eventually he merged with other gods, until in time he came to be regarded as the protector of children who had died young. He still graces many a roadside shrine in Japan today.

Amidism continued to attract an increasing following and devoted apostles such as Ryōnin (1072–1132), a Tendai monk who placed additional emphasis on the *nenbutsu.* As the Heian Period neared its end, the veneration of Amida and the use of the *nenbutsu* spread far and wide through existing temples, but eventually the new religious force established its own new schools. The break came when Hōnen (1133–1212) established Pure Land Buddhism as an independent school in the Kamakura era.

A World Permeated by Religion

No society is composed entirely of the devout—certainly not that of Heian Japan! The degree of piety felt by those who attended religious observances ranged widely. The diarist and essayist Sei Shōnagon famously recorded her belief that a priest should be handsome so that the audience will have no inducement to divert their eyes and thoughts. Frequently, then as now, a visit to a temple was primarily a pleasure trip. On the other hand, in the daily lives of all classes, religion and magic were inextricably interwoven with elements of Buddhism, yin-yang theory, geomancy, worship of local deities or *kami,* and popular beliefs of all kinds. (Geomancy, *feng shui* in Chinese, is the practice of selecting sites for graves, buildings, or cities according to the topographic configuration of yin and yang.) The inhabitants of the capital were forever purifying themselves; they studiously avoided traveling in certain directions on days for which such movement was inauspicious or even dangerous, and when ill they sought the services of a priest skilled in exorcism. The monastery on Mt. Hiei provides a good example of this fusion of beliefs. It was established northeast of the capital to guard the city against the evils that, according to Chinese beliefs, emanate from that direction. And before he built this Buddhist temple, Saichō was careful to pay his respect to the local *kami.*

As already noted, *kami* worship in early Japan was a complex mixture of indigenous cults of local deities; non-Buddhist gods and rituals imported from Korea and China; and notions and practices taken from or developed in opposition to Buddhism. This mixture provided the basis for the myths showcased in the *Kojiki* and *Nihon shoki,* and also the foundation of the state-supported shrine system. From the eighth century onward, and increasingly during the Heian Period, aspects of *kami* worship were combined with new and old Buddhist doctrines and deities, producing new configurations of ritual practice, sacred space, and systems of thought. All of these were strongly influenced by the esoteric practice of incorporating other beliefs into the Shingon spiritual hierarchy. The development of various mixtures of local deities and Buddhist concepts and practices, as worked out by Heian Period thinkers, eventually led to the emergence of a "Shinto" tradition that, ironically, claimed purely local roots. As Mark Teeuwen writes, "It was this *kami* thought and practice, pioneered by monks of the esoteric Buddhist sects, that opened the way for the *kami* cults to develop into something that may be meaningfully referred to as Shinto: a religious tradition that consciously and explicitly defined itself as non-Buddhist and self-contained."[3]

Literature

The Heian Period is celebrated for a literary efflorescence that produced works at the core of the canon of classical Japanese literature. Many of their authors are women, an extraordinary development at a time in world history when few women were even literate. These were elite women, of course: literacy remained largely confined to the upper reaches of society, though everyday administration and record-keeping became even more widespread than during the Nara Period.

The new styles and genres that are seen as most representative of the Heian Period emerged gradually, and many have clear precedents in eighth-century anthologies like the *Kaifūsō* and the *Man'yōshū.* One of the most important continuities was the lasting importance of Chinese-style poetry and prose. Although they are underrepresented in translations and scholarship, such texts remained, and were to remain, central to the tradition. They reveal dimensions of aesthetic, social, and political life not available elsewhere, partly because male courtiers wrote detailed diaries in the Chinese style, but also because it provided poetic and prose genres for dealing with topics and settings that are ignored in vernacular writings.

We can obtain a taste of Chinese-style prose and Heian urban life from the "Record of the Pond Pavilion," by Yoshishige no Yasutane (d. 1002). It extols the virtues of a house and garden constructed by the author late in life but begins by describing city life in general:

> In the eastern sector of the capital . . . there are huge crowds of people living, eminent and lowly alike. Towering mansions are lined up gate by gate, hall in sight of hall; little huts have only a wall between them, eaves all but touching. If a neighbor to the east suffers a fire, neighbors to the west seldom escape being burned out; if robbers attack the house to the south, the house to the north can't avoid the shower of stray arrows. . . . And how much the worse when some great mansion is first built and then begins bit by bit to broaden its gates and doors, swallowing up the little huts all around. Then how many of the poor people have occasion to complain, like sons forced to leave the land of their father and mother, like officials of paradise banished to the dusty world of men.[4]

Banishment of a less figurative sort was a theme in the work of one of the greatest Chinese-style poets of the age, Sugawara no Michizane. He is known for his sad fate, ousted from high position by his Fujiwara rivals and exiled to Kyushu, but he was also a famous scholar and a prolific poet who left hundreds of Chinese-style compositions, ranging from descriptions of elegant banquets, to vivid portrayals of the suffering poor, to long autobiographical accounts. The following short poem, titled "The Lamp Goes Out," was written from exile in 902, in the last year of his life.

> It was not the wind—the oil is gone;
> I hate the lamp that will not see me through the night.
> How hard—to make ashes of the mind, to still the body!
> I rise and move into the moonlight by the cold window.[5]

Chinese-style poetry continued to be a favorite medium of Japanese elites for a thousand years after Michizane's death.

Chinese style poetry and prose remained central, but literature in the vernacular was also much appreciated. Thousands of poems in the vernacular (*waka*) had already been included in the *Man'yōshū,* but this form of poetry received new official recognition in the early tenth century, with the compilation of the *Kokinshū,* (short for *Kokin wakashū, Collection of Ancient and Modern Poetry*) an imperially sponsored anthology that showcased work by Early Heian court poets and was the first of twenty-one imperial anthologies of *waka* compiled over the next five centuries.

As the inaugurator of this tradition, the *Kokinshū* had a shaping influence, dictating standards of taste, imagery, rhetoric, and even vocabulary. Its compilers not only considered the quality of the works that they included but also took pains in the arrangement and juxtaposition of poems in the anthology to create an overall aesthetic experience for the reader that framed and simultaneously transcended the individual short poems. Similarly, the prefaces of the *Kokinshū* set forth a vision of poetry as a natural response to emotion, and were as influential on subsequent poetic and aesthetic treatises as the content of the anthology itself was on poetic practice:

> Japanese poetry has the human heart as seed and myriads of words as leaves. It comes into being when men use the seen and the heard to give voice to feelings aroused by the innumerable events in their lives. The song of the warbler among the blossoms, the voice of the frog dwelling in the water—these teach us that every living creature sings. It is song that moves heaven and earth without effort, stirs emotions in the invisible spirits and gods, brings harmony to the relations between men and women, and calms the hearts of fierce warriors.[6]

The beauty of the seasons and the vicissitudes of love as it moves from infatuation to all-too-brief fruition and ends in embittered separation are the themes that dominate *waka*. Typical of the former is the following poem by Ki no Tsurayuki (d. c. 945), one of the compilers of the *Kokinshū* and a founder of its characteristic style:

> Ah, the autumn moon—
> shining forth with such brilliance
> that I can make out
> the shapes of the crimson leaves
> as they fall to earth.[7]

For the *Kokinshū* version of romance, we turn to Ono no Komachi, a mid-ninth-century woman who was renowned as a passionate poet of love and who later became the subject of a range of legends and anecdotes—some celebratory, others disapprovingly moralizing. In the following she takes up the common theme of lonely lovers reunited, fleetingly, in a dream:

> Did you come to me
> because I dropped off to sleep,
> tormented by love?
> If I had known I dreamed,
> I would not have awakened.[8]

Literary diaries in the vernacular, blending prose and poetry, truth and fiction, offer rich insights into the lives and thoughts of the elite women and men who wrote and are depicted in them. Many of the prose passages in these diaries provide settings for sparkling poetry exchanges. Other personal narratives are more concerned with describing the everyday life and opinions of the writer. The most famous of these is the *Pillow Book* of Sei Shōnagon (fl. late tenth–early eleventh century), which is filled with lush depictions of court life and snide commentaries on contemporary manners and taste.

A classic of the first half of the Heian Period valued for its prose and poetry was the *Tales of Ise,* which describe the putative exploits of a ninth century poet, Ariwara no Narihira, famous for romantic and literary exploits. The following passage finds Narihira and some friends boarding a rustic ferry to cross a river in remote eastern Japan, far from the capital, the undisputed center of the world for Heian elites:

> They embarked in wretched spirits, for not a soul among them but had left someone dear to him in the capital.
>
> A white bird about as big as a snipe, with a red bill and red legs, was idling on the water, eating a fish. Its like was not to be seen in the capital, and nobody could say what it was. When they consulted the ferryman, he answered, "Why, that's a capital-bird, of course." Someone composed this poem:
>
> If you are in truth
> What your name would tell us,
> let me ask you,
> capital-bird, about the health
> of the one for whom I yearn.
>
> Everyone in the boat shed tears.[9]

In addition to suggesting the Heian elite's sense of geography, this passage exemplifies the sentimentality and the humor of this influential collection.

As new forms of vernacular literature developed over the course of the ninth century, the scripts used to write them also changed dramatically. Earlier, it had been possible to write in Japanese by using Chinese characters to record words, syllables, or a combination of the two. As the syllabic use of characters increased, they were gradually abbreviated and simplified, eventually resulting in new syllabaries distinctive from Chinese graphs (see Figure 3.2).

Many texts continued to be written entirely or partially with characters, but the development of the new scripts allowed for innovative forms of calligraphy, and eventually helped promote the spread of new forms of literacy. Women are strongly associated with texts written in the cursive syllabary (the modern *hiragana* script), but men also wrote in it, and elite women had more access to and understanding of Chinese-style writings than they are often given credit for. The visual and stylistic variety of Heian Period writing does not map neatly onto divides between languages or genders, but it provided a rich repertoire of expressive strategies and techniques for Heian and later writers.

The crown jewel of Heian literature is the *Tale of Genji,* a long fictional narrative by Murasaki Shikibu (fl. late-tenth–early eleventh century), a court lady who served an empress who was one of Michinaga's daughters. The influence of this work on Japanese culture was enormous and varied. References to the *Genji* echo throughout Japanese literary history down to the present. Motoori Norinaga (1730–1801), who became its most influential interpreter, celebrated it as an expression of *mono-no-aware,* a word that defies translation but has been characterized as "that power inherent in things to make us respond not intellectually but with a gasp of emotion."[10] To make this classic accessible to a modern audience it has been translated into modern Japanese by such outstanding novelists as Tanizaki Junichiro (1886–1965) and Enchi Fumiko (1905–1986). It has also provided subject matter for the arts (see Figure 3.7) and left its mark on the writing of history.

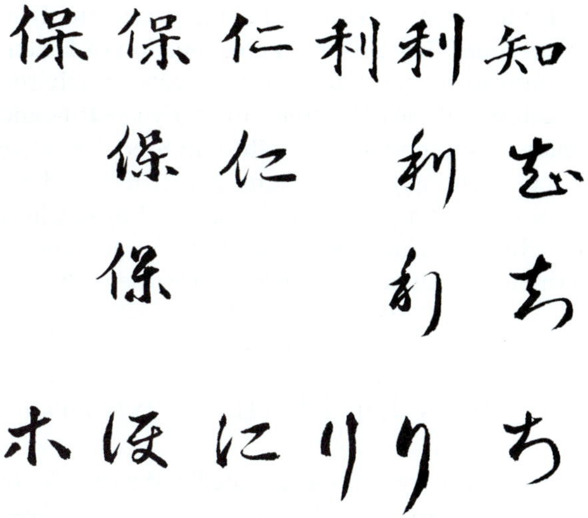

In her *Tale,* Murasaki tells the story of the peerless Genji, the son of an emperor and a low-ranking—and short-lived—consort. He is made a commoner by virtue of a lack of powerful maternal relatives, and is thus unable to inherit the throne, but with his intelligence, sensitivity, poetic and musical talent, and charisma he is the undisputed center of court society. The *Tale of Genji* traces his many affairs, his involvement in political intrigues, and the tragic consequences of his moral failings; after his death about three-quarters of the way through, the narrative continues on with the darker story of his children and grandchildren's generations. In addition to providing a panorama of the world of the Heian elites, replete with poetry, dance, musical performance, and all manner of pageantry, Murasaki Shikibu's masterpiece demonstrates a delicate but uncompromising understanding of human behavior and emotion. To quote her most recent English-language translator,

> The narrative is not extensively descriptive, but the telling touches it provides are just those that nourish a living image in the mind. Many people over the centuries have taken it for a record of life itself in its own time. The experience of reading it resembles that of looking through a small but very clear window into a complete and spacious world.[11]

保 保 仁 利 利 知

ホ ほ に り り ち

FIGURE 3.2 Development of *kana* syllabary. The top row contains Chinese characters, and the bottom row shows the *kana* into which they eventually developed. Reading from right to left, the *kana* are pronounced *chi, ri, ri, ni, ho,* and *ho.* In the bottom row, all except the third (from the right) and the last are *hiragana,* the most commonly used form; the third and last illustrate *katakana,* the form now primarily used for foreign terms and emphasis. (Calligraphy by Dr. Léon L. Y. Chang)

Late Heian vernacular tales also provide a window into another world, or at least into other realms of the world of the *Genji.* Some collections emerged from Buddhist contexts, motivated partly by preachers gathering material for sermons, but they soon came to include material simply because it was striking, funny, or scurrilous. They provide a cross-section of Heian society, revealing a wider vision of human pursuits than works devoted solely to the court and its concerns. The greatest of these collections, the early twelfth-century *Tales of Times Now Past,* contains over a thousand Buddhist and secular stories of India, China, and Japan. In its unrelentingly entertaining pages, the reader can encounter such memorable characters as a priest with a huge red nose who goes to absurd lengths to shrink it, a high-ranking court official with an irrational fear of cats, and a group of fishermen who aid a giant snake in a battle with an evil centipede.

Life of the Heian Aristocracy

Heian literature, with its detailed and varied accounts by elite men and women, is a rich source for the daily life of the upper classes, their values, and their tastes. The literary eminence of Heian ladies itself suggests something of their social status. They had ample leisure for reading and writing; the *Tale of Genji* is twice as long as Leo Tolstoy's *War and Peace.* Often, it seemed, they even suffered from an excess of leisure, becoming bored with long days of inactivity spent in the dimly lit interiors of their homes and welcoming the chance to exchange pleasantries and gossip with an occasional caller. If the caller was a man, he had to conduct the visit seated in front of a screen behind which the lady remained demurely hidden. Fortunately, there were numerous festivals to break the monotony of the daily routine, and pilgrimages to temples provided further diversion.

The world described in Heian literature is a small one, because it concerns only the tiny fraction of people at the pinnacle of society in the capital. Although there are descriptions of travel outside the capital area, the focus is on the capital itself. A provincial appointment, lucrative though it might be, was regarded as tantamount to exile. The provinces were viewed as an uncultured hinterland where even the governing classes were hopelessly vulgar. To these aristocratic ladies, the common people whose labor made society possible were so far removed in manners and appearance as to resemble the inhabitants of another world. At best, they seemed uncouth. At worst, they were regarded as not fully human, such as when Sei Shōnagon encountered a group of commoners on a pilgrimage and noted, "They looked like so many basket-worms as they crowded together in their hideous clothes, leaving hardly an inch of space between themselves and me. I really felt like pushing them all over sideways."[12]

Geographically limited and constricted in social scope, the Heian aristocracy was also less concerned than their predecessors with the rest of East Asia. The last official Heian government mission to China was sent in 838. When near the end of the ninth century it was proposed to send another and Sugawara no Michizane was chosen as ambassador, he successfully declined on the grounds that conditions in China were unsettled. Even after order had been restored in China with the establishment of the Song (960–1279), official relations were not resumed.

Even so, travel by priests and merchants continued, and the elites of the Heian capital were fascinated by valuable imported luxury goods from abroad.

In Heian court society, elite men and women developed keen sensitivity to beauty and subtle refinement in conduct. The perfect gentleman embodied by Murasaki's Genji is a fictional ideal rather than a real-life portrait, but it suggests the extent to which life and art could be fused through the cultivation of human sensibilities. In this world, where aesthetics reigned supreme, great attention was paid to pleasing the eye. Ladies dressed in numerous robes, one over the other (twelve was standard), which they displayed at the wrist in overlapping layers, and the blending of their colors was of the utmost importance in revealing a lady's taste. Often all a man saw of a lady were her sleeves, left hanging outside her carriage or spread beyond a screen behind which she remained invisible. The men were by no means to be outdone in the care they took over their own attire. The following description is from Sei Shōnagon's *Pillow Book:*

> His resplendent, cherry-colored court cloak was lined with material of the most delightful hue and lustre; he wore dark, grape-colored trousers, boldly splashed with designs of wisteria branches; his crimson under-robe was so glossy that it seemed to sparkle, while underneath one could make out layer upon layer of white and light violet robes.[13]

This concern for appearance extended to the features of the gentlemen and ladies. Both sexes used cosmetics, applying a white face powder, which in the case of the women was combined with a rosy tint. The ladies took great pride in their long, flowing, glossy hair but plucked their eyebrows and painted in a new set. Such customs are not unfamiliar to the modern world, but far more difficult for us to appreciate are the blackened teeth of the refined Heian beauty. Confined to the aristocracy during the Heian Period, this practice, like so many features of Heian taste and sensibility, later spread to the lower classes of society. It became the sign of a married woman and in the Edo Period was adopted by courtesans.

The emphasis on visual beauty did not mean the neglect of the other senses. Musical performances ranging from impromptu solos to marathon sessions involving many musicians played an important part in the lives of the Heian aristocracy, and aural and visual pleasure was often combined in courtly dances. Nor was the sense of smell neglected. The Heian ladies and gentlemen went to great lengths to blend perfumes, and a sensitive nose was a social asset second only to a good eye and ear.

The ideal Heian aristocrat was as sensitive in personal relations as in matters of aesthetics: feelings should be as beautiful as dress. Nowhere was this more important than in the love affairs that gave Heian vernacular literature its dominant theme. Marriages were arranged by and for the family in a game of marriage politics at which the Fujiwara excelled. But for a noble courtier to confine himself to one wife was the rare exception. He was much more likely to have one or more secondary wives and to conduct still other, more or less clandestine, love affairs. Nor were the ladies expected to remain true to one love for their whole lives, although few were as amorous as Ono no Komachi or Izumi Shikibu, another famously gifted poet with a reputation as a great lover. Nevertheless, jealousy posed a recurring problem for a lady of the Heian age, who might have to bear long waits between visits from her lover. For the less fortunate and less hardy, waiting could become a torture.

The qualities most valued in a lover were similar regardless of sex: beauty and grace, talent and sensibility, and personal thoughtfulness. Murasaki's Genji was ever gallant to one lady he had seduced even though he discovered she was unattractive. He found himself in this predicament because Heian men often had no clear idea of the appearance of the women they were wooing, hidden as they were behind screens with only their sleeves showing. Men fell in love with a woman's sense of beauty, her poetic talents, and her calligraphy. As in China, the latter was all-important because it was thought to reveal a person's character. The Heian version of love at first sight was of a gentleman falling hopelessly in love after catching a glimpse of a few beautifully drawn lines.

At every stage of a love affair, and for that matter in other social relationships, the aesthetics of writing were stressed. At least as important as the literary merits of the poems exchanged on all occasions were such matters as the color and texture of the paper, the way it was folded, and the selection of a spray of blossoms on which to tie the note. Most critical and most eagerly awaited of these poetic missives were the "morning-after letters" sent by a lover immediately upon returning home from a night of love, from which he had torn himself away just before dawn with a proper show of reluctance. In this world of sensitive people, men and women were expected to respond as readily to sadness as to joy. As we saw with Narihira and his boat mates, both sexes cried freely and frequently and neither hesitated to express self-pity. Tears were a sign of depth of feeling and of a genuine awareness of the ephemeral nature of beauty, the transient nature of all that is good and beautiful.

The Visual Arts

For the purposes of art history, the Heian Period is readily divided into two parts. "Early Heian," sometimes called the Kōnin or Jōgan Period, designates roughly the first century in Kyoto (794–897). In architecture, a transformation of taste is apparent in a variety of forms. It is particularly notable in the layout of the new temples, because when Saichō and Kūkai turned from the Nara Plain to build their monasteries in the mountains, they abandoned the symmetric temple plans used around Nara. Down on the plain, architecture could afford to ignore the terrain, but in the mountains, temple styles and layouts had to accommodate themselves to the physical features of the site. On Mt. Hiei and elsewhere, the natural setting, rock outcroppings, and trees became integral parts of the temple, as had long been the case with shrines devoted to *kami.* Even on Mt. Kōya, where there was enough space to build a Nara-style temple complex, the traditional plans were abandoned.

Changes were also made in building materials and decoration.

During the Nara Period, the main buildings, following continental practice, had been placed on stone platforms; the wood was painted; and the roofs were made of tile. In the Nara temples, only minor buildings had their wood left unpainted and had been fitted with roofs of thatch or bark shingles. Now, these techniques were also used for the main halls. An excellent site at which to observe the resulting aesthetic is Murōji, a temple set in the mountains some forty miles from Nara among magnificent straight, cedar-like trees (cryptomeria) found on Mt. Kōya and at other locations. Not only in the material but also in the size of its buildings, Murōji is more modest than the Nara temples. Its pagoda (see Figure 3.3) is only half the size of that at Hōryūji but makes up in charm and grace what it lacks in grandeur.

FIGURE 3.3 Pagoda of Murōji, Nara Prefecture. (© Lore Schirokauer)

In the Early Heian Period, wood replaced clay, bronze, dry lacquer, and stone as the material of choice for sculpture. Statues, and sometimes their pedestals, were carved from a single block of wood; frequently, the finished sculpture was painted or lacquered. Although some statues of *kami* survive from this period, most Early Heian statuary was Buddhist. Many reflect the demands of the new forms of that religion, particularly esoteric Buddhism. Usually, the statues are formal and symmetric. The flesh is full and firm. The faces are carved in a serious mien, creating an aura of mystery without the hint of a smile or the indication of friendliness. A famous example of Early Heian art is the figure of Sakyamuni (the historic Buddha) at Murōji (see Figure 3.4). It is, among other things, a fine example of "wave" drapery, so called because its lines flow like the sea.

The Shingon school demanded unusual iconographic exactitude in its art, just as it did in its rites. The result was a marked tendency toward formalism, both in reciting the mantras and in creating the religious art. This was especially true of Shingon mandalas, which became complex as artists tried to represent the cosmos graphically, including all the various deities that were emanations of Dainichi. Some altars, for example, at Tōji in Kyoto, were arranged in mandala fashion, but more usual were painted mandalas, such as that shown in Figure 3.5.

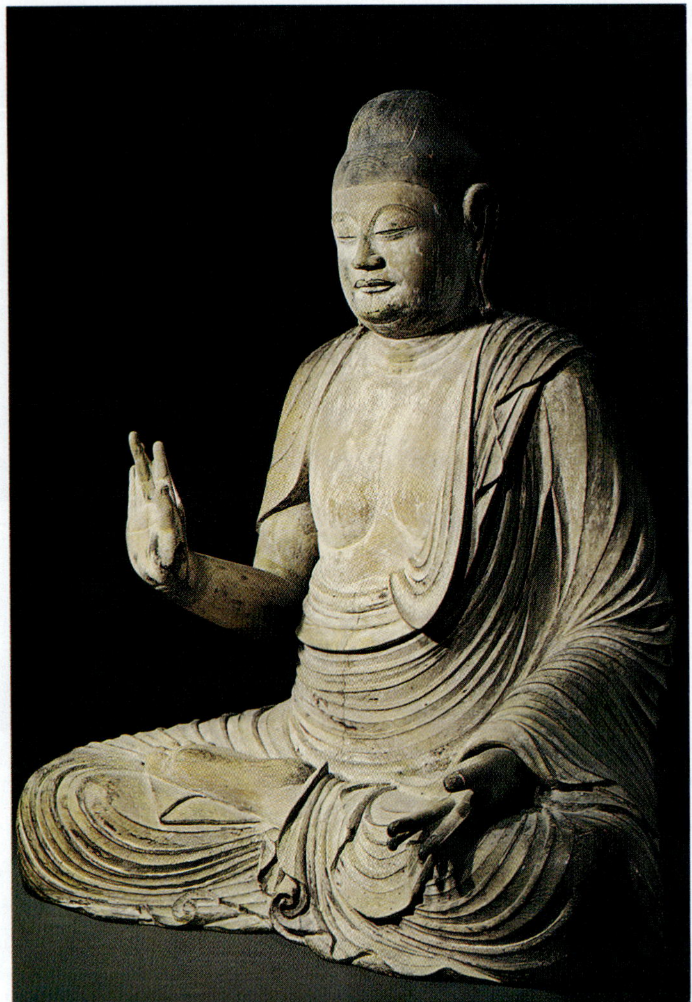

FIGURE 3.4 Sakyamuni, ninth century, 51 in high. Murōji, Nara Prefecture. It has been suggested that the curious swirls at the bottom may be the result of copying in wood an original calligraphic drawing. (© Murōji Publishers)

This is a depiction of the Womb Mandala, representing the world of phenomena. The red lotus at the center symbolizes the heart of the universe. Dainichi is seated on the seedpod of the lotus. Other Buddhas occupy the petals. Altogether there are 407 deities in the Womb Mandala. Its counterpart, the Diamond Mandala, centers on a white lotus and represents the world containing 1314 gods.

A frequent subject of painting and sculpture is Fudō, the Immovable, a ferocious deity bent on annihilating evil. In the *Red Fudō* at Mt. Kōya (see Figure 3.6),

FIGURE 3.5 Womb Mandala. Painting on silk, ninth century. Toji, Kyoto. (© Sakamoto Photo Research Laboratory/Corbis)

the red of the figure and the flames behind him dominate the color scheme and help create a terrifying atmosphere.

In his hand he holds a sword, the handle of which is a thunderbolt (*vajra*), a symbol originating in India as the weapon of the god Indra and in esoteric Buddhism thought to cut through ignorance just as lightning pierces the clouds. A dragon coiled around the blade of the sword adds to the threat. The proportions of the figures and the manner in which the picture fills the space produce a feeling of massiveness characteristic of the art of this age.

Early Heian art at its best achieved a certain majesty, but it has a forbidding quality about it that stands in striking contrast to the sweetness of Late Heian art. Shingon continued to influence the production of art after the ninth century, but

FIGURE 3.6 *Red Fudō*. Color on silk, Early Heian, 51.5 in. Myōin, Mt. Kōya, Wakayama. (© Red Fudō, Myooin, Koyasan, Wakayama)

much of the distinctive work of the period belonged to Amida—and to the Fujiwara. Michinaga had a great temple built in the capital reproducing Amida's paradise, containing "columns with bases of ivory, roof ridges of red gold, gilded doors, platforms of crystal."[14] This temple and a similar one built by Emperor Shirakawa are no longer extant. They have to be reconstructed from texts to give us some idea of what Heian Kyoto looked like.

The historical and artistic origins of such temples go back to Chinese images of the Western Paradise and to its closest terrestrial approximation, the Tang palace garden systematically laid out with its lake and bridges. Similarly, a major feature of the Heian

FIGURE 3.7 *Genji Monogatari*, section of hand-scroll. Color on paper, twelfth century, 8.5 in high. Tokugawa Museum, Nagoya. (© The Tokugawa Art Museum)

mansion (*shinden*) was a garden with one or two artificial hills, carefully placed trees and bamboo, and a pond in which a tiny island was reached by a bridge. A small stream fed the pond and was used to float wine cups at banquets in the Chinese manner. To the north of the garden were the living quarters: rectangular buildings joined by roofed corridors. Like all Japanese-style buildings, these structures were raised a few feet off the ground, and usually a little stream ran under a part of the mansion. Inside, the floors were of polished wood. Flexibility was provided by sliding paper screens, and shutters could be moved to combine small rooms into a larger one. Several kinds of screens (see Figure 3.7) provided some privacy.

Painting

Sliding doors in the Heian *shinden* mansion were frequently decorated with landscapes, such as the picture within a picture in Figure 3.7. In painting, as in the other arts, Heian artists added new styles and genres to those inherited from their Nara Period predecessors. This was not a rejection of continental influences but rather an expansion of possible methods of adapting and responding to them, in some cases in strikingly original ways. Japanese-style paintings (*Yamato-e*) depicted native, not Chinese, subjects, including views of the Japanese landscape. The greatest of such paintings still extant illustrate the *Tale of Genji.* In the Genji Scroll, unlike some later narrative scrolls, the individual scenes are separated by passages of text.

The scene reproduced in Figure 3.7 shows a lady (upper left) looking at pictures while one of her attendants reads aloud the story they illustrate. At the lower left, another lady is having her hair combed. In the foreground is a screen such as

FIGURE 3.8 *Animal Caricatures (Chōjū Giga)*, section of hand-scroll. Attributed to Kakuyū (Toba Sōjō). Late twelfth century, 12 in high. Kozanji, Kyoto. (© Kōzanji, Kyoto)

FIGURE 3.9 Cosmetic box. Lacquered wood, Late Heian, 8.86 in× 12 in × 5.12 in. Hōryūji, Nara Prefecture. (© Sakamoto Photo Research Laboratory/Corbis)

was used by a lady when receiving a gentleman caller. In this and similar paintings, the roofs are removed to afford a view from above into the rooms. The treatment of human features is conventionalized with what art historians refer to as "straight lines for eyes and hooks for noses." The colors were applied quite thickly to produce a richly decorative effect in keeping with aristocratic taste.

Late in the Heian Period there also appeared scrolls (*emaki*) in which no text interrupted the flow of pictorial narrative. Some represent Buddhist hells, but others display a gift for comic caricature. Particularly well known are the cartoon-like animal scrolls attributed to Kakuyū (Toba Sōjō, 1053–1140) but probably completed near the end of the twelfth century. Here frog-priests and rabbit-nobles gambol and disport themselves. In Figure 3.8, a monkey chants before an altar supporting not a Buddha but a frog.

The decorative arts also illustrate the taste of the Heian aristocrats. See, for example, the cosmetic box shown in Figure 3.9. It is adorned with cart wheels, made of mother-of-pearl and gold and half immersed in water. The asymmetry of the design and the unifying flow and rhythm, here supplied by the water, are characteristic of Heian achievements in decoration.

FIGURE 3.10 Byōdōin (Phoenix Pavilion). Uji, Kyoto prefecture. (© Lore Schirokauer)

The Phoenix Pavilion

Sometimes a single site offers a summary of a whole era; for Late Heian art this is true of the Phoenix Pavilion (Byōdōin) (see Figure 3.10). It is located in Uji, a locale some ten miles from Kyoto that figures prominently in the *Tale of Genji.*

The building is associated with the Fujiwaras: it was built by one of Michinaga's sons. It is dedicated to Amida, who occupied the center of a *raigō* in sculpture. Other versions of the *raigō,* painted on the doors and inner walls, show Amida and his entourage descending onto a Japanese landscape. Mother-of-pearl insets in the main dais and in some of the columns contribute to the overall richness of effect.

Amida himself is the work of the sculptor Jōchō. He is fashioned in the joined-wood technique, which affords greater freedom of expression than the Early Heian process of carving from a single piece of wood. It also allows greater and more varied exploitation of the grain. The halo, alive with angels, clouds, and flames, contrasts with the calm of Amida. As Robert Treat Paine so eloquently expressed it, "The tranquility of the Absolute is made to harmonize with the Buddha's sympathy for the finite."[15]

The design of the buildings suggests a bird coming in for a landing or ready for flight. Two bronze phoenixes grace its highest roof. It may be considered a mansion for the Buddha himself. To assure that Amida, too, will enjoy the beauty of the setting and the lovely sight of his hall reflected in the pond, the architect has thoughtfully provided an opening so that he can look out. Here is another example of the unity of building and site that was such a key feature of Heian architecture.

Notes

1. Elizabeth Sato, "The Early Development of the Shoen," in John W. Hall and Jeffrey P. Mass, *Medieval Japan: Essays in Institutional History* (New Haven: Yale Univ. Press, 1974), p. 105.
2. G. Cameron Hurst, Jr., "The Structure of the Heian Court," in John W. Hall and Jeffrey P. Mass, *Medieval Japan: Essays in Institutional History* (New Haven: Yale Univ. Press, 1974), p. 52.
3. Mark Teeuwen, "The *Kami* in Esoteric Buddhist Thought and Practice," Chapter 6, in John Breen and Mark Teeuwen, eds., *Shinto in History: Ways of the Kami* (Richmond, Surrey: Curzon, 2000), pp. 96–97.
4. Burton Watson, trans., *Japanese Literature in Chinese, Vol. 1* (New York: Columbia Univ. Press, 1975), p. 122.
5. Watson, *Japanese Literature in Chinese,* pp. 58–59.
6. Helen Craig McCullough, trans., *Kokin Wakashū: The First Imperial Anthology of Japanese Poetry* (Stanford: Stanford Univ. Press, 1985), p. 3.
7. Steven Carter, trans., *Traditional Japanese Poetry: An Anthology* (Stanford: Stanford Univ. Press, 1991), pp. 106–07.
8. Carter, *Traditional Japanese Poetry: An Anthology,* p. 84.

9. Helen McCullough, trans., *Classical Japanese Prose: An Anthology* (Stanford: Stanford Univ. Press, 1990), p. 43.
10. David Pollack, *The Fracture of Meaning: Japan's Synthesis of China from the Eighth through Eighteenth Centuries* (Princeton: Princeton Univ. Press, 1985), p. 37.
11. Royall Tyler, "Introduction," *The Tale of Genji* (New York: Penguin, 2001), p. xii.
12. Ivan Morris, *The Pillow Book of Sei Shonagon* (New York: Columbia Univ. Press, 1967), p. 258.
13. Morris, *The Pillow Book of Sei Shonagon,* p. 76.
14. Robert Treat Paine and Alexander Soper, *The Art and Architecture of Japan* (Baltimore: Penguin Books, 1955), p. 212.
15. Paine and Soper, *The Art and Architecture of Japan,* p. 45.

4

The Kamakura Period in Japan

Triumph and Fall of the Taira (1156–1185)

Establishment of the Bakufu

Local Governance

The Hōjō Regents

The Mongol Invasion and Its Aftermath

The Warrior and His Ideals

Religion: The Pure Land Sect

Nichiren

Zen

Kami Worship

Religious Art

Literature

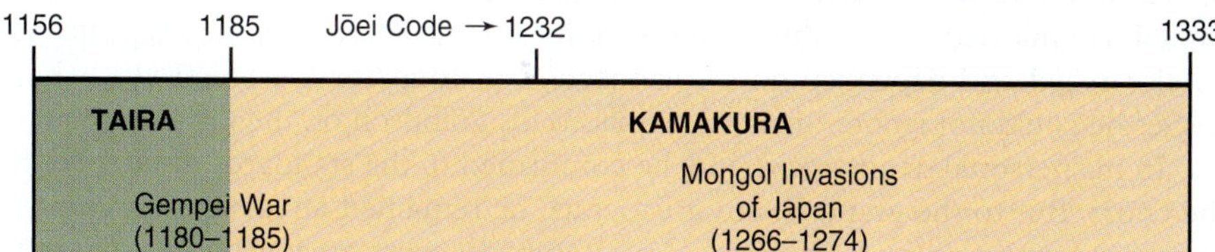

The ascent of the Japanese warrior was a slow process that began well before the Kamakura period and remained incomplete. Although the period, now often identified as early medieval, gets its name from the seat of warrior power at Kamakura in eastern Japan (Kantō), it was a time of shared power. The sanctity of the throne as the ultimate source of authority remained intact. Furthermore, the leaders of both the Minamoto and Taira groups were not just commanders of warriors pure and simple but also, to quote Jeffrey Mass, "bridging figures—military nobles in the truest sense—between the great central aristocrats, who were their patrons, and the great provincial warriors, who were their followers." This helps explain the slow development of warrior power and "the incompleteness of the warrior revolution."[1] Rivalries among the provincial fighting men overshadowed potential ties of common class interests or feelings of solidarity. The same was true of the imperial court. The political intrigues and fighting that marked this transitional period pitted not only warriors and aristocrats against each other but also warriors against warriors, court nobles against court nobles, and even fathers against sons in a complicated struggle for power.

Triumph and Fall of the Taira (1156–1185)

In 1156 open conflict broke out between the retired emperor and the reigning emperor, and military men were called in on both sides. On one side, supporting the cloistered emperor, was a force led by Minamoto no Tameyoshi (1096–1156); on the other side, the emperor, Go-Shirakawa, had the backing of a coalition led by Taira no Kiyomori (1118–1181), which also included among its leaders Tameyoshi's own son, Yoshitomo (1123–1160). Military victory in what is known as the Hōgen Conflict went to Kiyomori's coalition, but the real losers were the court and the old civil nobility.

The outcome left Kiyomori in a position of great power, but the victorious coalition was soon dissolved, and further fighting ensued in the Heiji War (1159–1160). Once again Kiyomori won, this time defeating his former ally, Yoshitomo. These Hōgen and Heiji conflicts were brief and localized but extremely bitter. They were followed by manhunts and executions, because warriors did not share the civilian aristocrats' qualms about taking life. Gone were the days when the usual penalty for being on the wrong side politically was exile.

These military victories gave Kiyomori a new power base, but he operated within the old framework, seeking to dominate the court and government machinery in the capital. He married his daughters into the imperial line and to Fujiwara regents, but he also relied and depended on his connection to Emperor Go-Shirakawa, whose wishes he could not ignore. In 1180 he placed his grandson on the throne.

In his personal deportment, too, he conformed to the standards of taste set by the court. But to the grand Kyoto aristocrats, he remained an arrogant provincial parvenu, worthy only of contempt. An attempt to exert greater control over the court by transferring it to a site near modern Kobe failed. More successful was Kiyomori's handling of the troublesome temple armies. He attacked and burned two of the worst offenders, both in Nara: the Tōdaiji and Kōfukuji, the prime temple of the Fujiwara family.

Conditions in the capital were unusually harsh during these years. Storms, earthquakes, and disease afflicted the city, which, as always, was also susceptible to the ravages of fire. A major conflagration destroyed a third of the city in 1177; in one two-month period after the fire, more than 40,000 corpses were found in the streets of the capital.

Kiyomori's most serious problem was that during his ascendancy the old institutions remained as weak as ever. He could no more exercise complete control over the provinces, where the sources of actual power now lay, than he could over the cloistered emperor. Led by Yoshitomo's son Yoritomo (1147–1199), the Minamoto took advantage of this situation to rebuild their power. With the support of many eastern Taira and Minamoto families, Yoritomo initiated the Gempei War (1180–1185), which culminated in the permanent defeat of the Taira. Contributing to this outcome was the brilliant generalship of Yoshitsune (1159–1189), Yoritomo's younger brother, who defeated the Taira at sea and on land. Later, Yoshitsune incurred the suspicion of his powerful brother, who, in the end, turned his armed might against him and brought about his death.

The wide extent of the fighting, a style of combat that placed a premium on personal valor, contrasts between the Taira (who had adopted many of the ways of Kyoto) and the rougher eastern warriors, and the effect of the war on subsequent developments have assured it a lasting place in the Japanese imagination and in literature. It is recounted in Japan's major literary epic, *The Tale of the Heike* (*Heike monogatari*), a tale widely chanted among all classes, and it generated a host of minor romances, including some that embellished the story of Yoshitsune, transforming it into a heroic legend.

Establishment of the Bakufu

Yoritomo was not a great general, but he was a good judge of men, a consummate politician, and an effective organizer. Carefully, he consolidated his position in the east. With his headquarters in the small fishing village of Kamakura, he built a se-

FIGURE 4.1 Japan, 1200–1600.

cure base for warrior power (see Figure 4.1). There he established his *bakufu*, literally "tent government," a term that evokes the military origins of his power. Legitimization for the new order came from the emperor, who in 1192 "appointed" Yoritomo shogun or, to use the full term, *seiï taishōgun* (barbarian-suppressing general). Under the theoretical sovereignty of the emperor, the shogun's government exercised substantial "delegated" power. This was the beginning of an institution (the shogunate) that lasted until 1868.

At the heart of Yoritomo's power in eastern Japan were ties of vassalage, aptly defined by Peter Duus as "a personal bond of loyalty and obedience by which a warrior promised service to a lord or chieftain in return for military protection, security, and assistance."[2] The ties of vassalage were more inclusive and expandable than the old kinship bonds, which, however, did not disappear. Vassalage was contractual in the sense that there was at least a tacit understanding of mutual obligations, but these were never spelled out or incorporated in legal documents. Nor were there legal mechanisms for altering or dissolving the arrangement. Ideally, it called for deep personal devotion of vassal to lord rather than the more abstract loyalty demanded in an impersonal bureaucratic state; but in practice, especially in turbulent and unsettled times, much depended on the individuals involved.

From his vassals (*gokenin,* "honorable housemen") Yoritomo demanded and expected absolute loyalty. Such loyalty was granted him partly as a result of the confidence he inspired in his men, some of whose families had served the Minamoto for generations. Others, particularly in western Japan, cast their lot with Yoritomo only after they had been impressed with his visible accomplishments. Calculations of military and political advantage on the part of the lesser lords played a role in augmenting Yoritomo's strength, which after the defeat of the Taira surpassed that of any possible rival, military or civil. Economic inducements also provided powerful motivation. Those who served him could expect confirmation of the land rights (*shiki*) they already held, and they could hope for further rewards in the form of rights over land confiscated from the enemies of the Minamoto. Economic self-interest reinforced the bonds of personal vassalage in Japan just as in feudal Europe; it was the cement that ensured the cohesiveness of the system.

There are certain striking resemblances between Kamakura Japan and feudal Europe. Both featured rule by a military aristocracy that held predominant local power, a system of vassalage, and land as a source of wealth. However, the Kamakura system functioned in uneasy tandem with the political and economic system centered on Kyoto. Yoritomo had neither the power nor the intent to eliminate the old order but used it to his own advantage in consolidating his power. His vassals received land rights, not land, and at least until the early thirteenth century the old Kyoto nobility and religious establishments retained much of their political influence and wealth.

Local Governance

The most important power "delegated" to Yoritomo was legal control over the staffing of provincial posts, which enabled him to appoint his own men to administrative positions in the provinces. He was also authorized to appoint his men to the newly created position of land steward or overseer (*jitō*) and as military governors (*shugō*).

Land stewards were appointed to estates and given official responsibility for the collection of rents and the forwarding of dues to the absentee holders of rights in the estates—that is, the court aristocracy, the imperial family, and the great religious establishments. The stewards also received considerable police and judicial authority over the estates and were rewarded by grants of rights (*shiki*) to a portion of the estate income. The function of the military governors, appointed to most provinces, was to provide liaison between the *bakufu* and its retainers and to maintain security. They were responsible for suppressing rebels and punishing major crimes. The appointment of stewards and military governors thus served both the cause of *bakufu* power and that of public order, but it left the imperial system of provincial governance basically intact.

The restoration of order benefited everyone, and the new system recognized the economic prerogatives and the continued legitimacy of the Kyoto establishment.

However, tensions inevitably resulted from the intrusion of a lord–vassal system into the old estate structure, as well as between the continued coexistence of private estates and publicly administered lands (*kokugaryo*). Disputes between stewards and estate proprietors were endemic. In the long run, the advantage clearly lay with the local warriors, but the *bakufu,* determined to uphold the system, frequently ruled against steward's attempts to extend their powers at the expense of proprietors or peasants. Tensions likewise arose between military governors and officials of the much older imperial provincial office. The former, with their military prowess, eventually eclipsed the latter in terms of de facto control, but this was a slow process and not necessarily accompanied by open conflict.

Early medieval peasants varied widely in status and wealth. At the top were the *myoshu,* managers and later owners of some land with responsibilities for tax collection who also derived wealth from entrepreneurial village activities such as money lending and sericulture. Cultivators received a share of the harvest. At the bottom were transient laborers and the hereditary household servants of wealthy families. There were no restrictions on geographic and social mobility. Peasants were free to leave, but when they did, they lost any claim to the land.

The coexistence between Kamakura and Kyoto was tested in 1221, when Emperor Go-Toba (1190–1229) used imperial lands and Buddhist monasteries to raise a force of dissatisfied warriors in an attempt to restore imperial power. He was soundly defeated. The end result was to strengthen the shogunate, which used the occasion to confiscate 3000 estates, appoint additional stewards in central and western Japan, and establish its own deputies in Kyoto. Faced with widespread general disorder, the *bakufu* sought to strengthen its own place within the system rather than to devise a new system.

The Hōjō Regents

Yoritomo established the Kamakura shogunate on a firm foundation but did not succeed in founding a dynasty of shoguns. He killed off rivals within his own family, but his death in 1199 was followed by a struggle for power.

Emerging victorious was the Hōjō, the family of Yoritomo's remarkable, strong-minded widow, Masako (1157–1225), who herself dominated shogunal politics for a time and was dubbed the "nun shogun." Her father became the first in a line of de facto Hōjō rulers, although they never assumed the office of shogun. That was held by a puppet, who after 1219 was not even a Minamoto, because in that year a Fujiwara infant received the appointment. Meanwhile, the Hōjō, by placing family members in key posts, exercised control over the *bakufu*. In this way, real power was doubly divorced from apparent authority: in theory, the country was ruled by an emperor, but this emperor was largely under the control of his abdicated father (the retired emperor); meanwhile, in Kamakura, the other locus of government, the power ostensibly "delegated" to the shogun was exercised by Hōjō ministers.

Although the overall structure seems complex, organization of the Kamakura shogunate remained relatively simple in keeping with its modest scope of government. An Office of Samurai looked after the affairs of the shogunate's vassals (*gokenin*) and generally supervised military and police matters. A board of inquiry (*monchūjo*) dealt with various judicial matters and under the Hōjō handled cases arising outside of Kamakura. General administration was under the jurisdiction of an Office of Administration similar to the household offices used by the great Heian families. Yoritomo designated it the *mandokoro*, the usual name for such a household bureau. The heads of these three bureaus participated in a council that advised Yoritomo, who made the final decisions himself. The council was led by the chief of the *mandokoro*, and it was in this capacity that the Hōjō exercised their power. In 1225 an innovative Hōjō statesman created a Council of State to allow broader warrior participation in government, but the Hōjō soon dominated this body.

The Hōjō concept of government is reflected in the law code of 1232, the Jōei Code, the first codification of warrior law. One of its purposes was to define the duties of stewards and military governors. Another major concern was to clarify matters of land tenure and succession. Included among the latter were the property rights of women. For example, women had some inheritance rights, and divorced women could retain the land they had originally brought into the marriage.

The code emphasized the impartial administration of justice in settling disputes among warriors, disputes that usually concerned land rights. The adjudication of such matters was one of the shogunate's prime functions, and much of its power and prestige rested on samurai confidence in the equity of its decisions. The Jōei Code sought to achieve this by setting forth its provisions in a simple and direct manner and by restricting itself to a small number of regulations. For cases not covered by precedent, it advised recourse to common sense. As the need arose, additional articles were added to the code. Its reputation as a symbol of justice was so strong that a revised version of it was adopted by the next shogunate in the fourteenth century.

Another indication of Hōjō effectiveness and the resilience of the institutions of the *bakufu* was the ability of the regime to withstand a most formidable military challenge and to survive the strains it produced in the body politic.

The Mongol Invasion and Its Aftermath

The Mongol conquest of East Asia was in full swing when the Jōei Code was issued, but it was another third of a century before the momentum of the Mongol conquest was felt in Japan. Before they were faced with the need to defend themselves against the Mongols, the Kamakura statesmen had successfully avoided political or military entanglement in continental affairs, although they did nothing to discourage trade with the Song, which flourished both before and after the founding of the shogunate. Although this trade consisted mostly of luxury items, for China it brought a drain of copper coinage, which posed a problem for Song finances. A major effect in Japan of the trade with China was to stimulate a renewed interest in Chinese culture. The shogunate also maintained cordial relations with Korea: when, in 1227, the depredations of Japanese pirates off the Korean coast prompted Korean complaints, the *bakufu* ordered the offenders arrested and executed.

The Mongols changed all that. In 1266, even before the conquest of the Southern Song had been completed, Khubilai Khan dispatched his first messenger to Japan demanding submission. This threat produced great consternation at court in Kyoto, but the shogunate remained calm, determined to resist. It took the Mongols until 1274 to organize a military expedition, but in that year a force of about 30,000 was sent to Japan. They landed near Hakata, in northern Kyushu, and fought briefly with a Japanese force assembled by the *bakufu* but consisting mostly of local warriors. Fortunately for the Japanese, a great storm destroyed this expedition. Heavy casualties did not deter Khubilai Khan from trying again. He renewed his demands only to meet with rebuff; the Japanese showed their determination to resist by executing his envoys. In 1281 Khubilai sent a much larger force, estimated at 140,000 men, to crush the Japanese. But the shogunate, too, had used the intervening years in military preparation: they built a stone wall along Hakata Bay, amassed troops, and trained them in the techniques of group fighting employed by the Mongols, which contrasted with the individual combat customary in Japanese warfare. They fought for seven weeks before nature intervened once more; another great storm, called the *kamikaze* ("divine wind") by the Japanese, settled the issue. About half the men sent by Khubilai perished in this fruitless attempt to add Japan to his empire.

Still the Great Khan did not give up. Preparations for a third attempt were in progress when he died in 1294. Only then was the project abandoned. But the *bakufu* did not know that: it continued the policy of military preparedness until 1312. In repulsing these attacks, the shogunate achieved a great success and further increased its power vis-à-vis the civilian court. But it had to share the glory of victory with temples and shrines, which claimed credit for securing divine intervention. Indeed, the notion of Japan as a special land protected by its deities gained currency from this time. This idea was central to the teachings of Nichiren (described later).

For the shogunate, however, the Mongol invasions proved its eventual undoing. Fighting the Mongol invaders, unlike internal warfare, brought in no new lands or booty with which to meet the expectations of warriors demanding their just rewards. When the shogunate proved unable to satisfy warrior claims, the *bushi* lost confidence in the regime. Their loyalty was weakened, and as they increasingly turned for support to local authorities (military governors and the stronger stewards), centrifugal forces came to the fore. The characteristic Hōjō response was to draw more power into their own hands, a policy not designed to deal with the underlying causes of their deteriorating situation. At the same time, economic pressures and the realities of power worked against aristocratic civilian interests, as military stewards proved increasingly reluctant to forward payments to Kyoto. Vis-à-vis the peasants, too, the stewards were assuming ever-greater powers. If a steward departed too far from custom in his demands, the peasants could appeal to higher authority (including Kamakura), or they could negotiate with the steward himself. However, the stewards' local authority was so extensive that increasingly they treated the estates as though they were their own property. The shogunal policy of balancing military with civilian prerogatives was breaking down. As the shogunate declined, the peculiar dual governance by court and *bakufu*, aristocrat and warrior, was also coming to an end.

The Warrior and His Ideals

By background and training, the ideal *bushi* was a man different from the Heian aristocrat. As a warrior, he was called upon to exhibit martial skills and to demonstrate valor and manly pride. Many of the features later idealized and incorporated into a "code of the samurai" are evident in medieval epics such as *The Tale of the Heike*. Virile, selfless, and incorruptible, the ideal samurai showed disdain for death and concern for maintaining his honor. It was even held that he should be ready to commit ritual suicide by disembowelment (*seppuku*) rather than face capture or dishonor.

In Kamakura Japan as elsewhere, the ideal must not be confused with the reality. Indeed, the more demanding an ideal, the rarer those who attained it. Even in the fictional *Tale of Genji* there is only one shining prince, and surely Heian Kyoto was not totally lacking in boors! Similarly, warriors who fled from combat, turned on allies, or allowed themselves to be captured were numerous. In practice, skills in negotiation and alliance building and careful management of the extended family and its property were as much hallmarks of the successful medieval warrior as martial ability and valor in battle. Moreover, there were cases of women successfully leading *bushi* houses without a male head.

Religion: The Pure Land Sect

The turbulence and uncertainties accompanying the transition from aristocratic to warrior rule tended to confirm the belief that history had indeed entered its final phase of degeneracy (*mappō*) and made people all the more receptive to the solace of religion. One result was the continuing growth and development of the popularizing and pietistic trends exemplified earlier by the activities and teachings of Kūya and Genshin. A major leader in this tradition was Hōnen, who advanced the

Pure Land School of Buddhism (Jōdo; Qingdu in Chinese), named after the paradise in the West over which presides Amida (Amitabha), the Buddha of Infinite Light. To the faithful it offered the hope of rebirth in the land of bliss. In practice, it stressed the *nembutsu,* and Hōnen carried the invocation of Amida further than his predecessors by teaching that the *nembutsu* was not just one method for attaining salvation but rather the best and indeed the only method suitable for the age.

When Hōnen expressed his ideas in writing, his book was burned by the monks on Mt. Hiei, the bastion of Buddhist orthodoxy. He remained a controversial person, suffering in his seventies an exile of four years from which he was allowed to return only a year before he died. Underlying the emphasis on the invocation of Amida was a belief in salvation through faith rather than through works or religious observances. Hōnen himself, on his deathbed, declined to hold the usual cord connected to an Amida to draw him to paradise. His persistent rejection of traditional ritual and scholasticism helps explain the hostility of the older schools.

Pure Land Amidism was further developed by Honen's greatest and most renowned disciple, Shinran (1173–1262), founder of the True Pure Land School (Jōdo Shinshu). Although he lived much earlier, Shinran has been compared with the founders of Christian Protestantism because, like them, he insisted that humans were so debased that they could not possibly gain salvation through their own efforts or "self-power" but must depend on the "other power" of Amida. Specifically, salvation comes through faith—frequently experienced by the individual in an act of conversion. The boundless compassion of Amida embraces the bad man or woman and the good. Indeed, bad individuals, conscious of their lack of worth, may be closer to salvation than good people who are incapable of resisting self-congratulation on their merits and who rely on their own efforts to attain rebirth in paradise. Once converted and granted faith, each person will naturally bring the message to others, repeating the *nembutsu* not out of a desire to be saved or for reassurance but out of gratitude and joy.

Shinran was himself filled with a sense of his own sinfulness. "A baldheaded old fool" is the name he adopted for himself. He also carried rejection of the old monastic observances further than any of his predecessors; he ate meat and even married. Exiled for his radical views, he spent his life proclaiming his religious message among the common people as one of themselves.

Shinran did not intend to found a new school, nor did he acknowledge having disciples. But he left many followers who further developed the True Pure Land School, attracting many adherents. In the fifteenth century, Rennyo (1415–1499) organized the community of believers into a disciplined body, ready and able to fight for their beliefs. The True Pure Land School is still one of the largest religious organizations in Japan, now divided into two branches, each headed by descendants of Shinran. This tradition of hereditary leadership was made possible by the abandonment of celibacy. It is also consistent with the value placed on family and with Jōdo faith in the benign "other power" of Amida.

Other popular forms of Pure Land Buddhism also flourished in medieval Japan. One of the best-known Pure Land evangelists was Ippen (1239–1289), who, like Kūya (see Figure 4.2), practiced the dancing *nembutsu* and who became

FIGURE 4.2 Kōshō, *Kūya.* Wood, Kamakura, approx. 46 in high. Rokuharamitsuji, Kyoto. (© National Commission for Protection of Cultural Properties of Japan)

the subject of a famous narrative scripture scroll.

Nichiren

Many older schools of Buddhism practiced invocation of the Buddha of the Western Paradise without, however, abandoning their older rituals or beliefs. But tolerance was not universal. A vociferous and vehement opponent of Pure Land teachings, as of the doctrines of all the other rival schools new and old, was Nichiren (1222–1282), one of Japan's most flamboyant religious leaders. Like Hōnen and Shinran, he was exiled for his advocacy of unacceptable beliefs, but unlike the others, he was almost put to death; he was saved, according to his followers, only by a miracle, as lightning struck the poised executioner's sword. Nichiren's conviction of the correctness of his teachings was buttressed by his belief that he was a reincarnation of a bodhisattva specially entrusted with the Lotus Sutra, the only text incorporating Buddha's teachings in all their dimensions.

Nichiren, although born into a family of poor fishermen, was a learned man. But like Hōnen and Shinran, his message was simple: faith in the Lotus Sutra, rather than a mastery of its contents, was the requirement for salvation. In place of the invocation of Amida practiced by Pure Land Buddhists, he substituted *namu myōhō renge-kyō* (hail to the Lotus Sutra of the wonderful law), usually chanted to the beat of a drum.

In adversity Nichiren demonstrated a depth of conviction and strength of character readily appreciated by warriors who valued similar virtues. Perhaps his origins in eastern Japan also enhanced his standing among the *bushi* who had established the shogunate. Furthermore, he was greatly attached to the land and was Japan-centered to an unusual degree, envisioning Japan as the headquarters for his faith, which from there would spread throughout the world. The very name he chose for himself, Nichiren (*nichi* = sun, *ren* = lotus), indicated his dual devotion to the Land of the Rising Sun and the Lotus Sutra. In his view, the one required the other. Repeatedly, he warned that the Lotus was essential for Japan and predicted dire consequences if other schools remained in favor. He prophesied the Mongol invasions, thereby increasing his credibility. Convinced that Buddhism had made its long journey across Asia to Japan to attain perfection, he cited the failed Mongol invasions as proof of Japan's special, divinely protected status. Nichiren's concern for state and country, his courage, and his zeal remained an inspiration for his followers in later times. One man is even said to have journeyed to Siberia as a missionary. Nichiren, the man and the faith, have retained their magnetism to the present. Today he is venerated not only by the traditional Lotus sect but also by the Sōka Gakkai (Value Creation Society), a religious body whose membership has burgeoned since World War II.

Zen

Pure Land Buddhism and the teachings of Nichiren appealed widely to warriors, but Zen, with a more limited following, enjoyed official favor and *bakufu* support. In Japan, as in China, Zen (Chan in Chinese) was taught and practiced before it became institutionalized with its own temples during the Kamakura shogunate. In Japan it was promoted by two monks, Eisai (1141–1215) and Dōgen (1200–1253), both of whom traveled to China.

Eisai made two trips and brought back not only religious ideas but also great enthusiasm for tea, thus initiating the long association between that beverage and Japanese Zen. He was a follower of the Rinzai (Linji in Chinese) school, practicing the use of the *kōan* riddles. Eisai found support in Kamakura, but in Kyoto he accommodated himself to the religious life of the old capital by observing Tendai and Shingon practices and Zen rules. He even recommended the *nembutsu* and allowed chants and prayers.

Dōgen, in contrast, was uncompromising in his attitude toward secular authority. He eventually settled in the mountains remote from Kamakura and Kyoto, consistently declined worldly honors, and built a small temple, which later grew into the great monastery of Eiheiji. Dōgen differed from Eisai also in the type of Zen he preached, because he brought back from China the doctrines of the Sōto (Caodao in Chinese) school, which emphasized sitting in silent meditation (*zazen*) without a specific object or goal in mind, a gradual process of realizing the Buddha nature through the body and the mind. In his attitude toward the transmission of the truth, Dōgen was a moderate, accepting scriptural authority and the authority of the personal transmission from patriarch to patriarch. The influence enjoyed by the Sōto school in Japan was much greater than that accorded Caodao in China.

The proper practice of Zen made great demands on its practitioners, demands no less severe than those encountered in military training. Seekers after illumination did not, like the second patriarch, have to sever an arm to demonstrate their seriousness of purpose, but they did have to endure a period of waiting and abuse

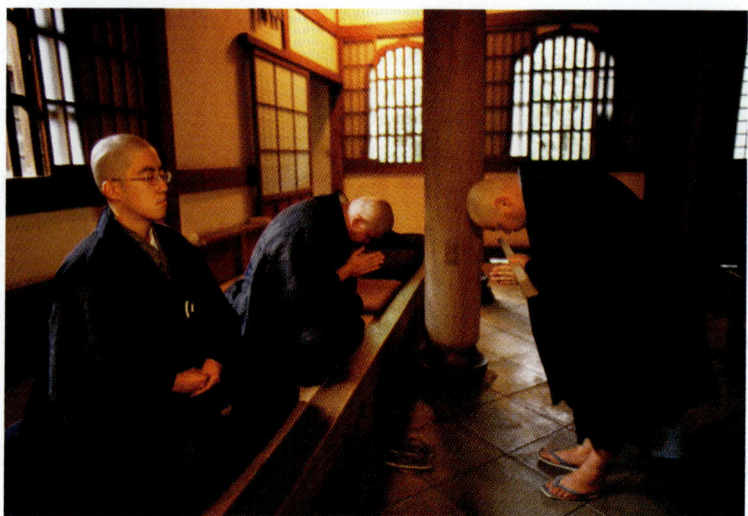

FIGURE 4.3 *Zazen.* Even now, the average day of the Zen Buddhist monk in Japan may run from 3 A.M. to 9 P.M. and is filled with a steady round of religious observances, manual labor, and *zazen.* The latter is itself a rigorous discipline, a period of formal meditation in which no bodily movement is allowed. A senior monk makes the rounds with a long flat stick to strike those who show signs of losing concentration. (© Michael S. Yamashita/Corbis)

before they were admitted to the spartan, rigorously regulated life of the temple (see Figure 4.3).

The fortunes of Zen were furthered not only by native Japanese monks but also by Chinese masters who traveled to Japan and won considerable influence in Kamakura. For example, the Kenchōji, one of the great Kamakura temples, was built by a Hōjō regent who invited a Chinese monk to become its abbot. Several of the regents became deeply versed in Zen. With Zen, the monks brought from China a variety of artistic and cultural influences of which tea is just one example. The secular influence of Zen became even more marked in the succeeding Muromachi period. The continuity of Zen influence is reflected in the career of Musō Soseki (1275–1351), also known as Musō Kokushi (Musō the National Master), who successively enjoyed the favor of the Hōjō regent, the emperor Go-Daigo, and the Ashikaga shogunal house (see Chapter 5).

Kami Worship

No account of the religious scene in the Kamakura period is complete without mentioning the continuing appeal of the native spirits, in the so-called Shinto tradition. In the medieval period, *kami* worship had been subsumed within Buddhism institutionally, doctrinally, and even to a great extent physically, with temple compounds typically containing a shrine. Shinto's influence on Buddhism in turn was profound: Ippen, for example, identified individual Buddhas and bodhisattvas with *kami*, and Tendai and Shingon remained hospitable to the *kami*. *Kami* worship in turn borrowed freely from Buddhism. The Inner and Outer Shrines at Ise were regarded as Shingon mandalas. It may well be that there was a special affinity between Shingon and Shinto; indeed, the major Shinto writer and champion of the imperial house, Kitabatake Chikafusa (1293–1354), ascribed the success of Shingon in Japan, as opposed to in China, to its compatibility with Shinto.

Another syncretic religion was preached by mountain priests (*yamabushi*), who embodied a combination of shamans, monks, and Daoist mountain ascetics. They identified mountain *kami* with Buddhist incarnations and emphasized the role of religious retreats in the mountains. In their ceremonials and incantations they blended Shinto and Buddhist elements. This mountain religion (Shugendō) had enjoyed aristocratic patronage during the Heian period but now turned increasingly toward the common people for support. In the process, it furthered the spread of Buddhism to northern Japan.

Religious Art

When the Taira destroyed the Tōdaiji and Kōfukuji temples in Nara, they inadvertently prepared the way for a great revival of Buddhist sculpture, stimulated by a happy conjunction of artistic talent and generous patronage. Old works that were damaged or destroyed had to be restored or replaced. Patronage for this effort came from both the *bakufu* and the court, giving rise to a school of highly talented artists (all of whom chose names ending in "kei"). Artistic inspiration came partly from the sculpture in the old capital area, but the best Kamakura sculptures also convey a new realism and robust vigor. The leading figure of the new school was Unkei (active 1163–1223), whose career exemplified the blending of the old and the new. He participated in the restoration of some traditional Nara sculptures, but he also traveled and worked in eastern Japan, where he was exposed to the values and tastes of the warrior class. Both experiences influenced his work.

A good example of the new style is provided by the guardian figures flanking the main entrance of Tōdaiji, a joint enterprise in which Unkei participated (see Figure 4.4). In such guardian figures, ferocity tends to take precedence over realism, but this is not the case in sculpture portraits of milder Buddhist saints and monks. A new device that appeared at this time was the use of crystal for the eyes to give them a life-like sparkle. The figure of Kūya (see Figure 4.2) goes beyond realism: even the words of the priest were portrayed as a string of small Amidas emerging from his mouth. Amidas came in all sizes. In his compassionate benevolence the massive Kamakura Amida, paid for by funds raised from the common people, leans forward to look down on pilgrim and sightseer (see Figure 4.5).

FIGURE 4.4 *Niō* (Guardian Figure), Great South Gate. Wood, approx. 30 ft high. Tōdaiji, Nara. These figures are constructed of many pieces of wood carefully fitted together. Kamakura sculptors rejected the delicate serenity of Late Heian sculpture but not its new technique. The wood is undercut to emphasize tendons and muscle, imparting an effect of virility and strength. (© Mark Schumacher)

Along with Amida, Kannon continued to enjoy great popularity. Dating from the middle of the thirteenth century, and thus roughly contemporary with the Kamakura Amida, are the breathtaking contents of the Sanjusangendō (Rengeōin) in Kyoto. It features a seated "thousand-armed" Kannon, which is flanked by a thousand standing statues of the same Kannon in ranks, a Kamakura manifestation of the Buddhist proclivity for repetition. Of greater artistic appeal are some of the realistic Kamakura sculptures also found in this hall.

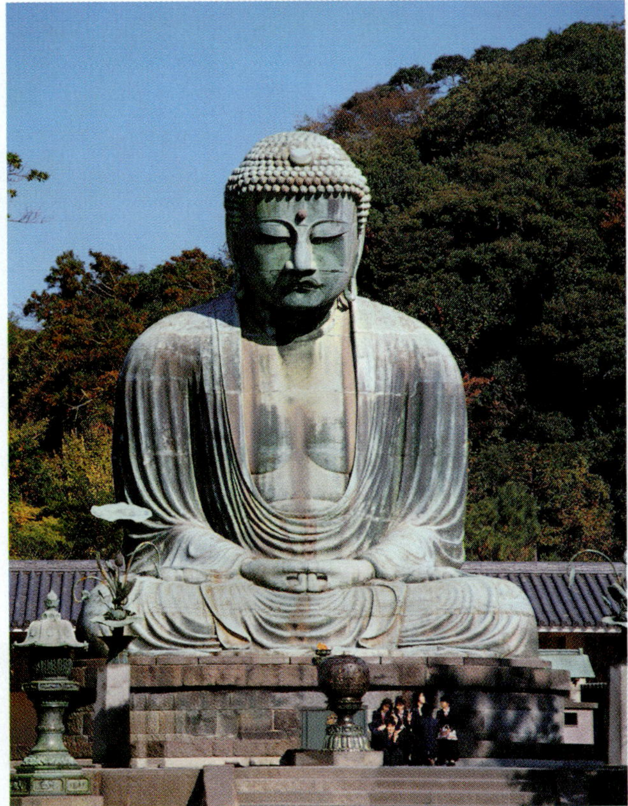

FIGURE 4.5 *Amida*. Bronze, Kamakura, approx. 49 ft high, completed in 1252. Artistically, this figure compares favorably with the poorly restored giant Buddha at Nara, but its effectiveness is probably more a function of its dimensions than of any inherent artistic excellence. It is partially hollow; inside, steps lead to a little window in Amida's back, through which visitors may look out. (© Royalty-Free/ Corbis)

The vitality of early Kamakura sculpture gradually waned, and the decline in the quality of Buddhist sculpture turned out to be permanent. Craftsmen continued to produce Buddhist figures in imitation of older styles, but there was a dearth of new departures or even creative revivals. The Buddhist religion and the visual arts continued to enrich each other, but after the Kamakura period the relationship between them took a new form.

Chinese influence, visible in some fourteenth-century religious sculpture, can also be seen in architecture, which drew on at least two distinctive Chinese traditions. One style of great power was known in Japan as the "Indian style"

a

b

FIGURE 4.6 The Great South Gate. Tōdaiji, Nara, with detail showing the hallmark of the "Indian style" bracketing constructed along a single, transverse axis and inserted through, rather than mounted on, the supporting columns. As Sherman Lee observes, "The gate structure is logical but simple, almost heavy rather than lucid, with a brute strength that overpowers memories of the refined Heian architectural style and which finds no later repetition." Sherman Lee, *A History of Far Eastern Art* (New York: Harry N. Abrams, 1964), p. 324. (a and b: © Lore Schirokauer)

FIGURE 4.7 Engakuji Relic Hall. Thirteenth century, Kamakura. Unfortunately, the Chinese prototypes have not survived, and the building is now covered with an incongruous Japanese-style thatched roof. (a and b: From Robert Treat Paine and Alexander Soper, *The Art and Architecture of Japan* [Pelican History of Art, 2nd Edition. 1974]. Reprinted with permission of Penguin Books Ltd.)

(Tenjikuyō), although it was actually imported from Fujian in China. Its best example is the gate of Tōdaiji (see Figure 4.6), which shelters the two guardian figures described previously. This style was short lived in Japan but survived in Fujian, from which a later version was reintroduced to Japan in the seventeenth century with the Ōbakusan (Huangboshan) sect of Zen.

Perhaps the Japanese called this style "Indian" because it ran counter to the prevailing fashions of Song architecture and taste. In any case, they reserved the term "Chinese style" (Karayō) for buildings modeled on the prevailing continental style. In Kamakura, the Kenchōji (1253) was supposed to be a copy of a famous Chan temple in Hangzhou, and the Engakuji (see Figure 4.7) is said to have been built by an architect who had traveled to Hangzhou to study the Chinese model.

Literature

The crosscurrents of Kamakura history and the styles of life prevalent at court, in the military, and in the temple found expression in a rich and varied literature, much of it of the highest quality. Collections such as the late Heian *Tales of Times Now Past* gained popularity. Among the best known is the thirteenth-century *Tales from the Uji Collection,* which in vivid and direct language recounts tales of the morals and miracles of Buddhism and a range of other, nonreligious anecdotes. One story, made famous by a twelfth-century narrative scroll, concerns the holy man of Mt. Shigi who obtained his daily food by sending his begging bowl flying down from his mountain to be filled. When one day the bowl was disdained by a wealthy man, it flew back up the mountain with his entire rice-filled warehouse. The painter had great fun depicting the consternation of the rich man as his storehouse flies off. The episode ends happily when the holy man decides to return the rice, and the bowl flies back down the mountain carrying one bag, followed by all the other bags flying through the air in single file.

The *Confessions of Lady Nijō,* completed in the first decade of the fourteenth century and thus quite late in the Kamakura period, takes us back to the familiar world of the court lady. In the early chapters we find her conducting her love affairs and paying attention to the fine points of aesthetics against a general background of melancholy awareness that reminds us of the *Tale of Genji.* The last two sections, however, are an account of her life as a Buddhist nun, fulfilling vows to copy the sutras, and traveling to holy sites (including Ise). She also travels to Kamakura, where her advice on dress and decoration is eagerly sought, because in these matters the prestige of the court remained paramount.

Poetry, too, remained an integral part of court life. Some fine poetry was produced in the late twelfth and early thirteenth centuries under the auspices of two great poets, father and son: Fujiwara Shunzei (1114–1204) and Fujiwara Teika (1162–1241). They were descendants of Michinaga, although poetry, not politics, was their world.

In addition to his fame as a poet, Shunzei was recognized by his contemporaries as an arbiter of poetic taste and was influential in developing a new aesthetic, which sought to deepen the expression of melancholy (*aware*) by adding to it a new dimension of profound mystery (*yūgen*). A mood of sadness also colors the word *sabi,* first used as a term of praise by Shunzei, for whom it basically meant "loneliness." These qualities permeated the aesthetic climate of the subsequent Ashikaga period and will be encountered again in our description of the characteristic achievements of that era.

Teika presided over the committee that compiled the *Shinkokinshū* (*New Kokinshu,* 1205), one of the great collections of Japanese verse and often considered the last of the great imperial anthologies. The following poem by the priest Saigyō (1118–1190) is an example of the poetic qualities found in the best court poetry:

> Even one who claims
> to no longer have a heart

feels this sad beauty:
snipes flying up from the marsh
on an evening in autumn dusk.[3]

Buddhism demands that a devout man give up the feelings of his own heart even when they are humbly aesthetic.

One of Teika's poems included in the anthology is from a series of 100 poems on the moon. (The composition of such series was one way Japanese poets transcended the limitations of the *tanka.*)

On her straw of straw
she waits as the autumn wind
deepens the night,
spreading moonlight for her robe—
the maiden of the Uji River.[4]

Even in translation the beauty of the original imagery remains apparent. In contrast, the following is just one example of a poem that dispenses with imagery—a practice not unusual in *tanka.* It was written by Lady Jusammi Chikaku, who lived around 1300 (after the great age of Saigyū, Shunzei, and Teika). It is included here to remind us that poetry did not end with them and that ladies and gentlemen continued to excel in this medium. It deals with one of the recurrent motifs in statements of the woman's side of love, the breaking of love's promises.

In recent days
I can no longer say of wretchedness
That it is wretched,
For I feel my grief has made me
No longer truly capable of grief.[5]

The theme is ageless. The private, delicate yet resilient world of the court poet seemed far removed from the hurly-burly of politics and warfare; affected though these poets were by the events of their age, in their poetry they did not deign to notice the intrigue and the fighting.

A literary man who wrote excellent prose and fine poetry was Kamo no Chōmei (1153–1216), who withdrew from the turbulent world to live quietly in a hut on a mountainside near Kyoto. His *An Account of My Hut* is a carefully constructed essay about the world around him: the calamities such as fire, famine, and earthquake suffered by those who remained behind in the world and observations on the simplicity and solitude of his own life. Deeply religious, he fell short of the complete detachment taught by Buddhism but found consolation in repeating the *nembutsu.*

Kamakura literature also devotes much attention to the world of the warrior, as reflected in the military tales and romances. We have already mentioned the tales that grew around Yoshitsune, the younger brother of Yoritomo. Often retold were accounts of his heroic exploits and those of his right-hand man, the stout monk and formidable fighter Benkei, who became his lifelong follower after the young Yoshitsune bested him in a sword fight on a bridge. Stories extolling bravery in battle, engaging accounts of clever stratagems, and celebrations of victory were as appreciated by the Kamakura warrior as by warriors everywhere, but the ultimate tone of the tales is somber. Yoshitsune was, in the end, vanquished (even if one legend has him fleeing to the continent to become Chinggis Khan). Defeat is also the fate of the Taira in *The Tale of the Heike,* an oratorio given its final, classic form after the Kamakura *bakufu* had passed away by the blind musician-priest Akashi no Kakuichi (d. 1371), praised by Barbara Ruch as "one of the greatest composer-performers in history."[6] The main theme of his work is the fall of Taira pride, not the glory of the victorious Minamoto.

Underlying *The Tale of the Heike* is a sense of the transience of victory, the ultimate emptiness of success. Buddhist consciousness of the fleeting nature of all that is best in life saved the age of the Heian courtier from sinking into mere shallow hedonism and likewise rescued the world of the Kamakura warrior from the futile pomposity of the vainglorious. The sweetness of the warrior's triumph is just as ephemeral as the joy of lovers. The opening words of *The Tale of the Heike* sound a note that reverberates throughout the medieval period:

> In the sound of the bell of the Gion Temple echoes the impermanence of all things. The pale hue of the flowers of the teak-tree show the truth that they who prosper must fall. The proud do not last long, but vanish like a spring-night's dream. And the mighty ones too will perish in the end, like dust before the wind.[7]

Notes

1. Jeffrey Mass, "The Kamakura *Bakufu*," in Kozo Yamamura, ed., *The Cambridge History of Japan, Vol. 3: Medieval Japan* (Cambridge: Cambridge Univ. Press, 1990), p. 49.
2. Peter Duus, *Feudalism in Japan* (New York: Alfred A. Knopf, 1969), p. 8.
3. Steven Carter, *Traditional Japanese Poetry: An Anthology* (Stanford: Stanford Univ. Press, 1991), p. 161.
4. Carter, *Traditional Japanese Poetry: An Anthology*, p. 197.
5. Earl Miner, *An Introduction to Japanese Court Poetry* (Stanford: Stanford Univ. Press, 1968), p. 133.
6. Barbara Ruch in *The Cambridge History of Japan, Vol. 3: Medieval Japan*, p. 531.
7. Donald Keene, *Japanese Literature* (New York: Grove Press, 1955), p. 78.

5

Muromachi Japan

The Kenmu Restoration (1333–1336)

The Establishment of the Ashikaga Shogunate (1336–1368)

Japanese and Continental Culture

Government and Politics

Yoshimitsu and His Age

The Nō Drama

Political Decline and Cultural Brilliance

Poetry and Painting

Economic Growth

War and the Rise of the Daimyo

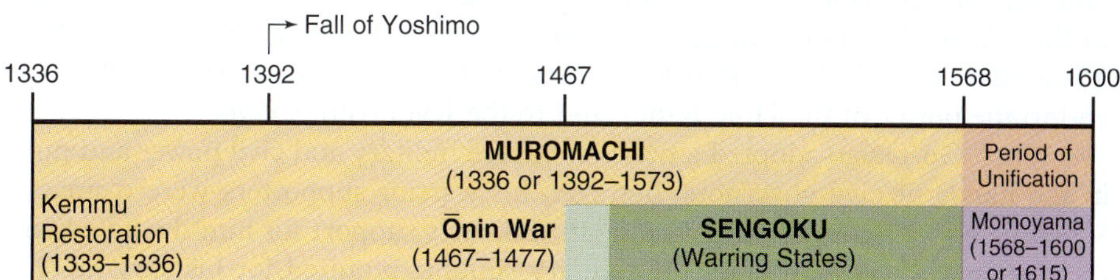

Culturally and politically, the more than two centuries described in this chapter were an unusually rich and complex time in the history of Japan. The political ascendancy of warriors, so long in the making, was completed, but the period's cultural efflorescence owed much to elements of aristocratic and commoner culture as the Ashikaga *bakufu* took up residence in Kyoto. The period is called Muromachi after the section of northeast Kyoto where the Ashikaga shoguns resided, although it is sometimes applied only to the time after 1392. It is also crucial to bear in mind that after 1477 the *bakufu's* area of effective control shrank to the capital area, even if a shogun continued to play some political role until 1573.

The Kenmu Restoration (1333–1336)

Between the Kamakura and the Ashikaga shogunates, as earlier between the Heian and the Kamakura Periods, there was a brief interlude. The Kenmu (Kemmu) Restoration of Emperor Go-Daigo (1288–1339) was an attempt to reassert the prerogatives of the throne similar to the earlier efforts of Emperor Go-Toba. Because it confronted a much-weakened shogunate, the restoration had considerable initial success. Even after Kyoto was lost, there was sufficient momentum to sustain a government in exile in the mountains of Yoshino, south of Nara, which for more than half a century provided at least a potential rallying point for those opposed to the Ashikaga. Not until 1392 did it come to an end.

The origins of the restoration go back to an imperial succession dispute in the middle of the thirteenth century. After the reluctant intervention of the *bakufu,* a compromise was reached whereby the two disputing branches, northern and southern, would alternately occupy the throne. Go-Daigo was determined to break this agreement and retain the succession in his own line. To that end, he gathered a coalition of warriors to defy the *bakufu.*

Fighting began in 1331 when the shogunate tried to force Go-Daigo to abdicate. At first Go-Daigo suffered setbacks, including capture and exile to the Oki

Islands in the Sea of Japan. But the *bakufu* was unable to suppress Go-Daigo's coalition, and in 1332 the emperor escaped from the Oki. He returned to Kyoto in triumph after Ashikaga Takauji (1305–1358), commander of a *bakufu* force sent to destroy him, changed sides. Behind Takauji was the wealth and prestige of the Ashikaga family, which, like Yoritomo, the founder of the first shogunate, belonged to the Seiwa Minamoto lineage. Another important Go-Daigo warrior ally, Nitta Yoshisada (1301–1338), seized Kamakura in the name of Go-Daigo and put an end to the power of the Hōjō family and to the Kamakura *bakufu*.

When Go-Daigo adopted a policy to merge military and civil power and put it in the hands of civil governors, however, his warrior supporters were dismayed. When he appointed his own son shogun, Takauji's support for him dwindled, and the throne's policies cost him the military support required for his survival. The Kenmu Restoration came to an end in 1336 when Takauji defeated Nitta Yoshisada and then dethroned Go-Daigo. Go-Daigo escaped south to the mountains of Yoshino, and with his remaining followers occasionally mounted an offense against the Ashikaga forces for more than fifty years. Ironically, a major casualty of the military turbulence was the civil provincial administration that had survived the Kamakura Period, because now the *shugō* increasingly assumed control of public land. The emperor's attempt to turn back the clock misfired badly.

Go-Daigo's significance is still debated. Some see him as an anachronism, desiring restoration of imperial power and thus a reduction of warrior power. Others, however, credit him with a vision for the future, including an understanding of the importance of commerce in national life and of reviving relations with China, then under Mongol rule. Still others point to his policies as despotic beyond anything seen previously in an emperor.

The Establishment of the Ashikaga Shogunate (1336–1368)

The power of the Ashikaga, enhanced after the defeat of Nitta Yoshisada, was legitimated in 1338, when Takauji received the coveted title of shogun from the new emperor he had installed in Kyoto. Go-Daigo's rival court continued in exile for another twenty-two years until 1392, when Yoshimitsu, the third and very vigorous Ashikaga shogun, brokered an end to the conflict and to the so-called period of the northern and southern courts (Nambokucho, 1336–1392). The basic foundations of the new shogunate were firmly in place.

The de facto defeat of an emperor by warriors was an event that stirred discussion among contemporary intellectuals. The genealogical and theoretical bases for Go-Daigo's claims to legitimacy were supplied by the aristocrat Kitabatake Chikafusa. In his *The Records of the Legitimate Succession of the Divine Sovereigns*, Chikafusa argued not only for the legitimacy of Go-Daigo but also for the sanctity of correct imperial succession leading back all the way to the Sun Goddess. It was this, he claimed, that made Japan uniquely divine and set it apart from other lands.

Meanwhile, the *Taiheiki,* a military epic, supplied stirring accounts of the feats of imperial loyalists, such as Kusunoki Masashige (d. 1336), an early and faithful adherent to Go-Daigo's cause, and Nitta Yoshisada. It turned these men into popular heroes, adding luster to the cause they served. Thus, one legacy of the Kenmu Restoration and the Yoshino court was an embellished and fortified imperial myth.

In contrast, Ashikaga Takauji was somewhat unreasonably cast as the villain of this historical drama. After all, although they denied the throne any real power, he and his successors wanted to preserve the status of the throne, the theoretical source of Takauji's own authority. For his part, even Chikafusa admitted that the warriors had a legitimate role given the ineffectiveness of the imperial course. A contemporary anecdote vividly illustrates its tarnished reputation: a warrior, probably under the influence of alcohol, refusing to dismount when he encountered the procession of the abdicated emperor, is quoted as saying, "Did you say 'cloistered emperor' (*in*) or 'dog' (*inu*)? If it's a dog, perhaps I'd better shoot it."[1] He then struck the retired emperor's carriage with an arrow. The upshot was that the carriage overturned and its occupant tumbled into the street. Takauji promptly had the warrior beheaded.

Japanese and Continental Culture

As mentioned in the preceding chapter, the life of Zen Master Musō Soseki is an indication that the vicissitudes of political and military fortune did not disrupt all careers, because he enjoyed in turn the favor and patronage of the Hōjō, Go-Daigo, and Takauji. Of the latter it is said that he often practiced Zen before going to sleep after a heavy dinner party. Musō was responsible for the fine garden at Tenryūji, the great Zen monastery built by Takauji for Musō and dedicated to the memory of Go-Daigo. Its building and grounds covered almost 100 acres west of the capital. Musō also deserves much of the credit for the Saihōji, popularly known as the "moss garden." He also persuaded Takauji to establish a nationwide system of Zen temples.

Musō's role extended beyond that of spiritual mentor: it was on his advice that Go-Daigo in 1325 had sent an official embassy to China, resuming relations broken off almost 500 years earlier. Similarly, his influence is seen in Takauji's decision to send another mission in 1339. In the latter case, the ship was named after the monastery Tenryūji, which was involved in lucrative voyages to China, and Zen monks provided the major impetus for renewed interest in Chinese culture.

In the arts, as elsewhere, the Japanese selected from China what appealed to them. They ignored the monumental Northern Song landscapes, preferring the more intimate Southern Song painting of Ma Yuan and Xia Gui and especially the vigorous brushwork and bold imagery in the paintings by Zen monks such as Muqi. Even though these artists never traveled to Japan, much of their work has been preserved only there. For Muqi, six persimmons mirrored the truth as faithfully as any portrait of the Buddha (see Figure 5.1). This painting is still owned by the Daitokuji temple, founded in 1326 with the backing of the retired emperor and Go-Daigo.

Monasteries and nunneries continued to provide a haven for those seeking to retire from the trials and tribulations of an unstable world. Among them was

FIGURE 5.1 *Six Persimmons,* Muqi. Ink on paper, 14.2 in wide. Daitokuji, Kyoto. (© Daitokuji Temple)

Yoshida Kenkō (1283–1350), poet, court official, and author of *Essays in Idleness* (*Tsurezuregusa*), a collection of brief jottings long admired in Japan as a repository of good taste in social conduct as in art. Despite the randomness of its organization, like Sei Shōnagon's *Pillow Book* and Kamo no Chōmei's *An Account of My Hut,* Kenkō's work is held together by recurrent themes. Particularly significant is his celebration of the aesthetics of the impermanent, because to Kenkō perishability is an essential component and a necessary precondition for beauty. And he voices aesthetic judgments that have since become closely associated with Japanese taste, displaying a preference for objects that bear the signs of wear and have acquired the patina of age (*sabi*). He loves the old literature and reiterates the value of *yūgen.* His antiquarianism is pervasive: he admires the old whether it be in poetry, carpentry, or even torture racks for criminals. As we can see in the following excerpts, his style is fresh and succinct, observant yet detached:

> To sit alone in lamplight with a book spread out before you, and hold intimate converse with men of unseen generations—such is a pleasure beyond compare.
>
> Are we to look only at flowers in full bloom, at the moon when it is clear? Nay, to look out on the rain and long for the moon, to draw the blinds and not to be aware of the passing of the spring—these arouse even deeper feelings. There is much to be seen in young boughs about to flower, in gardens strewn with withered blossoms.

Government and Politics

Unlike their predecessors, the Ashikaga shoguns did not establish a new center of power but conducted their affairs from Kyoto and appointed a deputy to look after their interests in the Kantō region. Other deputies were established in Kyūshū, west-central Japan, and in the north. Although the shoguns held the highest civil offices, their power depended on their control over their vassals. But the old bonds had been weakened, and the system of loyalties on which the Ashikaga depended proved highly unstable.

The military protectors of the Kamakura Period developed into provincial military governors, although their title, *shugō,* remained the same. At its height, the Kamakura *bakufu* had limited the power of the *shugō* by assigning men to provinces in which they had no family roots or property; by asserting its right to dismiss and confirm the *shugō*, even though the positions eventually became hereditary; and by maintaining direct control over lesser vassals. In the Ashikaga age, however, warriors in the provinces steadily whittled down the absentee proprietors' control of land. The Ashikaga, eager to obtain warrior support, played into the hands of the military governors in particular by assigning them virtually unlimited rights to taxation and adjudication. Increasingly, the *shugō* were able to turn local warriors into vassals. Frequently, the term *shugō-daimyo* is applied to these provincial power holders who, like the later full-fledged daimyo, held extensive territory and grew increasingly autonomous of the *bakufu* in Kyoto.

Bakufu and *shugō* were involved in a complicated balance of power, which all parties tried to manipulate to their own advantage. Until the Onin War, the fulcrum of this balance remained in Kyoto. The situation offered military governors and their deputies opportunities, but it also posed dangers. They might be able to recruit local warriors as vassals to augment their own military power, but they could not count on the loyalty of these men, who put family interests first and were not reluctant to switch sides.

On a lower level, too, the trend favored local warriors. Instead of retaining *shiki* in scattered areas, *jitō* gradually consolidated their holdings. They became strong enough to make peasant leaders their vassals, and they took on the character of local overlords. The estate system, badly battered by the conflict of the fourteenth century, was severely damaged, and aristocratic and religious control of land dwindled as a result. The old system did not disappear completely, however, until the period of reunification (see Chapter 6).

To complicate matters still further, the great military families (*shugō* and *jitō*) faced internal family conflicts as single inheritance became common. The old tradition of dividing an estate equally among heirs, feasible in times of peace and security, created fragmentation that was too dangerous in a period of unrest. Therefore, to secure the family's future, the property was left intact and passed to a single heir designated by the family head. This was not necessarily the eldest son, but it was always a son: a daughter would be unable to protect the property militarily. This system frequently led to bitter rivalries and hard-fought family succession disputes. These, like all serious conflicts in this period, were settled by force of arms.

John Whitney Hall succinctly defined the Ashikaga body politic when he wrote, "The imperial system was now in effect dead, but the system of military allegiances and feudal controls had not fully matured."[3] Based on unstable alliances, the system nevertheless worked, at least to a degree, and was indeed the closest thing to a government in an era of political diffuseness. It neither hampered considerable economic growth nor inhibited fine cultural achievements. Indeed, under Ashikaga Yoshimitsu (1358–1408), Japan experienced a cultural and political renewal.

Yoshimitsu and His Age

In 1368 Yoshimitsu, not yet ten, became the third shogun. Initially, however, the shogunate was controlled by the capable Hosokawa Yoriyuki, a member of one of the Ashikaga collateral families powerful in Kyoto and the provinces. Yoriyuki's official appointment was as chief administrator (*kanrei*), the top position in the *bakufu*, which was always assigned to one of the three most powerful vassal families (Hosokawa, Shiba, or Hatakeyama). His services to the *bakufu* included administrative reform, settlement of conflicting land claims, and a strengthening of the shogunate's finances. Spending was reduced, and new sources of revenue were opened by taxing the wealth of commercial enterprises such as sake breweries and moneylenders. (These two establishments frequently belonged to the same proprietor because the original capital of the pawnshops often came from the profits of the sake trade.) Indeed, the Ashikaga shogunate, unlike either the Kamakura or the Tokugawa shogunates, drew substantial revenues from commercial sources in the capital.

When Yoshimitsu took power into his own hands, he continued efforts to strengthen the shogunate. He successfully met several military challenges, and in 1392 he secured the reunification of the two imperial courts. A final campaign in 1399 achieved a workable balance of power in the country. Through a series of impressive processionals to religious sites, such as Mount Kōya and Ise, Yoshimitsu further displayed his power and inspected local conditions firsthand. His lavish patronage of religious establishments no doubt helped win him support in those quarters.

Yoshimitsu, unlike the first two Ashikaga shoguns, was born and raised in Kyoto and sought to combine his warrior heritage with the values long cherished there. In gratifying his taste for fine architecture and beautiful gardens, he spared no expense. Unfortunately, his Palace of Flowers (Hana no Gosho) has not survived. Politically, he demonstrated his dual legacy by assuming the title of chancellor and shogun, and he even managed to have his wife made empress dowager! Yoshimitsu truly believed in doing things in royal style: once he entertained the emperor with twenty days of banqueting, music, and theatrical performances, a display of wealth that the emperor could not match. In this period the shogunate controlled the imperial budget through its tax collecting authority and did not hesitate to demonstrate to the emperor its ability to withhold needed funds. Yoshimitsu and his successors expressed formal deference toward the emperor but kept his finances rather underfunded.

Many of Yoshimitsu's entertainments took place on his estate in the northern hills (Kitayama) just beyond Kyoto, graced by the Golden Pavilion (Kinkakuji), a symbol of his good taste and affluence. Although the roofline and parts of the building were covered with gold leaf, the plain surfaces of natural wood, the pavilion's shingled roofs, and the grilled shutters and solid doors of the second floor preserved the Japanese tradition of natural simplicity. On the other hand, the paneled doors and arched windows of the top story derive from the standard repertoire of Chinese Zen architecture. With artful casualness, the building is set on an artificial platform in a pond. It combined Chinese and native elements harmoniously and tastefully.

Chinese elements in the Golden Pavilion are but one facet of Song influence on Ashikaga art. Indeed, without the patronage of such men as Yoshimitsu, many valuable Chinese paintings would have been lost. The shogun's fondness for things Chinese extended to Chinese dress. He even reported that the emperor of China visited him in his sleep. When awake, he made an effort to cultivate good relations with the Ming, and diplomatic communiqués between him and the Chinese court referred to Yoshimitsu as the "king" of Japan. As usual, the Chinese responded to foreign tribute by giving even more impressive gifts in return. A lucrative trade ensued, in which the officially patronized Five Zen Temples of Kyoto (gozan) played a leading role and from which they derived much wealth. Along with the Zen temple Tenryūji, Shōkokuji played a prominent part in these undertakings. Here, communications intended for the Ming were drafted by monks in Chinese. At Chinese request, Yoshimitsu took measures against unofficial Japanese traders ("pirates") in East Asia.

It is characteristic of the age that Zen monks were welcomed by the Ashikaga rulers not only for their religious insights but also for their managerial abilities, their command of Chinese learning, their poetic talents, and their expertise in the various arts. For example, the Zen monk Josetsu of the Shōkokuji was famous as an ink painter and was patronized by both Yoshimitsu and his successor. His *Patriarchs of the Three Creeds* (see Figure 5.2) reflects the religious, cultural, and artistic ambiance of the period. In it, the three great teachers Sakyamuni, Confucius, and Laozi are shown in harmonious agreement. The "abbreviated" brushwork is in the manner beloved by Zen artists. Each figure is rendered in its own style, and every stroke, every line, counts. The style of this painting is Chinese, and its subject inspired Song artists, although none of their paintings survive. It is a theme that reflects the Chinese trend toward religious and philosophical syncretism. Such syncretism was readily accepted in Japan, which had never experienced an institutionalized Daoism competing with a Buddhist establishment, and where Buddhism had from the first been mixed with Confucianism. The close relationship between Daoism and Zen has already been noted. Josetsu's own name is a case in point. It was given to him by a great priest of the Shōkokuji and was derived from the *Daodejing* passage, "the greatest skill is like clumsiness (*josetsu*)."[4] This was his artistic ideal and his achievement.

The Nō Drama

When Yoshimitsu hosted the emperor for twenty days, among the entertainments offered were performances of Nō, the classic drama of Japan. The roots of Nō are in less-formal singing, dancing, music, and mime, but its developed form was truly the creation of a remarkable father and son, Kan'ami (1333–1384), a Shinto priest, and Zeami (or Seami, 1363–1443). Both composed plays and acted in them, and Zeami formulated the critical and aesthetic criteria of the art. When Yoshimitsu first saw them performed, he was especially captivated by Zeami, then a good-looking boy of eleven, because the shogun was eclectic in his sexual as in his artistic preferences.

FIGURE 5.2 *Patriarchs of the Three Creeds.* Attributed to Josetsu. Hanging scroll, ink on paper, 8.58 in × 38.7 in. (© "Patriarchs of the Three Creeds," by Josetsu Ryosokuin, Kyoto)

A performance of Nō is presented on a highly polished square wooden stage open to the audience on three sides. A raised passageway leads from the actors' dressing room through the audience to the stage. Both stage and passageway are roofed. Three small pine trees in front of the passageway and a band of pebbles in front of the stage replicate the drainage area surrounding gutterless buildings, symbolic reminders that Nō performances were originally held outdoors. The stage is bare or almost bare. Occasionally, there are symbolic representations of scenery: an outline of a boat, a cube to suggest a well. Likewise, stage properties are few and generally symbolic.

The Nō is often compared with Greek drama, but the differences are as important as the similarities. For example, both use a chorus, but the chorus in Nō does not participate in the dramatic action. Seated at the side of the stage, the chorus expresses what is in the actor's mind and sings his lines when he dances. The music, produced by a flute and some drums, provides accompaniment and accent.

The actors and the chorus are all male. Some actors wear highly stylized and exquisitely fashioned masks. The carving of these masks is a prized art. The one reproduced in Figure 5.3 represents a young woman. It illustrates the characteristic features of a classic Heian beauty, with her powdered complexion, artificial eyebrows, and blackened teeth. By subtle body movements and just the right tilt of the head, a great actor can suggest remarkable nuances of mood and emotion, and the frozen faces of the unmasked actors attain a mask-like anonymity. The effect allows full concentration on the spiritual message of the play and not on the identity of the actor. Attired in all the elegance of Heian courtier costumes, the actors "dance" their roles, moving with slow and deliberate grace.

Nō plays are classified by the Japanese according to subject matter: plays about a god, a warrior, a woman, a mad person, or a demon. It later became customary to include one of each type, in this order, in a full program that would take about six hours to perform. The texts are short, and although they contain some fine poetry, they were always meant for the stage. The plots draw heavily on the literary tradition,

FIGURE 5.3 Nō mask. (© Tokyo National Museum)

recreating some of the most poignant scenes from earlier literature, including the *Tale of Genji, The Tale of the Heike,* and the *Tales of Ise*. As one might expect, there are plays about Yoshitsune and other notable figures, including the great poetess Komachi, who is portrayed as an old woman suffering because she caused others to suffer when she was young and beautiful. Others deal with legends; the story of the fishermen who stole the angel's cloak (Hagomoro) is a favorite.

The tone is serious; the presentation symbolic. The typical Nō play is not an enactment of a dramatic episode or a dramatic rendition of a historical or mythological occurrence; it is a retelling after the event. Consider the play based on the death of the young Atsumori, reluctantly slain in battle by the warrior Kumagai, as recounted in *The Tale of the Heike*. The main actors in Zeami's play on this theme are the priest who was once Kumagai and a young reaper who is actually the ghost of Atsumori. Here, the purpose of art is not to mirror life but to transform it; setting the action in the play's own past allows a meditation on the Buddhist themes of permanence and the folly of worldly ties. It is an art that eschews realism and aspires to convey a sense of profound meaning beyond the words and scenes on stage. The ultimate criterion, according to Zeami, is a play's success in creating *yūgen,* the sense of underlying mystery.

A tone of grave sadness is hard to sustain for hours. Even a refined Kyoto aristocrat with his penchant for melancholy must have welcomed the comic relief provided by *kyōgen* (mad or wild words), performed in the interlude between Nō plays. Often in the nature of farce, they show a fondness for broad humor and foolery: servants outwitting their master, a dull country bumpkin sent to purchase a sculpture of the Buddha and taken in by the trickery of an apprentice posing as a statue, and so on. Livelier than Nō, *kyōgen* are less demanding of the audience, but they lack the aura of profundity and poetic mystery that has sustained the Nō tradition in Japan.

Political Decline and Cultural Brilliance

When Yoshimitsu died in 1408 and was succeeded by his son, there was no radical discontinuity in shogunal politics or even in cultural policies, although his death brought an end to the favor shown to Zeami. Under the fifth shogun there were signs of fiscal and political weakness, but the following shogun, Yoshinori (r. 1428–1441), was able to rally the Ashikaga fortunes. However, Yoshinori's policy of strengthening the *bakufu* necessarily involved checking the power of strong military governors (*shugō*), and this turned out to be a dangerous and difficult game. It cost Yoshinori his life when he was lured to a mansion by a military governor and assassinated.

Yoshinori was the last strong and vigorous Ashikaga shogun. His son was eight when he inherited the office and died two years later. He was followed by another child, Yoshimasa (1436–1490). Yoshimasa remained shogun for thirty years (1443–1473) then retired, having presided over the political collapse of the regime. From Yoshinori's assassination in 1441 through the Onin War (1467–1477), governance, such as it was, disintegrated. But the Ashikaga shogunate benefited from its historical momentum and the absence of a viable alternative, because the power of the provincial families, afflicted by succession disputes, was also declining. It is characteristic of the age that the Ashikaga downfall came not at the hands of a more powerful family or coalition but as the result of disputes within its own ranks. In 1464 Yoshimasa, still without an heir, designated his brother as next in line, but the following year his ambitious and strong-minded wife Masako bore him a son. Anxious to have her son be the next shogun, she found support in a powerful provincial governor's family, and another family backed the older claimant. Thus, the ground was prepared for the succession struggle that set off the disastrous Onin War. The outcome of the war did not lead to the triumph of either family, but it did destroy the authority of the Ashikaga and half of the city of Kyoto, and it wreaked havoc on much of the surrounding country. During these violent years, Yoshimasa continued to emulate Yoshimitsu in patronizing the arts; he had the exquisite aesthetic sensibilities long cultivated in Kyoto. But he lacked the qualities of command and decisiveness required of a shogun, a holder of what was, after all, a military office.

Yoshimasa was as lavish as Yoshimitsu in financing building projects and in giving entertainments. He, too, was a great patron of Nō and an admirer of Heian and Song aesthetics. Like Yoshimitsu, his name is associated with a district in the outskirts of Kyoto to which he retired (Higashiyama). As a counterpart to Yoshimitsu's Golden Pavilion, there is Yoshimasa's Silver Pavilion (Ginkakuji), somewhat smaller, more intimate, and more subdued than its predecessor, having two stories instead of three (see Figure 5.4). It, too, combines, or at least juxtaposes, Chinese and native elements, featuring a continental second story placed on a Japanese first story.

A Chinese theme is echoed in the Ginkakuji's sand garden, identified as a rendition of the West Lake outside Hangzhou, frequented by Song painters and poets such as Su Shi on their pleasure outings. Near one bank, however, stands a volcano, also of sand—a miniature Mount Fuji. Such gardens were the objects of much care and careful planning. Wealthy patrons such as Yoshimasa went to great expense to obtain just the right effect. Transportation costs were disregarded when a stone was discovered precisely right in shape and texture and presenting the exact contrast between its rough and its smooth surfaces required for the composition of the garden. As in

China, stones themselves were objects of connoisseurship. Similar care went into the selection and pruning of plants and into performing the myriad chores necessary for maintaining a garden at its aesthetic best.

FIGURE 5.4 Ginkakuji (Silver Pavilion), Kyoto. (© Lore Schirokauer)

In Japan as in China, the aesthetics of garden design and landscape painting were closely related. Like the painter, the garden artist could choose rich, colorful landscapes—using tree and shrub, rivulet and waterfall, pond and bridge—or he could confine himself to stone and carefully raked sand, much like the ink painter who rejected color. Such sand and stone gardens can be viewed as three-dimensional monochrome landscapes with the sand representing water and the rocks functioning as mountains, or they can be enjoyed as abstract sculptures inviting the viewer to exercise imagination. Like Zen, they concentrate on the essentials. The finest are found in the Zen temples of Kyoto (see Figure 5.5). Not all of the Ryōanji's fifteen stones are visible in this photograph because the garden is designed so that there is no single point from which they can all be seen at once.

The compound of the Silver Pavilion also contains a small hall, the interior of which is divided between a Buddhist chapel and a new element: a room for the performance of the tea ceremony. Tea grew in popularity after its enthusiastic advocacy by Eisai, the Zen monk who introduced Rinzai to Japan. Even Kyoto commoners enjoyed creating formal occasions for its consumption. It was not until the time of Yoshimasa, however, that it developed into a ritual art with its own strict rules and regulations.

The accent in the classic tea ceremony is on simplicity and tranquility of spirit. Through a small doorway no bigger than a window, the guests crawl into a room about nine feet square to enjoy in silent calm the movements of their host as he prepares the tea with motions as deliberate as those of an actor on the Nō stage. After they have drunk the deep green tea, they may exchange a few remarks about the bowl or the flower arrangement prepared for the ceremony. Among the unrefined, the ceremony may be exaggerated into ostentation; in incapable hands it easily degenerates into an empty and pedantic formalism. But when performed with an easy grace by a master, it can convey Japanese good taste at its best. The

FIGURE 5.5 Sand and Stone Garden. Ryōanji, Kyoto. (© Lore Schirokauer)

cult of tea—for such it was—reached perhaps its greatest height during the Momoyama Period (1568–1600).

The tea ceremony influenced secular architecture, which during the Ashikaga Period adopted many of the features of the tea room. Rush matting (*tatami*) now covered the whole floor—previously, individual mats had been placed on wooden floors as needed to provide a place for people to sit. Sliding doors consisting of paper pasted on a wooden frame (*shoji*) came into common use, supplementing the earlier sliding partitions (*fusuma*) with their painted surfaces. Another standard feature is the alcove (*tokonoma*) with its hanging scroll and flower arrangement. Flower arrangement, like tea, became an art, with its own rules and styles passed through the generations by the masters of distinct schools. It became one of the polite accomplishments expected of those with a claim to refinement.

In all the arts, the influence of Zen aesthetics remained strong even after the Onin War disrupted the network centered on the Five Zen Temples of Kyoto, which by then included some 300 monasteries, or several thousand institutions if sub- and branch-temple affiliates are counted separately.

Poetry and Painting

In Yoshimasa's time, poetry continued to be an important part of Kyoto life. In the Heian Period it was not uncommon for one poet to supply the first three lines of a *tanka* (a thirty-one-syllable poem), leaving it to his companion to complete the poem with a suitable couplet. From such origins grew the linked verse (*renga*), which became a favorite Muromachi pastime. Its instability was an important part of its appeal. Nijō Yoshimoto (1320–1388), a champion of *renga,* put it this way:

> The poet of *renga* does not seek to tie the idea of one moment in with that of the next but, like this fleeting world, shifts through phases of both waxing and waning, of sadness and joy. No sooner does he reflect on yesterday than today has passed; while thinking about spring it becomes autumn, and even as he admires a scene of new blossoms it turns into one of crimson leaves. Is this not proof that everything is impermanent, like scattered flowers and fallen leaves?[5]

Reflecting its social nature, the composition of *renga* came to be governed by complicated rules:

> Of the opening verse (the *hokku*) it was said, "The hokku should not be at variance with the topography of the place, whether the mountains or the sea dominate, with the flying flowers or falling leaves of the grasses and trees of the season, with the wind, clouds, mist, fog, rain, dew, frost, snow, heat, cold, or quarter of the moon. Objects which excite a ready response possess the greatest interest for inclusion in a *hokku,* such as spring birds or autumn insects. But the *hokku* is not of merit if it looks as though it had been previously prepared." The requirements for the second verse were somewhat less demanding; it had to be closely related to the first and to end in a noun. The third verse was more independent and ended in a particle; the fourth had to be "smooth"; the moon had to occur in a certain verse; cherry-blossoms could not be mentioned before a certain point; autumn and spring had to be repeated in at least three but not more than five successive verses, while summer and winter could be dropped after one mention, etc.[6]

A master such as the Zen monk Sōgi (1421–1502), the greatest of the *renga* poets, was able to create fine poetry within this framework. Sōgi also composed *tanka* in the old tradition of court poetry, now coming to an end. The last imperial anthology was compiled in the fifteenth century. The *renga* may not have been a great poetic form, but it pointed in new directions.

In painting as in poetry, Zen monks continued to contribute greatly. Josetsu's style of monochrome painting was continued by two Zen monks, Shubun (d. 1450) and Sesshū (1420–1506), both trained at the Shōkokuji. In their work the influence of Song painting remains clearly visible. The fifteenth-century painter-monks in the great Zen temples could draw on Japanese ink paintings in the Chinese manner going back to the Kamakura Period, and the more eminent or fortunate among them might also see the Chinese paintings kept in Japan. The prime source for these was the shogunal collection systematized and catalogued for the first time under Yoshimasa. Most fortunate were those who were able to travel abroad. Thus, Shubun drew inspiration from a journey to Korea, and Sesshū

FIGURE 5.6 *Ama-no-Hashidate*, Sesshū. Hanging scroll, ink and light color on paper, 70 in long. (© Shimizu Kohgeisha Co., Ltd.)

was able to travel to and in China. There was no need for him to paint Chinese landscapes from imagination alone.

Sesshū's versatile genius expressed itself in a variety of styles. One of his greatest paintings shows the man who was to become the second Zen patriarch offering his severed arm as a token of religious commitment to Bodhidharma, the reputed Indian founder of Zen in China. Another is a long landscape scroll (more than fifty-two feet long) guiding the viewer on a leisurely trip through scenery and seasons. Reproduced in Figure 5.6 is his painting of a renowned beauty spot on the Sea of Japan, Ama-no-Hashidate (the Bridge of Heaven). It was evidently painted on the basis of personal observation shortly before his death. The written identification of the various localities confirms the realism of this solidly constructed painting, and the softness of the painter's brush technique is appropriate for the gentle Japanese landscape.

Although Zen monks and temples had the greatest influence on the arts, some major contributions were made by believers in the nembutsu, who demonstrated their faith in Amida by incorporating his name in theirs. The aesthetics of Nō may be compatible with the teachings of Zen, but the greatest names in this theater were, as we have seen, Kan'ami and Zeami. And among the main painters in the monochrome style imported from the continent were the three Ami: Nōami (ca. 1394–1471), Geiami (1431–1485), and Sōami (d. 1525)—father, son, and grandson. These three men not only were fine painters but also served as the shogun's advisers in aesthetic matters, cataloguing and evaluating his art collection and passing as masters in the gamut of Ashikaga art from flower arranging, tea, and incense to music and the stage.

Also part of the artistic scene were professional painters. Two names that were to remain important as major schools of painting enjoying official favor first appear in the fifteenth century. These schools, like the schools of Nō and other arts, were continued from father to son or, if necessary, to adopted son, perpetuating their traditions much like warrior or merchant families. Their secrets were just as carefully guarded as the formulae of sake brewers or pharmacists. Painting in the old native style (Yamatōe), Tosa Mitsunobu (1434–1525) became official painter to both the imperial court and the *bakufu.* Provided with a generous grant of land, he was able to establish the social and economic position of his family. Meanwhile, his contemporary Kanō Masanobu (1434–1530) painted in the Chinese manner, although without all the religious and literary associations found in the work of the nonprofessional artists. Of the two, the Kanō line was the more creative. Masanobu's son Motonobu (1476–1559) added color to his paintings. In this he was likely influenced by the Tosa school.

Especially in the city of Kyoto, commoners enjoyed various cultural pursuits. Wealthy merchants such as moneylenders collected objects including ceramics, illustrated screens, poetry books, and kimono. Some commoners rubbed elbows with aristocrats at cultural events such as tea ceremonies, poetry rounds, and the more sophisticated linked-verse competitions. Commoners could be found in the audience at Nō performances, at public recitations of literary epics, and sometimes even as actor participants in comic *kyōgen* and in *sarugaku,* a mime-based theatrical art. Some wealthier commoners produced amateur ink paintings. Festivals, usually based at a local shrine, were a very visible and popular cultural activity; Kyoto's Gion Festival is the main example of this genre. A religious ceremonial core was lavishly elaborated by the townspeople, who prepared the ornate floats for the festival parade. The ostentatious display of wealth and a street-level energy were important elements of the culture of commoners.

This rich hybrid culture of Muromachi—the blending of the imported and the native, the high and the low—was new to Japan. The interpersonal contact that was a feature of tea ceremony and linked-verse gatherings imparted a socially mixed character to the culture of the age. Muromachi taste was exquisite, expressed in the aesthetic of the Nō mask, the sand garden, the tea ceremony, and a Sesshū landscape, a taste for the old (*sabi*), the solitary and poor (*wabi*), the astringent (*shibui*), and the profound (*yūgen*). The prestige of Chinese culture was enormous, and Sinophiles versified and painted in Chinese. But, unlike their predecessors of the Nara Period, they were selective in their borrowing and rapidly assimilated the new. In later ages Muromachi aesthetic sensibility was challenged, assailed, and even displaced, but it never disappeared entirely.

Economic Growth

The economy grew during the Kamakura epoch, and in Ashikaga times there was considerable if unevenly distributed prosperity. Frequently, developments that originated in the earlier period reached fruition in the later. The basis of the economy remained agricultural, and an increasing agricultural yield provided the means for growth. Improvements in farm technology employing better tools and devices such as the waterwheel, new crops, double-cropping, and new strains of rice and greater use of draft animals were some of the major developments that increased the productivity of the land. This, in turn, positively affected commerce and manufacturing. Technical progress in such endeavors as mining, sake brewing, and paper production, to mention just a few, further contributed to this process. The resulting wealth produced a prosperous stratum of peasants and townspeople, many of whom engaged in several livelihoods simultaneously and including moneylending, sericulture, estate management, and transportation. However, poor laborers and peasants were forced to live at subsistence level, led precarious lives, and famine was still frequent. At the very bottom of society was the outcast class, especially numerous in the Kyoto area, where they were employed especially by religious institutions as manual laborers and security guards.

An added economic stimulus came from trade with China and Korea. Initiated by Yoshimitsu, it continued, with minor interruptions, to grow and flourish. To control this commerce and keep the number of ships within agreed-upon limits, the Ming issued official tallies valid for trading at a specified port. This system also had the effect of restricting unofficial trade; it lasted until the middle of the sixteenth century. Japanese imports included cotton from Korea, and from China came great quantities of copper coins as well as porcelain, paintings, medicine, and books. A major Japanese export was fine swords. Japan also exported copper, sulfur, folding fans (a Japanese invention), screens, and so forth. The ability to trade products of sophisticated craftsmanship is another index of Japanese accomplishments during this period.

With the growth of commerce, of markets, and of market towns, there appeared guilds (*za*)—product-specific groups of merchants and artisans exercising monopoly rights over the exchange and production of various commodities. In return for protection of their rights and privileges, these guilds paid taxes to their overlords, great religious institutions, and powerful families. The moneylenders of Kyoto, for example, enjoyed the protection of the Tendai monastery on Mount Hiei, which occasionally sent its armed agents into the capital on behalf of its clients. Temples and shrines, aristocratic families, and the *bakufu* itself, as their hold on the provinces loosened, welcomed the guilds as an additional source of revenue and increasingly depended on income from this source. As noted earlier, already under Yoshimitsu the Ashikaga shogun relied heavily on income from these quarters, and this trend continued. The prosperity of the moneylenders is only one of several signs of the increasing use of money, a development both a product of and a stimulus to commercial growth. To facilitate transactions between places distant from each other, bills of exchange also came into use.

Around ports and markets, cities grew. The most impressive was Sakai, near modern Osaka, which in the sixteenth century became an autonomous political unit governed by a group of elders who were mostly merchants. Hakata in Kyūshū, the center for trade with Korea, also flourished, as did several other well-placed cities.

The growth of cities and similar economic developments suggest parallels with European history, but such parallels hold only to a limited degree. Japanese merchants and cities did not achieve autonomy; instead, the merchants provided a source of revenue for feudal lords. Social and political institutions were not shattered, but society was enriched by the emergence of a new urban population. One result of political decentralization combined with economic growth was the diffusion of higher culture to the provinces. Conversely, students of Nō and linked verse have pointed out that these arts owe much to popular culture. Sōgi, the great master of linked verse, was himself of obscure parentage. Many more opportunities for men of low birth were created during the warfare that marked the last phase of Ashikaga rule.

War and the Rise of the Daimyo

The Onin War (1467–1477) was a major turning point in Japanese history. It drastically curtailed the power of the Ashikaga *bakufu,* ending the system of alliances on which it was precariously based. The *shugō,* who had been drawn into Kyoto, were mostly superseded by local deputies. Not only was the old balance of power demolished but its very constituents were also eliminated. The Onin War was the first decade of a century of sporadic warfare and political instability. Kyoto was beset by attacks from without and disorder within: "The landscape was stark: residents of a repeatedly assailed and burned city retreated into two separate enclaves that they protected with moats, wells, and watchtowers."[7]

Gekokujō—those above overthrown by those below—was the watchword of the day. During this period, the shogun was unable to control even the provinces near Kyoto and occasionally was driven out of the capital temporarily by warlords. Even so, the Ashikaga *bakufu* could not be counted out completely as late as the 1550s; in Kyoto, at least, the *bakufu* remained the only recognized authority to adjudicate disputes.

Disruption and uncertainty affected the people at the bottom of society at least as much as the elites. This was a period of great popular unrest. During the middle of the fifteenth century, there were numerous peasant uprisings demanding debt cancellation. Characterized by skillful organization and timing, some of these even laid siege to the city of Kyoto, stopping commercial activity there until debt amnesties could be negotiated. In earlier times as well, villages had banded together in leagues to press demands against estate overlords. By the late fifteenth century, large-scale peasant uprisings against local warriors could dominate entire provinces. In the most famous case, in Yamashiro province near Kyoto, peasants were able to hold power for eight years (1485–1493).

The proliferation of popular Buddhist movements, some with a militant character, was another feature of the age. Particularly prominent was the well-organized Ikkō sect, whose members followed Shinran's True Pure Land Buddhism. In the sixteenth century, these sectarians were able to obtain control of the province of Kaga, on the Sea of Japan; extend their power into neighboring Echizen; and maintain a strategic stronghold in the Kyoto–Osaka area. The Lotus sect followers of Nichiren, commoners and elites alike, multiplied rapidly in the fifteenth century and were dominant in Kyoto by the early sixteenth century. In the authority vacuum of the 1530s, they established loose rule of the city through a confederation of congregations only to be brutally suppressed by an alliance of warriors and Enryakuji monks in 1536.

What had been decentralized governance gave way in the mid-sixteenth century to radical fragmentation as Japan was divided into many separate principalities, directed by feudal lords known as daimyo.

These lords competed with each other to preserve their territories and, if possible, to expand them. The sizes of these principalities varied widely; some were no larger than a small castle town, while others might be as large as one of the old provinces. Regardless of the size of his holdings, the daimyo's fate depended on his success in the field of battle. What counted was power. Although some of the mid-sixteenth-century daimyo belonged to the old families, many emerged from the class of local warriers. In these strenuous, difficult times, capable, ambitious, and unscrupulous men struggled to the top using any means at hand; frequently, betrayal was the price of upward mobility. The introduction of formal oaths, unnecessary in an older and simpler age, did not change the situation. Vassals could be counted on for their loyalty only as long as it was in their own best interests to be loyal.

To obtain and hold their vassals, the daimyo granted or confirmed landholdings, much like European fiefs, thereby bringing to a final end the old and complicated system of estates and *shiki.* In return for these grants of land, the vassals were obliged to render military service to their lord and provide the services of a set number of their own fighting men. The traditional elites in the capital area, aristocrats and religious institutions, could not compete with local warriors for control of land, and so the old estate system disappeared.

The future was to belong to warriors, not peasants or religious institutions. In the long run, success in this precarious age went to those daimyo who could most effectively mobilize the resources of their domains, turning them into small states. The ultimate consequence of the breakdown of central unity was the creation of smaller, more highly integrated political entities. Daimyo normally asserted their authority over the succession of their vassals, and since political combinations were involved, they also had a say concerning their vassals' marriages. Some daimyo, in their house laws, asserted rights to tax the land in their territory and to regulate economic activities. Frequently, spies were employed to keep the lord informed of the activities and plans of his vassals.

A potent force for integration was the changing nature of warfare. It was found that massed foot soldiers, recruited from the peasantry and armed with spears and the like, were an effective force against the traditional, proud, and expensive mounted warriors. Armies grew larger, and vassals tended to serve as officers commanding troops of commoners.

Sixteenth-century Japan was no exception to the rule that change in offense sooner or later stimulates new developments in defense. The Japanese answer to the new armies was the castle. It was often built on a hill, crowned with a tower, protected by walls, and surrounded by a moat or a natural body of water. These castles often served as the centers of daimyo-states, and warriors tended to be gathered there and removed from the land.

An added impetus to the use of the new type of armies came after the Portuguese introduced European firearms to Japan in 1543. Within ten years the daimyo of Western Japan were using imported and domestic muskets in their armies. In repsonse, bigger and more elaborate castles became necessary, so that in defense as well in offense, the larger daimyo with ample means had a decisive advantage.

By the middle of the sixteenth century, trends towards political consolidation were apparent, but that did not come quickly or easily.

Notes

1. H. Paul Varley, *Imperial Restoration in Medieval Japan* (New York: Columbia Univ. Press, 1971), p. 131.
2. Donald Keene, trans., *Essays in Idleness: The Tsurezuregusa of Kenko* (New York: Columbia Univ. Press, 1967), p. 12.
3. John W. Hall, *Japan from Prehistory to Modern Times* (New York: Dell Publishing, 1970), p. 110.
4. Jan Fontein and Money L. Hickman, *Zen Painting and Calligraphy* (Boston: Museum of Fine Arts, 1970), p. 93.
5. Quoted by H. Paul Varley, in Kozo Yamamura, ed., *The Cambridge History of Japan, Vol. 3: Medieval Japan* (Cambridge: Cambridge Univ. Press, 1990), p. 475.
6. Donald Keene, *Japanese Literature* (New York: Grove Press, 1955), pp. 34-35.
7. Mary Elizabeth Berry, *The Culture of Civil War in Kyoto* (Berkeley: Univ. of California Press, 1994), p. xviii.

Part Three

Early Modern/ Late Traditional Japan

In this and in the following chapter, we will consider Japan during the period of unification and the first two centuries of the Tokugawa shogunate. During these momentous years in world history, European civilization was transformed in ways that were to have profound effects all over the globe. But that came later. For now, Japan was left free to deal with overseas challenges on its own terms and to develop according to its own internal dynamics. In the process, Japan underwent changes so deep that some scholars have described this period as "early modern" (kinsei), *comparable to the European Renaissance. This designation is useful in that it highlights the continuities with what was to come as well as the very considerable discontinuities with earlier history. Conversely, however, it may distract from what the Tokugawa shared with its past or cause us to overestimate its links to the future.*

Harunobu, Boy Water Vendor. Calendar Print. 1765. © Tokyo National Museum. Urban life and woodblock printing flourished during the Tokugawa Period. Balancing two buckets of pure water on a carrying pole, the young boy in this print also provides tea ceremony bowls and utensils.

6

The Formation of a New Order

I. Consolidation (1573–1600)

Consolidation (1573–1600)

Oda Nobunaga

Toyotomi Hideyoshi

The Invasion of Korea

Grand Castles and the Arts

II. Japan and Europe: First Encounters (1543–1630)

The Portuguese in East Asia

The Jesuits in Japan: Initial Success

Persecution and Closure to the West

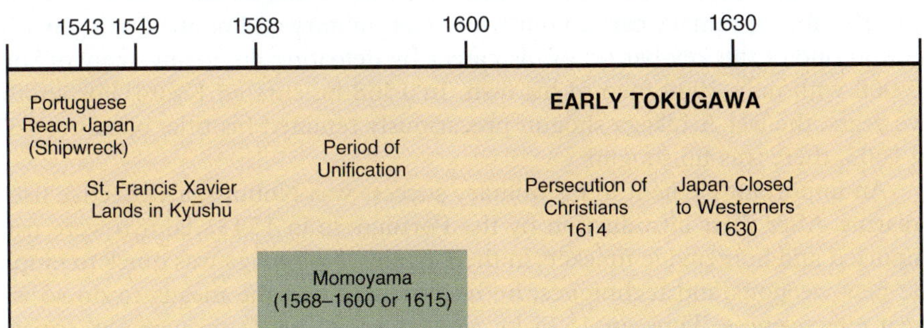

During the last thirty years of the sixteenth century, Japan was reunified, and the foundations were laid for an orderly political and social system as well as for economic growth. This was also a time of vigorous interaction between Japan and the outside world. We begin with internal developments and then consider the arrival of Europeans in Japan in the light of East Asian and world history.

Consolidation (1573–1600)

After the demise of the last Ashikaga shogun, there was not another for thirty years, but there was always an emperor. The imperial court, although impoverished and dependent on warrior patronage, was generally well led and succeeded in remaining Japan's most prestigious ceremonial and cultural center, setting standards of refined taste in poetry, flower viewing, kickball, and other arts and conferring honors and ranks on warriors eager for recognition. In a period with numerous complex crosscurrents in values and ideas as in politics and society, the court benefited from what Lee Butler has called "an ideology that upheld the traditional social order and confirmed the centrality of the court in the political and social world of medieval Japan."[1]

When Tokugawa Ieyasu (1542–1616) had himself appointed shogun in 1603, he confirmed the status of the emperor as well as the hegemony he had established at the decisive battle of Sekigahara in 1600, a victory marking the effective beginning of the Tokugawa rule. In establishing a new order, he built on the work of two forceful predecessors: Oda Nobunaga (1534–1582) and especially Toyotomi Hideyoshi (1542–1616).

Oda Nobunaga

Nobunaga inherited control of Owari, not one of the great territories but one of strategic importance in central Honshū. From this base, he embarked on a ruthless drive for supremacy carried out with great military and political skill. In 1560 he won one of the key battles of his career by defeating an enemy army of some 25,000 with only 2000 men of his own. In 1568 he entered Kyoto. For another five years, the last Ashikaga shogun precariously retained his title, but from 1573 to 1603, there was no shogun.

An important element in his military success was Nobunaga's effective use of firearms. After their introduction by the Portuguese in 1543, daimyo were using imported and homemade muskets in their armies. Nobunaga was quick to employ the new weapons and techniques; he had the will and the means to do so with great effectiveness. Thus, in 1575 he won a crucial battle through the superior firepower of his 3000 musketeers. For defense he built a great castle at Azuchi on the shore of Lake Biwa.

Secular opponents were not alone in feeling the full force of Nobunaga's wrath. After he seized Kyoto, he turned his attention to the monks on Mount Hiei and ended the military proclivities of the great Tendai monastery. He did this by destroying its buildings, slaughtering its monks, and eliminating the unfortunate inhabitants of nearby villages. "The roar of the huge burning monastery, magnified by the cries of countless numbers of the old and young, sounded and resounded to the ends of heaven and earth."[2] An estimated 1600 people lost their lives in this terrible bloodletting. Nobunaga was similarly set in his hostility toward the Ikkō sect. In Echizen province, he was responsible for the deaths of 30,000 to 40,000 Ikkō adherents, although he did not eradicate the sect completely. Even Mount Kōya only narrowly escaped Nobunaga's wrath. His hostility toward organized Buddhism was one of the factors influencing the friendly reception he accorded the first Jesuit missionaries to enter Japan.

Nobunaga was politically adroit. He forged valuable alliances through his marriage policies, managed to keep his enemies divided, and retained his followers and allies. A major element in his growing power was his ability to attract new vassals, frequently men who had been the vassals of his rivals. By going over to Nobunaga, they could secure their own positions and hope to participate in future gains. Thus, success fed on success.

By opening markets, breaking up guild monopolies, destroying toll stations, and encouraging road construction and shipbuilding, Nobunaga fostered trade. He also reorganized the administration of his lands, introducing a new system of tax collection and initiating a land survey. And he began to disarm the peasantry. Both were in full swing when Nobunaga died, betrayed by one of his own generals avenging a wrong. At the time of his death, he controlled about a third of Japan but clearly indicated his intent to be master of all.

Toyotomi Hideyoshi

Hideyoshi was born a peasant but rose to become one of Nobunaga's foremost generals. After Nobunaga's death, he defeated other contenders for the succession and then continued to increase his power much in the manner of Nobunaga, inducing daimyo to acknowledge his supremacy. Hideyoshi continued to increase his power by diplomacy. Unable to subdue the strongest daimyo, Tokugawa Ieyasu, he gave his sister to Ieyasu in marriage and assigned him substantial holdings in Kantō in exchange for domains of less value in central Japan. In this way, he saw to it that Ieyasu was both content and at a distance.

Hideyoshi also relocated his own vassals to assure maximum security. Those he trusted most were placed in strategic positions, and those thought to harbor territorial ambitions were provided with hostile neighbors to discourage them. To demonstrate their loyalty, vassals were sometimes required to leave wives and children with Hideyoshi as virtual hostages. Feudal bonds were further strengthened through marriage alliances. Thus, through conquest, diplomacy, and manipulation Hideyoshi became, in effect, overlord of all Japan. By 1590 all daimyo swore oaths of loyalty to him. Because he did not belong to the Minamoto lineage, he was ineligible to become shogun. He did have himself adopted into the Fujiwara family, and in 1585 he was appointed regent (*kanpaku*). This association with the imperial throne gave added legitimacy to his place at the apex of a system of feudal loyalties.

Hideyoshi was intent on keeping the daimyo in their places but not eliminating them. On the contrary, his policies strengthened the daimyo locally vis-à-vis their warriors and farmers even as he took steps to assure their subordination. When a daimyo was relocated, he took many of his vassals with him into his new domain, where they had no hereditary links to the land. This accelerated a tendency, already visible earlier, for samurai to be concentrated in castle towns where they received stipends collected from land but were divorced from direct supervision of the land. On the one hand, this severed the samurai from an independent power base and made them dependent on the daimyo. On the other, villages were left to provide their own leadership and to run their own affairs with little outside interference as long as they fulfilled their tax obligations. The village was freed from samurai control even as it was deprived of warrior leadership in case of conflict.

One of Hideyoshi's most important acts was the great "sword hunt" of 1588, when all peasants who had not already done so were ordered to surrender their weapons, the metal to be used in building a great statue of the Buddha. By depriving peasants of their weapons he did more than discourage them from rioting or rebelling—although he did that, too. A major, and intentional, consequence of the measure was to draw a sharp line between peasant and samurai, to create an unbridgeable gulf between the tiller of the soil and the bearer of arms where hitherto there had been low-ranking samurai who had also worked the land.

By this time, Hideyoshi's land survey, begun in 1582 but not completed for all of Japan until 1598, was well under way. In this great survey the value of cultivated land was assessed in terms of average annual productivity, measured in *koku* of rice, a *koku* being equal to 4.96 bushels. The resulting listings were used to assess the taxes due from each village, and the holdings of the daimyo were calculated in terms of the assessed value rather than acreage. From this time on, a daimyo, by definition, held land assessed at a minimum of 10,000 *koku*. Large daimyo held much more than that. Some of the greatest had several hundred thousand *koku*, and there were a few with more than 1 million. Hideyoshi personally held 2 million, not including the lands of his most trustworthy vassals. Tokugawa Ieyasu held 2.56 million. Like the confiscation of weapons, the land survey, which listed the names of the peasant proprietors, effectively separated farmers and fighters.

An edict of 1591 carried the process further. The first of its three articles prohibited fighting men from becoming peasants or townsmen, and the second banned peasants from leaving their fields and becoming merchants or artisans and prohibited the latter from becoming farmers. The third prohibited anyone from employing a samurai who had left his master without permission. If discovered, the offender was to be returned to his master. If this was not done and the culprit was knowingly allowed to go free, then the edict declared that "three persons shall be beheaded in place of the one, and their heads sent to the offender's original master. If this threefold substitution is not effected, then there is no alternative but to punish the new master."[3] In this way, Hideyoshi, who had himself risen from the peasantry to the greatest heights, did his best to make sure that henceforth everyone would remain within his hereditary social status.

The Invasion of Korea

Hideyoshi's vision of the world and his own place in it extended well beyond Japan. He took an active interest in overseas trade. After he subjugated the Kyushu daimyo, he undertook suppressing the pirates and freebooters who had long plagued the Chinese and Korean coasts. In East Asia as elsewhere, the line between trade and piracy was often obscure, as was the actual nationality of the so-called Japanese pirates (*wako*), many of whom were Chinese. Hideyoshi undertook other measures to encourage international commerce. One of his two great castles was at Osaka, which soon eclipsed Sakai as a trading center and remains today the second largest city in Japan.

But Hideyoshi looked abroad for more than trade: he thought in terms of empire. In the 1590s, he demanded the submission of the Philippines by their Spanish governor, although no steps were ever taken to enforce the demand. He also made plans to conquer China, which he then intended to divide among his vassals, much in the same way he had dealt with his Japanese conquests. After China would come India and, indeed, the rest of the world as he knew it. Hideyoshi's invasion of the continent can partially be seen as an attempt to satisfy the perpetual land hunger of his vassals or, at least, to find employment for restive samurai. It would also convince the Japanese and the rest of the world of Hideyoshi's power and glory. Another factor surely was his personality, but Jurgis Elisonas has suggested that "not so much megalomania as ignorance moved the entire enterprise."[4]

Whatever Hideyoshi's motivation, he dispatched a force of 150,000 men to Korea in 1592, after Korea had refused free passage for his troops to march to China. The Japanese force had great initial success and captured Seoul within a month. But they ran into difficulties further north and were bested at sea by the superior ships and seamanship of the Korean fleet under Admiral Yi Sun-sin, famous for his armed "turtle ships." Chinese military intervention and Korean guerrilla fighting also took their toll, and in 1593 peace negotiations were under way. These talks were fruitless, however, and in 1597 Hideyoshi sent another force of 140,000 men to Korea. This time they met with stronger resistance. The whole attempt was suddenly abandoned when Hideyoshi died in 1598, and the Japanese forces immediately returned home.

The expense of the campaign helped undermine the Ming dynasty in China, but the real losers were the Korean people, who suffered pillage and rape at the hands of their Chinese allies as well as their Japanese enemies. In the second campaign, the Japanese announced that all Korean officials along with their wives and children would be killed, as would any farmer who did not return to his house and land. Following through, the Japanese conducted manhunts, and as proof of their exploits commanders sent back to Hideyoshi casks filled with noses preserved in salt. Careful records were kept, and nose counts figured in determining promotions and rewards. Other Koreans were brought back to Japan in bondage. One result was an infusion of Korean influence on Japanese pottery and printing.

Hideyoshi never joined the Korean campaigns but left command to his vassals, several of whom were seriously weakened as a result. As it turned out, not only his continental ambitions but also his hopes to found a lasting dynasty at home came to naught. Before he died, he made his most powerful vassals solemnly swear allegiance to his five-year-old son, Hideyori, whom he left in their care as regents. But this proved useless, and in the ensuing struggle for power Ieyasu emerged the winner. His victory at Sekigahara in 1600 was followed by his designation as shogun in 1603, after he had acquired a suitable Minamoto ancestry. Final confirmation of Ieyasu's triumph came with the fall of Osaka Castle and the death of Hideyori in 1615. Ieyasu inherited Hideyoshi's power, but unlike Hideyoshi, he concentrated on building a lasting state at home.

Grand Castles and the Arts

The period of unification is usually called the Azuchi–Momoyama Epoch (or Momoyama for short) after Nobunaga's Azuchi Castle near Lake Biwa and Hideyoshi's Momoyama Castle in Fushimi, close to Kyoto. In many ways, these castles, along with those of the daimyo, are fitting representatives of the age. Dominating the surrounding countryside, they featured massive keeps and strong fortifications designed to withstand the new armies and weapons. Their great size was made possible by the wealth obtained by the unifiers and the daimyo as they achieved greater local control. The castles formed nuclei around which grew new cities, as first samurai and then merchants and artisans were attracted to castle towns. The most grandiose of all the castles was built by Hideyoshi in Osaka and boasted forty-eight towers. Unfortunately, Hideyoshi's and Nobunaga's castles were all destroyed, although the Osaka Castle was later rebuilt.

Most admired among Japan's castles is that at Himeji, which dates from the early seventeenth century. In recognition of its suggestive white silhouette, it is commonly known as the "Heron Castle" (see Figure 6.1). Like European castles, it is a stronghold surrounded by moat and wall and protected by massive foundations. Aesthetics were an important consideration in building a castle, and not only to please its owner, because "its purpose was to impress rivals by its elegant interiors as well as to frighten them by its strength."[5] One way to impress people was through richness of decor. The dark interiors of the castle were "lavish to the point of absurdity."[6] Hideyoshi's castle even had locks and bolts of gold and columns and ceilings covered with the precious metal.

Paintings on walls, sliding doors, and screens decorated and brightened the castle interiors. To meet new needs and tastes, the paintings were frequently large and used striking colors. Gold leaf was employed to create a flat background with the result that "its unreality reinforces the assertive substance of painted objects."[7] The artist Kanō Eitoku (1543–1590) epitomized the new style and spirit. Generously patronized by both Nobunaga and Hideyoshi, Eitoku worked at both the Azuchi and the Momoyama castles. The Eitoku screen shown in Figure 6.2 was originally one of a pair, but its companion is now lost. It is about twenty feet long and eight feet high and was obviously intended for use in a large room.

The Kanō school was continued by Eitoku's adopted son, Sanraku (1559–1653), in a trend that culminated in the great decorative screens of the early Tokugawa Period. In another medium, Momoyama fondness for rich decoration produced elaborate wood carvings such as those on the Kara Gate of the Nishi Honganji in Kyoto, popularly known as the gate that requires a whole day to be properly seen.

Ostentatious and profuse, the Momoyama aesthetic is far removed from Ashikaga restraint. Nothing could be more alien to the aesthetics of the tea ceremony than the monster tea party given by Hideyoshi in 1587 to which literally everyone was invited for ten days of music, theater, and art viewing.

This was not the only occasion on which Hideyoshi displayed a penchant for great gatherings and lavish entertainment; however, he also patronized Sen no Rikyu (1522–1591), greatest of the tea masters, who stressed harmony, respect, purity, and tranquility in his writings on tea. A story told about the great tea master and his son has them visiting another practitioner of the art. When they entered the garden, the son admired the wooden gate, covered with moss, at the end of the path leading to the tea hut, but the father disagreed:

FIGURE 6.1 Himeji Castle. Himeji, Hyōgo. (© Lore Schirokauer)

FIGURE 6.2 *Chinese Lions* (*Kara-shiki*), Kanō Eitoku. Section of sixfold screen, 88.58 in high. (Imperial Household Collection, Tokyo.) (© Sakamoto Photo Research Laboratory/Corbis)

That gate must have been brought from some distant mountain at obvious expense. A rough wicket made by the local farmer would give the place a really quiet and lonely look, and not offend us by bringing up thoughts of difficulty and expense. I doubt if we shall find here any very sensitive or interesting tea ceremony.[8]

FIGURE 6.3 Chōjirō, *Tea Bowl Named "Shobu."* Rakuware, sixteenth century, 8.9 cm high, Hakone Art Museum.

Sen no Rikyu is said to have influenced the potter Chōjirō (1576–1592), originator of Raku ware, illustrated by the tea bowl (see Figure 6.3). Eschewing the technical virtuosity of Chinese ceramics, the Japanese potter delights in bringing out the earthiness of the clay. The tea master, Furuta Oribe (1544–1615), originated a ceramic tradition characterized by thick glazes and rough brushwork and not only intentionally made misshaped bowls but even broke some so he could mend them.

Yet, as Lee Butler has written of Sen no Rikyu, "His practice of tea was at the same time very simple and deeply complex: it presented an image of poverty while revealing and requiring considerable wealth, and it adopted and revered the simplest of objects, thereby giving them great value."[9] From the beginning, a tendency toward wealth and ostentation coexisted with the aesthetics of poverty and simplicity, although the fantastic prices paid by wealthy daimyo competing for ownership of a famous bowl or jar were not exactly in keeping with the original spirit of tea. It is also worth noting that both tea masters became embroiled in the world of power and politics to the point that they were ordered to commit suicide. Tea survived, worldly yet refined. The second Tokugawa shogun was a connoisseur, and it remained the occasion for the display and appreciation of the best of taste.

As in China, painters in Japan often worked in more than one style. Both Eitoku and his great contemporary, Hasegawa Tōhaku (1539–1610), worked both in monochrome and in color. In scale, Tōhaku's masterly *Pine Grove* (see Figure 6.4) is typically Momoyama, because it occupies two screens more than five feet (sixty-one inches) high; but it is ink on paper and subtle rather than ostentatious.

FIGURE 6.4 *Pine Grove,* Hasegawa Tōhaku. Section of a sixfold screen. 136.6 in × 61 in. (© Tokyo National Museum)

II. Japan and Europe: First Encounters (1543–1630)

The Portuguese in East Asia

The Jesuits in Japan: Initial Success

Persecution and Closure to the West

The early contacts between post-Renaissance Europe and East Asia had nothing like the impact of those which were to follow in the nineteenth century. Even the introduction of firearms merely hastened the unification of Japan, accelerating but not changing the course of history. Yet these early relations form more than just an overture, introducing themes to be developed in later history. They provide an opportunity for comparisons of how different civilizations responded to similar foreign stimuli. More significantly for our purposes, the ultimate failure of the Catholic missionaries and the reduction of Western influence to a trickle left Japan, like China, comparatively isolated from Europe. This occurred just before developments in Europe that, for the first time in world history, were to affect all humanity inexorably.

The Portuguese in East Asia

The pioneers of European expansion in East Asia, as elsewhere at this time, were the Portuguese, who reached India in 1498, China in 1514, and Japan in 1543. Having wrested control of the seas from their Arab rivals, they established their Asian headquarters in 1510 at Goa, a small island off the coast of West India. In 1511, they captured Malacca, a vital center for the lucrative spice trade, located on the straits separating the Malay Peninsula from Sumatra (see Figure 6.5).

The desire to break the Arab spice monopoly supplied the economic motive for this initial European expansion. Spices were highly valuable relative to their bulk and weight. Easily transported and fetching a high price, they formed an attractive cargo. And there was an assured market for them in Europe, where they added flavor to an otherwise dull diet and made meat palatable in an age when animals were slaughtered in the fall for want of sufficient fodder to sustain them through the winter. They were also used in medicine and in religious ceremonies.

Prospects for trade were hampered, however, by the absence of any European commodities that could be marketed in Asia. Lacking access to silver, the Portuguese initially financed themselves by a mixture of trade and piracy, taking advantage of their superior ships, weapons, and seamanship. They derived income from transporting goods from one Asian country to another: Southeast Asian

FIGURE 6.5 Eastern Europe and Asia in the sixteenth and seventeenth centuries.

wares to China, Chinese silk to Japan, and Japanese silver to China. They used their profits from this trade to purchase spices and other products for European markets. But before this trade could prosper, they had to secure entry to China and Japan. This posed problems quite different from those they had encountered in seizing a small island off the coast of politically divided India or in driving the Arabs from Malacca.

In China they got off to a very bad start. Not waiting for official permission to trade, they engaged in illegal commerce and even built a fort on Lintin Island, located at the mouth of the river that connects Canton to the sea. Their unruly behavior did not endear them to the Ming authorities and served to confirm the opinion that these "ocean devils" were a new kind of barbarian. The outrageous behavior of the Portuguese traders was further embellished by the Chinese imagination. When the Portuguese bought kidnapped Chinese children as slaves, the Chinese concluded that their purpose was to eat them. They long continued in the firm belief that they were dealing with barbarous child-eaters. More than just a popular rumor held by the ignorant, this belief found its way into the official history of the Ming dynasty.

The first Portuguese envoy to China not only failed to obtain commercial concessions, but he also ended his life in a Cantonese prison. It was a most inauspicious beginning. But the Portuguese would not leave, and their superiority on the seas made it impossible for the Chinese to drive them out. A modus vivendi was reached in 1557 when the Portuguese were permitted to establish themselves in

Macao in exchange for an annual payment. There the Portuguese administered their own affairs, but the territory remained under Chinese jurisdiction until Macao was ceded to Portugal in 1887.

The Jesuits in Japan: Initial Success

Trade and booty were not the only objectives of the Europeans who ventured into Asian waters. Missionary work was also important: mid-sixteenth-century Goa boasted some eighty churches and convents. From the beginning, the missionary impulse provided a strong incentive as well as religious sanction for European expansion, and it was the missionary rather than the trader who served as the prime intermediary between the civilizations of East Asia and the West from the sixteenth to the twentieth centuries.

Among the early missionaries, the great pioneers and the most impressive leaders were members of the Society of Jesus (Jesuits). Founded in 1540, this tightly disciplined religious order formed the vanguard of the Catholic Counter-Reformation. They were the "cavalry of the church," prepared to do battle with Protestant heretics in Europe or the heathen in the world beyond. Along with its stress on martial discipline and intensive religious training, the Society was noted for its insistence on intellectual vigor and depth of learning. The latter included secular as well as sacred studies, and the ideal Jesuit was as learned as he was disciplined and devout.

In 1549, less than ten years after the founding of the Jesuit order, St. Francis Xavier (1506–1552), one of the original members of the Society, landed in Kyūshū on a vessel captained by a Chinese wako. This was just six years after the Japanese had first encountered Europeans, some shipwrecked Portuguese who had landed on the island of Tanegashima. Xavier was well received and was soon able to establish cordial relations with important men in Kyūshū. First impressions on both sides were favorable. Xavier and his successors liked the Japanese; he himself referred to them as "the best [people] who have yet been discovered."[10] Likewise, the Japanese were impressed by the strong character and dignified bearing of the European priests. The Jesuit combination of martial pride, stern self-discipline, and religious piety fit well with the ethos of sixteenth-century Japan, and the Christian religion did not seem altogether strange. On the contrary, Christianity, when initially brought to Japan from Goa, seemed like just another type of Buddhism. Some of its ceremonies were similar to those found in Buddhism, and it was difficult for the early priests to convey the subtleties of theology, to explain the difference between God and the cosmic Buddha, for example, or to distinguish Paradise from the Buddhist Pure Land. At last the Jesuit fathers concluded that the devil, in all of his malicious cleverness, had deliberately fashioned Buddhism to resemble the true faith so as to confound and confuse the people.

The initial meeting of the Jesuits and the Japanese was facilitated by similarities in their feudal backgrounds. In Japan, Xavier and other Europeans found a society that resembled their own far more than did any other outside Europe. "The people," wrote Alessandro Valignano (1539–1606), "are all white, courteous and highly civilized, so much so that they surpass all the other known races of the world."[11] Only the Chinese were to receive similar praise—and, indeed, to be regarded as "white." Donald F. Lach has summarized the qualities the Jesuits found to admire in the Japanese: "their courtesy, propriety, dignity, endurance, frugality, equanimity, industriousness, sagaciousness, cleanliness, simplicity, discipline, and rationality."[12] On the negative side, besides paganism, the Jesuits were appalled at the prevalence of sodomy among the military aristocracy and the monks. They criticized the Japanese propensity to commit suicide and also found fault with the "disloyalty of vassal to master, their dissimulation, ambiguity, and lack of openness in their dealings, their bellicose nature, their inhuman treatment of enemies and unwanted children, their failure to respect the rule of law, and finally their unwillingness to give up the system of concubinage."[13] Nevertheless, the similarities between Japanese culture and their own gave the Jesuits high hopes for the success of their mission.

In their everyday behavior the Jesuits tried to win acceptance by adapting themselves to local manners and customs, as long as these did not run counter to their own creed. "Thus," Valignano observed, "we who come hither from Europe find ourselves as veritable children who have to learn to eat, sit, converse, dress, act politely, and so on. . . ."[14] They learned how to squat Japanese style, learned to employ the Japanese language with its various levels of politeness, and mastered the art of tea—the Jesuit dwelling was usually equipped with a tea room so that their guests could be properly entertained. C. R. Boxer has pointed out that the Christian monks came from a land with rather different standards of personal cleanliness: "Physical dirt and religious poverty tended to be closely associated in Catholic Europe where lice were regarded as the inseparable companions of monks and soldiers."[15] But in Japan the devoted monks even learned to wash, a major concession to Japanese sensibilities. Still there were limits: Valignano could not bring himself to endorse the Japanese custom of taking a hot bath every day. That would really be going too far!

Careful attention to the niceties of etiquette was required of the Jesuit fathers in their strategy of working from the top down. It was their hope to transform Japan into a Christian land by first converting the rulers and then allowing the faith to seep down to the populace at large. The purpose of their labors was not to Europeanize Japan or China but to save souls. They realized that the enthusiastic support of the ruling authority would be an invaluable asset, whereas without at least the ruler's tacit approval they could do nothing.

This approach met with considerable success in Kyūshū, where they converted important local daimyo, who ordered their people to adopt the foreign faith. Although there were numerous cases of genuine conversion, some daimyo simply saw the light of commerce, adopting a Christian stance in the hope of attracting the Portuguese trade to their ports. On at least one occasion, when the great Portuguese ship did not appear, they promptly turned their backs on the new faith.

In the end, Christianity did gain an impressive number of genuine converts, but the strategy of steering trade to friendly daimyo had grave political consequences. Since it strengthened some daimyo at the expense of others, the Jesuits inevitably became embroiled in the complicated, and often bloody, power struggles that continued in Kyūshū, until Hideyoshi put an end to them. Nor was the Jesuit involvement always indirect. For seven years Nagasaki, which had developed into the major port for the Portuguese trade, was ruled by the Jesuits, overlords by virtue of a grant from an embattled Christian daimyo. Thus, the Jesuits became minor players in a deadly secular game.

From the beginning, the Jesuits had realized that real progress for their mission depended on the goodwill not only of local Kyūshū daimyo but also of the central government. Xavier's initial trip to Kyoto came at an unpropitious time—the city was in disorder. But Nobunaga soon became a friend of the Jesuits. Attracted by their character and interested in hearing about foreign lands, perhaps he was also happy to talk with someone not part of the hierarchical order that he himself headed. This personal predilection coincided nicely with reasons of state. It was consistent with his hostility toward the Buddhist orders and with his desire to keep up the flow of overseas trade. Hideyoshi, sharing Nobunaga's desire for trade as well as his hostility toward militant Buddhism, was similarly well-disposed toward the new foreigners and curious about their religion. He liked dressing up in Portuguese clothes, complete with rosary, and he once said that the only thing that kept him from converting was the Christian insistence on monogamy.

The political and economic success of the Jesuits helped the spread of Christianity, but power, or the semblance of power, always entails risks. There was the danger that the ruler might perceive the activities of the monks not as assets bolstering his own position but as liabilities, actual or potential threats to his authority. Why should a man who had stringently suppressed Buddhist religious organizations exercising military and political power have been more favorable to a Christian society engaged in similar activities? Initially, Hideyoshi may have seemed to welcome a Jesuit vice provincial's promise of help in subduing Kyūshū and in the subsequent conquest of the mainland, but such political maneuvers proved harmful in the long run. Even if Jesuit plans for a coalition of Christian daimyo never materialized, Hideyoshi came to view them as a danger. In 1587 he issued an order expelling the monks. Soon thereafter he seized Nagasaki. Yet, since he did not really feel threatened and continued to want trade, he did not enforce the expulsion decree.

There was, instead, a surge of popularity for things Western, such as "Southern barbarian screens" (*Namban byobu*), showing the giant black ships of the foreigners and the foreigners themselves. The barbarians were depicted as exceedingly tall and rather ungainly, with sharp long noses and red hair, wearing the ballooning pantaloons that formed the standard Portuguese fashion (see Figure 6.6). Other scenes, based on paintings from Europe, depicted various barbarian topics: the battle of Lepanto, an Italian court, European cities, and maps of the world, not to mention religious subjects. Whereas some artists painted European subjects Japanese style, others experimented with Western perspective and techniques of shading to produce three-dimensional effects.

FIGURE 6.6 "Southern Barbarians" in Japan. Namban screen. (© Freer Gallery of Art, Smithsonian Institution, Washington, DC. [F1965.22])

Western motifs were not limited to painting. Western symbols were widely used in decoration: a cross on a bowl, a few words of Latin on a saddle, and so forth. In a letter written in 1594, a missionary described the foreign fad. Writing of non-Christian daimyo, he stated:

> They wear rosaries of driftwood on their breasts, hang a crucifix from their shoulder or waist, and sometimes even a handkerchief. Some, who are especially kindly disposed, have memorized the Our Father and the Hail Mary, and recite them as they walk in the streets. This is not done in ridicule of the Christians, but simply to show off their familiarity with the latest fashion, or because they think it good and effective in bringing success in daily life. This has led them to spend no small sums in ordering oval earrings bearing the likeness of Our Lord and the Holy Mother.[16]

This was a passing fashion, but some new products entered Japan to stay, and new words were added to the language, for instance tabako (tobacco), pan (bread), and karuta (playing cards). Another Portuguese contribution was tempura, the popular Japanese dish prepared by deep fat frying vegetables and seafood dipped in batter. The Japanese word is derived from temporas (meatless Friday).

Persecution and Closure to the West

Since the final chapter of these early encounters straddles the transition from Hideyoshi to Tokugawa rule, our discussion will similarly overlap into the Tokugawa Period, whose beginning is discussed in the following section. Despite the order of 1587, Western influences continued to enter Japan: religious, commercial, and cultural. The situation was complicated, however, by the arrival of other Europeans. The first Spaniards arrived from the Philippines, headquarters of the Spanish in Asia, in 1587; and the first Franciscans came from Manila in 1592. By the early 1600s, representatives of the Protestant Dutch and English had also arrived. Although the prospects for trade were attractive, the proliferation of foreigners was disturbing. The various nations competed with each other for Japanese trade. The Dutch and English sought to encourage Japanese suspicions of their Catholic rivals. Moreover, the Japanese were not unaware that the Spanish role in the Philippines was that of colonial master, and that the Spaniards might harbor imperial ambitions with regard to Japan as well. Finally, the Japanese became increasingly concerned that growing Catholic influence might prove subversive of internal stability. The Jesuits had been unable to avoid a degree of involvement in Japanese politics; now the Franciscans, working among the poor, seemed to threaten the traditional social order.

The Jesuits had sought to carry out their missionary activities within the framework of Japanese society and social values. They associated primarily with the upper classes, with a view to working their way down. The Franciscans were suspicious of the Jesuit approach. They were much less well informed concerning conditions in Japan and also much less discreet in their work. Instead of associating with the samurai, the Franciscans worked among the poor and forgotten, the sick and miserable, those at the very bottom of society. The Jesuits did not disguise their contempt for the ignorance and poverty of the Franciscans, the "crazy friars" (frailes idiotas) as they called them, and these sentiments were heartily reciprocated by the friars, who scoffed at Jesuit pretensions.

Rivalry between the Portuguese and the Spanish, between Goa and Manila, compounded the instability of the situation. On the one hand, Manila presented the possibility of a new source of profitable trade; on the other, the colonization of the Philippines demonstrated the imperialistic ambitions of the Europeans and the connection between Christian evangelism and colonialism. It was an omen of things to come when Hideyoshi, in 1597, crucified six Franciscan missionaries and eighteen of their Japanese converts after the pilot of a Spanish ship driven ashore in Japan reportedly boasted about the power and ambitions of his king. Ieyasu, the founder of the Tokugawa shogunate, was at first friendly to the Christians, but he too turned against them. In 1606 Christianity was declared illegal, and in 1614 he undertook a serious campaign to expel the missionaries.

By 1614 there were more than 300,000 converts in Japan. The destruction of Christianity was long and painful. Tortures, such as hanging a man upside down with his head in a pit filled with excrement, were used to induce people to renounce their faith. Before it was all over, more than 3000 persons were recognized as martyrs by the Vatican, of whom fewer than seventy were Europeans. Others died without achieving martyrdom. From 1637 to 1638 there was a rebellion in Shimabara, near Nagasaki, against a daimyo who combined merciless taxation with cruel suppression of Christianity. Fought under banners on which Christian slogans were written in Portuguese and led by some masterless samurai, it was a Christian version of the rural uprisings characteristic of the century of warfare before Nobunaga. In its suppression, some 37,000 Christians lost their lives.

Persuasion as well as violence was employed in the campaign against Christianity. Opponents of Christian dogma argued that the idea of a personal creator was absurd and asked why, if God was both omnipotent and good, he should have tempted Adam and Eve and devised eternal punishment in Hell for non-Christians even though they led exemplary lives. According to Christian teaching, even the sage emperors Yao and Shun would end in hell. The First Commandment was attacked as leading to disobedience of parents and lord; a loyal retainer should accompany his lord even into hell.

Such arguments suggest that the Japanese saw Christianity as potentially subversive, not only of the political order, but of the basic social structure, for it challenged accepted values and beliefs and demanded a radical reappraisal of long-revered traditions. Its association with European expansionism posed a threat from abroad, and, as exemplified by the Shimabara Rebellion, it also harbored the seeds of radical disruption at home. Thus, the motivation for the government's suppression of Christianity was secular, not religious. The government was not worried about the state of its subjects' souls, but it was determined to wipe out a dangerous doctrine. An indication that the government's concerns were secular is provided by the oath of apostasy demanded of all former Christians. In it the recanters had to swear that if they had the slightest thought of renouncing their apostasy, "then let us be punished by God the Father, God the Son, and God the Holy Ghost, St. Mary, and all the Angels and Saints."[17] Thus, they had to take a Christian oath that they no longer believed in Christianity! The persecutions succeeded in destroying all but a small underground group of secret Christians, who passed from generation to generation a faith increasingly infused with native elements. Meanwhile, every Japanese family was registered with a Buddhist temple, and once a year the family head had to swear that there were no Christians in his household. Incidentally, the resulting demographic data, the most complete for any premodern society, constitutes an invaluable resource for modern scholars.

Not only Christianity but all foreign influences were potentially subversive, including trade that would tend to the advantage of the Kyūshū daimyo rather than the Tokugawa. Gradually, the *bakufu* further restricted foreign contacts. The Spaniards were expelled in 1624, one year after the English had left voluntarily. In 1630 Japanese were forbidden to go overseas or to return from there or to build ships capable of long voyages. The Portuguese were expelled after the Shimabara

FIGURE 6.7 *A Dutch Dinner Party.* Prints such as this satisfied the public's curiosity about the strange customs of the Westerners—and may or may not have been accurate portrayals. Color print, 12.99 in × 8.66 in. (© Charles E. Tuttle & Company, Tokyo)

Rebellion on the grounds of complicity with that uprising. When they sent an embassy in 1640, its members were executed.

The only Europeans left were the Dutch (see Figure 6.7), trying their luck in Japan until the English and Russians challenged Dutch naval supremacy in the late eighteenth and early nineteenth centuries. The Dutch themselves were moved to Deshima in 1641, a tiny artificial island in Nagasaki Harbor where they were virtually confined as in a prison. The annual Dutch vessel to Deshima was all that remained of Japan's contact with Europe, but an annual average of almost twenty-six Chinese ships came to Nagasaki, and Japan also maintained indirect diplomatic links with Korea. The "closing" was by no means complete.

The story of early contacts with Europe is one of promise unfulfilled. Neither the West nor the Japanese turned out to have been ready for fruitful discourse or exchange. In terms of world history, opportunities were missed. In terms of Japanese history, the exclusion of disruptive forces from abroad can be seen as an integral part of a broader effort by Ieyasu and his immediate successors to achieve stability in a land that had suffered a surfeit of warfare and disorder.

Notes

1. Lee Butler, *Emperor and Aristocracy in Japan, 1467–1680: Resilience and Renewal* (Cambridge, MA: Harvard Univ. Asia Center, 2002), p. 287.
2. Ryusaku Tsunoda, Wm. Theodore de Bary, and Donald Keene, comps., *Sources of Japanese Tradition* (New York: Columbia Univ. Press, 1958), p. 316.
3. David John Lu, *Sources of Japanese History* (New York: McGraw-Hill, 1974), 1:189. Trans. from Okubo Toshiaki et al., eds., *Shiryo ni yoru Nihon no Ayumi (Japanese History Through Documents) Kinseihen (Early Modern Period)* (Tokyo: Toshikawa Kobunkan, 1955), pp. 40–41.
4. Jurgis Elisonas, "The Inseparable Trinity: Japan's Relation with China and Korea," in John W. Hall, ed., *The Cambridge History of Japan, Vol. 4: Early Modern Japan* (New York: Cambridge Univ. Press, 1991), p. 271.
5. Sir George Sansom, *A History of Japan, 1334–1615* (Stanford: Stanford Univ. Press, 1961), p. 380.
6. Sir George Sansom, *Japan: A Short Cultural History* (New York: Appleton-Century-Crofts, 1931), p. 437.
7. Carolyn Wheelwright, "A Visualization of Eitoku's Lost Paintings at Azuchi Castle," in George Ellison and Bardwell L. Smith, eds., *Warlords, Artists, & Commoners: Japan in the Sixteenth Century* (Honolulu: Univ. of Hawaii Press, 1981), p. 99.
8. Langdon Warner, *The Enduring Art of Japan* (Cambridge: Harvard Univ. Press, 1958), p. 95.
9. Butler, *Emperor and Aristocracy in Japan,* p. 264.

10. C. R. Boxer, *The Christian Century in Japan* (Berkeley: Univ. of California Press, 1951), Appendix I, p. 401. Also quoted in Donald F. Lach, *Asia in the Making of Europe, Vol. I: The Century of Discovery* (Chicago: Univ. of Chicago Press, 1965), p. 284, also pp. 663–64.
11. Ibid., p. 74.
12. Lach, *Asia in the Making of Europe,* 1:728.
13. Ibid.
14. Quoted in Boxer, *The Christian Century in Japan,* p. 5.
15. Ibid., p. 214.
16. Yoshitomo Okamoto, *The Namban Art of Japan* (Tokyo and New York: John Weatherhill, 1972), p. 77.
17. Boxer, *The Christian Century in Japan,* p. 441.

7

Tokugawa Shogunate

- Founding and Consolidation
- Bakufu–Han Relations
- Economic and Social Change
- Classes and Values
- The Aesthetic Culture of the Aristocracy
- Genroku Urban Culture
  - The Print
  - Theater and Literature
- Intellectual Currents: Confucianism
  - Historiography and Nativism
  - Dutch Learning
- Reform and Its Limits
- Art and Literature After the Genroku Period

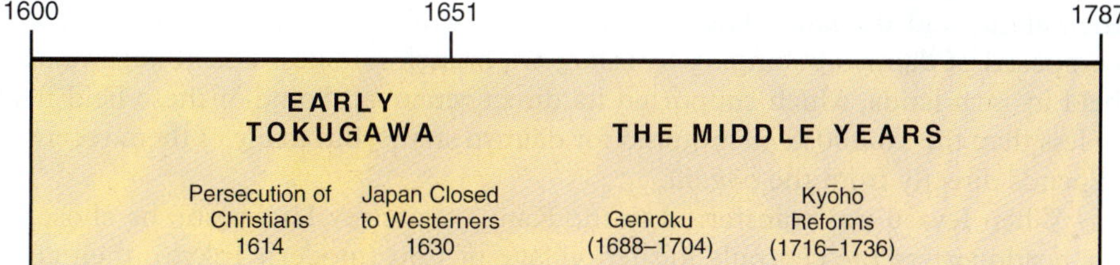

Ieyasu founded a long dynasty of shoguns and found the stability he sought, but that stability in itself generated change. Under the Tokugawa Japan enjoyed peace, experienced economic growth, and developed a flourishing urban culture. At the same time, there were stresses inherent in the system and, over time, new conditions arose to strain the body politic and society.

Founding and Consolidation

The essential structure of the Tokugawa political system was devised by Ieyasu and completed by his two immediate successors, Hidetada (1616–1623) and Iemitsu (1623–1651). By the middle of the seventeenth century, the system was in full operation.

Ieyasu rose to supremacy as the leader of a group of daimyo, each of whom was backed by his own vassals and supported by his independent power base. The daimyo were by no means all deeply committed to the Tokugawa. Hideyoshi's recent failure to establish a dynasty had demonstrated, if any demonstration was needed, the folly of relying solely on the loyalty of such men, especially when passing the succession to a minor. Ieyasu assured the smooth transfer of power to his son by resigning from the office of shogun in 1605, after holding it for only two years. But he continued in actual control until his death, working to ensure the continuity of Tokugawa rule.

All the daimyo were the shogun's vassals, bound to him by solemn oath, and when a daimyo's heir succeeded to his domain, the new daimyo had to sign his pledge of vassalage to the shogun in blood. Still, some vassals were more reliable than others, and the Tokugawa classified them into three groups. Least trusted and potentially the most dangerous were the "outside," or allied, daimyo (*tozama*), who were too powerful to be considered Tokugawa subordinates. Virtually all of these, like Ieyasu, had been vassals of Hideyoshi. Some had supported Ieyasu at the battle of Sekigahara, but others came over to the Tokugawa only after the outcome of that battle left them no choice. More trustworthy were the house daimyo (*fudai*), most of whom had been Tokugawa family vassals raised to daimyo status by the Tokugawa; thus, unlike the *tozama,* they were indebted to the *bakufu* for their status and domains. The third group, the collateral daimyo (*shimpan*), was composed of daimyo belonging to Tokugawa branch families. The Tokugawa also held its own lands, which supported its direct retainers. Some of these held fiefs of less than the 10,000 *koku* required for daimyo status, but many of them received stipends directly from the *bakufu.*

When Ieyasu was transferred to the Kantō region by Hideyoshi, he chose as his headquarters the centrally located village of Edo (modern Tokyo), then consisting of about a hundred houses but destined to become one of the world's great cities. The shogunate also maintained castles at Osaka and Shizuoka (then called Sumpu) and the Nijō Castle in Kyoto, residence of a *bakufu* deputy responsible for the government of the capital city and serving concurrently as the shogun's representative at the imperial court.

To secure itself militarily, the Tokugawa placed its *fudai* in strategic areas. It dominated the Kantō, central Japan, and Kyoto–Osaka regions, and the *tozama* had their territories in the outer areas. Several policies were initiated to keep the daimyo from acquiring too much strength. They were restricted to one castle each and had to secure *bakufu* permission before they could repair this castle. They were allowed to maintain only a fixed number of men at arms and, in line with the seclusion policy, were forbidden to build large ships. To keep the daimyo from forming political alliances that might threaten the *bakufu,* they were required to obtain *bakufu* consent for their marriage plans.

During the first half of the seventeenth century, the shogunate enacted a vigorous policy of increasing its own strength at the expense of the daimyo. In this period there were 281 cases in which daimyo were transferred from one fief to another, shuffles that strengthened some and weakened others. Another 213 domains were confiscated outright. This happened sometimes as a disciplinary measure, such as when a lord proved incompetent or the domain was torn by a succession dispute. More often, confiscation resulted from failure to produce an heir. Deathbed adoptions of an heir were not recognized. By such means, the Tokugawa more than tripled the size of its holdings, until its own domain was calculated as worth 6.8 million *koku* of rice (see Figure 7.1). The distribution of their holdings also favored the Tokugawa economically, as it did militarily, because they possessed many of Japan's mines and most of the important cities, such as Osaka, Kyoto, and Nagasaki. In the mid-Tokugawa Period, *shimpan* held land worth 2.6 million *koku; fudai,* 6.7 million; and *tozama,* 9.8 million. It is indicative of the decline of their economic and political power that religious institutions held only around 600,000 *koku,* and the emperor and the court nobility could draw on land worth only 187,000 *koku.*

To see to it that the daimyo obeyed *bakufu* orders, the shogunate sent out its own inspectors. It also devised a highly effective system of strengthening itself po-

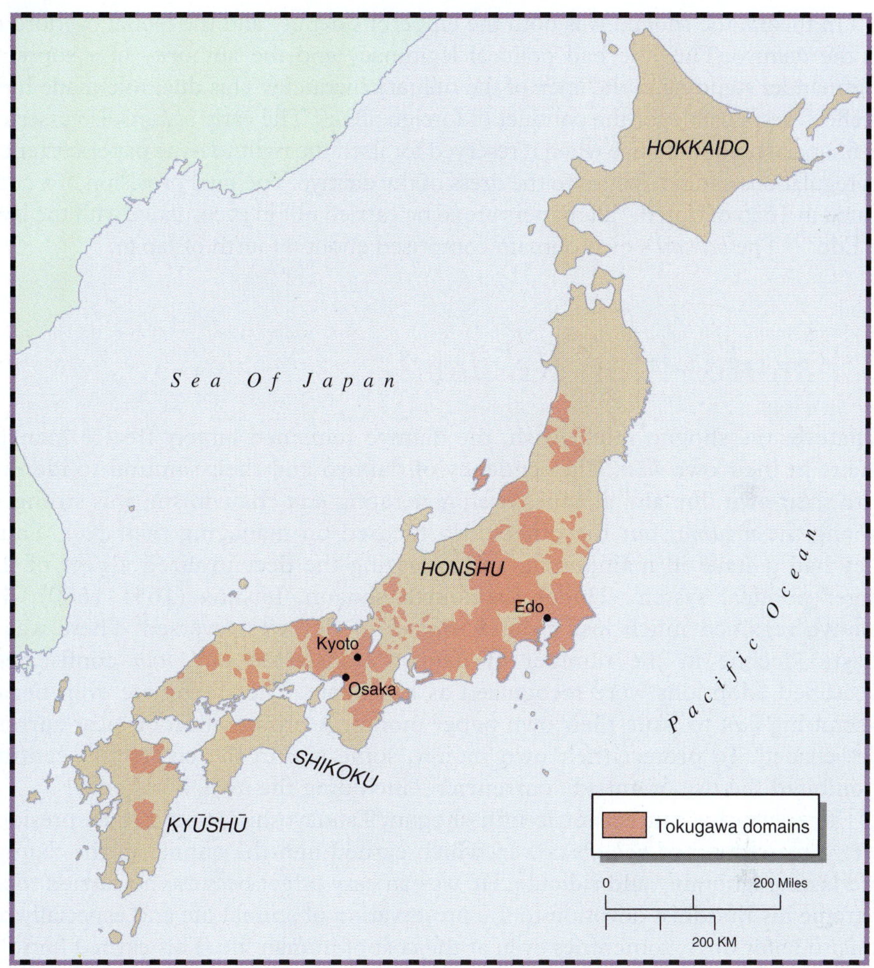

FIGURE 7.1 Japan c. 1664.

litically (while draining the daimyo financially) by requiring them to spend alternate years in residence in Edo, where the *bakufu* could keep them under surveillance. When they did go back home to their domains, they had to leave their wives and children behind as hostages. This system of alternate attendance (*sankin kotai*) forced the daimyo to spend large sums traveling with their retinues. The maintenance of suitably elaborate residences in Edo was a further strain on daimyo resources. The daimyo were also called upon to support public projects such as waterworks or the repair of the shogun's castle at Edo, but such exactions were not as burdensome as the constant expense of alternate attendance. The residence requirement had the additional effect of turning Edo into a capital not only of the *bakufu* but of all Japan.

In theory, the shogun was both the emperor's deputy and the feudal overlord of all the daimyo. Thus, he had political legitimacy and the authority of a supreme commander standing at the apex of the military hierarchy. This dual role made him, in effect, responsible for the conduct of foreign affairs. The early *bakufu* also asserted its financial predominance when it reserved for itself the right to issue paper currency. Its regulations extended even to the dress of the daimyo. The final provision of a code issued in 1635 declared, "all matters are to be carried out in accordance with the laws of Edo."[10] The *bakufu's* own domain comprised about a fourth of Japan.

Bakufu–Han *Relations*

Whatever the shogun might wish, the daimyo remained largely free to manage affairs in their own *han*. The tendency of daimyo and their samurai to identify with their own domain, at times even generating *han* chauvinism, was strongest among the *tozama,* but the others also focused on managing their *han*. Thus, they had a stake in maintaining and enlarging the decentralized aspect of the larger political system. Under the fourth shogun, Ietsuna (1651–1680), the daimyo regained much lost ground. *Bakufu* policy was reversed. There was a drastic decline in the number of daimyo transferred and *han* confiscated. Deathbed adoptions were recognized as legitimate. The shogunate even began permitting *han* to issue their own paper money. A proliferation of local currencies ensued. To protect their own money, some *han* in the eighteenth century prohibited the use of outside currencies—including the *bakufu's* money!

The vigorous but eccentric fifth shogun, Tsunayoshi (1680–1709), presided over a reassertion of *bakufu* power, which earned him the enmity of the daimyo and lasting ignominy and ridicule. He was an easy target because he carried to an extreme his Buddhist devotion to the preservation of animal life and especially his solicitude for dogs, sometimes even at the cost of human life. This earned him the epithet "dog shogun." Nevertheless, his period saw a great flowering of culture and a resurgence of centralizing activity. But this did not lead to a permanent shift in the power balance, nor did it initiate a long-term trend toward greater *bakufu* control. If it had, this shogun's historical image would have been different.

Until the end of the Tokugawa, the pendulum continued to swing between the *bakufu* and the *han*. In his analysis of the history and dynamics of this process, Harold Bolitho has shown that periods of *bakufu* assertiveness tended to occur under vigorous shoguns working with trusted advisers drawn from among the shogunate's low-ranking retainers. Unencumbered by fief or vassals, totally dependent on the shogun, they became his men, free from potential conflicts of interest. Under such regimes, the high-ranking senior councilors, always selected from among the *fudai* were treated with an outward show of respect while they were actually bypassed and disregarded. Little love was lost between the *fudai* and the new men.

When the shogun was a minor or incompetent, control over the *bakufu* reverted to the senior councilors, descendants of the Tokugawa's most favored and highly trusted vassals. The service of these vassals had formed the core of Ieyasu's strength, and he relied on their descendants for continued loyal service to his house. Although these men were conscious of their heritage of special obligations toward the shogunate, they also had responsibilities and opportunities as daimyo.

The tensions between shogunate and *han* were mirrored in their own persons as they faced the often-conflicting demands of *bakufu* and *han*. The usual pattern was for them to act more as daimyo than as *bakufu* officials. Such senior councilors were not prepared to sacrifice *han* privileges for the sake of the larger body politic. There were even cases of *han* held by incumbent senior councilors refusing to export grain badly needed to combat famine elsewhere. There were periodic shifts in the balance of power between the *bakufu* and the *han*, but the issue was never lastingly resolved in favor of one or the other. It can be argued that this proved beneficial in the long run because it allowed considerable divergence yet still maintained a center.

The more than 250 *han* varied widely in size, natural resources, and local conditions. All the lands held by a daimyo were not necessarily contiguous; some domains were more easily organized than others. But in general, operating on a smaller scale than the *bakufu*, the daimyo were more successful in controlling their retainers. The trend for the samurai to be concentrated in the *han* capitals divorced from the land continued strong. By the last decade of the seventeenth century, more than 80 percent of the daimyo were paying stipends to their samurai. By the end of the eighteenth century, 90 percent of samurai depended entirely on their stipends. Only 10 percent retained local roots in the country.

Economic and Social Change

During the Tokugawa, peace made economic growth possible. There was a rise in demand to meet the needs of the samurai and the growing expenses of the daimyo. The system of alternate attendance stimulated the commercialization of agriculture, and agricultural productivity increased substantially, especially in the seventeenth century. Cultivated acreage doubled because of vigorous irrigation and land reclamation. Technological improvements, the practice of multiple-cropping, better seed strains, and improved fertilizers helped, as did the dissemination of knowledge through agricultural handbooks and manuals. The spread of market networks was accompanied by regional specialization in cash crops such as cotton, mulberry trees for rearing silk worms, indigo, tobacco, and sugar cane, but grain continued to be grown in all parts of Japan.

Population rose from about 18 million at the beginning of the Tokugawa to around 30 million by the middle of the period. Afterward, there were fluctuations in population, but there was no major long-term increase during the rest of Tokugawa; in 1872 the population stood at only 33.1 million. Although famine and disease took their toll, mortality rates were comparatively low, and the average life span was likely longer than that in premodern Europe because Japan was free from war and was less susceptible to epidemics. Late marriage, the custom of having only one son marry and inherit, and abortion and infanticide kept population growth under control. Family planning was widespread. Even when times were good, life was by no means easy for Japanese peasants who remained at the mercy of the elements. Many were poor, but for most of the period, the standard of living rose.

With samurai now largely removed from the land, the villages were left virtually free to collect the taxes due their overlord. Within the village, neither the benefits of agricultural growth nor the burdens of taxation were shared equally: there were wide gradations in wealth, status, and power backed by the state. Because tax reassessments were infrequent, wealthy peasants who were able to open new lands and otherwise increase their yields found their incomes rising.

Traditionally, the main house of an extended family had claims on the services of the lesser households and some obligations to look after the poorer members. Furthermore, the heads of the main houses formed the traditional village leadership. Now, with more money in circulation, wealthy villagers turned increasingly to hired laborers or tenant farmers to work their land. They also put their money to work in rural commerce, money lending, and such rural industries as processing vegetable oils, brewing sake, producing soy sauce, and making paper. Because the wealthy villagers did not necessarily belong to the old main houses, tensions ensued.

These tensions were aggravated by economic disparities, because poorer villagers and the landless did not share in the prosperity of the countryside but suffered as contractual relationships replaced those based on family. Most often they endured in silence, but at times they vented their resentment in uprisings. Peasant unrest was on the increase in the late Tokugawa. In contrast to early Tokugawa rural uprisings, often led by village headmen, those of the later period were frequently directed against those wealthy and powerful villagers. However, neither the uprisings nor the changes in agricultural technology seriously threatened the basic stability of the village. Violence was a form of protest, not a means toward revolution.

Changes in agriculture increased yield but did not alter the basic pattern of rice farming, with its need for intensive labor and community cooperation. At the same time, the experience of calculating work in terms of money and time was to prove a legacy useful in the future.

Internal peace and economic vigor were conducive to expansion of the Japanese presence in the far north, homeland of the non-Japanese Ainu people who, by the end of the eighteenth century, accounted for only about half the population of Hokkaido. The Japanese presence then accelerated, partly out of concern over Russian expansion. In the early nineteenth century in eastern Hokkaido, they pursued a policy of turning the Ainu into Japanese, forcing them to abandon their bear festival, to cut their hair in the Japanese manner, and to give up tattooing and ear piercing. The decline in Ainu numbers and identity proved a long-term trend.

Economic expansion also left a dubious ecological legacy. In the seventeenth century, both the *bakufu* and the domains promoted land clearance. Old-growth forests were cut. By the end of the century, producers and consumers were faced with a lumber shortage. In the eighteenth century, there was a countervailing move to save natural resources and even to reforest cleared areas. However, government policies were inconsistent, because agriculture brought in more much needed tax revenue than did forestry. Conrad Totman concludes, "How best to balance the need for both woodland and arable was a dilemma that early modern Japan never resolved."[1]

Much of the lumber went to the cities, home not only of officials but also of merchants, who became rich as the economy flourished and the political authorities found their services indispensable. Merchants supplied an economic link between the cities and the rural hinterlands and between the localities and the capital. They handled the transport, warehousing, and sale of rice and other commodities. Frequently, they were licensed to operate *han* monopolies and organize commodity production. Important merchants acted as financial and forwarding agents for the daimyo, handling shipments to Osaka for exchange or to Edo for the daimyo's consumption. They supplied banking services, dealing in the manifold *han* currencies, transferring funds, and issuing loans to political authorities and hard-pressed samurai. They were the backbone of widespread and diverse commercial networks. The position of individual commercial establishments could be precarious—in extreme cases, a wealthy merchant with heavy loans out to the powerful might suffer confiscation so that the loans could go unpaid, as happened to a great Osaka merchant in 1705. However, these cases were exceptions. Government measures forcing creditors to settle for less than full repayment, or even cancellation, simply had the effect of raising the cost of new loans, because the authorities never found a way to eliminate the need for such borrowing.

With the *bakufu,* daimyo, and samurai dependent on them, the merchants prospered; in the second half of the eighteenth century, there were more than 200 mercantile establishments valued at more than 200,000 gold *ryō,* a monetary unit worth roughly a *koku* of rice. Such merchants were fully the economic equals of daimyo. Some of the great modern commercial and financial empires go back to the early Tokugawa, including the house of Mitsui, founded in 1620.

By the beginning of the eighteenth century, Edo had a population of about a million, a little more than half of them townspeople (*chōnin*). Osaka, too, developed as a prosperous commercial and shipping center, and Kyoto remained a major city. The capitals of the *han* also became trade centers, with merchants and artisans playing an active role in shaping the character of each city. The most prominent merchants, as city elders, ward representatives, and the like, had a role in administration.

As in the villages, there were also great differences in status and wealth among the town dwellers; for every great merchant, there were many more humble shopkeepers, peddlers, artisans, laborers, and servants. At the bottom of society, constituting less than 2 percent of the population at the end of the Tokugawa Period, were *hinin* (nonpeople), mostly beggars, and *eta,* or outcasts (today called *burakumin* because *eta* is considered pejorative), who, most prominently, engaged in butchering and tanning, tasks considered unclean. The *bakufu* supported one powerful outcast house to lord over all outcasts in its domain in return for supplying leather goods and men to serve as prison guards and executioners. As Eiko Ikegami has pointed out, "The identical action of killing, whether human beings or animals, was, however, interpreted variously as either a source of pollution and exclusion (in the case of the outcasts) or a source of honor and power (in the case of the samurai)."[2]

Classes and Values

To create an enduring order, Ieyasu followed Hideyoshi in drawing a clear line between samurai and commoners. It did happen that destitute *rōnin,* masterless samurai, dropped out of their class or that through marriage an alliance was formed between a wealthy merchant family and that of an impoverished samurai, but such cases remained uncommon.

Assigned to various duties, the samurai staffed the increasingly bureaucratized administrative machinery of the domains and the *bakufu.* Most were now occupied more with civil than with military affairs. The most visible sign of the samurai's privilege was his sole right to wear swords, symbols of his status even after they had ceased to be his major tools. Although he was expected to acquire some proficiency in at least one of the martial arts, these became "a matter of formal gymnastics and disciplined choreography."[3] Nevertheless, the ethos of the samurai remained that of a loyal military vassal imbued with a strong and prickly sense of personal honor and a proclivity to violence that the *bakufu* needed to tame as well as exploit. Success in civil office depended on study. Although Ieyasu patronized the Confucian scholar Hayashi Razan (1583–1657), whose family continued to supply the heads of the *bakufu*'s Confucian academy, it was not until the end of the century that Confucianism came to prevail. The ideal was for the samurai to combine the virtues of Confucian scholar and old-time warrior. An early proponent of a fusion of Confucian and warrior values was Yamaga Sokō (1622–1695). A student of Hayashi Razan and of the martial arts, he is considered a founding father of the modern way of the warrior (*bushidō*).

One of his followers became the leader of the famed forty-seven *rōnin* who persevered in seeking vengeance for the wrong done their dead lord. In 1703 their carefully nurtured plans were rewarded with success as they stormed into the Kyoto mansion of the offending daimyo and killed him. They were immediately considered heroes and have remained popular examples of ideal loyalty. Theirs was an act of warrior courage and devotion, but it was also illegal! For a time the shogunate debated what should be done but then found a solution that would both uphold the substance of civil law and preserve the warriors' honor: they were ordered to commit ritual suicide. Playwrights lost no time in adapting the story for the stage. *Chūshingura* (*Treasury of Royal Retainers*), to give the drama its proper title, was popular with commoners and samurai alike and has remained a Japanese favorite; in the twentieth century both the cinema and the television versions enjoyed great success.

In Tokugawa times, there was much on which samurai and commoner could agree. The official morality was promoted in periodic lectures and spread by the many schools founded during the Tokugawa Period so that by 1800, 40 to 50 percent of Japanese males were literate to some degree. Fewer girls went to school, but, as in China, special texts were published for their benefit. It is estimated that 10 percent of girls were in school by the end of Tokugawa in 1868.

Hierarchical principles of organization operated throughout the society, as did a tendency to rank people in grades. Like samurai, even the inhabitants of the demimonde of the urban pleasure quarters were carefully ranked. The great merchant houses resembled feudal fiefs not only in their wealth but also in their expectation of lifelong loyal service from their employees, who in turn were entitled to be treated with paternalistic solicitude. A similar relationship survives in Japanese industry to this day.

Although merchant and samurai held many values in common, it was a mark of samurai pride to regard financial considerations with contempt. Fukuzawa Yukichi (1853–1901), in his famous autobiography, tells how his father took his children out of school when, to his horror, their teacher began to teach them arithmetic, a subject fit only for merchants and their offspring. But business had its defenders, including the Kaitoku Academy in Osaka, which taught the importance of trade and of those who engaged in it. Also legitimating the merchants' calling was the strain of Buddhism that considered all occupations valid forms of devotion. Heart Learning (Shingaku), a religion founded by the Kyoto merchant and philosopher Ishida Baigan (1685–1744), combined elements of Shinto, Confucianism, and Buddhism to create an ethic for the artisan and merchant stressing honesty, frugality, and devotion to one's trade. Diversity in classes and lifestyles made for similar diversity in the visual, literary, and performing arts and in thought.

The Aesthetic Culture of the Aristocracy

The aristocracy inherited a rich cultural tradition. The subtle arts of the tea ceremony and flower arranging continued, and the Nō drama that had flourished in Muromachi times had its devotees, including the shogun Tsunayoshi, who performed in Nō plays. In architecture, the classic aesthetic of restraint was exemplified by the imperial villa at Katsura, outside Kyoto, but it coexisted with a love for the ornate, displayed at Nikko, the mausoleum north of Tokyo where Ieyasu's remains are interred. Here, brightly painted and gilded decorations luxuriate in chaotic flamboyance, saved from empty vulgarity by their setting in a magnificent forest and creating, in Alexander Soper's words, "a serene depth of shadow into which their tumult sinks without an echo."[4]

FIGURE 7.2 *Thousand Cranes.* Section of a hand-scroll. Painting by Tawaraya Sōtatsu, calligraphy by Hon'ami Kōetsu. Gold and silver underpainting on paper, 11.2 feet × 47.9 feet. (© Kyoto National Museum.)

In Kyoto, aristocratic aesthetics enjoyed a surge of vitality in a movement led by Hon'ami Kōetsu (1558–1637) who established a community of artists and craftsmen on a site granted him by Ieyasu in recognition of his prominence as a member of that city's Nichiren Buddhist community. Kōetsu was trained in his family's hereditary art of sword repair and connoisseurship, but his far-reaching talents found masterly expression in tea bowls, lacquer inlay work, and cast metal vessels; in painting; and, above all, in calligraphy. Frequently, he collaborated with other artists, such as in the bold and free calligraphy he contributed to the hand-scroll *Thousand Cranes,* painted by Tawaraya Sōtatsu, a highly gifted younger contemporary (see Figure 7.2). The result is a decorative elegance that honors an aristocratic tradition going back to the Heian Period (794–1185).

The third great Kyoto artist was Ogata Kōrin (1658–1716), represented here by a pair of iris screens, which Elise Grilli has compared with Mozart's variations on a musical theme, the artist "first stating his motif, then adding variations, shifts, repetitions, pauses, leaps, intervals, changes of tempo, accents, chords, rise and fall, with changes of mood from major to minor."[5] Kōrin's color orchestration and his superb eye for the decorative are clearly apparent even in a reproduction, which by its very nature cannot completely capture the vibrant original (see Figure 7.3).

FIGURE 7.3 *Irises,* from a scene of the *Tales of Ise,* Ogata Korin. One of a pair of sixfold screens. Color on gold foil over paper, 11.8 feet × 5 feet. (© Nezu Institute of Fine Arts, Tokyo, Japan.)

Genroku Urban Culture

Urban culture reached a high point during the Genroku Era, technically the era name for the sixteen years from 1688 to 1704 but more broadly used for the cultural life of the fifty-year period beginning in the last quarter of the seventeenth century, when some of Japan's most creative artists were at work. These include the playwright Chikamatsu (1653–1724); the short story writer Saikaku (1642–1693); Moronobu (1618–1694), generally credited with developing the Japanese print; and Matsuo Bashō (1644–1694), master of the haiku.

Most large cities have "pleasure districts," parts of town devoted to bohemian life, erotic activities, entertainment, and gambling. Tokugawa cities were no exception. But rarely, if ever, have such quarters produced a first-rate aesthetic as they did in seventeenth-century Yoshiwara, the home of Edo's "floating world." Here, and in similar quarters in the other large towns, was a world that savored sophisticated stylishness in dress, coiffure, perfume, gesture, and life itself. The tone was set by the worldly flair of the man-about-town and the elegance of the spirited courtesans who presided over this world and who looked down with disdain on the country boor.

The Print

Courtesans and actors were favorite subjects of the *ukiyo-e,* "pictures of the floating world," woodcut prints preceded by *ukiyo-e* paintings and by illustrations for books such as the *Yoshiwara Pillow* (1660), a combination sex manual and "courtesan critique." To produce the prints, portraits of courtesans, theater

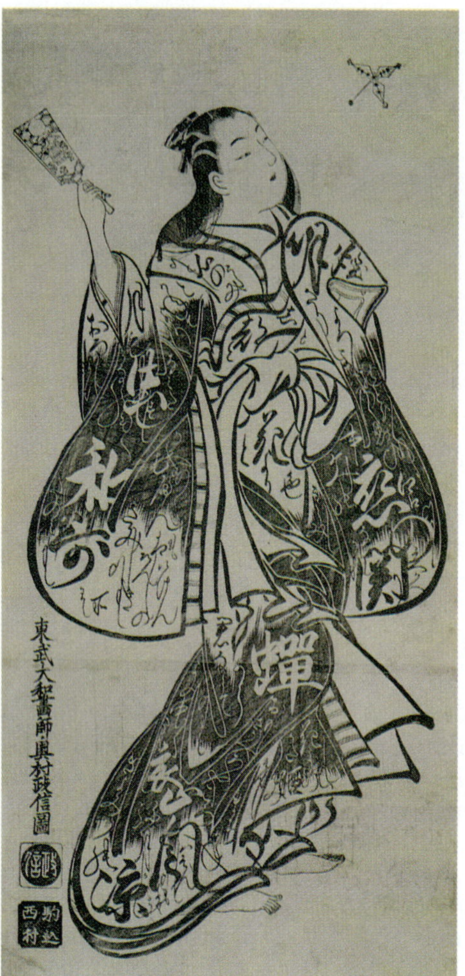

FIGURE 7.4 *Courtesan Striking a Shuttlecock with a Battledore,* Okumura Masanobu (1710s). Poetic verses written in calligraphic script decorate the courtesan's kimono. Hanging scroll, woodblock print, ink on paper, 12.7 in × 25.7 in. (© Allen Memorial Art Museum, Oberlin College, Ohio. Mary A. Ainsworth bequest [1950.202].)

scenes, nature subjects, or scenes from urban life were carved into wood blocks. These were then inked and printed on paper. The process was highly experimental until Hishikawa Moronobu consolidated the early efforts.

At the beginning the prints were in black and white, but soon color was added, first by hand, then by developing techniques for printing red and green. By the eighteenth century, three- or four-color prints were produced. A versatile master and major contributor to the development of the print was Okumura Masanobu (c. 1686–1764), who, in Figure 7.4, shows an eighteenth-century beauty, dressed in a characteristically sumptuous kimono, gracefully at play.

Masanobu, a master of a variety of styles, influenced other artists, including the creator of the handcolored print shown in Figure 7.5, which conveys a wealth of information about the material culture. Depicting the interior of a house in Yoshiwara, the composition experiments with the receding perspective of European painting.

Masanobu was a publisher and an artist, but usually these functions were carried out by different people. Numerous people had a hand in creating a print. The publisher not only distributed and sold the prints but also commissioned them from the artist with more or less explicit instructions on subject and style. The artist drew the picture and designed the print but then turned it over to the engraver and the printer. The craftsmanship of these men helped determine the quality of a print, but the artist contributed the essential vision.

FIGURE 7.5 *A Tea House in the Yoshiwara, with a Game of Backgammon.* Attributed to Torii Kiyotada (fl. c. 1720–1750). The image shows such standard features of Japanese interior architecture as rooms separated by sliding partitions, the *tatami* floor, and the sense of spaciousness created by the virtual absence of furniture. Color woodcut, 25.2 in × 17 in. (© Fine Arts Museums of San Francisco, Achenbach Foundation for Graphic Arts Purchase [A057901 1970.25.14].)

Theater and Literature

An unceasing source of inspiration for the print artist was the kabuki theater, whose celebrated actors enjoyed as much acclaim and attracted as avid a following as did the most elegant of Yoshiwara courtesans. Kabuki originated in the dances and skits performed in Kyoto early in the seventeenth century by a troupe of female performers. But this women's kabuki lasted only until 1629, when it was banned by the *bakufu* to put an end to the outbursts of violence that erupted as rivals competed for the favors of these ladies. For the next two decades young men's kabuki flourished, until it ran into similar difficulties and was prohibited in 1652. After that, all actors were mature men. Even then, kabuki continued to be under restrictions, tolerated but licensed and controlled because, like other indecorous pleasures, it could not be suppressed.

Kabuki's spectacular scenery, gorgeous costumes, and scenes of violent passion enchanted audiences. It was an actor's art, dominated by dynasties of actors who felt free to take liberties with the texts of plays. The audience greeted the virtuoso performances of the stars with shouts of approval. Particularly esteemed was the artistry of the men who played the female roles. These masters devoted their lives to achieving stylizations of posture, gesture, and voice, conveying the quintessence of femininity, always operating in that "slender margin between the real and unreal"[6] that Chikamatsu, sometimes called Japan's Shakespeare, defined as the true province of art.

Chikamatsu wrote for the kabuki stage but preferred the puppet theater (*bunraku*), where his lines were not at the mercy of the actors. In *bunraku*, large wooden puppets, each manipulated by a three-man team, enacted a story told by a group of chanters accompanied by three-stringed samisen. This theater became so popular that live actors came to imitate the movements of the puppets. Even after kabuki carried the day in Edo, *bunraku* continued to flourish in Osaka. The puppets, like the masks employed in Nō, assured that the action on stage would not be a mere mirror of ordinary life but would be more stylized and symbolic. It also made possible scenes of violence and fantastic stage business that, impossible for live actors, pose no problems for figures that do not bleed and are not bound by the usual limits of human physiology. Chikamatsu frequently used spectacular elements in his plays on historical subjects, such as *The Battle of Coxinga,* his most famous work in this genre.

Chikamatsu also wrote more subtle domestic plays. These center on conflicts between moral obligation (*giri*) and human emotion (*ninjō*). Feeling usually wins out over duty, but at a heavy price. One play, for example, tells of the tragic love of a shopkeeper and a lovely courtesan whom he cannot ransom from her house for lack of funds. Frequently, the poetic high point of the play is the lovers' flight to death. Often, the women exhibit greater strength of character than the men, but both are turned into romantic heroes through the purity and intensity of their emotions. Art imitates life, but life also imitates art: the plays produced such a rash of love suicides that the *bakufu* finally banned all plays with the words "love suicide" in the title.

Ihara Saikaku loved to write about love in his stories and books. Sometimes he wrote about samurai, but his best works deal with recognizable city types: the miser and money-grubber, the playboy who squanders his patrimony, the young beauty mismatched to an elderly husband, men and women in love with love. Exuberant and witty, he mixed humor and sex and wrote with a robust directness. He was also a prolific composer of *haikai,* light verse that grew out of *renga,* linked verse in which one poet started off, leaving it up to friends to continue.

Enlivened by infusions of everyday speech and humor, *haikai* turned its back on aristocratic refinement, as seen in this famous pair of links in a sixteenth-century anthology:

Bitter, bitter it was
And yet somehow funny.
Even when
My father lay dying
I went on farting.[7]

Vulgar as it is, the second verse contrasts sharply with the first, as required in this poetic form. The popularity of *haikai* is attested by several seventeenth-century anthologies, one containing verses by more than 650 contributors.

Classical poems (*tanka*) and *renga* often began with seventeen syllables arranged in three lines (five/seven/five), which, when standing alone, form a *haiku.* The greatest haiku master was Matsuo Bashō, who was born a samurai but gave up his rank to live the life of a commoner, earning his living as a master poet with pupils from all strata of society.

Not every seventeen-syllable poem is a true haiku, because the real measure of a haiku lies not in its formal structure or surface meaning but in its resonance, not in what it says but in what is left unsaid. It presents the reader with a series of images, which, when connected in the imagination, yield a wealth of associations, visions, and emotions. Consider, for example, Bashō's best-known haiku:

> An old pond
> Frog jumps in
> Sound of water.

The inner spring of the poem is the juxtaposition of two contrasting natural elements, a juxtaposition that (like the frog in the water) sets off waves in the reader's mind. The old pond supplies the setting, but implies a condition of ancient stillness that contrasts with the sudden action and results in a delightful image. It raises the question, "How does one explain the relationship between the pond, which has been there for centuries, and a tiny splash that disappears in a moment?" This question was raised by Professor Makoto Ueda, who commented, "Different people will give different answers, though they will all experience the same sort of 'loneliness' when they try to give an explanation. It seems that Bashō was more concerned with the loneliness than with the answer."[8] Some of his finest poems were composed on his travels and are contained in his *The Narrow Road of Oku.* One reads as follows:

> At Yoshino
> I'll show you cherry blossoms
> Cypress umbrella.[9]

He wrote the poem on his umbrella, and there is a gentle whimsy in Bashō's idea of sharing the beauty of the cherry blossoms with his umbrella. The word translated "umbrella" can also mean "hat." Figure 7.6 is a portrait of Bashō dressed for travel with this haiku inscribed on it.

This painting is an example of the genre known as *haiga* in which a *haiku* and a painting (*ga*) are integrated. It is by Yokoi Kinkoku (1761–1832), in the general manner of Yosa Buson (1716–1783), the most eminent artist in the literati mode. Like Chinese gentleman painters, the creators of Japanese "literati painting" (*bunjinga,* Chinese *wenrenhua*) cultivated calligraphy and poetry as means of self-expression. They looked to China for inspiration but did not limit themselves to Chinese subjects in their art.

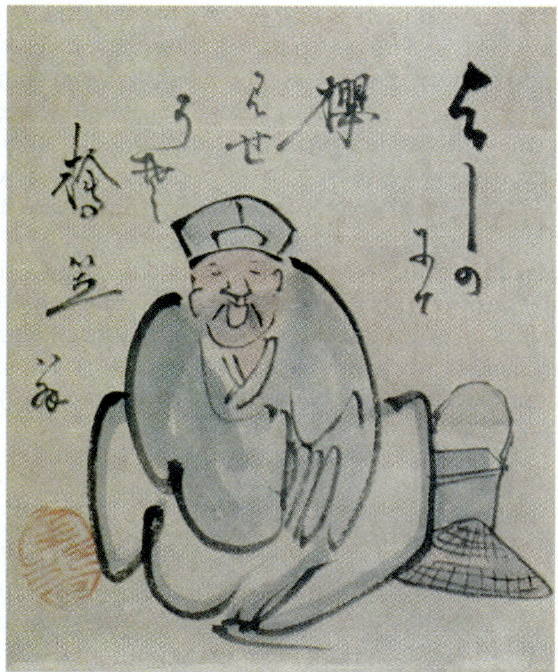

FIGURE 7.6 *Portrait of the poet Bashō,* Yokoi Kinkoku (1761–1832). Matsuo Bashō, the greatest haiku master, composed some of his finest poems on his travels and appears here ready for his next trip with his traveling hat. Ink and color on paper, hanging scroll, 7.2 in × 8.5 in. (© University of Michigan Museum of Art. Museum purchase, gift of the Margaret Watson Parker Art Collection [1968/2.22].)

Intellectual Currents: Confucianism

Tokugawa Confucians were deeply influenced by developments in China, but their writings also reflect the vast differences between the two countries. In Japan there was no civil service examination system to reward mastery of Confucian texts. Most Confucian scholars came from lower samurai or commoner ranks and made their living as teachers or doctors. One attraction of Confucianism to such men was its advocacy of government by the meritorious rather than the well-born. At the same time, even the Sinophiles among them took pride in Japan. Some argued that Japan came closer to Confucian ideals than Qing China, and others played an ingenious "game of one-upmanship."[10]

The beginnings of Tokugawa Confucianism are usually traced back to Fujiwara Seika (1561–1619), an aristocrat who did not find it beneath his dignity to write a letter for a Kyoto merchant sending a trade mission to Vietnam. He drew up a ship's oath, which began: "Commerce is the business of selling and buying in order to bring profit to both parties." He defined profit as "the outcome of righteousness" and admonished merchants not to be greedy.[11]

In Japan, as in China and Korea, Confucian teachings found a home in academies. Edo's premier Confucian academy was founded by Hayashi Razan (1583–1657) under *bakufu* patronage, but Edo did not dominate Tokugawa thought. The fragmentation of political authority made for intellectual diversity.

An outstanding early exponent of Song Confucianism was Yamazaki Ansai (1618–1682), a stern and forceful teacher who stressed "devotion within, righteousness without" and was so dedicated to Zhu Xi that he said he would follow the master even into error. When asked the hypothetical question, What should be done if Confucius and Mencius were to lead a Chinese invasion of Japan? he answered that he would capture the two sages and put them at the service of his own land. Deeply versed in Shinto, Ansai attempted to fuse Confucian ethics with Shinto religion. Most Confucians justified the shogunate by incorporating it into the hierarchy of loyalty, but Ansai's contemporary Muro Kyūso (1658–1734) argued that the Tokugawa ruled because of a heavenly mandate.

Muro Kyūso found it necessary to defend the thoughts of Zhu Xi against increasingly vigorous challenges from other schools. The man considered to be the founder of the rival Wang Yangming school in Japan was Nakae Tōjū (1608–1648). Like the Chinese philosopher, he stressed the inner light and insisted on the importance of action. His lofty and unselfish character attracted the admiration of his contemporaries and of later activist intellectuals. His best-known disciple, Kumazawa Banzan (1619–1691), ran into political trouble, not because of his philosophical ideas but because of such policy recommendations as relaxing the daimyo's attendance requirements to save expenses. His deep concern for the well-being of the peasantry went hand in hand with lack of sympathy for the merchant class, as reflected in his advocacy of a return to a barter economy using rice in place of money.

Like Yamazaki Ansai and Kumazawa Banzan, Kaibara Ekken (1630–1714) found much of value in Shinto, but his philosophy of nature was based on *qi*. The writings of this remarkable man range from botany to ethics, from farming to philology, and include precepts for daily life and a primer for women. They express his breadth of mind, commitment to the welfare of society, and faith in the unity and value of knowledge.

In Japan, as in China, there were men who denied the authority of Song thinkers and insisted on going back to the foundation texts. This was the stance of Yamaga Sokō, the formulator of *bushidō,* and of Itō Jinsai (1627–1705) who drew inspiration from the *Analects:* "The *Analects* is like the boundless universe which men live in without comprehending its full magnitude. Enduring and immutable throughout the ages, in every part of the world it serves as an infallible guide. Is it not, indeed, great!"[12] Jinsai rejected the distinction between *li* (principle) and *qi* and stressed self-cultivation with an emphasis on *ren* (humaneness).

Another opponent of Song philosophy was Ogyū Sorai (1666–1728), who insisted on going back even earlier than the *Analects* to the classics, has been described by Kate Nakai as effecting an intellectual "sea-change." Rejecting the unity of the inner human realm and the outer world of heaven and earth, "Sorai challenged the notion that through the practice of *li* [rites and propriety] the individual realized an innate capacity for alignment with a natural order."[13] A complex, many-sided thinker and prolific writer, he emphasized rites and institutions all the more and wrote on many topics: philosophy and politics; literature, linguistics, and music; military science; and economics.

A younger contemporary of Sorai, Goi Ranshū (1697–1762), head of the Kaitokudo Academy, did not believe that the ancients had exhausted all knowledge and even envisioned intellectual progress. A member of the next generation who studied at the academy was Tominaga Nakamoto (1715–1746), a skeptic who argued that all historical texts were unreliable. In the work of these and others were the roots for ideas that exceeded the confines of the Tokugawa order and, indeed, the normal bounds of Confucian thought. But Confucian thought, too, could take men's minds in unanticipated directions.

Historiography and Nativism

A perennial field of Confucian scholarship was the study of history. Hayashi Razan began work on a history of Japan that was completed by his son and accepted as the official history of the shogunate. Another major contributor to scholarship was the statesman and scholar Arai Hakuseki (1657–1725), noted for his careful attention to evidence and willingness to reexamine traditional beliefs.

A different emphasis appeared in *The Great History of Japan* (*Dainihonshi*), begun in the seventeenth century and sponsored by Mito, a Tokugawa collateral house. Begun under the lord of Mito, Tokugawa Mitsukuni (1628–1700), it was not completed until the twentieth century. Mitsukuni, a grandson of Ieyasu, enlisted the services of a Chinese émigré and Ming loyalist, Zhu Shunshui (1600–1682). The resulting history was highly moralistic and exalted the Japanese imperial house. Because the shogun derived his legitimacy from the emperor, there was nothing inherently anti-*bakufu* in this, but its focus on the emperor rather than on the shogun was potentially subversive. Indeed, it later became an emperor-centered source for nationalistic sentiments and eventually supplied intellectual ammunition for the anti-*bakufu* movement to "restore the emperor," which culminated in the Meiji Restoration of 1868.

Interest in Japan's past often went hand in hand with a new appreciation of native traditions. Ansai had advocated both Confucianism and Shinto, but Kada Azumamaro (1669–1736) urged a return to a Shinto purified of Confucian elements. Rejection of Confucianism and celebration of the native tradition became a defining theme in the nativist thought of the National Learning (*kokugtaku*) scholars.

Frequently, this was linked to a championship of Japanese literature and aesthetics. Thus Tokugawa Mitsukuni commissioned the Shingon priest Keichū (1640–1701), a great philologist, to write a commentary on the Man'yōshū, the oldest anthology of Japanese poetry. Motoori Norinaga (1730–1801), a gifted philologist, enjoyed wide influence as a teacher, political adviser, and champion of a supposedly pure Shinto found in antiquity and as yet uncorrupted by Buddhist and Confucian influences. He also is famous as an interpreter and admirer of *The Tale of Genji*. Admitting that it contained much that was immoral, he borrowed the lotus image much used by Buddhists to praise the novel:

> Genji's conduct is like the lotus flower that grows in muddy water yet blooms with a beauty and fragrance unlike any other in the world. Nothing is said about the water's filth; the monogatari [that is, the *Tale*] concentrates instead on Genji's deep compassion and his awareness of what it means to be moved by things and holds him up as the model of a good man.[14]

His life's work, however, was the study of the Kōjiki (*Record of Ancient Matters*), by then a thousand years old. Motoori thought it wrong to understand its accounts of the *kami* rationally and arrogant not to recognize the limitations of the human intellect. Indeed, the irrationality of the old legends was a sign of their truth, because "who would fabricate such shallow sounding, incredible things?"[15] Supreme among the *kami* was the Sun Goddess, and although she spread her favor everywhere, foremost among the countries of the world was the land of her birth. Motoori left a dual heritage: academic philology and ideological nativism. Of those who drew on the latter aspect of his thought, the most influential was Hirata Atsutane (1776–1843), whose narrow Japanism proved attractive to many nineteenth- and twentieth-century ultranationalists.

Dutch Learning

Because the Dutch were the only Westerners allowed even limited access to Japan (see Chapter 13), it is from them that the Japanese got their information about the West. Their annual audience with the shogun allowed the Japanese to satisfy their curiosity about the exotic:

> He [the shogun, mistaken for the emperor by the Dutch chronicle] order'd us to take off our Cappa, or Cloak, being our Garment of Ceremony, then to stand upright, that he might have a full view of us; again to walk, to stand still, to compliment each other, to dance, to jump, to play the drunkard, to speak broken Japanese, to read Dutch, to paint, to sing, to put our cloaks on and off. . . . I join'd to my dance a lovesong in High German. In this manner, and with innumerable such other apish tricks, we must suffer ourselves to contribute to the Emperor's and Court's diversion.[16]

This is from a report of the embassy of 1691 or 1692. "The red-haired barbarians," as the Dutch were commonly known, continued to be the objects of wild rumor. But they also drew the attention of serious scholars after 1720, when the *bakufu* permitted the import of books on all subjects except Christianity. These scholars wrestled with the difficulties of the Dutch language, laboriously made translations, compiled the first dictionaries, and wrote treatises on geography, astronomy, medicine, and other Western subjects. Shiba Kōkan (1738–1818), the first in Japan to produce copper engravings, was fascinated by the ability of Western art to portray objects as they appear to the eye. Arai Hakuseki had earlier recognized the practical value of Western studies, and this, too, is what Shiba valued. For spiritual nourishment, such men continued to turn to their own heritage, thus foreshadowing the nineteenth-century formula "Eastern ethics–Western science." Because of *bakufu* policy, they knew little about Western political, philosophical, or religious thought.

By the end of the eighteenth century, there were also scholars of Dutch Learning who, alarmed by Western expansionism, discussed political, military, and economic matters at considerable personal risk. Hayashi Shihei (1738–1793) was arrested for defying a *bakufu* prohibition by publishing a book dealing with political issues: he advocated defense preparations against the threat he saw impending from abroad. Honda Toshiaki (1744–1821), who wanted to turn Japan into the England of the East, complete with mercantile empire, escaped persecution by not publishing his ideas.

Implicit in the views of the scholars of Dutch Learning was dissatisfaction with the Tokugawa seclusion policy, which stood in the way of their learning more about Western civilization and prevented them from traveling overseas. Meanwhile, by stressing the royal line, Mito Confucians and National Learning scholars helped weaken the *bakufu* ideologically. And even orthodox Confucianism did not really require a shogun or a *bakufu*. Thus, by 1800 there were fissures in the Tokugawa's intellectual, as well as in its political and economic, foundations.

Reform and Its Limits

The underlying discrepancy between official theory and socioeconomic reality was brought home to the *bakufu* in a series of financial crises, some aggravated by poor harvests resulting from natural causes. Major famines during 1732 to 1733 and again after 1783 brought death and starvation, as well as rural uprisings and urban riots, highlighting the government's ineptness.

Repeatedly, revenue failed to keep up with government needs. Retrenchment was one standard response. Often, as in the Kyōhō Reforms (1716–1736), a spending cut was seen as morally desirable and as fiscally necessary. Calls for reduction in government spending were accompanied by admonitions for samurai to revive warrior morality and detailed laws to limit merchant expenditure. More effective was the granting of merchant monopolies in exchange for an annual fee. To make it easier to fill high offices with capable men of low inherited rank, the practice of granting such men permanent high hereditary rank was abandoned in favor of raising their rank and stipends only during their tenure of office.

Among the sources of needed revenue were special payments imposed on the daimyo, programs of land reclamation, and campaigns to squeeze more taxes out of the peasantry, but in the long run these yielded diminishing returns. The same can be said of the *bakufu*'s attempts to set prices of essential commodities. Some initially successful measures backfired, such as when monetary deflation quelled a destructive inflation only to bring on a deflation so severe that it provoked urban riots in 1733.

Later in the century, the *bakufu* made some additions to its reform repertoire—such as when, under the leadership of Tanuma Okitsugu (1719–1788), it encouraged foreign trade, tried to develop mines, created new monopolies, imposed new merchant licenses, and showed interest in developing Hokkaido. Tanuma, however, was resented for favoring the *bakufu* vis-à-vis the *han,* and his enemies emphasized his corruption. In 1787, food shortages caused by crop failures the previous year led to uprisings throughout Japan and violent rioting in Edo. Tanuma died in disgrace. Whether the *bakufu* was capable of leading the country in new directions remained a question for the future.

Art and Literature After the Genroku Period

Genroku was the classic age of popular theater, prints, fiction, and haiku, but artists and writers continued to work in these genres and create works that are often considered to mark another high point in cultural history. Notable among the later *ukiyo-e* artists was Tōshūsai Sharaku, famous for the psychologically penetrating and bitterly satiric prints of actors he turned out during a ten-month outburst of creativity in 1794. More in keeping with the spirit of the time was Suzuki Harunobu (1724–1770), who excelled in the subtle use of color and the freshness of his young beauties. Controversial and uneven was the prolific Kitagawa Utamaro (1754–1806), who achieved great popularity with his prints of the ladies of the "floating world" (see Figure 7.7).

Toward the end of the eighteenth century, there was a falling off in the quality of the figure print, but, as if in compensation, the landscape print flourished. A master of this art was the "old man mad with painting," Katsushika Hokusai (1760–1849), an eclectic genius. He is represented here by one of his depictions of Mount Fuji (see Figure 7.8). Less versatile, but at his best producing works imbued with a delicate lyricism, was Andō Hiroshige (1797–1858), who lived to see Commodore Matthew C. Perry of the United States Navy arrive in Japan in 1853.

Various genres of literature, energized by a "complex fusion of Japanese and Chinese cultures, and by a mixture of popular and elite culture"[17] continued to

FIGURE 7.7 *A Flirt,* from the series *Ten Studies in Female Physiognomy,* Kitagawa Utamaro. Woodblock print, ink, color, and mica on paper, 9.9 in × 14.9 in. (© Mr. and Mrs. John D. Rockefeller, third collection of Asian Art 1979.219. Asia Society, New York: Photograph by Lynton Gardiner.)

flourish and delight, as did the haiku, that most Japanese of poetic forms. Perhaps the best loved of the later haiku poets was Kobayashi Issa (1763–1827). He achieved wide identification with nature and showed sympathy for even the humblest animals and insects.

> Lean frog,
> don't give up the fight!
> Issa is here![18]

FIGURE 7.8 "Fuji at Torigoe" from *Fugaku Hyokkei,* Katsushika Hokusai. The instrument shown here is an orrery, a mechanical model of the solar system. (© Spencer Collection [SOR579: Hokusai], New York Public Library, Astor, Lenox, and Tilden Foundations.)

Notes

1. Conrad Totman, *Early Modern Japan* (Berkeley: Univ. of California Press, 1993), p. 229.
2. Eiko Ikegami, *The Taming of the Samurai: Honorific Individualism and the Making of Modern Japan* (Cambridge: Harvard Univ. Press, 1995), p. 116.
3. Ronald P. Dore, *Education in Tokugawa Japan* (Berkeley: Univ. of California Press, 1965), p. 151.
4. Robert Treat Paine and Alexander Soper, *The Art and Architecture of Japan* (Baltimore: Penguin Books, 1955), p. 274.
5. Elise Grilli, *The Art of the Japanese Screen* (Tokyo and New York: John Weatherhill, 1970), pp. 111–12.

6. Attributed to Chikamatsu by his friend Hozumi Ikan. Hozumi's account of Chikamatsu's views has been translated by Donald Keene as "Chikamatsu on the Art of The Puppet Stage," in Donald Keene, ed., *Anthology of Japanese Literature* (New York: Grove Press, 1955), p. 389.
7. Ryusaku Tsunoda, W. Theodore de Bary, and Donald Keene, comps., *Sources of Japanese Tradition* (New York: Columbia Univ. Press, 1958), p. 454.
8. Makoto Ueda, *Matsuo Basho* (New York: Twayne, 1970), p. 53.
9. Calvin French, *The Poet-Painters: Buson and His Followers,* exhibition catalog (Ann Arbor: Univ. of Michigan Museum of Art, 1974), p. 132.
10. See Kate Wildman Nakai, "The Naturalization of Confucianism in Tokugawa Japan: The Problem of Sinocentrism," *Harvard Journal of Asiatic Studies,* 40 (1980): 157–99.
11. Tsunoda, *Sources of Japanese Tradition,* p. 349.
12. Ibid., p. 419
13. Kate Nakai, "Chinese Ritual and Japanese Identity in Tokugawa Confucianism," in *Rethinking Confucianism: Past and Present in China, Japan, Korea, and Vietnam* (Los Angeles: UCLA Asian Pacific Monograph Series, Univ. of California, 2002), p. 272.
14. Haruo Shirane, ed., *Early Modern Japanese Literature: An Anthology, 1600–1900,* trans. Thomas Harper (New York: Columbia Univ. Press, 2002), pp. 624–25.
15. Ibid., p. 524.
16. E. Kaempfer, quoted in Donald Keene, *The Japanese Discovery of Europe* (Stanford: Stanford Univ. Press, 1969), p. 4.
17. Shirane, *Early Modern Japanese Literature,* p. 91.
18. Harold G. Henderson, *An Introduction to Haiku* (New York: Doubleday, 1958), p. 133.

Part Four

Japan and the Modern World

During the roughly two hundred years discussed in this section, Japan was increasingly drawn into world history as pressure from the outside world, armed with new technologies and ideas, became irresistible. Japan became the stage for the complex interplay of the dynamics of its own unfolding history and that of the rest of the world, each with its own multiple crosscurrents. In this the story of Japan resembles that of the rest of the world, except Japan became the major player in international and transnational life it is today.

Yokohama prints such as these were popular in early Meiji. This one juxtaposes a train and paddle-wheel steamer with traditional boats and dress and, of course, Mt. Fuji (once clearly visible from downtown Edo as well as Yokohama). Though the parts (except Fuji) changed, such juxtapositions remained characteristic.

8

Endings and Beginnings: From Tokugawa to Meiji, 1787–1873

Internal crisis and Western intrusion are the main themes of this chapter. Although there were some good years before the 1830s, the Tokugawa system was showing many symptoms of stress even before challenges from abroad put the old order to a final test. However, the dynamism of the forces subverting the Tokugawa state and society ultimately helped Japan develop into a modern country.

I. Late Tokugawa

The Bakufu *(1787–1841)*

Economy and Society

Reforms

Intellectual Currents

The "Opening" of Japan

Domestic Politics

Sonnō Jōi

Mixed Responses to the West

Last Years of the Shogunate (1860–1867)

II. The Meiji Restoration

Formation of a New Government: The Meiji Restoration

The Charter Oath

Dismantling the Old Order

Disaffection and Opposition

The Crisis of 1873

The Meaning of the Restoration

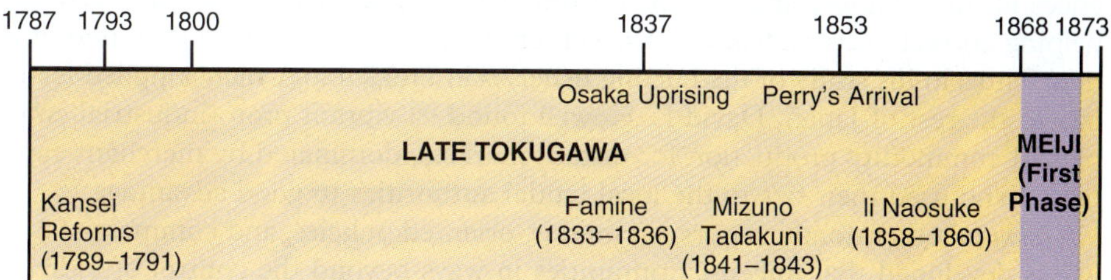

The Bakufu (1787–1841)

Nature rescued the land from the famine of the 1780s, but it took government action to relieve the *bakufu*'s financial distress. The Kansei Reforms (1789–1791) were led by Matsudaira Sadanobu (1787–1793), an earnest Confucian who served a young shogun and owed his position as head of the *bakufu* to the support he received from an inner circle of daimyo. Matsudaira encouraged a return to simpler times. He launched a much-needed campaign against corruption and made an effort to improve public services in Edo, but his fiscal and economic program relied on edicts mandating lower prices for rice, restrictions on merchant guilds, cancellation of some samurai loans, and rent control. Matsudaira also sought to freeze foreign policy, reducing contact with the Dutch and proposing to leave Hokkaido undeveloped as a buffer to foreign intervention.

To improve administration, he not only sought to advance "men of ability" but also tried to control what they thought by furthering education and by making the Neo-Confucianism of Zhu Xi the official doctrine. He proscribed heterodoxy for the official *bakufu* school, but this had little effect elsewhere. There was also a hardening of censorship. All told, these measures "institutionalized and hardened tradition . . . and left a regime less flexible and more concerned with preserving a tradition that had now been defined."[1]

It did not take long for the *bakufu*'s systemic fiscal ills to reappear. By 1800 its annual budget showed a small deficit, the beginning of a trend. Forced loans and nineteen currency devaluations between 1819 and 1837 brought only temporary relief. The political authorities remained dependent on the market and on the merchants, who understood and manipulated the market. The government could not simply borrow, because there was no system of deficit financing. When famine struck again, beginning in 1833 and reaching a crescendo in 1836, the *bakufu*'s response was again inadequate. As before, reform was urgently needed.

Economy and Society

Reflecting Japan's geographic and political diversity, there were major local differences in the economy and society. Fortunately, several local studies are currently helping correct overemphasis on the center, which was less central then than it is now. Thus, in his study of the herring fisheries in Hokkaido, which supplied fertilizer to the rest of Japan, David L. Howell found "a vibrant proto-industrial complex of commodity production for distant markets, dominated by merchant capitalists who used their ties to the local feudal authorities to good advantage."[2]

Several other domains pursued market-oriented policies, and commercial networks developed that linked communities in ways beyond the control of individual political authorities.

Change varied geographically and was complex socially. Some flourished; others suffered. Among the losers were lower-ranking samurai who had to convert a substantial portion of their rice stipend into cash and who were constantly at the mercy of a fluctuating market that they did not understand and would not study. When daimyo, burdened with periodic attendance in Edo and the need to maintain establishments in both Edo and their own *han* capitals, found themselves in financial difficulty, they frequently reduced samurai stipends. This hurt even the small minority of high-ranking men with large stipends but was devastating for the bulk of samurai, who ranked low in status and stipend.

Some samurai married daughters of wealthy merchants, but many lived in increasingly desperate circumstances. They pawned their swords, worked at humble crafts such as umbrella making and sandal weaving, and tried to hide their misery from the world. A samurai was taught that his mouth should display a toothpick even when he had not eaten. The samurai were not dissatisfied with the premises of a social system in which, after all, they formed the ruling class, but they were enraged by the discrepancy between the theoretical elevation of their status and the reality of their poverty. Not only was their poverty demeaning, but the spectacle of merchant wealth also hurt their pride. It seemed the height of injustice that society should reward the selfish moneymakers and condemn to indigence the warriors whose lives were ones of service. They harbored deep resentment against incompetence and corruption in high places, and they called on governments to employ more capable men from the lower samurai ranks.

City merchants and rural entrepreneurs flourished, but the increasing scope of the market had diverse effects on ordinary folk. In Kantō there were villages left with untilled fields as people fled rural poverty in the hope of a better life in industry or commerce, but the market often proved a hard taskmaster. Consolation when things turned out badly and hope for a better future were offered by charismatic religious teachers and by cults such as Fujiko, which centered on a pilgrimage to Mount Fuji and worship of Maitreya, associated in Japan as elsewhere with millenarianism.

When, as during a famine, things became unbearable, people resorted to violence. The best estimate has it that during 1830–1844 there were 465 rural disputes, 445 peasant uprisings, and 101 urban riots. A great impression was made by the 1837 uprising led by Ōshio Heihachiro (1793–1837), a low-ranking *bakufu* official and follower of Wang Yangming's philosophy of action. Although poorly planned and quickly suppressed, the uprising expressed a general sense of malaise and of the disintegration of authority. This was the case also in the countryside, where, in earlier conflicts, villagers had united behind their headmen, but now the gap between the rich and the poor had reached the point at which interests diverged too widely for the village to speak with a single voice.

Reforms

In response to the financial and social crisis, there was one more concerted effort at reform both in the domains and at the center. On both levels, large doses of antiquated remedies such as economic retrenchment, bureaucratic reform, and moral rearmament were administered, but there were also some innovative policies. In the *bakufu,* reforms began in 1841 under Mizuno Tadakuni (1793–1851), a house daimyo who rose to *bakufu* leadership. His measures included recoinage, forced loans, dismissal of officials to reduce costs, and sumptuary laws intended to preserve morals and save money. Censorship became stricter. An effort (by no means the first) was made to force peasants to return to their lands. This was in keeping with the Confucian view of the primacy of agriculture and with the Tokugawa policy of strict class separation—but it hardly solved any problems.

A program to create a solid area of *bakufu* control around Edo and Osaka called for the creation of a *bakufu*-controlled zone of twenty-five square miles around Edo and twelve square miles around Osaka by moving certain daimyo and direct retainers out of these areas. This could have rationalized administration and strengthened the shogunate, but the plan proved too ambitious and could not be carried out. In the hope of fighting inflation, merchant monopolies were broken up and an attempt was made to bar the daimyo from engaging in commercial monopolies. Despite the retrenchment policy, an expensive and ostentatious formal procession to the Tokugawa mausoleum at Nikko was organized in an effort to reassert the *bakufu'*s preeminence. But the daimyo were not easily bridled, and the reform lasted only two years.

Various domains, faced with similar problems, attempted local reform programs of their own. Here and there *han* government machinery was reformed, stipends and other costs were cut, and some domains even rewarded the expert assistance of outstanding members of the merchant community by promoting them to samurai status. Agriculture was encouraged and commercial policies were changed. In general, in the *han* as in the *bakufu,* the reforms ended, "some whimpering their way into oblivion, others culminating in an explosion in which the reformers were dismissed . . . and sometimes thrown into prison as well. . . . Whatever the end, they were ignored until their resurrection as models for fresh reforms in the 1850s and 1860s."[3]

FIGURE 8.1 Map showing Satsuma in Kyūshū and Chōshū in southwest Honshu, 1850s–1860s.

A major domain in which the reforms did take hold was Satsuma in Kyūshū (see Figure 8.1). Subsequently, Chōshū in southwest Honshū enjoyed similar success. In important ways these were untypical domains. For one, they were both large, outside *han* that had accepted Tokugawa supremacy only when they had no other alternative. Both had had their domains transferred and reduced in size. One consequence was that they kept alive an anti-Tokugawa tradition. Another was that the reduction in the size of their domains left them with a higher-than-average ratio of samurai to the land. In Satsuma, this led to the formation of a class of samurai who worked the land (*goshi*) and maintained a tight control of the countryside, which experienced not a single peasant uprising throughout the Tokugawa Period. Satsuma backwardness was also an asset to the domain in the sense that it worked against the erosion of samurai values found in economically more advanced and urbane regions. Both Chōshū and Satsuma also had special family ties with the court in Kyoto, the most likely focus for any anti-*bakufu* movement.

In both *han,* finances were put in order and a budget surplus was built up, although by different means. In Chōshū, rigorous cost cutting was initiated, major improvements were made in *han* financial administration, and the land tax was reformed. Most monopolies were abolished because they were unprofitable for the government and unpopular among the people. Only the profitable shipping and warehouse monopolies at Shimonoseki were continued. Otherwise, commodity transactions were turned over to merchants for a fee. Satsuma, in contrast, derived much of its income from its monopolies, especially the monopoly on sugar from the Ryukyu Islands, a Satsuma dependency, which was directed to continue sending tribute to China to foster trade. Thus, the Ryukyu Islands were a source of Chinese goods for Satsuma. The sugar monopoly was strictly enforced: private sale of sugar was a crime punishable by death. The sugar was brought to market in Osaka in the *han's* own ships, and at every stage, from production to sale, everything was done to maximize profit for the Satsuma treasury.

These programs required vigorous leadership, because they naturally ran up against the opposition of merchants and others who benefited from doing things the old way. Both Chōshū and Satsuma were fortunate in having reform-minded daimyo who raised to power young samurai of middle or low rank, men who tended to be much more innovative and energetic than conservative samurai of high rank. Particularly in Chōshū, such differences in background and outlook among the samurai class led to bitter antagonism and political turbulence.

That reform was more successful in Chōshū and Satsuma than in the *bakufu* suggests that it was easier to implement reform in a well-organized, remote domain than in the central region, where the economic changes were most advanced and political pressures and responsibilities were far greater. Reform attempts in other *han* varied in success, but Chōshū and Satsuma are particularly important because these two large and wealthy domains were to play a crucial role in the eventual overthrow of the Tokugawa.

Intellectual Currents

Economic, social, and political changes were accompanied by intellectual restiveness. Perceptions and ideas advanced by Shinto Revivalists of the School of National Learning, the Mito school with its emphasis on the centrality of the emperor, followers of Dutch Learning, and advocates of social restructuring ate away at the intellectual foundations of Tokugawa rule.

From the world of Osaka merchants came the bold ideas of Yamagata Bantō (1748–1821), a great Osaka financier with a well-established place in society. Yamagata based his ideas on astronomy and formulated a view of the world that allowed achievements to occur anywhere on the globe. He had great regard for utility and trust. One of his recommendations was to make written Japanese more accessible by using only the phonetic *kana* script and eliminating all Chinese characters.

An even more unorthodox thinker was Kaihō Seiryō (1748–1821), who spent his life traveling Japan free from encumbrances of status or family and saw all relations, including that between lord and samurai, in economic terms: the samurai sells his service to the lord in exchange for a stipend. For Kaihō, this was merely accommodating to *li* (principle). Here, a key Neo-Confucian concept is employed to structure a new theory of social conduct. The old bottles were capable of holding remarkably new wine.

In political thought, the respective roles of emperor and shogun continued to be subjects of discussion. In Mito, noted for its work on history, scholars emphasized that the emperor ruled because of his unique descent and that the shogun's legitimacy came from the mandate he derived from the emperor. Aizawa Seishisai (1782–1863), a leading Mito thinker, combined Confucian values and *bushidō* with Shinto mythology in discussing Japan's unique polity (*kokutai*). In 1825 he wanted the emperor to create in Japan the kind of unity that he saw as the basis for the strength of Western states and attributed to (iniquitous) Christianity. As Bob Tadashi Wakabayashi has indicated, in 1825 Aizawa's "argument for using the emperor's religious authority to bolster *bakufu* political supremacy was sensible and compelling."[4] But thirty years later the emperor and shogun had grown so far apart that this would have been inconceivable. Aizawa's glorification of the emperor, however, was to outlast the very idea of a *bakufu*.

Attitudes toward the West varied widely. Hirata Atsutane (1776–1843), for example, drew on the ideas of Motoori Norinaga and advocated an irrational and frequently naive nativism, but as a physician he admired Western medicine and studied Dutch medical texts. To reconcile his adulation of Japan with his appreciation for the foreign science, Hirata maintained that Japan had originally been pure and free of disease: the need for a powerful medical science arose only after Japan was infected by foreign contacts.

Most students of Dutch Learning took a more positive attitude. Interest in practical Western sciences such as astronomy, medicine, and mathematics continued to grow. The *bakufu* itself, in 1811, set up a bureau to translate Dutch books even though it maintained its closed-door policies toward the West. Takano Chōei (1804–1850) and Watanabe Kazan (1795–1841), persecuted for disagreeing with the *bakufu*'s seclusion policy, ended as suicides.

Outstanding among the students of Western science was the Confucian scholar Sakuma Shōzan (1811–1864), who conducted experiments in chemistry and glassmaking and later became an expert in the casting of guns; he was a serious thinker about the principles and the products of Western technology. There was ample room in his thought for Western learning, which he saw as part of the ultimate unity of *li* as taught by Zhu Xi; supplementing, not supplanting, his own tradition. His formula, "Eastern ethics and Western science," conveying the primacy of Japanese values and the compatibility of Western science, became an influential slogan after the Meiji Restoration. But Sakuma did not live to see the day; he was murdered by an antiforeign extremist from Chōshū in 1864.

Sakuma's intellectual strategy was essentially one of compartmentalization. The basic framework was left intact, with native and foreign traditions assigned different functions. Each had its distinct role. Most students of Dutch painting would have agreed, because they valued Western techniques more for their practical results than for any aesthetic merit. Yet, like all generalizations, this demands qualification. Hokusai, who lived until 1849, once contrasted the use of shading for decorative purposes in Chinese and Japanese art with its employment to create an effect of three-dimensionality in the West. He concluded, "One must understand both methods: there must be life and death in everything one paints."[5]

FIGURE 8.2 Commodore Matthew C. Perry (1794–1858) of the United States Navy. Artist unknown. In 1853–1854, Perry successfully led an armed mission to force isolationist Japan's agreement to open trade and diplomatic relations with the United States. Woodcut, nineteenth century, 9.6 in × 10.2 in. (© Courtesy Peabody Essex Museum, Salem, Massachusetts)

The "Opening" of Japan

The opening of China to the West was a result of the Opium War and subsequent treaties with European powers. In Japan, the opening resulted from an armed mission by Commodore Matthew C. Perry of the United States Navy in 1853 (see Figure 8.2). The treaties that followed that momentous event ended the Tokugawa policy of seclusion. This undermined the authority not only of the *bakufu* but also of the entire Tokugawa system.

Before 1853 there were several Western attempts to induce the Japanese to broaden their foreign policy, but these efforts were sporadic, because they were not supported by substantial economic and political interests of the kind at work in China. Regarded as poor and remote, Japan was considered a low priority by the great powers. The first approaches came from Japan's nearest Eurasian neighbor, the Russian Empire, and took place in the north, in the Kurile Islands, Sakhalin, and Hokkaido. In 1778 and again in 1792 the Russians requested trade relations in Hokkaido, and in 1804 a similar request was made in Nagasaki. All were refused. British ships seeking trade or ship's stores were also turned away. British whaling ships sometimes requested supplies, but in 1825 the *bakufu* ordered that all foreign ships should be driven from Japanese waters. In 1837 a private American–British attempt to open relations with Japan fared no better. But in 1842 the shogunate relaxed the edicts of 1825 and ordered that foreign ships accidentally arriving in Japan were to be provided with water, food, and fuel before being sent on their way.

China's defeat in the Opium War and the opening of new ports increased the number of Western vessels in East Asia and hence the pressure on Japan. This changing situation could not be ignored. To begin with, the lessons of Chinese weakness and Western strength were not lost on Japanese observers. Information concerning Western science, industry, and military capabilities continued to be provided by scholars of Dutch Learning and by the Dutch at Nagasaki. Information also came from China: Wei Yuan's *Illustrated Treatise on the Sea Kingdoms* was widely read after it appeared in a Japanese edition in 1847. Furthermore, the Japanese were making progress in mastering Western technology. By the 1840s, Mito, Hizen, and Satsuma were casting guns using Western methods. In 1850 Hizen possessed the first reverberatory furnace needed to produce iron suitable for making modern cannons. As already noted, a few courageous students of the West had suggested abandoning the policy of seclusion well before the arrival of Perry. The Dutch, too, had warned the *bakufu* of the designs of the stronger Western nations.

In 1846 an American mission to Japan ended in failure, but with the acquisition of California in 1848, the interest of the United States increased because Nagasaki, 500 miles from Shanghai, was a convenient fueling stop for ships bound from San Francisco to that port. Thus, the United States, rather than Britain or Russia, whose interests remained marginal, took the lead, sending Perry with four ships. Perry and his fleet reached Japan in July 1853, forced the Japanese to accept a letter from the American president to the emperor, and announced that he would return for an answer the following spring.

No match militarily for the American fleet, the *bakufu* realized that it would have to accede at least partly to American demands. In preparation for that unpopular move, it took the unprecedented step of soliciting the opinions of even the outside daimyo. This turned out to be a serious miscalculation, because instead of hoped-for support, the *bakufu* received only divided and unhelpful advice and seriously undermined its exclusive right to determine foreign policy.

When Perry returned in February 1854 with eight ships, an initial treaty was signed that provided for the opening of Shimoda and Hakodate to ships seeking provisions, assured that the shipwrecked would receive good treatment, and per-

FIGURE 8.3 *Harris's Procession on the Way to Edo.* Artist unknown. Townsend Harris, first American consul to Japan, traveled to Edo (Tokyo) in 1856 to negotiate a commercial treaty with Japan—a treaty that contained terms unfavorable to Japan. Watercolor, 21 in × 15.3 in. (© Peabody Essex Museum, Salem, Massachusetts)

mitted the United States later to send a consul to Japan. Similar treaties with Britain and France followed in 1855, and the Dutch and Russians negotiated broader agreements in 1857. The task of negotiating a commercial treaty was left to the first American consul, Townsend Harris, who arrived in Japan in 1856 and gradually succeeded in persuading the shogunate to make concessions (see Figure 8.3). The resulting treaty was signed in 1858, and another round of treaties with the Dutch, Russians, British, and French followed.

At the end of this process, Japan's international situation was essentially that of China under the unequal treaty system. First there was the matter of opening ports. This began with Shimoda on the Izu Peninsula and Hakodate in Hokkaido; it was extended to Nagasaki and Kanagawa (for which Yokohama was substituted). Dates were set for the opening of Niigata, Hyogo (modern Kobe), and the admission of foreign residents, but not trade, into Osaka and Edo. As in China, the treaties gave foreigners the right to be tried by their own consular courts under their own laws (extraterritoriality). Japan lost its tariff autonomy and was limited to relatively low import duties. Most-favored-nation treatment obliged Japan to extend to all states any concession it granted to any one of the others.

Domestic Politics

For the *bakufu,* forced to accede to foreign demands without enjoying support at home, these were difficult years. Each concession to the powers provided additional ammunition to its domestic enemies. Compounding its difficulties, the *bakufu* itself was divided by factionalism and policy differences. An attempt was made after Perry's arrival to broaden the shogunate's base by drawing on the advice of nonhouse daimyo. The lord of Mito, Tokugawa Nariaki (1800–1860), a persistent advocate of resistance to the West, was placed in charge of national defense. These measures, however, failed to strengthen the *bakufu*—too many men were pulling in opposite directions.

When the shogun died without an heir in 1858, a bitter dispute took place over the rival claims of two candidates for the succession. One was still a boy but had the strongest claim by descent. He also had the backing of most of the house daimyo (*fudai*) including that of Ii Naosuke, greatest of the *fudai.* The other candidate was Tokugawa Yoshinobu (then known as Hitotsubashi Keiki), the capable son of the lord of Mito.

The immediate issue in the succession dispute concerned control over the *bakufu,* because Keiki's accession was seen as a threat to the continued control over the shogunate by the *fudai.* Foreign policy was also involved because the *bakufu* officials, as men on the spot, were inclined to make concessions to the foreigners. The great lords, however, demanded a vigorous defense policy against the intruders from the West. Furthermore, the lord of Mito and some of his peers envisioned their own *han* as playing important roles in building military strength. Thus, his advocacy of a strong foreign policy was consistent with his desire to strengthen his own domain at the expense of the center. Meanwhile, the split in the *bakufu* increased the political importance of the imperial court. Nariaki even appealed to Kyoto for support for his son's candidacy. And when the shogun tried to obtain imperial approval for the treaty negotiated with Harris, he failed.

The crisis of 1858 was temporarily resolved when Ii Naosuke took charge of the *bakufu* as grand councilor (*tairo*), a high post more often than not left vacant and one that had previously been held by several members of the Ii family. The effective power of this position depended on the authority of the incumbent, and the strong-minded Ii Naosuke used it to dominate the shogunate. He proceeded to sign the treaty with the United States without prior imperial approval; vigorously reassert *bakufu* power; purge his enemies; force into retirement or house arrest the daimyo who had opposed him and were on the losing side in the succession dispute, including the lord of Mito; and punish some of the court nobles and Mito loyalists. For a moment, the *bakufu* was revitalized. But only for a moment: in March 1860, Ii was assassinated by a group of samurai, mostly from Mito. They were advocates of *sonnō,* "revere the emperor," and *jōi,* "expel the barbarians."

Sonnō Jōi

As we observed earlier, Mito was the home of an emperor-centered school of historiography and political thought, and its lord was one of the most fervent advocates of a strong military policy to "expel the barbarians." It is therefore not surprising that Mito thought influenced the passionate and brilliant young man who became the main spokesman and hero of the Sonnō Jōi movement. This was Yoshida Shōin (1830–1859), the son of a low-ranking Chōshū samurai. Yoshida was influenced by *bushidō* in the tradition of Yamaga Sokō, by books on military science, and by Confucianism. From Sakuma Shōzan he learned about the West. Then he became acquainted with Mito ideas on a study trip to northern Japan, which, because it was unauthorized, cost him his samurai rank. Apprehensive of the West and convinced of the importance of knowing one's enemy, he tried to stow away on one of Perry's ships but was caught and placed under house arrest in Chōshū. After his release he started a school there and attracted disciples, including Kido Kōin (or Takamasa, 1834–1877), one of the three leading statesmen of the Meiji Restoration, and the future leaders Itō Hirobumi and Yamagata Aritomo. Yoshida condemned the *bakufu* for its handling of the foreign problem. He charged that its failure to expel the barbarians reflected incompetence, dereliction of duty, and a lack of proper reverence for the throne. Like many men of lower samurai origins, he resented a system that rewarded birth more than ability or talent, and he blamed the *bakufu*'s inability to reject the foreigners on this system. What was needed to redress the situation were pure and selfless officials who would act out of true loyalty rather than mindless obedience. Thus, Yoshida's teaching combined elements of moral revival at home, opposition to the foreigner, and championship of the throne.

Initially, Yoshida favored the appointment of new men to the *bakufu,* but after the signing of the treaty with the United States in 1858, he concluded that the *bakufu* must be overthrown. Both personal fulfillment and national salvation required an act of unselfish self-sacrifice by a national hero. In 1858, Yoshida, seeking to achieve both aims, plotted the assassination of the emissary sent by the shogun to the imperial court to persuade the emperor to agree to the commercial treaty with the United States. Word leaked out. Yoshida was arrested and sent to Edo, where he was beheaded the following year.

Mixed Responses to the West

In this turbulent era, Japanese reactions to the West varied widely. Some Japanese, like the Confucian Shinoya Tōin (1810–1867), had an absolute hatred for everything Western. Shinoya even belittled the script in which the foreigners wrote, describing it as follows:

> [It is] confused and irregular, wriggling like snakes or larvae of mosquitoes. The straight ones are like dog's teeth, the round ones are like worms. The crooked ones are like the forelegs of a mantis, the stretched ones are like slime lines left by snails. They resemble dried bones or decaying skulls, rotten bellies of dead snakes or parched vipers.[6]

It is not surprising that a culture that prized calligraphy should find the strictly utilitarian Western script aesthetically unappetizing, but Shinoya's invective goes beyond mere distaste. Every word betrays, and indeed is meant to express, horror and disgust at the beasts that had come among them.

But there were others who were determined to learn from the West, even if only to use that knowledge to defeat the foreigner. Their slogan was *kaikoku joi:* "open the country to drive out the barbarians." The learning process continued. In 1857 the *bakufu* opened the Institute for the Investigation of Barbarian Books near Edo Castle. Not only the *bakufu* but also some of the domains sent men on study trips abroad; in the case of the *han,* this was often done illegally. The process of adopting Western technology, begun even before Perry's arrival, was accelerated.

An indication of the people's receptivity to the new knowledge is provided by the popularity of the writings of Fukuzawa Yukichi (1835–1901), who went abroad twice in the early 1860s and published seven books before the restoration, beginning in 1866 with the first volume of *Conditions in the West* (*Seiyō jijō*), which appeared in 1866 and promptly sold 150,000 copies. Another 100,000 copies were sold in pirated editions. These works, written in a simple style easy enough for Fukuzawa's housemaid to read, were filled with detailed descriptions of Western institutions and life: hospitals and schools, tax systems and museums, climate and clothes, cutlery, beds, and chamber pots. Fukuzawa went on to become a leading Meiji intellectual, but the turbulent years just before the restoration were dangerous for men of his outlook.

Unlike Yoshida Shōin, some people hoped for a reconciliation of the court and *bakufu,* and there were some who still hoped the *bakufu* could transform itself and take the lead in creating a more modern state. These issues, at work during the 1860s, were finally buried in the restoration.

Last Years of the Shogunate (1860–1867)

After the assassination of Ii Naosuke in 1860, the *bakufu* leadership tried compromise. An effort was made to effect a "union of the court and military" that was confirmed by the shogun's marriage to the emperor's sister. In return for affirming the emperor's primacy, the *bakufu* obtained assent for its foreign policy. It also sought to win daimyo support by relaxing the requirements for attendance at Edo. However, this policy ran into the opposition of Kyoto loyalists, activists of the Sonnō Jōi persuasion, samurai, and voluntary rōnin who had escaped the bonds of feudal discipline by requesting to leave their lords' service. Psychologically, this was not difficult, because their loyalty to their lords had become bureaucratized and they now felt the claims of a higher loyalty to the throne.

Men of extremist dedication, ready to sacrifice their lives, to kill and be killed for the cause, terrorized the streets of Kyoto in the early 1860s and made the capital unsafe for moderates, who risked losing their heads and having them displayed as a warning to others. This also happened to statues: their location in a temple did not save the statues of Ashikaga shoguns from decapitation at the hands of some followers of Hirata Atsutane who, unable to reach prominent living targets, exercised vengeance on the Ashikaga for wronging the emperor in the fourteenth century. Mito, too, was notably unsafe for moderates.

For ordinary people this was a time when their frustrations came to a head, a time of messianic visions and religious fervor, of amulets falling from the sky, and of people finding temporary escape from misery by dancing wildly in the streets, shouting *ee ja nai ka* ("ain't it great," or "what the hell"), barging into the houses of the rich and powerful demanding food and drink, forcing them to join the dance, and wreaking general havoc. Beginning in the cities of central Japan and spreading along the Tokaidō, these riots showed that the Tokugawa order was falling apart. George M. Wilson says of the Meiji Restoration that "a pervasive urge to remedy distress at home was just as compelling to most participants as the patriotic intent to elevate Japan in the international area."[7]

Westerners, too, were blamed for the distress because the opening of the ports was followed by a marked rise in the price of rice, causing great hardship and reinforcing nativistic hatred of foreigners. Several foreigners were assassinated by fervent samurai in 1859, and in 1861 Townsend Harris's Dutch interpreter was cut down and the British legation in Edo was attacked. In 1862 a British merchant lost his life at the hands of Satsuma samurai. When the British were unable to obtain satisfaction from the *bakufu,* they took matters into their own hands. In August 1863, they bombarded Kagoshima, the Satsuma capital, to force punishment of the guilty and payment of an indemnity.

A similar incident involving Chōshū took place in the summer of 1863. By that time, extremists had won control of the imperial court and, with Chōshū backing, had forced the shogun to accept June 25, 1863, as the date for the expulsion of the barbarians. The *bakufu,* caught between the intransigent foreigners and the insistent court, interpreted the agreement to mean that negotiations for the closing of the ports would begin on that day, but Chōshū and the loyalists interpreted it more literally. When Chōshū guns began firing on foreign ships in the Straits of Shimonoseki, the foreign ships fired back. First American warships came to shell the fortifications, then French ships landed parties that destroyed the fort and ammunition. Still Chōshū persisted in firing on foreign vessels, until in September 1864 a combined French, Dutch, and American fleet demolished the forts and forced Chōshū to come to terms. These losses, plus a defeat inflicted on

Chōshū adherents by a Satsuma–Aizu force in Kyoto in August 1864, stimulated Chōshū to overhaul its military forces. It had already arranged to purchase arms and ships. Now peasant militia were organized and mixed rifle units were formed, staffed by commoners and samurai, a radical departure from Tokugawa practice and from the basic principles of Tokugawa society. One of these units was commanded by Itō Hirobumi, recently returned from study in England.

Satsuma's response to defeat, although not as radical as Chōshū's, was similar in its appreciation of the superiority of Western weapons. With British help, the domain began acquiring Western ships, forming the nucleus of what was to become the Imperial Japanese Navy. The British supported Satsuma partly because they were disillusioned with the *bakufu* and partly because the French were supporting the shogunate with arms, hoping to lay the foundations for future influence in a reconstituted shogunate. By now many *bakufu* officials appreciated the need for institutional change and for modernization. During the closing years of the Tokugawa, the issue changed from preserving the old system to determining who would take the lead in building the new. In Chōshū and Satsuma, too, there was less talk about "expelling the barbarians" and more about "enriching the country and strengthening the army," at least among the leaders.

The politics of these years were even more than usually full of complications and intrigues, and as long as Chōshū and Satsuma remained on opposite sides, the situation remained fluid. Traditionally unfriendly to each other, competing for power in Kyoto, and differing in their policy recommendations, they were nevertheless unified in their opposition to a restoration of Tokugawa power. There were two wars against Chōshū. In the first, 1864–1865, a large *bakufu* force with men from many domains defeated Chōshū. This set off a civil war in Chōshū from which the revolutionaries, with their mixed rifle regiments, emerged victorious.

This led to a second *bakufu* war against Chōshū, but before this second war began, in 1866, Chōshū and Satsuma made a secret alliance. When war came, Satsuma and some other powerful *han* remained on the sidelines. Although outnumbered, the Chōshū forces, better trained, better armed, and higher in morale, defeated the *bakufu.*

After this defeat by a single *han,* the *bakufu,* under Tokugawa Yoshinobu (who inherited the position of shogun in 1866), tried to save what it could. There were attempts to work out a daimyo coalition and calls for imperial restoration. In November the shogun accepted a proposal that he resign in favor of a council of daimyo under the emperor. According to this arrangement, he was to retain his lands and, as the most powerful lord in Japan, serve as prime minister. However, this was unacceptable to the *sonno* advocates in Satsuma and Chōshū and to the restorationists at court, including the court noble Iwakura Tonomi (1825–1883), a master politician. On January 3, 1868, forces from Satsuma and other *han* seized the palace and proclaimed the restoration. The shogunate was destroyed. Tokugawa lands were confiscated, and the shogun himself was reduced to the status of an ordinary daimyo. A short civil war ensued. There was fighting in Edo and in northern Honshū, but no real contest. Last to surrender was the *bakufu* navy in May 1869.

II. The Meiji Restoration

Formation of a New Government: The Meiji Restoration

The Charter Oath

Dismantling the Old Order

Disaffection and Opposition

The Crisis of 1873

The Meaning of the Restoration

The end of the shogunate brought to the fore new leaders to deal with a world full of dangers and opportunities—perhaps in equal measure.

Formation of a New Government: The Meiji Restoration

The men who overthrew the Tokugawa in January 1868 did not subscribe to any clear and well-defined program. There was general agreement about the abolition of the shogunate and "restoration" of the emperor, but this meant no more than that the emperor should once again be at the center of the political system, functioning as the source of legitimacy and providing a sense of continuity. It most certainly did not mean that actual power should be given to the sixteen-year-old Meiji Emperor (1852–1912; r. 1867–1912),* nor did it necessarily imply the destruction of feudalism, because there were those who envisioned the restoration in terms of a new feudal system headed by the emperor. On the other hand, Japanese scholars had long been aware that the Chinese system provided a bureaucratic alternative to feudalism. This surely eased the shift to bureaucratic centralization.

The new leaders did not always see eye to eye, but they shared certain qualities: they were all of similar age (thirty-five to forty-three years) and rank, and they came from the victorious *han* or the court aristocracy, although the *han* coalition was soon broadened to include men from Tosa and Hizen. The three most emi-

* His name was Mutsuhito, but as in the case of the Qing emperors in China, it is customary to refer to him and his successors by the designation given to their reign periods.

nent leaders in the early years of the restoration were Ōkubo Toshimichi (1830–1878), Kido Kōin (1833–1877), and Saigō Takamori (1827–1877). Both Ōkubo and Kido had risen to leadership in their own domains (Satsuma and Chōshū) through their influence in the domain's bureaucratic establishment and among the loyalist activists. Of the two, Ōkubo was the stronger personality—disciplined, formal, and somewhat intimidating; dedicated to the nation, cautious, and practical. Kido was livelier but more volatile, less self-confident but more concerned than Ōkubo with strengthening the popular base of the government. But he was just as devoted to building a strong state.

Ōkubo's was the single strongest voice in government from 1873 to 1878. One of his initial tasks was to retain the cooperation of Saigō, the military leader of the Satsuma forces who had joined with Chōshū to overthrow the Tokugawa. Saigō was a man of imposing physique and great physical strength. He was known for his outstanding courage and possessed many of the traditional warrior virtues, such as generosity and contempt for money. More conservative than the others, he was devoted to Satsuma and its samurai but worked with the others at least until 1873. They were united in their conviction that the country must be strengthened to resist the West.

For national self-preservation, the leaders were prepared to enact vast changes, but it took time to plan and carry these out and, indeed, to consolidate their own power in a land where, as Kido complained, "we are surrounded on four sides by little *bakufu*."[8] To insure that the emperor would not become a focus of opposition to reform, Ōkubo argued that he should be moved to Edo, renamed Tokyo (Eastern Capital) in September 1868. This took place the following year when the emperor moved into the shogun's former castle, which in 1871, after much debate, was renamed the "imperial palace."

The Charter Oath

Even before the move, in April 1868, while the emperor was still in Kyoto, a Charter Oath was issued in his name to provide a general, if vague, statement of purpose for the new regime. It consisted of five articles:

1. An assembly widely convoked shall be established and all matters of state shall be decided by public discussion.
2. All classes high and low shall unite in vigorously promoting the economy and welfare of the nation.
3. All civil and military officials and the common people as well shall be allowed to fulfill their aspirations so that there may be no discontent among them.
4. Base customs of former times shall be abandoned and all actions shall conform to the principles of international justice.
5. Knowledge shall be sought throughout the world and thus shall be strengthened the foundation of the imperial polity.[9]

Although the government was reorganized to provide an assembly in keeping with the first article, power remained with the original leadership and the attempt to implement this provision was soon abandoned. In contrast, the end of seclusion, the acceptance of international law, and the openness to foreign ideas conveyed by the last two articles took place. Symbolic of this shift was the audience granted to representatives of the foreign powers by the emperor in Kyoto just a month before the Charter Oath was issued. The document itself was drafted by two men familiar with Western thought; it was then revised by Kido. The ramifications of the Charter Oath were far from clear, but the last article, to seek for knowledge "throughout the world," was taken very seriously. Furthermore, with its call for an assembly and its strong internationalism, the entire document illustrates the gulf between Japanese and Chinese leaders at this time. No Chinese government would have issued such a document in an attempt to gain political strength.

Dismantling the Old Order

Although the machinery of the central government underwent various reorganizations, the prime need was for the government to extend and consolidate its authority and ability to collect taxes. Because the continued existence of the feudal domains was a major obstacle to this, the government leaders undertook the delicate but essential task of abolishing the *han.* In March 1869, Kido and Ōkubo were able to use their influence to induce the daimyo of Chōshū and Satsuma to return their domains to the emperor. They were joined in this act by the lords of Tosa and Hizen. Many others followed suit, anxious to be in the good graces of the new government and expecting to be appointed governors of their former domains, which they were. The real blow came in 1871 when, in the name of national unity, the domains were abolished and the whole country was reorganized into prefectures. This was made palatable to the daimyo by generous financial arrangements. They were allowed to retain a tenth of the former domain revenue as personal income while the government assumed responsibility for *han* debts and financial obligations. The daimyo were also assured continued high social standing and prestige. Finally, in 1884, they were elevated to the peerage.

By background and experience, the new leadership was keenly sensitive to the importance of military power. Initially, the new government depended entirely on forces from the supporting domains, but this would hardly do for a government truly national in scope. Accordingly, the leaders set about forming a new army freed from local ties. Rejecting the views of Saigō, who envisioned a samurai army that would ensure the warrior class a useful and, he hoped, brilliant role in Japan's future, the leaders decided in 1872 to build their army on the basis of commoner conscription. In January 1873, the new measure, largely the work of Yamagata Aritomo (1838–1922), "father of the Japanese Army," became law.

The restoration had a profound effect on the samurai. The new army, by eliminating distinctions between commoners and samurai, cut to the heart of the status system. Anyone could become a warrior now. Other marks of samurai distinctiveness were eliminated or eroded. In 1870 commoners were allowed to acquire surnames and were released from previous occupational and residential restrictions. In 1871 the wearing of swords by samurai became optional; five years later it was prohibited entirely.

The samurai's position was further undermined by the abolition of the *han,* which left them without political or social function. Furthermore, continued payment of their stipends at the customary rate was more than the central government could afford. Accordingly, they were pensioned off. But in view of their number, the government could not afford to treat them as generously as it did the daimyo. At first, samurai stipends were reduced on a sliding scale from half to a tenth of what they had been, then they were given the right to commute these into twenty-year bonds (1873), and finally they were forced to accept the bonds (1876).

Reduction and commutation of samurai stipends was only one of the measures taken to establish the new government on a sound financial basis. In addition to monetary and banking reform, a tax system was created (1873). The fiscal measures were largely the work of Ōkuma Shigenobu (1838–1922), a man from Hizen who was to remain prominent in Meiji politics, and Itō Hirobumi (1841–1909) of Chōshū. The main source of government revenue was, as before, agriculture, but in place of the old percentage of the crop payable by the village to the daimyo, the tax was now collected by the government in money in accordance with the assessed value of the land. It was payable by the owner, and for this purpose ownership rights had to be clearly established. This was not done in favor of the absentee feudal interest long divorced from the land, nor did ownership pass equitably to all peasants. Instead, certificates were issued to the cultivators and wealthy villagers who had paid the tax during Tokugawa times. In this way tenancy was perpetuated. Because poor peasants, often unable to meet their taxes, were forced to mortgage their land, the rate of tenancy increased, rising from about 25 percent before the new system to about 40 percent twenty years later.

Disaffection and Opposition

The creation of a modern political, military, and fiscal system benefited the state but hurt some of the people. The peasantry was unhappy not only about the land system but also about forced military service and showed its bitter displeasure by staging uprisings with increasing frequency from 1866 to 1873. Many large merchant houses that had developed symbiotic relationships with the *bakufu* or daimyo also suffered during these years, and some went bankrupt.

More serious for the regime was samurai discontent. The new government was led by former samurai, and for many men the new order meant a release from old restrictions and the opening of new opportunities. Because the samurai were the educated class with administrative experience, they supplied the personnel for local and national government, officers for the army, teachers for the schools, and colonists for Hokkaido. Casting aside tradition, some entered the world of business and finance. Yet there were many who did not make a successful transition, who were unable to take advantage of the new vocations opened to them or to use their payments to establish themselves in new lines of endeavor. And among the leaders and the supporters of the Meiji government were men who firmly believed that its purpose was literally the restoration of the old, not the creation of the new. A split between conservatives and modernizers developed early in the restoration and came to a head in 1873.

The Crisis of 1873

The crisis of 1873 centered on the issue of going to war with Korea to force it to open its doors to Japan. Those who advocated war, such as Saigō and Itagaki Taisuke (1836–1919) from Tosa, did so not only out of nationalist motives but also because they saw war as a way to provide employment for the samurai, an opportunity to give them a greater role in the new society and a means to preserve their military heritage. Saigō, a military leader with great charisma and devotion to the way of the warrior, asked to be sent to Korea as ambassador so that he could deliberately get himself killed and thus provide a cause for going to war.

A decision for war was made in the summer of 1873 in the absence of Ōkubo, Kido, and other important leaders who were abroad in America and Europe. They were on a diplomatic and study mission headed by Iwakura Tonomi, the noble who had played a leading role at court in bringing about the Meiji Restoration. The purposes of the Iwakura mission were to convey the Meiji Emperor's respects to the heads of state of the treaty powers and build goodwill, to discuss subjects for later treaty revision, and to provide its distinguished members with an opportunity to observe and study the West at first hand. It took 631 days, including seven months in the United States, four in England, and seven in continental Europe. The Japanese leaders did not just have audiences with heads of state and observe parliaments and courts. They were interested in everything:

> They toured cotton mills, iron foundries, shipyards, newspaper plants, breweries, prisons, banks, stock exchanges, cathedrals, telegraph offices, military fortifications, lunatic asylums, libraries and art galleries. . . . [They] visited zoos; attended the theater and opera; and took in endless concerts, ballets, and an occasional masked ball, circus performance, and fox hunt.[10]

They returned home in September 1873 with a new appreciation of the importance and complexity of modernization and new realization of the magnitude of the task facing Japan in its quest for equality. They were convinced of the urgent priority of domestic change.

When the mission returned, Ōkubo led the opposition to the Korean venture on the grounds that Japan could not yet afford such an undertaking. Ōkubo,

Kido, and Iwakura prevailed, with the support of many officials and the court. In October it was decided to abandon the Korean expedition and to concentrate on internal development. The decision split the government. Bitterly disappointed, the war advocates, including Saigō and Itagaki, resigned. They provided leadership for those disaffected by the new government and its policies, an opposition that would prove troublesome to those in power. But their departure left the government in the hands of a group of men unified by a commitment to modernization. Most prominent among them were Ōkubo, Itō, Ōkuma, and Iwakura.

By 1873 the Meiji government had survived the difficult period of initial consolidation. It had established the institutional foundations for the new state, had found a means of defense and national security, and with the resolution of the 1873 crisis had charted the basic course of development at home and peace abroad that was to dominate Japanese policies during the next twenty years.

The Meaning of the Restoration

Like other major historical events, the Meiji Restoration meant and continued to mean different things to different people. Most visible was increased openness to the West in matters small and large. Already in the early 1870s the gentleman of fashion sported a foreign umbrella and watch and, as recommended by Fukuzawa Yukichi, strengthened his body by eating beef. Faddish Westernism was satirized in one of the best-sellers of the day, *Aguranabe (Sitting around the Stew Pan)* (1871) by Kanagaki Robun (1829–1903). Ōkubo ate bread, drank dark tea for breakfast, and wore Western clothes even at home. In 1872 Western dress was made mandatory at court and other official functions. The Gregorian calendar was adopted the same year. After the Tokyo fire of 1872, the city's main avenue, the Ginza, was rebuilt under the supervision of an English architect. It boasted brick buildings, colonnades, and gas lamps (see Figure 8.4). The inhabitants of Tokyo could take pleasure and pride in the Ginza, but the glitter of the capital was not shared by the countryside. Already in 1874, the widening contrast between the prosperous modern capital and the hinterland prompted Fukuzawa Yukichi to warn of the following:

> The purpose [of the government] seems to be to use the fruits of rural labor to make flowers for Tokyo. Steel bridges glisten in the capital, and horse-drawn carriages run on the streets, but in the country the wooden bridges are so rotten one cannot cross them. The cherry blossoms bloom in Kyōbashi [in Tokyo] but weeds grow in the country fields. Billows of smoke such as rise from city stoves do not rise from the farmer's furnace. . . . We must cease making Tokyo richer and concentrate on rural districts.[11]

Unfortunately for those at the bottom of society, this was not to be.

Ideologically, the main thrust was to use the old to justify the new, a process that produced new visions of the past and of the future. Invoking the name of the em-

FIGURE 8.4 The Ginza, 1873. The Ginza's facade and lampposts represent the Meiji Restoration's most visible feature—an increased openness to the West in matters small and large. (© Tsisei Corporation, Japan. Used by permission)

peror, a symbol of continuity with the old, the Meiji leaders were able to innovate even as they assured the survival, in new forms, of old values and ideas. Along these lines, there was an effort to turn Japan into a Shinto state. In 1868 Shinto was proclaimed the basis for the government and a Department of Shinto was established, with precedence over the other departments. There was a drive to purify Shinto, to eliminate Buddhist influences that had steadily seeped into Shinto, and to make Shinto the only religion of Japan. This drive, however, ran into opposition from Buddhists and conflicted with Western pressures for the legalization of Christianity. In 1872 the Department of Shinto was abolished, and in 1873 the ban on Christianity was lifted. Settlement of the legal status of Shinto had to wait until 1882.

The restoration was revolutionary in that it destroyed the old system and created a centralized state. It eliminated the old class lines and legally opened all careers to all men. In all areas of human activity it prepared the way for the profound changes that, during the next century, were to transform the very countryside of Japan. But if it was a revolution, it was a revolution from above, an "aristocratic revolution," to borrow a term from Thomas C. Smith.[12] Although popular unrest helped undermine the Tokugawa, the restoration was not the product of a mass movement or of a radical social ideology. It did not radically change the structure of village life or the mode of agricultural production. It eliminated the samurai elite as a legally defined, privileged class but, led by men who were themselves samurai, did so in terms samurai could understand.

The legacy of the restoration was complex and perhaps is not even yet fully played out, because it provided a base for both the successes and the failures that were to come.

Notes

1. Marius Jansen, ed., *The Cambridge History of Japan, Vol. 5: The Nineteenth Century* (Cambridge: Cambridge Univ. Press, 1989), p. 60.
2. David L. Howell, *Capitalism from Within: Economy, Society, and the State in a Japanese Fishery* (Berkeley: Univ. of California Press, 1995), p. 91.
3. Harold Bolitho, in Howell, *Capitalism from Within,* p. 159.
4. Bob Tadashi Wakabayashi, *Anti-Foreignism and Western Learning in Early Modern Japan: The New Theses of 1825* (Cambridge: Harvard Univ. Press, 1986), p. 134.
5. Michiaki Kawakita, *Modern Currents in Japanese Art: Heibonsha Survey of Japanese Art, Vol. 24,* Charles S. Terry, trans. (New York and Tokyo: Weatherhill/Heibonsha, 1974), p. 29.
6. Marius Jansen, ed., *Changing Japanese Attitudes toward Modernization* (Princeton: Princeton Univ. Press, 1969), pp. 57–58; quoting van Gulik, "Kakkaron: A Japanese Echo of the Opium War," *Monumenta Serica* 4 (1939): 542–43.

7. George M. Wilson, *Patriots and Redeemers in Japan: Motives in the Meiji Restoration* (Chicago: Univ. of Chicago Press, 1992), p. 2. For *ee ja nai ka,* see p. 98.
8. Albert Craig and Donald H. Shively, eds., *Personality in Japanese History* (Berkeley and Los Angeles: Univ. of California Press, 1970), p. 297.
9. Ishii Ryosuke, *Japanese Legislation in the Meiji Era,* William J. Chai, trans. (Tokyo: Pan-Pacific Press, 1958), p. 145.
10. John Hunter Boyle, *Modern Japan: The American Nexus* (Fort Worth: Harcourt Brace Jovanovich, 1993), p. 92.
11. Quoted in Mikiso Hane, *Peasants, Rebels, and Outcastes: The Underside of Modern Japan* (New York: Pantheon Books, 1982), p. 33.
12. See Thomas C. Smith, "Japan's Aristocratic Revolution," *Yale Review* 50 (Spring 1961), 370–83. Also see Marius Jansen, "The Meiji State: 1868–1912," in James B. Crowley, ed., *Modern East Asia: Essays in Interpretation* (New York: Harcourt Brace Jovanovich, 1970), pp. 95–121, which cites Smith on p. 103.

9

The Emergence of Modern Japan: 1874–1894

Political Developments
Formation of Parties
The Emperor and the Constitution
Western Influences on Values and Ideas
"Civilization and Enlightenment"
Social Darwinism
The Arts
Conservatism and Nationalism
Education
Modernizing the Economy
The Zaibatsu
The Military
Korea and the Sino-Japanese War of 1894–1895
The Treaty of Shimonoseki (April 1895)

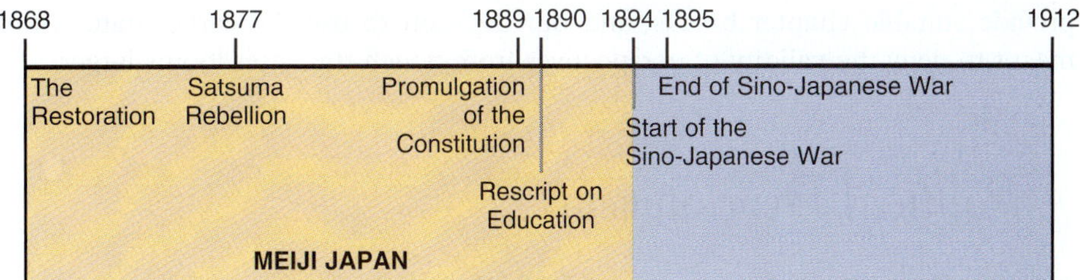

After the Meiji leaders consolidated their new regime, their top priority was to transform Japan into a modern nation accepted as an equal by the powers of the world. During the next twenty years, a new political framework was devised, the foundations for a modern economy were laid, and profound change occurred in institutions as in values and ideas. Just as tradition meant different things to different people, throughout the nineteenth and twentieth centuries there were diverse (and changing) versions of modernity. Rather than attempting a substantive definition of modern, we use the term in a purely temporal sense, to mean "up to date." During the nineteenth and twentieth centuries, modernity was largely defined by the West because of its great power.

Change was neither smooth nor simple. In the intricate interweaving of old and new, some old customs went the way of the samurai's sword and topknot, but others were retained or transformed and put to new uses. Early Meiji saw not only the appearance of what was patently new and seen as such, but also the emergence of new versions of the past. John W. Downer, summarizing a body of recent scholarship, has written the following:

> Thus they [recent scholars] called attention to the careful and adroit manner by which elites and molders of popular opinion, in Japan as elsewhere, routinely create modern myths under the rubric of "tradition" or cultural uniqueness—whether these be myths involving the emperor, or an idealized hierarchical "family system," or a code of "obedience and filial piety," or a harmonious "traditional employment system," or a simple and egalitarian rural community, or a pure "national essence" rooted in the past before the corruption of foreign influences from China and the West.[1]

As we have seen, myths centered on a "national essence" could draw on Tokugawa nativist thought, but they became modern myths participating in Japan's process of becoming modern. That process knows no end, but Japan's victory over China in 1895 marked the conclusion of the crucial initial phase, because by then it had achieved many of its initial objectives: a centralized government, a modernizing economy, and sufficient military strength to warrant international respect. This was confirmed and augmented by Japan's defeat of Russia in the Russo-Japanese War of 1904–1905, another major break in modern Japanese history that had repercussions beyond Japan and even East Asia. Both provide suitable chapter breaks, and our decision to use the earlier date is not meant to deny the validity of perspectives from which the latter looms larger.

Political Developments

Acting in the name of the emperor, a small inner circle dominated the government during the 1870s and 1880s, but not without opposition. To mollify those disappointed by the abandonment of the Korean expedition so earnestly sought by Saigō Takamori and his friends, in 1874 Japan sent a military force to Taiwan, ostensibly to punish aborigines who had killed some shipwrecked Okinawans. This expedition was a smaller and less dangerous undertaking than a military confrontation with Korea. It was successful, with the result that China was forced to pay an indemnity and to recognize Japanese sovereignty over the Ryukyu Islands, thus ending the ties that the Ryukyus had maintained with China even while they were Satsuma vassals.

The success of the expedition, however, did not alleviate the situation of disoriented and embittered samurai who felt betrayed by the Meiji leaders. Such men resorted to arms in an uprising in Hizen in 1874, western Kyūshū in 1876, and, most seriously, in Satsuma in 1877. The Satsuma Rebellion was led by Saigō, who had withdrawn from the government after the 1873 decision against the Korean expedition. The number of those who threw in their lot with the rebellion rose as high as 42,000. Its suppression strained the military resources of the restoration government, but after half a year the rebellion was crushed.

The Satsuma Rebellion was the last stand of the samurai. When the military situation became hopeless, Saigō committed ritual suicide. His was a martyr's death for a lost cause.

Saigō died under official condemnation as a traitor, but the Meiji government soon rehabilitated him, and government leaders joined in expressions of admiration and acclaim. Not only conservatives but also representatives of the most diverse political persuasions praised the magnanimity of his spirit and transformed Saigō into a legendary hero celebrated in poems and songs (including an army marching song), portrayed on stage and in an extensive literature, depicted in portraits and prints, and even identified with the planet Mars.

Protest against the government continued, on occasion, to take a violent turn. Less than half a year after Saigō's death, some of his sympathizers assassinated Ōkubo Toshimichi, also from Satsuma, who had worked so hard and successfully to create the new Japanese state. There were other assassination attempts, both successful and not. More important in the long run, however, was the formation of nonviolent political opposition, animated not only by objections to one or another aspect of government policy but also by protest against the political domination exercised by a few men from Chōshū and Satsuma who had exclusive control over the centers of power. Basing their position on the first article of the 1868 Charter Oath, early in 1874 opposition leaders demanded the creation of an elected legislature. Prominent among them was Itagaki Taisuke, the Tosa leader who, with Saigō, had left the government over the Korean issue.

In Tosa and elsewhere, antigovernment organizations voiced the discontent of local interests, demanding political rights, local self-government, and formation of a national assembly. The advocates of a constitution and the leaders of what became known as the movement for popular rights drew upon Western political theories. Constitutionalism itself was an idea with wide currency and long pedigree in the West, where it was associated with ideas concerning the supremacy of law, a "social contract," and human rights highlighted in eighteenth-century political thought. In the West, constitutions limited the powers exercised by heads of state by providing representative institutions to share in governing, but a strong argument advanced in Japan was that representative institutions would create greater unity between the people and the emperor. In this view, a constitution was needed not to limit the emperor's powers but to control his advisers. The men in power were not averse to some kind of constitution as a necessary and even desirable component of modernization. Indeed, Kido, as a participant in the Iwakura mission to Europe, became persuaded of the need for a constitution.

By 1878, Kido, Ōkubo, and Saigō were all dead. Of the older men only Iwakura remained important, and three younger men who had already contributed significantly to the Meiji state assumed leadership: Itō Hirobumi and Yamagata Aritomo, both from Chōshū, and Ōkuma Shigenobu from Hizen. Yamagata was the creator of the new army, Itō took the lead in political modernization, and Ōkuma served as finance minister. They agreed that Japan should have a constitution, but they could not agree on the structure of the constitution or on a schedule for drawing up and implementing it. Tensions between Itō and Ōkuma came to a head in 1881 when the latter wrote a memorandum advocating the adoption of an English-style political system. His proposals that the majority party in parliament form the government, that the Cabinet be responsible to parliament, and that the first elections be held in 1883 clashed with the conservative and gradualist views of his colleagues. First, his proposals were rejected; then, when Ōkuma joined in public criticism of the government over its sale of a certain government project in Hokkaido, the emperor consented to having Ōkuma ousted from the government. At the same time, the government announced that the emperor would grant a constitution, to take effect in 1890.

Formation of Parties

In response, Itagaki and his associates formed the Jiyutō (Liberal party), and Ōkuma followed by organizing the Kaishintō (Progressive party). Both parties advocated constitutional government with meaningful powers exercised by a parliament, but they differed somewhat in ideology and especially in composition. The

Jiyutō, linked to Tosa, drew much of its support from rural areas, where peasants and landlords were unhappy that their taxes were as high as they had been under the Tokugawa and resented bearing a heavier tax burden than that required of commerce and industry. The Jiyutō proclaimed itself "devoted to the expansion of liberty, protection of rights, promotion of happiness, and reform of society."[2] Ōkuma's party (linked to Hizen) was, in contrast, more urban and more moderate, advocating English-style liberalism and setting forth more specific proposals. It had the backing of merchants and industrialists. Although both opposed the government and advocated representative government, the two parties fought each other energetically. At the same time, the parties were troubled by internal factionalism; party splits were based on master–follower and patron–client relations rather than on differences in programs.

The organized opposition was further hampered by the need to operate under restrictive laws, including those promulgated to control political criticism. One source of such criticism was the press. The first newspaper appeared in 1871. Early papers had a small but elite readership and focused on politics, but restrictive press laws enacted in 1875 and revised in 1877 gave the home minister power to suppress publications and fine or imprison offenders. The 1880 Public Meeting Law placed all political meetings under police supervision. Included among those prohibited from attending such meetings were teachers and students. Nor were political associations allowed to recruit members or to combine or correspond with similar bodies. Finally, the 1887 Peace Preservation Law increased the home minister's powers of censorship and gave the police authority to expel people from a given area if they were deemed a threat to public tranquility. Some of the 570 shortly removed from Tokyo were criminals, but many were party members.

The Jiyutō was hurt not only by differences among its leaders but by antagonism within its membership, including conflicts between tenants and landlords. It proved impossible to contain within one party both the radicals who supported and even led peasant riots and the substantial landowners who were the objects of these attacks. In 1884 the party was dissolved. At the end of the same year, Ōkuma and his followers left the Kaishintō, although others stayed to keep it in existence. Criticism of the government continued, but this initial attempt to organize political parties turned out to have been premature.

In addition to suppressing its critics, the government was taking steps to increase its effectiveness. A system of centralized local administration was established that ended the Tokugawa tradition of local self-government. Villages and towns were now headed by officials appointed by the Home Ministry in Tokyo, which also controlled the police. From 1878 to 1880, local assemblies were created as sounding boards of public opinion, but their rights were limited to debate and their membership was restricted to men of means. The details of bureaucratic procedure were worked out and a civil service system was fashioned. A new code of criminal law was enacted, and work began on civil and commercial codes.

For the parties and the government alike, the promulgation of a constitution was seen as an essential component in fashioning a modern state uniting the people and the nation, as exemplified by the advanced countries of the West. However, the West offered a range of ways to accomplish this, with varying degrees of popular participation and power. To prepare for drawing up a constitution, Itō spent a year and a half in Europe during 1882 and 1883, mostly studying German theories and practices, which were most in keeping with the kind of constitution he and the other oligarchs wanted. After his return, several steps were taken in preparation for the constitution: a new peerage was created in 1884 composed of the old court nobility, former daimyo, and some members of the oligarchy; in 1885 a European-style Cabinet was created with Itō as premier; and in 1888 the Privy Council was organized as the highest government advisory board.

The Emperor and the Constitution

In the last chapter we noted the abandonment of the original effort to turn Japan into a Shinto state and the granting of religious tolerance, but this did not settle how such tolerance was to coexist with the belief in the divine descent of the emperor and in the legends in which it was grounded. The matter was settled in 1882 with the division of Shinto into Shrine Shinto and Sect Shinto. Most Shinto shrines, including the most prominent, such as Ise and Izumo, sacred to the Sun Goddess and her brother, respectively, came under Shrine Shinto. Thus, they were transformed into state institutions operating on a higher plane than the merely "religious" bodies, such as the various forms of Buddhism, Christianity (legalized in 1873), and ordinary Shinto shrines subsumed under Sect Shinto. This formula permitted the government to identify itself with the Shinto tradition from which it derived the mystique of the emperor, source of its own authority, and also meet the demands for religious tolerance voiced by Japanese reformers and Western nations.

In the name of the "restoration" of the emperor, strands of nativist thought and notions of modern monarchy were combined to form an image of the emperor—promoted by careful manipulation of the emperor himself and spread by word and picture. In his person, he represented both old and new: he was a divine being embodying a timeless spirit, but this was a modern divinity, resplendent in his flashy, new, world-class uniform (see Figure 9.1).

In 1889, after work on the constitution was completed, it was promulgated as a "gift" from the emperor to his people. The Meiji constitution remained in force until 1945. The emperor, "sacred and inviolable" father of the family state, was supreme. He was the locus and source of sovereignty: the land and people belonged to him. He had the power to declare war, conclude treaties, and command the army. He also had the right to open, recess, and dissolve the legislature, the power to veto its decisions, and the right to issue his own ordinances. The ministers were responsible not to the legislature but to the emperor. The legislature, called the Diet (derived from *dieta,* Late Latin for public assembly) consisted of two houses, the House of Peers and the House of Representatives. The latter was

FIGURE 9.1 *Portrait of the Meiji Emperor,* Takahashi Yuichi. Oil, 1880. Emperor Meiji—the reign name of the emperor of Japan from 1867 to 1912 (his given name was Mutsuhito)—ascended the throne when he was fifteen. He is depicted here in a modern medium, dressed in a manner appropriate to an emperor appearing on the world stage during the "long nineteenth century" that ended in 1914. (© Collection Imperial Household, Tokyo, Japan.)

elected by a constituency of tax-paying property owners amounting to about 450,000 men, or 1.1 percent of the total population. The most consequential power of the Diet was the power of the purse, but following the example of the Prussian constitution, the Meiji constitution provided for automatic renewal of the previous year's budget whenever the Diet failed to pass a new budget.

Only the emperor could take the initiative to revise the constitution. The emperor was the final authority, but he was also above politics; the actual exercise of imperial authority was divided between the Privy Council, the Cabinet, the Diet, and the general staff. Because the constitution failed to provide for coordination among these bodies, this was done by the men who had been governing in the emperor's name all along. Gradually, the practice developed of deciding on the selection of prime minister and other major questions by consulting the *genrō*—elder statesmen and leaders of the Meiji Restoration, such as Itō and Yamagata, who talked things out in private. Obviously, this could work only as long as there were *genrō* to consult.

The oligarchs who framed the constitution viewed the government, like the emperor in whose name it functioned, as above the divisive and unedifying world of party politics. But the parties turned out to be stronger than the oligarchs had expected. In the first election of 1890, the reconstituted Jiyutō won 130 seats; the Kaishintō, led again by Ōkuma, won 47; and only 79 members favoring the government were elected. As a result of this growing party strength, there was a stiff parliamentary battle over the budget in the first session of the Diet, which was resolved only after the premier, Yamagata, resorted to bribery and force. When the budget failed to pass the following year, the Diet was dissolved. During the subsequent elections (1892), the government used the police to discourage the opposition but failed to obtain a more tractable Diet. Imperial intervention in 1893 worked only temporarily. Another election was held in 1894, but the majority remained opposed to the government, and the Diet was dissolved after only a month and a half.

The war with China over Korea broke the political deadlock and provided temporary unity in the body politic. During the war, the government enjoyed enthusiastic support at home. By that time, Japan was quite different from what it had been twenty years earlier, when the oligarchs rejected intervention in Korea. The political developments were just one dimension of the transformation of Japan.

Western Influences on Values and Ideas

Enthusiasm for aspects of Western science and technology went back, as we have seen, to Tokugawa proponents of Dutch Learning, and from the start of Meiji there was a fashion of Western styles, including styles of dress. Representative of Japanese attitudes, the Meiji Emperor himself wore Western clothes and dressed his hair in the Western manner, as in his portrait by Takahashi Yuichi (1828–1894), shown in Figure 9.1. Not only the subject but also the artist was influenced by Western styles. Takahashi was conscious of his precursors: he revered Shiba Kōkan. Like Shiba and his own teacher, the prominent Western-style painter Kawakami Tōgai (1827–1881), Takahashi placed great value on realism. Most of his works, unlike the emperor's portrait, were still-life studies of familiar objects, and his most famous work is a realistic painting of a salmon. A major difference between Kawakami and Takahashi is that whereas the former saw Western art as no more than a necessary component of Western learning to be mastered for technical reasons, Takahashi also valued it as art.

Similarly, men turned to the West in other fields, not only because of practical reasons but also because they were attracted by the intrinsic nature of Western achievements. Prominent among such men were the intellectuals who, in 1873, formed the Meirokusha, a prestigious society devoted to all aspects of Western knowledge. These same men led what was known as the movement for "civilization and enlightenment" (*bummei kaika*). A leading theorist of this movement was Fukuzawa Yukichi, whose books on the West were mentioned earlier.

"Civilization and Enlightenment"

In eighteenth-century Europe, the intellectual movement known as the Enlightenment sought to put all traditional ideas and institutions to the test of reason. Impressed by the achievements of science as exemplified in the work of Sir

Isaac Newton (1642–1727), such philosophers as Voltaire (1694–1778) and Diderot (1713–1784) believed that reason could produce similar progress in solving human problems and that the main obstacles to truth and happiness were irrationality and superstition. Their greatest monument was the encyclopedia compiled by Diderot and his associates, a summation of the accomplishments of reason in all fields of human knowledge.

Japanese intellectuals such as Fukuzawa were strongly influenced by the European Enlightenment, particularly the emphasis on reason as an instrument for achieving progress. Their faith in progress was also confirmed by influential Western historians such as H. T. Buckle (1821–1862) and Francois Guizot (1787–1874). Firm belief in progress remained widespread during the nineteenth century, even after faith in reason had faded.

A corollary to this new concept of historical progress, in Japan as in the West, was a negative reevaluation of Chinese civilization, now regarded as unchanging and therefore decadent. No longer did the Japanese look up to China as the land of classical civilization; on the contrary, China was now a negative model, and, as China's troubles continued, the Japanese tended to regard it with condescension and concern. Now the source of "enlightenment" was in the West.

One of Fukuzawa's prime goals in advancing the cause of "civilization and enlightenment" was to stimulate in Japan the development of an independent and responsible citizenry. "It would not be far from wrong," he complained, "to say that Japan has a government but no people."[3] Tracing the lack of individual independence back to the traditional family, Fukuzawa advocated fundamental changes in that basic social institution. Ridiculing the ancient paragons of filial piety, he urged limitations on parental demands and authority. Although he viewed the role of women in terms of family and home, Fukuzawa also, on occasion, recommended greater equality between the sexes, championed monogamy, argued that women should be educated and allowed to hold property, and compared the Japanese woman with a dwarfed ornamental tree, artificially stunted.

According to Fukuzawa, history was made by the people, not by a few great leaders, and he thought it wrong to place too much faith in government or to give the political authorities too much power. His view of the role of government resembled the concept of the minimal state held by early European liberals. Consistent with these ideas, he did not enter government himself but disseminated his views in books and through a newspaper he founded. He also established what became Keiō University, a distinguished private university in Tokyo whose graduates played an important part in the world of business and industry.

In Fukuzawa's mind, the independence of the people and the independence of the country were linked; indeed, the former was a prerequisite for the latter. This view was widely held among the proponents of "enlightenment." For instance, the translator of the best-seller *Self-Help* by Samuel Smiles, whose Japanese version was published in Tokyo in 1871, explained that Western nations were strong because they possessed the spirit of liberty. John Stuart Mill's *On Liberty* appeared in Japanese translation the same year; Rousseau's *The Social Contract* was published in installments from 1882 to 1884. Fukuzawa, with his faith in progress, believed that the ultimate universal movement of history is in the direction of democracy and that individual liberty makes for national strength.

Fukuzawa's liberalism of the early 1870s was based on the Western Enlightenment concept of natural law, that is, that human affairs are governed by inherent concepts of right just as the physical world is governed by the laws of nature. This belief resembled the Neo-Confucian concept of *li* (principle) in linking the natural and human orders, but the European doctrine, unlike the Chinese, included the affirmation of innate human rights. It postulated an affirmative body of law stating the inherent rights of people in society, in whose name societies could overthrow unjust governments and establish new ones. It was to natural law that the American colonists appealed when they declared their independence in 1776; this was also the case when the French revolutionaries promulgated their Declaration of the Rights of Man in 1789.

Social Darwinism

After the "civilization and enlightenment" of the 1870s, discourse became more many-sided, but the concept of natural law was soon displaced by another, more recent, Western import: Social Darwinism. There were various versions of this doctrine, most notably those developed by the enormously influential Herbert Spencer (1820–1903), but all were based on the theory of evolution by natural selection presented in Charles Darwin's famous *On the Origin of Species* (1859). Darwin held that over time the various forms of life adapt to changing natural conditions and that those that adapt best are most likely to survive. This theory was summarized by the catch phrase "survival of the fittest." Social Darwinism was the application of these doctrines to the human realm. Applied to the success or failure of individuals within society, it justified brutal competition. Similarly, applied to the rise and fall of nations, it focused on military and civil competition. In both cases, "the fittest" were those who came out on top and thereby contributed to human progress.

Social Darwinism, purporting to have a scientific basis, offered a persuasive explanation of the present yet held out hope for a different future. It explained why Japan had been unable to resist the Western powers but held out the promise that a nation did not have to accept permanent inferiority. Thus, it justified Japanese efforts to develop national strength by mastering the learning and techniques of the West. Unlike natural law with its moral rules, it turned strength itself into a moral criterion and justified not only resisting foreign aggression but also engaging in aggressive expansionism.

In the mid-1870s, Fukuzawa first became skeptical of natural law and then abandoned it. He lost confidence in international law and formed a new view of international relations as an arena in which nations struggle for survival. In 1876 Fukuzawa remarked, "a few cannons are worth more than a hundred volumes of international law."[4] By 1882 he was willing to accept even autocracy if it meant strengthening the nation. Furthermore, he favored imperialist expansion, both to assure Japan's safety and to bring the benefits of "civilization" to neighboring countries such as Korea. Thus, he welcomed the war when it came in 1894.

Fukuzawa found words of praise for some aspects of the Japanese tradition, including the samurai value of loyal service, but continued to look primarily to the West for his models and ideas. However, he avoided the extremes of Westernization. In early Meiji some thinkers allowed their enthusiasm to get the better of their judgment, and there were all kinds of extreme proposals for radical Westernization, including one to abolish the national language and another to intermarry with Europeans. However, not all supporters of Westernization were genuine enthusiasts. Many desired to impress Westerners to be accepted as equals and to speed treaty revision. This was the motive behind a variety of movements, ranging from a drive to reform public morals to the revision of the legal code. It also accounts for one of the symbols of the era, the Rokumeikan, a hall completed in 1883 to accommodate mixed foreign and Japanese social gatherings. Designed by an English architect in the elaborate manner of the European Renaissance, it provided the setting for dinners, card parties, and fancy dress balls.

The Arts

In the arts, Western influence was both audible and visible. It affected the music taught in the schools and that performed in military bands. In literature, the 1870s and 1880s have been defined as "the age of translation,"[5] during which Japanese versions of European novels were published and read with great enthusiasm to be joined, in the mid-1880s, by the first modern Japanese novels, worthy forerunners of great achievements to come. In painting, we have already noted the work of Takahashi, but the presence of the West was also visible in more traditional genres. Sometimes called the last of the major *ukiyo-e* artists was Kobayashi Kiochika (1847–1915). He introduced Western light and shading into *ukiyo-e,* using the principles of Western perspective yet retaining a traditional Japanese sense of color (see Figure 9.2).

Western styles of painting were advanced by foreign artists who taught in Japan and by Japanese who studied abroad, particularly in France, bringing back new styles and ways of looking at the world. Kuroda Seiki (1866–1924) studied in France from 1884 to 1893, and it was there that he painted *Morning Toilet* (see Figure 9.3), which caused a stir when exhibited in Tokyo in 1894 and unleashed a storm of controversy when shown in more conservative Kyoto the following year. Japan and East Asia had no tradition of painting the nude. There were protests that Kuroda's painting was pornography, not art. But Kuroda won the battle and went on to become one of Japan's most influential Western-style painters.

The initial enthusiasm for Western art led to the neglect of, and even disdain for, traditional art. This shocked the American Ernest Fenollosa (1853–1908) when he came to Japan in 1878 to teach at Tokyo University. Fenollosa did what

FIGURE 9.2 *Train at Night,* Kobayashi Kiyochika. Woodcut. This was the great age of the railway, a force and a symbol of technological and economic transformation. With his unique techniques of light and shadow, the artist sets his train rushing through the night against a calm, seemingly eternal Japanese landscape. (© Arthur M. Sackler Gallery, Smithsonian Institution, Washington, D.C. Robert O. Muller Collection.)

he could to make the new generation of Westernized Japanese aware of the greatness of their artistic heritage. He was an admirer of the last of the masters of the China-influenced Kanō school, Kanō Hogai (1828–1898) and, with the younger Okakura Tenshin (1862–1913), sparked a revived interest in traditional styles. Meanwhile, Japanese art fascinated such Western artists as Gaugin, van Gogh, and Whistler.

Conservatism and Nationalism

The reaction against the enthusiasm of the early Meiji Westernizers was not limited to the arts. Starting in the late 1880s, there was a tide of conservative thought. Many were attracted by the old formula, "Eastern ethics and Western science," a concept earlier advanced by Sakuma Shōzan.

Some feared that acceptance of a foreign culture was a step toward national decline and sought ways to be both modern and Japanese, to adopt universalist aspects of Western culture yet retain what was of value in their own past. The

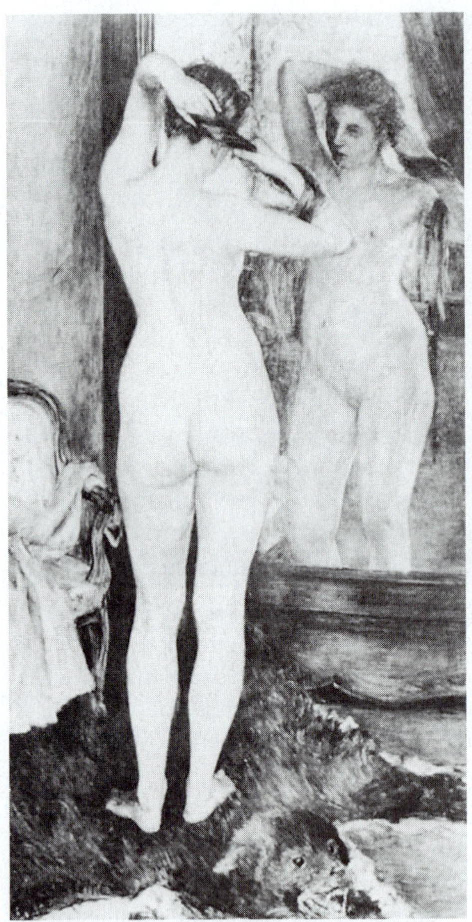

FIGURE 9.3 *Morning Toilet,* Kuroda Seiki. Kuroda learned an academic style under the French painter Louis-Joseph-Raphael Collin but also acquired an Impressionist vision that incorporated bright outdoor light. Oil, 1893, 38.6 in × 70.3 in. (© National Research Institute of Cultural Properties, Tokyo.)

educated and sensitive were especially troubled by the tensions inherent in a program of modernization under traditionalist auspices. Western scientific rationalism could, by questioning the founding myth, undermine the throne and polity. In 1892, a Tokyo University professor was forced to resign after he wrote that Shinto was a "survival of a primitive form of worship."[6] That was sacrilege. Similarly, Western individualism, fostered by the policy of modernization, clashed with the old family values that, Fukuzawa notwithstanding, continued strong and remained in official favor.

Drawing on German thought, new conservative voices affirmed Japanese uniqueness and their belief in national progress, arguing that change should come about gradually, growing organically out of past traditions, with emphasis not on the individual but on the state. There was talk about a national "essence," although little agreement on how it should be defined.

Akira Iriye has drawn attention to the weakness in Japan of the liberal elements that Western nationalism inherited from its origins, when it "had been part of the democratic revolution in which national identity was sought less in a country's ethnic and historical uniqueness than in the belief that it embodied certain universal values such as freedom and human rights." Such a nationalism "could often be transformed into internationalism because a nation could envision a world order that embodied some of the universalistic principles that it exemplified itself."[7] Japanese particularism often took a benign form but was also prone to lead to cultural exceptionalism and political chauvinism, even if Japanese nationalists were hardly unique in celebrating (and exaggerating) the uniqueness of their nation. Such views could easily lead to a sense of special national mission.

Some Japanese intellectuals, notably Okakura, soon went on to define a wider world role for Japan by emphasizing Japan's Asian roots. Thus, in a book bearing the revealing title, *The Ideals of the East* (1902), Okakura presented the nation's mission in terms of preserving an "Asian" cultural essence. Not only Japan's cultural place in the world but also its political mission remained key issues throughout modern times.

Education

Japanese intellectual and political leaders were quick to realize the importance of education in fashioning a new Japan capable of competing with the West. In this, as in other areas, they showed great interest in the practices and institutions of European countries and of the United States. One member of the Iwakura mission paid special attention to education and wrote fifteen volumes on the subject after his return from abroad.

At the beginning of the Meiji Period, Japan sent many students overseas to obtain the advanced training it could not provide at home. One-eighth of the Ministry of Education's first budget (1873) was designated for this purpose, and 250 students were sent to the United States and Europe on government scholarships that year. Furthermore, many foreign instructors from the same countries were brought to Japan to teach in various specialized schools. However, these were temporary expedients to be used until Japan's own modern educational system was in operation. By the late 1880s, the number of foreign instructors was down, and only fifty to eighty students were being sent abroad by the government annually. A landmark in the history of higher education was the establishment of Tokyo University in 1877 with four faculties: physical science, law, literature, and medicine.

Considerable progress was made in building a complete educational system to replace the uncoordinated network of now-outdated academies and *han,* temple, and family schools. Yet actual accomplishments fell short of the ambitious plan drawn up in 1872 calling for 8 universities, 256 middle schools (equivalent to American high and junior high schools), and 53,760 elementary schools. Thirty years later, in 1902, there were only 2 universities, 222 middle schools, and 27,076 elementary schools. Similarly, the government had to retreat from its 1872 ordinance making four years of education compulsory for all children. Among the difficulties this program encountered were money problems (elementary education was locally financed), teacher shortages, and the reluctance of rural parents to send their children to school. However, by the time four years of compulsory education were reintroduced in 1900, most children who were supposed to be in school were in attendance, and in 1907 the government was able to increase the period to six years. By that time the teachers were predominantly graduates of Japanese Normal Schools (teacher training institutes), the first of which was established in Tokyo in 1872 with the assistance of Marion M. Scott, an American educator.

When the Ministry of Education was first established in 1871, the French system of highly centralized administration was adopted. Although local schools were locally financed, the ministry not only determined the general direction of education but also prescribed textbooks, supervised teacher training, and generally controlled the curriculum of schools throughout the country. Government educational policy therefore was decisive in determining what was taught.

There was wide agreement among political leaders that an essential function of the educational system was to provide the people with the skills necessary for modernization. They realized that not only factories and businesses but also armies and navies require a certain level of literacy and command of simple arithmetic among the rank and file, as well as higher education for managers and officers. Beyond that, the leaders recognized that schools foster values and looked to them to help mold the Japanese people into a nation. On the question of specific moral content, however, there were intense disagreements reflecting different visions of Japan's future. In the 1870s, when enthusiasm for the West ran high, even elementary readers and moral texts were frequently translated from English and French for use in Japanese schools. But there were also critics who insisted that the schools should preserve traditional Confucian/Japanese values. Another influential position was opposed to both Western liberal values and to traditionalist ideals but looked to the schools to indoctrinate the populace with modern nationalist values. An influential proponent of this last position was Mori Arinori (1847–1889), minister of education from 1885 until he was assassinated by a nationalist fanatic in 1889.

Although Mori had a strong hand in shaping the educational system, the most important Meiji pronouncement on the subject was drafted under the influence of Motoda Eifu (1818–1891), the emperor's lecturer on Chinese books, who for twenty years provided Confucian guidance and advice. This was the *Rescript on Education,* issued in 1890. For half a century it remained the basic statement of the purpose of education, memorized by generations of schoolchildren. It begins by attributing "the glory of the fundamental character of Our Empire" to the imperial ancestors who "deeply and firmly implanted virtue," calls on his majesty's subjects to observe the usual Confucian virtues beginning with filiality toward their parents, and enjoins them to "pursue learning and cultivate arts" for intellectual and moral development and "to advance public good and promote common interests." Furthermore, "should emergency arise, offer yourselves courageously to the State, and thus guard and maintain the prosperity of Our Imperial Throne coeval with heaven and earth."[8] In this document, Confucianism is identified with the throne (no mention is made of its foreign origins), and a premium is placed on patriotic service to the state and to the throne. These values were further drummed into schoolchildren in compulsory ethics classes. Education was intended to prepare Japan for the future in the name of the past.

Modernizing the Economy

In the twenty years that followed consolidation of the Meiji regime, Japan laid the foundations for a modern industrial economy. The nation was still primarily agrarian, but Western experience had shown that capital accumulated through the sale of surplus agricultural production and labor obtained through the migration of surplus rural population to the cities were necessary conditions for industrial development. Both conditions existed in Meiji Japan.

Japanese agriculture had become more efficient because of the introduction of new seed strains, new fertilizers, and new methods of cultivation. New land for farming was being opened, especially in Hokkaido. New applications of science to agriculture were being tried at experimental stations and agricultural colleges. In consequence, during the fourteen years preceding the Sino-Japanese War, rice yields increased by 30 percent, and other crops showed comparable gains; per capita rice consumption increased. Agriculture was further stimulated by the development of a substantial export market for silk and tea and a growing domestic demand for cotton. Thus, trade also helped generate capital needed for investment in manufacturing.

Increased agricultural production did not result in major changes for the grower. Village government and the organization of village labor remained largely the same. Rents remained high: it was not unusual for a peasant's rent to equal half his rice crop. Profits resulting from the commercialization of agriculture went to the landlord, who handled the sale, rather than to the tenant. Even the creation of factory jobs did little to relieve population pressure on the land.

Much of the factory labor was performed by peasant girls sent to the city to supplement farm incomes for several years before they were married. Housed in company dormitories and strictly supervised, they were an inexpensive workforce. When times were bad and factory operations slowed, they could be laid off and returned to their villages. It was a system advantageous to both the landlord and the industrialist.

In Western countries, the industrial revolution was largely carried out by private enterprise. In Japan, however, where it was government policy to modernize so as to catch up with the West, the government took the initiative. The Meiji regime invested heavily in the economic infrastructure—those basic public services that must be in place before an industrial economy can grow: education, transportation, communication, and so forth. As previously mentioned, students were sent abroad at public expense to study Western technologies and techniques, and foreigners were brought to Japan to teach in their areas of expertise. A major effort went into railroads. The first line was completed in 1872, running between Tokyo and Yokohama. By the mid-1890s there were 2000 miles of track, much of it privately owned, because government initiative was followed by private investment once the feasibility, and especially the profitability, of railroads had been established. Transportation within cities began to quicken as Kyoto, in 1895, became the first Japanese city to have trolleys.

This sequence of state initiative followed by private development can also be observed in manufacturing. The government took the lead in establishing and operating cement works, plants manufacturing tiles, textile mills (silk and cotton), shipyards, mines, and munitions works. The government felt these industries were essential, but private interests were unwilling to risk their capital in untried ventures with little prospect of profits in the near term. Thus, if such ventures were to be started, the government had to start them and finance the initial period of operations.

The Zaibatsu

The expenditure of capital required for this effort, the payment due to samurai on their bonds, the costs of the Satsuma Rebellion, and an adverse balance of trade combined to create a government financial crisis. Rising inflation damaged the government's purchasing power and hurt the samurai, whose income depended on the interest paid on their bonds. These problems came to a head in 1880. The government's response was mainly to cut back on expenditures, leading to a deflation generally seen as preparing the way for a period of economic growth sustained to the end of World War I.

As part of its economy move, the government decided, late in 1880, to sell at public auction all its enterprises with the exception of the munitions plants. Most buyers were men who were friendly with government leaders and who recognized the long-term advantages of buying the factories, which were selling at bargain prices. These enterprises did not become profitable immediately, but when they did, this small group of well-connected companies enjoyed a controlling position in the modern sector of the economy. These were the *zaibatsu,* huge financial and industrial combines.

The *zaibatsu* were usually organized by new entrepreneurs, because most of the old Tokugawa merchant houses were too set in their ways to make a successful transition into the new world of Meiji. The outstanding exception to this generalization was the house of Mitsui, originally established in Edo as a textile house and enriched by its banking activities. When it became apparent that government initiatives were creating new economic opportunities in commerce and industry, Mitsui brought new men into the company to take advantage of them. The new leadership was vigorous and capable, establishing first a bank and then a trading company. These institutions became important factors in Japan's foreign commerce; they also engaged in domestic transactions, profiting handsomely from handling army supply contracts during the Satsuma Rebellion. In 1881, Mitsui bought government coal mines, which ultimately contributed greatly to its wealth and power. By that time, the traditional drapery business had been relegated to a sideline and delegated to a subordinate house.

In contrast to Mitsui, the Mitsubishi *zaibatsu* was founded by a former samurai from Tosa, bold and ruthless in the wars of commerce. This was Iwasaki Yatarō

(1834–1885) who developed a strong shipping business by obtaining government contracts, government subsidies, and for a time, even government guarantee of its dividend payments. At one point the government lent the company ships, a loan that eventually became a gift. Mitsubishi also benefited greatly from doing government business during the Taiwan expedition of 1874 and again during the Satsuma Rebellion. The company grew strong enough to displace some of its foreign competitors, and around its shipping business it developed banking and insurance facilities and entered foreign trade. It also went into mining, and its acquisition of the government-established Nagasaki shipyard assured its future as the leader in shipbuilding and heavy industry, although Iwasaki did not live long enough to see the shipyard turn a profit. Iwasaki ruled the combine like a personal domain, but he also recruited an able managerial staff composed largely of graduates of Fukuzawa's Keiō University.

For Iwasaki, personal ambition and patriotism were fused. As he conceived it, his mission was to compete with the great foreign shipping companies, and he was convinced that whatever benefited his company was also good for the nation. Not everyone, however, agreed with this assessment. For a time Iwasaki had to face the competition of a rival company, one of whose organizers was Shibusawa Eiichi (1840–1931), one of the great Meiji entrepreneurs and bankers, founder of the Tokyo Chamber of Commerce and Bankers' Association, and a believer in joint-stock companies, in competition, and in business independence from government. Iwasaki won this battle, but Shibusawa remained enormously influential, not only because of his economic power but also because of his energetic advocacy of higher business standards and the view that business could contribute to public good by remaining independent of government.

The success of such men as Iwasaki and Shibusawa should not obscure the fact that new ventures continued to entail risk. Not all new ventures were successful. For example, the attempt to introduce sheep raising into Japan was a failure. Initial attempts at organizing insurance companies were similarly ill conceived because they used rates and tables appropriate for European rather than Japanese conditions. But insurance companies were finally established, and altogether successes outnumbered failures.

One reason for the success of the *zaibatsu* and other new companies was their ability to attract capable and dedicated executives. Formerly, many capable members of the samurai class had refused to enter the business world because concern with moneymaking was considered abhorrent. But this obstacle was largely overcome after the restoration, not merely because these were now ex-samurai families but also because commercial and industrial development was required for the good of the state. Those who helped build a strong bank, trading company, or manufacturing industry were seen as rendering a service to the emperor and to Japan. Indeed, the government's initial sponsorship of many enterprises lent them some of the prestige of government service. Many companies were created by men of samurai origins, helping make business socially acceptable.

The association of business with government also influenced business ideology in Japan. From the beginning, the ethos of modern Japan business focused on its contributions to the Japanese nation, not on the notions of economic liberalism that prevailed in the West. The company did not exist only, or even primarily, to make a profit for its shareholders. Likewise, provisions were made in the internal organization of the business to encourage group solidarity and mutual responsibility, to give participants in the venture a strong sense of company loyalty, and to keep workers in their place. The association of business and government also helped justify the government's influence on business and helped account for continued acceptance of policies that kept consumption low even as national income rose.

In somewhat similar fashion, in the 1890s the argument first appeared that Japanese factories were "exceptional sites of warm-hearted social relations,"[9] a contention that grew more insistent in the early twentieth century as movements for legislation concerning factory conditions, working hours, child labor, and so on gained momentum.

In describing the *zaibatsu* and other modern companies, it should not be supposed that large-scale trading, mining, and manufacturing represented the whole of Japanese business. On the contrary, many small-scale establishments continued to function well past the early Meiji era. But the new companies did represent major growth and change in economic activity, and they signaled a change in Japanese perceptions of Japan's role in international affairs. This was reflected in economic terms by efforts to preserve economic independence—for example, by protecting home markets, conserving foreign exchange, and avoiding dependence on foreign capital to assure Japanese ownership of railways and other large-scale enterprises. It was also reflected in Japanese foreign policy and especially in the modernization and deployment of the Japanese military.

The Military

Japanese military forces engaged in three major operations in the twenty years following the restoration: the Taiwan expedition of 1874, the Satsuma Rebellion of 1877, and the Sino-Japanese War of 1894–1895. The first two operations were fought primarily for domestic purposes as the new Meiji government sought to consolidate its power. The Sino-Japanese War, on the other hand, was an outward-looking venture from the start, a test of strength with China on the Korean Peninsula. An even more striking difference was in the quality of Japanese military organization, armament, and tactical skill.

The Taiwan expedition of 1874 was far from brilliant. The landing was poorly executed, hygiene was so defective that disease took a great toll, and equipment had to be abandoned because it was unsuitable for use in a tropical climate. Similarly, the force that suppressed the Satsuma Rebellion did so because of its superiority in numbers and equipment rather than its military excellence.

To improve the quality of the army, Yamagata directed a major reorganization in 1878. He established a general staff along German lines, and Germany became the overall model for the army, which had previously been influenced by France. By strengthening the reserves, the military potential was greatly increased. During the ten or fifteen years before the Sino-Japanese War, generous military appropriations enabled the army to acquire modern equipment, mostly manufactured in Japanese arsenals and plants, and the creation of a staff college and improved training methods further strengthened the army and made it more modern. Like Yamagata, most leading generals were from Chōshū.

Naval modernization was similar to that of the army, except that England was the model and continued to be a source from which some larger vessels were purchased. In 1894 the navy possessed twenty-eight modern ships with a total displacement of 57,000 tons and twenty-four torpedo boats. Most importantly, Japan had the facilities to maintain, repair, and arm its fleet. From the start, most naval leadership came from Satsuma.

The military is a good example of the way in which the various facets of modernization were intertwined and supported each other, because the armed forces both benefited from and contributed to the process. Not only did they stimulate new industries, ranging from armaments to tin cans, but it was also in the army that the rural conscript was first exposed to a wider and more modern world. Indeed, when conscription was first introduced, many men from backward districts were bewildered by the accouterments of modern life. There are reports that some bowed in reverence to the stove in their barracks, taking it for some kind of god. For many men, the army provided the introduction to shoes. Before the spread of education, some men learned to read and write in the army. All were exposed to the new values of nationalism and loyalty to the emperor. Most also learned to smoke (cigarettes were first reported in 1877) and to drink native alcoholic beverages and excellent Japanese beer, first brewed in the 1870s. Most had their first experience with the modern city. Soldiers enjoyed a better diet, receiving more meat than the average Japanese. But discipline was harsh, and draft dodging was rampant. Nevertheless, the majority served.

In this and other ways life was changing for that majority, but compared with later times, it was changing slowly. There were changes in style, such as glass replacing paper inside the house or the use of Western umbrellas outside, but as Susan B. Hanley has shown, the essential consumption patterns and basic components of the material culture of the Japanese people remained traditional and stable.[10]

Korea and the Sino-Japanese War of 1894–1895

Like Vietnam, Korea had adopted Chinese political institutions and ideology and maintained a tributary relationship with China yet guarded its political independence. Again, as in Vietnam, differences in size, social organization, and cultural tradition insured the development of a distinct Sino-Korean culture. In the nineteenth century, however, Korea was sorely troubled by internal problems and external pressures. The Yi dynasty (1392–1910), then in its fifth century, was in serious decline. Korea's peasantry suffered from "a skewered or concentrated pattern of landholding; small average per capita holdings; high rates of tenancy; a regressive tax structure; false registration of taxable land; extortion and illegal charges and gratuities at tax collection time; and usury, especially official usury in the management of the grain loan system."[11] There was a serious uprising in the North in 1811. In 1833 there were rice riots in Seoul. And in 1862 there were rebellions in the South.

From 1864 to 1873, there was a last attempt to save the situation through a traditional program of reform initiated by the regent, or Taewongun (Grand Prince, 1821–1898), who was the father of the king. The reform program proved strong enough to provoke a reaction but was not sufficiently drastic, even in conception, to transform Korea into a strong and viable state capable of dealing with the dangers of the modern world. That world was gradually closing in on Korea.

During the first two-thirds of the century, several incidents occurred involving Western ships and foreign demands. Korea's initial policy was to resist all attempts to "open" the country by referring those seeking to establish diplomatic relations back to Beijing. This policy was successful as long as it was directed at countries for which Korea was of peripheral concern, but this had never been the case for Japan. Japan, therefore, was the most insistent of the powers trying to pry Korea from the Chinese orbit. In 1876 Japan forced Korea to sign a treaty establishing diplomatic relations and providing for the opening of three ports to trade. The treaty also stipulated that Korea was now "independent," but this did not settle matters because China still considered Korea a tributary. Insurrections in Seoul in 1882 and 1884 led to increased Chinese and Japanese involvement in Korea, including military involvement, always on opposing sides. But outright war was averted by talks between Itō Hirobumi and Li Hongzhang, which led to a formal agreement between China and Japan to withdraw their forces and inform each other if either decided in the future that it was necessary to send in troops.

During the next years the Chinese Resident in Korea was Yuan Shikai (1859–1916), a protégé of Li, originally sent to Korea to train Korean troops. Yuan successfully executed Li's policy of vigorous assertion of Chinese control, dominating the court, effecting a partial union of Korean and Chinese commercial customs, and setting up a telegraph service and a merchant route between Korea and China.

Conflicting ambitions in Korea made war between China and Japan highly probable; the catalyst was the Tonghak Rebellion. Tonghak, literally "Eastern Learning," was an amalgam of Chinese, Buddhist, and native Korean religious ideas and practices. As so often before in East Asian history, the religious organization took on a political dimension, serving as a vehicle for expressions of discontent with a regime in decay and for agitation against government corruption and foreign encroachments. Finally outlawed, it was involved in considerable rioting in 1893, which turned to rebellion the following year when Korea was struck by famine. When the Korean government requested Chinese assistance, Li responded by sending 1500 men and informing the Japanese, whose troops were already on the way. The rebellion was quickly suppressed, but it proved easier to send than to remove the troops.

When Japanese soldiers entered Seoul, broke into the palace, and kidnapped the king and queen, Li responded by sending more troops, and war was inevitable. It was a war that everyone, except the Japanese, expected China to win, but all parties were stunned when Japan defeated China on sea and on land. Begun in July 1894, the war was over by March 1895. In retrospect, the reasons for the outcome are easy to see: Japan was better equipped, better led, and more united than China, a country hampered by internal division, corruption, and inadequate leadership in the field. Equipped with shells, some of which were filled with sawdust rather than gunpowder, and commanded by an old general who lined up the fleet as though he were still organizing a cavalry charge, it is no wonder that China lost the war at sea. Furthermore, powerful governors-general considered it Li's war, not theirs, and were slow in participating; the southern navy remained aloof.

The Treaty of Shimonoseki (April 1895)

The war was terminated by the Treaty of Shimonoseki. China relinquished all claims to a special role in Korea and recognized that country as an independent state (although its troubles were far from over). In addition, China paid Japan an indemnity and ceded it Taiwan and the Pescadores, thus starting the formation of the Japanese Empire. A further indication that the Japanese had now joined the ranks of the imperialist nations was the extension to Japan of most-favored-nation status, along with the opening of seven additional Chinese ports. Japan was also to receive the Liaodong Peninsula but, after diplomatic intervention by Russia, Germany, and France, had to settle for an additional indemnity instead. The effects of the treaty on Korea, on domestic Chinese politics, and on international relations in the area are considered in the following chapters. Here, it should be noted that the treaty marked an unprecedented shift in the East Asian balance of power, a shift from China to Japan that was to continue until Japan's defeat in World War II.

Notes

1. John W. Downer, "Sizing Up (and Breaking Down) Japan," in Helen Hardacre, ed., *The Postwar Development of Japanese Studies in the United States* (Leiden: Brill, 1998), p. 14.
2. First article of the party platform as quoted by Kyu Hyun Kim, "Political Ideologies of the Early Meiji Parties," in *Hardacre, The Postwar Development of Japanese Studies in the United States,* p. 400.
3. Quoted in Carmen Blacker, *The Japanese Enlightenment: A Study of Fukuzawa Yukichi* (London: Cambridge Univ. Press, 1964), p. 111.
4. Quoted in Blacker, *The Japanese Enlightenment: A Study of Fukuzawa Yukichi,* p. 128.
5. Donald Keene, "The Age of Translation," Chapter 3, in *Dawn to the West: Japanese Literature of the Modern Era—Fiction* (New York: Holt, Rinehart and Winston, 1984), pp. 55–75.
6. Quoted in Kenneth B. Pyle, *The New Generation in Meiji Japan: Problems in Cultural Identity, 1885–1895* (Stanford: Stanford Univ. Press, 1969), p. 124.

7. Akira Iriye, in Marius Jansen, ed., *The Cambridge History of Japan, Vol. 5: The Nineteenth Century* (Cambridge: Cambridge Univ. Press, 1989), p. 754.
8. "Rescript on Education," in David John Lu, *Sources of Japanese History, Vol. 1* (New York: McGraw-Hill, 1974), pp. 70–71.
9. Andrew Gordon, "The Invention of Japanese-Style Labor Management," in Stephen Vlastos, *Mirror of Modernity: Invented Traditions of Modern Japan* (Berkeley: Univ. of California Press, 1998), p. 19.
10. Susan B. Hanley, "The Material Culture: Stability in Transition," in Marius Jansen and Gilbert Rozman, eds., *Japan in Transition: From Tokugawa to Meiji* (Princeton Univ. Press, 1986), pp. 467–69 sic passim.
11. James B. Palais, *Politics and Policy in Traditional Korea* (Cambridge: Harvard Univ. Press, 1975), p. 63.

10

Imperial Japan: 1895–1931

I. Late Meiji (1895–1912)

II. The Taishō Period (1912–1926) and the 1920s

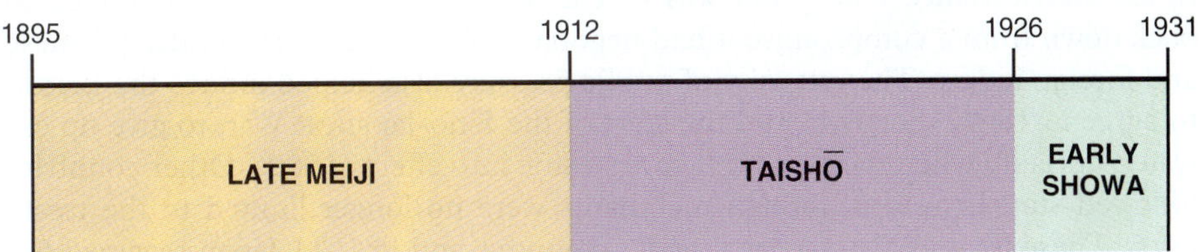

Between the founding of the empire in 1895 and the advent of militarism in 1931, Japan increasingly participated in world history. It was in many respects a success story, but later history was to reveal the potential for disaster. The death of the Meiji Emperor in July 1912, although not as momentous as the abdication of China's last emperor earlier that year, marked something of a watershed and was experienced as such. People at the time felt that the passing of the emperor, who had presided over Japan's transformation for more than forty years, signified the end of an era, a judgment with which many later scholars have concurred. We have divided this chapter accordingly.

Foreign Policy and Empire Building

From the beginning, Meiji foreign policy aimed to achieve national security and equality of national status. But how were these to be defined and attained? As Louise Young put it, "In an international order where the 'strong devour the weak,' Japanese concluded they could either join with the West as a 'guest at the table' or be served up with China and Korea as part of the feast."[1] Both the army's German adviser and Yamagata Aritomo, the hardheaded, realistic architect of Japan's modern army, held that Korea was the key to Japan's security and in 1890 propounded the thesis that Japan must defend its "line of sovereignty" and secure its "line of interest," which ran through Korea. The Japanese navy, heavily influenced by the ideas of Admiral Alfred T. Mahan (1840–1914), an American advocate of the importance of sea power, demanded Japanese naval domination of the surrounding seas. Colonies were desired as "the ultimate status symbol" and for strategic reasons. Economic and other considerations also played a part, but an authority on the subject concluded "no colonial empire of modern times was as clearly shaped by strategic considerations."[2]

Equality was as elusive a concept as security, but at a minimum it required the end of extraterritoriality and the restoration of tariff autonomy. In the 1870s work began on revision of the law codes to bring them into line with Western practices so that the powers would no longer have reason to insist on maintaining jurisdiction over their own subjects. Even before the lengthy process of revising the codes had been completed, there was strong and vociferous public demand for an end to extraterritoriality. One result was that in 1886 the government was forced to back down from a compromise it had negotiated for mixed courts under Japanese and foreign judges. The intensity of public pressure also helped induce the British to agree in 1894, shortly before the start of the Sino-Japanese War, to give up extraterritoriality when the new legal codes came into effect (1889). Other countries followed suit. In return, foreign merchants were no longer limited to the treaty ports. These treaties also secured tariff autonomy, and in 1911 Japan regained full control over its customs duties.

By that time, Japan, under the most-favored-nation clause of the Treaty of Shimonoseki, was enjoying extraterritorial rights in China and benefiting from China's lack of tariff autonomy. As a result, Japan's exports to China increased both absolutely and in proportion of total exports, rising from less than 10 percent before 1894 to 25 percent by World War I. A commercial treaty negotiated with China in 1896 gave Japan and other nations enjoying most-favored-nations treatment the right to establish factories in the treaty ports, spurring investment in China but limiting China's ability to nurture its own industries.

The acquisition of Taiwan gratified the navy, but most of the public shared the army's disappointment and outrage when French, German, and Russian intervention forced Japan to give up the strategic Liaodong Peninsula. The government's response to this setback was to follow a prudent foreign policy but increase military spending. Accordingly, Japan exercised careful restraint during the Boxer Rebellion (1900) and earned respect for the disciplined behavior of its soldiers.

Japan's chief rival in northeast Asia was Russia, which had demonstrated its intent to become a major power in the area by constructing the Trans-Siberian Railway (1891–1903). In 1896 Russia had obtained permission to run tracks across northern Manchuria directly to Vladivostok, and in 1898 it obtained the lease of Port Arthur on the Liaodong Peninsula, thereby acquiring a much-needed warm-water port but further alienating the Japanese, who had so recently been denied the peninsula and were concerned to hold their own in the scramble to gain concessions from China.

Russia also interfered in Korea, allying itself with conservative opponents of Japanese-backed reformers. Agreements reached in 1896, 1897, and 1898 kept the Russo-Japanese rivalry from exploding into immediate war, but Russian use of the Boxer Rebellion to entrench its interests in Manchuria intensified Japanese apprehensions.

Japan was not alone in its concern over Russian expansion. Great Britain, which had not joined the intervention after the Sino-Japanese War, had long been alarmed over Russia's eastward expansion. In 1902 it abandoned its policy of "splendid isolation" to form an alliance with Japan. Great Britain recognized Japan's special interest in Korea, and each nation recognized the other's interests in China. Britain and Japan agreed that each would remain neutral in any war

FIGURE 10.1 *Sea Battle near Port Arthur, March 10, 1904: A Sailor from the Sazanami Jumps to the Russian Ship and Kicks Its Captain into the Sea,* Migita Toshihide (1866–1905). Woodcut print triptych, ink and color on paper, 1904. (© Arthur M. Sackler Gallery of Art, Smithsonian Institution, Washington, D.C. Gift of Gregory and Patricia Krugla [S1999.131a-c])

fought by the other against a single enemy in East Asia and that each would assist the other if either were attacked by two powers at once. This meant that if Japan and Russia went to war, British forces would join Japan if France or Germany supported Russia. Japan would not have to face a European coalition alone. This alliance with the foremost world power gave Japan new prestige and confidence. But Russia remained determined to maintain and expand its position in East Asia.

These conflicting ambitions led to the Russo-Japanese War of 1904–1905, fought both on land (mostly in Manchuria, which was Chinese territory) and at sea. For both belligerents the cost was heavy, but victory went to Japan. Despite some hard fighting, Russian troops were driven back on land, and in two separate naval actions the Japanese destroyed virtually the entire Russian navy. The naval war was spectacular and much celebrated in Japan (see Figure 10.1). Japan attacked the Russian Pacific fleet at Port Arthur just before the declaration of war. Russia's Baltic fleet then embarked on an 18,000-mile trip, sailing around Africa because Britain refused passage through the Suez Canal. Its destination was Vladivostok, but it was demolished by the Japanese in a decisive battle in the Tsushima Straits, between Japan and Korea. Only four of the thirty-five Russian ships reached Vladivostok.

Not only in Japan but throughout Asia people were deeply impressed by this first victory of a non-Western nation over a European power. In Russia, these defeats had fateful consequences. The failed Revolution of 1905 was a precursor of the successful Revolution of 1917. Although victorious, the Japanese were exhausted. Thus, both sides were happy to accept the offer from the United States to mediate and to participate at a peace conference in Portsmouth, New Hampshire.

In the resulting Portsmouth Treaty, Japan gained recognition of its supremacy in Korea, the transfer of Russian interests in Manchuria (railways and leaseholds on the Liaodong Peninsula), and cession of the southern half of Sakhalin Island (north of Hokkaido). Japan had demanded all of Sakhalin and a war indemnity, but Russia successfully resisted these demands. This aroused the anger of the Japanese public, which, drunk on victory and uninformed of their country's inability to continue the war, had expected more. In Tokyo the treaty was greeted by three days of rioting.

One immediate result of Japan's victory was economic expansion in Manchuria, where the semiofficial South Manchurian Railway Company was soon engaged in shipping, public utilities, and mining, as well as railroading. From the start, the Japanese government held half of the company's shares and appointed its officers. Although private Japanese companies also entered Manchuria, it has been calculated that in 1914, 79 percent of all Japanese investments in Manchuria were in the South Manchurian Railway. Furthermore, 69 percent of all Japanese investments in China before World War I were in Manchuria. Japan's economic reach stretched beyond its formal empire.

Economic and Social Developments

Both the Sino-Japanese War and the Russo-Japanese War stimulated the Japanese economy. Both wars were followed by an outburst of nationalist sentiment that gave a strong boost to heavy industry (for example, Yawata Steel Works, established in 1897) and to armaments, including shipbuilding. After 1906, Japan produced ships comparable in size and quality to any in the world. Japanese technology continued to progress, with advances in new fields such as electrical engineering. Light industry, particularly textiles, continued to flourish and dominate the modern sector. The most important item of export, amounting to nearly half the total, was in partly finished goods, especially silk. (Because of superior quality control, Japanese silk exports overtook those of China.) Trade figures revealing an increasing emphasis on the import of raw materials and the export of manufactured goods are indicative of economic change, and in 1912 the industrial sector accounted for 36 percent of the gross national product (GNP). Other statistics indicate increases in labor productivity and in urbanization, widening the gulf between city and country. The government, guided by pragmatic conservative reformers, sponsored a program of rural cooperatives, which were established by an act of the Diet in 1899. Through the cooperatives—which helped with credit, marketing, and production—and through intense propaganda, the government hoped to avoid class conflict.

Not everyone in the industrial sector benefited from economic growth. Those working in the numerous small, traditional establishments experienced little change in their living conditions. Especially harsh were the working and living conditions of those who labored in the factories and shops. These were comparable to those in Western countries at a similar early stage of industrialization. During the first decade of the twentieth century, 60 percent of the workforce was still female. An act promulgated in 1900 outlawed strikes, but when conditions became too bad, male workers, for whom a factory job was not an interlude before marriage but a lifelong occupation, rebelled, sometimes violently. Thus, in 1909, three infantry companies were required to quell violence in the Ashio Copper Mines. Another labor action that made a deep impression was the 1912 Tokyo streetcar strike.

Conservative reformers, mindful of the social legislation of Bismarckian Germany, insisted early on that the government had the responsibility to ensure a balance between capital and labor, but the first factory laws were not passed until 1911. Efforts to improve the lot of women and children working in the factories also made headway only slowly. Not until 1916 did a law take effect that gave them some protection, such as limiting their working day to eleven hours.

The distress of the workers was much on the minds of radicals. Beginning in the early 1890s, there was a small group of radicals composed of Christian socialists and anarchists. They courageously opposed the war with Russia, holding antiwar rallies in the Tokyo YMCA even after the war began. However, barred by the government from forming a political party and facing government repression, they were unable to expand their influence beyond the world of intellectuals and college students. In 1911, twelve of their leaders were convicted, on mostly flimsy evidence, of plotting the death of the emperor and were executed.

Among the main beneficiaries of economic growth were the huge industrial–financial combines (*zaibatsu*), which retained close ties with government. The dominant political party during this period, the Seiyūkai (Association of Friends of Constitutional Government), also had a stake in economic development, because projects for railway and harbor development were a major means by which it won regional support and built local power.

Politics

During the Sino-Japanese War, the oligarchs and the party-controlled Diet were united in pursuit of common national aims, but after the war, political struggles resumed. A handful of men, enjoying the prerogatives of elder statesmen (*genrō*), advised the emperor on all major matters. They tended to see themselves as guardians of the public good in contrast to the private interests represented by the parties and to stress the need for unity in face of a hostile world. As participants in fashioning the new state and architects of its major institutions, they enjoyed great prestige and the support of their protégés and associates. The party politicians, on the other hand, resented the perpetuation of the *genrō*'s power and their propensity to limit political decision making to a few handpicked insiders.

The politicians' main weapon against a prime minister who defied them was that under the constitution only the Diet could authorize increases in the budget.

Complicating the political situation were divisions within both the oligarchy and the party leadership. Among the former, Yamagata, a disciplined, rather austere military man, was committed to "transcendental government"—dedicated to emperor and nation and above political partisanship. His main *genrō* rival was Itō Hirobumi, the more flexible conservative who had supervised the writing of the constitution. Itō was more willing than Yamagata to compromise with the parties. Similarly, not all Diet members were adamantly opposed to collaborating with the *genrō*. Some lost their enthusiasm for opposing a government that could dissolve the Diet and thereby subject them to costly reelection campaigns. Also, the oligarchs could trade office for support. Accommodation had its appeal, but initially it was an uneasy accommodation; there were four dissolutions of the Diet between 1895 and 1900.

Another political factor was the influence of the military. As stipulated by the constitution, the chief of the general staff reported directly to the emperor concerning command matters, thus bypassing the minister of war and the Cabinet. In 1900 the military's power was further strengthened when Yamagata obtained imperial ordinances specifying that only officers on active duty could serve as minister of the army or minister of the navy. In effect, this gave the military veto power over any Cabinet, because it could break a Cabinet simply by ordering the army or navy minister to resign. Still, control over funds for army expansion remained in the hands of the lower house.

Up to 1901 the oligarchs themselves served as prime minister, but after that date Yamagata's protégé Katsura Tarō (1847–1913) and Itō's protégé Saionji Kimmochi (1849–1940) alternated as prime minister for the remainder of the Meiji Period. Katsura, like Yamagata, was a general from Chōshū; Saionji was a court noble with liberal views but little inclination to political leadership.

Katsura and Saionji were able to govern because they had the cooperation of the Seiyūkai, which Itō had founded in 1900 as a means to obtain assured support in the Diet. In 1903 Itō turned the presidency of the party over to Saionji, but the real organizing force within the party was Hara Kei (1856–1921), an ex-bureaucrat who became the leading party politician of his generation. Hara greatly strengthened the party by building support within the bureaucracy during his first term as home minister (1906–1908), and he used his power to appoint energetic partymen as prefectural governors. He linked the party to the provinces and freely resorted to the pork barrel to build constituencies among the local men of means who formed the limited electorate.

The business community, including the *zaibatsu*, was interested in maintaining a political atmosphere favorable to itself, and political leaders welcomed business support. Thus, Itō, when he organized the Seiyūkai, obtained the support of Shibusawa Eiichi and other prominent business leaders, although many remained aloof. The head of Mitsui was so intent on establishing his company's independence from government that he even discontinued the practice of extending loans to Itō without collateral. However, the trend was toward closer association between the *zaibatsu* and politics, as exemplified by the relationship between Mitsubishi and Katsura after 1908. During Katsura's second ministry (1908–1911), his chief economic adviser was the head of the Mitsubishi Bank.

The relative strength of the participants in the political process did not remain unchanged. The *genrō* enjoyed great influence as long as they remained active, but theirs was a personal, not an institutional, power. It tended to diminish with time. As the number of living participants in the restoration decreased, the power of the oligarchs to orchestrate politics declined. As prime minister, Katsura did not always follow Yamagata's advice. Furthermore, the *genrō* lost an important source of support when a new generation of bureaucrats came to the fore. These men did not owe their positions to *genrō* patronage because, after 1885, entrance to and promotion in the bureaucracy were determined by examinations. As servants of the emperor, bureaucrats enjoyed high prestige and considerable influence.

Political compromise eroded much of the idealism found in the early movement for people's rights, but the Seiyūkai prospered. Its strength in the Diet alarmed the parliamentary opposition, which was divided and diverse. It included not only men opposed in principle to the Seiyūkai's compromises but also small and shifting groups of independents and a series of "loyalist" parties that habitually supported the Cabinet. Decision making was complicated, because government policies were determined by the interaction of various power centers, none of which could rule alone. The arrangement functioned as long as funds were sufficient to finance both the military's and the Seiyūkai's highest priority projects and as long as none of the participants felt their essential interests threatened. When that ceased to be the case, it brought on the Taishō political crisis.

Literature and the Arts

The beginnings of modern Japanese literature can be traced to Tsubouchi Shōyō (1859–1935), a translator and the author of *The Essence of the Novel* (1885), in which he opposed both didacticism and writing solely for entertainment and advocated Western realism, that is, the view that literature should portray actual life. From 1887 to 1889, Futabatei Shimei (1864–1909) followed with *Drifting Cloud,* a psychological study of an ordinary man told in a style more colloquial than usual.

Following the introduction of realism came Western romanticism with its emphasis on expression of feelings and of naturalism, which aimed at scientific detachment as advocated by the French writer Emile Zola. Although in Europe naturalism was hostile to romanticism, this was not necessarily the case in Japan, where Shimazaki Tōson (1873–1943) won fame for his romantic poetry and for *The Broken Commandment* (1906), a naturalistic account of a member of the pariah class (*burakumin*) who tries to keep his pledge to his father never to reveal that he was born into this group, which continued to suffer discrimination and contempt even though it was not subject to legal restrictions.

Two late Meiji writers, Mori Ōgai (1862–1922) and Natsume Sōseki (1867–1916), produced works of lasting literary merit. Ōgai identified with his family's samurai heritage, while Soseki was a proud son of plebeian Edo. Their writings differed in substance and style, but both men, although deeply influenced by the West, achieved greatness by drawing on their Japanese heritage. Both spent time abroad. Ōgai was sent by the army to study medicine in Germany. After returning to Japan, he had a distinguished career as an army surgeon, rising in 1907 to the post of surgeon-general. He was both a modern intellectual profoundly influenced by his time in Europe and a samurai-style army officer, not an easy combination but one that stimulated major achievements. Admired for the masculine, restrained style of his original works, he was also a prolific and excellent translator. Among his finest translations are his renderings of Goethe, including the full *Faust,* and of Shakespeare, which he translated from the German. He also translated modern German poetry with the result that more modern German verse was available in Japanese translation than in English. Furthermore, he introduced German aesthetic philosophy to Japan and influenced the development of modern Japanese theater; the performance of his translation of an Ibsen play in 1908 was a major cultural event.

Mori Ōgai's first story, "Maihime" ("The Dancing Girl," 1890), recounts the doomed romance between a Japanese student sent by his government to Germany and a German girl named Alice. It became a precursor of the many "I novels," thinly disguised autobiographical works, which became one of the standard genres of modern Japanese fiction and owe something to the Heian tradition of literary diaries. After his initial romantic period, Ōgai went on to write works of increasing psychological insight and philosophical depth. He increasingly turned to Japanese themes, as in his novel *The Wild Goose.* Ōgai was greatly moved when his friend General Nogi (1849–1912), hero of the Russo-Japanese War, followed the Meiji Emperor into death by committing ritual suicide with his wife. Afterward, Ōgai published painstakingly researched accounts of samurai. A particularly acclaimed late work is his *Chibu Chūsai,* an account of a late Tokugawa physician with whom Ōgai identified.

Natsume Sōseki studied in England, where a meager government stipend forced him to live in poverty, and he had virtually no friends. Later he described himself as having been "as lonely as a stray dog in a pack of wolves."[3] Both this experience of loneliness and the extensive reading he did while in England were reflected in his subsequent work. Sōseki returned from Europe to teach English literature at Tokyo Imperial University before resigning this position to devote himself wholly to writing. He was acclaimed not only for his fiction but also for his poetry in Chinese, his haiku, and his literary criticism. He once described his mind as half Japanese and half Western, and his early novels reflect English influence, particularly that of George Meredith, but in his mature work the Japanese element predominates.

Sōseki's early novels, *I Am a Cat* (1905) and *Botchan* (1906), present slices of Meiji life with affectionate good humor. Also in 1906, in a mere week, he wrote the remarkable painterly and diary-like *The Grass Pillow,* also translated as *The Three-Cornered World* because "an artist is a person who lives in the triangle which remains after the angle which we may call common sense has been removed from this four-cornered world."[4] Travel in that world was by railway train:

> It is an unsympathetic and heartless contraption which rumbles along, carrying hundreds of people crammed together in one box. . . . People are said to board and travel by train, but I call it being loaded and transported. Nothing shows greater contempt for the individual than the train. Modern civilization uses every possible means to develop individuality and then having done so, tries everything to stamp it out. It allots a few square yards to each person within that area. At the same time, it erects railings around him, and threatens him with all sorts of dire consequences if he should dare to take but one step beyond their compass.[5]

The main theme of Sōseki's mature works is human isolation, studied in characters given to deep introspection. Like Mori Ōgai, Natsume Sōseki was stricken by the death of the Meiji Emperor and General Nogi's suicide, which entered into *Kokoro* (1914), a novel concerning the relationship between a young man and his mentor, called "Sensei" (master or teacher). Sōseki links Sensei's personal tragedy and suicide to the deaths of the emperor and general and to the larger tragedy of the passing of a generation—and with it the loss of the old ethical values. Sensei perceives he has become an anachronism.

FIGURE 10.2 *Tao Qian* (Chinese poet, 365–427). Detail from one of a pair of six-fold screens, *Master Five Willows,* by Yokoyama Taikan. Taikan favored tradition, but his style resonates with his own time. Color on paper, 1912, 5.6 feet × 11.9 feet. (Tokyo National Museum. © Shokodo C. Ltd./APG-Japan 2002)

Painters, like writers, were grouped in several schools. The disciples of Okakura Tenshin, for example, continued to avoid the extremes of formalistic traditionalism and imitative modernism, seeking a middle ground that would be both modern and Japanese. One such was Yokoyama Taikan (1868–1958). His screen shown in Figure 10.2 depicts the Chinese poet Tao Qian (365–427), whose blend of regret and relief at withdrawal from public life continued to strike a responsive chord.

Among the artists working in European styles was Kuroda Seiki, whose nude had so shocked Kyoto in the 1890s. Kuroda continued to paint

FIGURE 10.3 *Concert Using Japanese and Western Instruments,* Sakaki Teitoku (1858–1925). Playing the violin while kneeling must have taken much practice—one can only hope the ensemble's music was as charming as the painting. Oil, 1910. (© Nagasaki Prefectural Art Museum)

in a Western manner, and he had many students. At the time of his death in 1924, he had come to be "the Grand Old Man of Western painting in Japan."[6] Some attempts at rendering Japanese themes in Western style produced paintings that are little more than historical curiosities, but in other cases there was a happier result. The painting by Sakaki Teitoku (1858–1925) shown in Figure 10.3 was executed in oil around 1910. While young men blow traditional bamboo flutes, two young women play violins.

Western influence on the visual arts was often direct and immediate, as it was for Umehara Ryūzaburō (1888–1986), who studied in France, met Renoir in 1909, and became his favorite pupil. The strongest influence on Japanese sculpture during this period was Rodin, who enjoyed a great vogue in Japan, especially after a major exhibition of his work in Tokyo in 1912.

Music also changed. The Meiji government early on sponsored Western military music, and in 1879 the Ministry of Education agreed to a proposal made by Izawa Shūji (1851–1917) to combine Japanese and Western music in the schools. Izawa had studied vocal physiology in the United States and persuaded the Ministry of Education to bring Luther Whiting Mason (1828–1896) from Boston to Japan to help develop songs for use in elementary schools. The first songbook (1881) consisted half of Western songs supplied with Japanese words ("Auld Lang Syne," for example, turned into a song about fireflies) and half of Japanese pieces harmonized in the Western manner.

Meiji popular music was more freely eclectic than that taught in schools. Beginning during the last decade of the nineteenth century, Japanese composers began working with sonatas, cantatas, and other Western forms, and, because of the Tokyo School of Music, good performers were available on the piano and violin, as well as on the koto and other traditional instruments taught at the school. However, performers made greater progress than composers. As suggested by William P. Malm, training in Western harmonics "created a series of mental blocks which shut out the special musical potentialities of traditional styles."[7] The rediscovery of the latter and their creative employment did not take place until after World War II.

II. The Taishō Period (1912–1926) and the 1920s

The Taishō Political Crisis (1912–1913)

Japan during World War I

Politics and Policies (1918–1924)

Party Government (1924–1931)

Popular Culture

Fine Arts

Mingei

Literature

Intellectual Trends

The Taishō Political Crisis (1912–1913)

The Taishō Period began with a political crisis, when financial conditions forced a cutback in government spending that made it impossible to fund both the Seiyūkai's domestic program and two new divisions for the army. Although the Seiyūkai won support at the polls, Prime Minister Saionji was forced out of office in December 1912 when the army ordered the minister of the army to resign. Although the *genrō* deliberated about a successor to Saionji, a number of politicians, journalists, and businessmen organized a movement "to protect constitutional government." The ensuing mass demonstrations were reminiscent of those protesting the Portsmouth Treaty in 1905.

Called on to form a government once more, Katsura, no longer willing to compromise with the Seiyūkai, attempted to organize a party strong enough to defeat it but failed. When the Seiyūkai threatened a vote of no confidence, Katsura tried to save the situation by obtaining an imperial order forcing the Seiyūkai to give up its planned no-confidence motion. This was a stratagem previously employed by embattled prime ministers, but this time it did not work: the Seiyūkai turned down the order. The crisis ended with Katsura's resignation. Such use of an imperial order was discredited and never tried again.

For the first time, a party majority in the Diet, backed by public opinion and a vociferous press, had overthrown a Cabinet. Katsura died in 1913, but the coalition he had created held together under the leadership of Katō Kōmei (Katō Takaaki, 1860–1926) whose background included graduation from Tokyo Imperial University, service in Mitsubishi, and a career in the Foreign Office capped by an appointment as foreign minister at the age of forty. He enjoyed a financial advantage from his marriage into the family that controlled Mitsubishi. A capable and determined man, he was personally reserved. But this was no handicap, because there was no need for party leaders like Katō or Hara to cultivate mass support. The power of a party leader depended on his strength within his party, although this was influenced by the party's showing at the polls.

The emergence of a strong second party meant that now the Seiyūkai faced a rival for control of the lower house. The parties represented a cross section of skills and resources needed to make participation in government viable. Arthur E. Tiedemann described it as follows:

> Each party had associated with it the three essential ingredients for achieving political power: professional politicians to do the nitty-gritty of day-to-day party management; former bureaucrats who had the administrative talents required to form a viable alternative government acceptable to the *genrō;* and businessmen who could supply the funds and influence essential to successful election campaigns.[8]

Although the Taishō political crisis confirmed the importance of the Diet and the parties, they were not the only power center. Again there were compromises: not until Hara became prime minister in 1918 did the top government post go to a man who had made his career as a party politician. Before Hara, there were three prime ministers: Admiral Yamamoto Gombei (1913–1914), a military bureaucrat from Satsuma whose government was brought down by a scandal in naval procurement; the septuagenarian Ōkuma Shigenobu (1914–1916), who was intent on destroying the Seiyūkai but failed; and Terauchi Masatake (1916–1918), a Yamagata-backed Chōshū general who had been governor-general of Korea. It was the Ōkuma and Terauchi governments that guided Japan during World War I.

Japan during World War I

When the Western powers became immersed in war, new opportunities opened up for Japan. In August 1914 Japan declared war on Germany and within the next three months seized German holdings in Shandong and the German islands in the Pacific. In January 1915 the Ōkuma government presented the Twenty-One Demands to China. Japan had to compromise but obtained additional rights at the cost of stirring up strong Chinese resentment. A prominent critic of this policy was the pro-German Yamagata, who wanted Japan to be on good terms with China to prepare for the war he anticipated against the West.

Much larger and more costly than the military effort against Germany during World War I was Japan's attempt to prevent the extension of Bolshevik power over territory that had belonged to the Russian Empire but had become a battleground after the Revolution of 1917. Russia and Japan had been wartime allies, but in March 1918 the Bolsheviks signed a separate peace with Germany (the Treaty of Brest-Litovsk). Complicating the situation in the East was the presence of Czech troops fighting their way out of Russia and determined to continue the war against Germany.

The Japanese intervened and by midsummer 1918 controlled the eastern Trans-Siberian Railway and Vladivostok. The United States then changed its earlier opposition to intervention, although President Woodrow Wilson envisioned only a limited military operation. The Japanese, however, sent 75,000 troops, triple the number sent by the Allies (United States, Britain, France, and Canada). Faced with Russian Communist victories and the absence of a viable alternative, the United States withdrew its forces in January 1919. The other Allies soon did likewise, leaving only the Japanese, who continued their efforts in the vain hope of at least keeping the Bolsheviks from controlling eastern Siberia. Although failure was apparent by 1920, the last Japanese troop did not withdraw until 1922.

Japan could pay for such a costly undertaking largely because its economy boomed during the war, which brought an unprecedented demand for its industrial products and the withdrawal of European competition. Old industries expanded, new ones grew up, and exports surged, turning Japan from a debtor into a creditor. But while some prospered, others suffered. The sudden economic expansion produced inflation, but workers' wages, as well as the income of those in fishing and other traditional occupations, failed to keep pace. The price of rice rose until people could no longer afford this most basic food. In August 1918, rice riots erupted in cities, towns, and villages all over Japan. Even as Japanese troops were setting off for Siberia, other soldiers were firing on hungry people rioting at home. The bitter irony was not lost on Japanese radicals. The immediate effect of the turbulence was to bring down the Terauchi government. When the *genrō* met to choose the next prime minister, they settled on Hara.

Politics and Policies (1918–1924)

Hara Kei had spent his career building up the Seiyūkai in preparation for the day of party rule, but by 1918 he was too set in his ways to embark on significant new policies or initiate meaningful change. From then until his assassination by a demented fanatic in November 1921, he initiated only minor changes and remained partisan in his concerns. Democratic intellectuals, students, and leaders of labor and farmer unions were disillusioned when the government turned a deaf ear to their demands for universal suffrage and instead passed an election law that retained a tax qualification for voting and reconstructed local electoral districts to favor the Seiyūkai. Abuse of office, financial scandals, and narrow partisanship had damaged the public image of the parties for years, and the record of the first party prime minister did nothing to alter this. Liberals who had placed their hopes in parliamentary reform either became cynical or looked elsewhere, and the public was apathetic.

In foreign affairs, Hara's prime ministership began with the peace conference at Versailles, where Japan failed to obtain a declaration of universal racial equality but did gain acquiescence to its claims in China and the Pacific. His government then adopted a policy of cooperation with the United States, the only possible source for capital badly needed by Japanese industry facing difficult adjustments after peace brought an end to wartime prosperity. The first product of the new policy was the Washington Conference of 1921–1922, as a result of which Japan's alliance with Britain was replaced by a Four Power Pact signed by France, Great Britain, Japan, and the United States. The signatories also agreed to limit construction of capital ships (ships over 10,000 tons with guns over eight inches) to maintain the existing balance of naval power at a 3:5:5 ratio for Japan, the United States, and Britain, calculated in tonnage. In February 1922, Japan further agreed to a Nine Power Treaty, acceding to the American Open Door Policy. In October 1922, Japan agreed to withdraw from Siberia.

That October Japan also reached an agreement with China, where nationalist sentiment had turned bitterly anti-Japanese. At Versailles, Japan had agreed, in principle, to the restoration of Chinese sovereignty in Shandong provided that it retained economic rights there. This was now officially agreed upon. To secure and advance Japanese interests in Manchuria, Zhang Zuolin, the local warlord, was supported by the Japanese army. However, Shidehara Kijūrō followed a general policy of getting along with the United States and conciliating China during his tenure as foreign minister from 1924 to 1927 and again from 1929 to December 1931.

The purpose of this policy was to avert another anti-Japanese outburst and costly boycotts of Japanese goods, which would hinder continued Japanese economic expansion. After 1914, Japanese investments in China accelerated. By 1931 more than 80 percent of Japan's total foreign investments were in China, where they amounted to 35.1 percent of all foreign investments in that country.* In 1930, 63 percent of Japanese investments in China were in Manchuria and another 25 percent were in Shanghai, where Japanese engaged in trade, banking, and textile manufacturing. In 1930 Japanese owned 39.6 percent of the Chinese textile industry (calculated in number of spindles). They were also a major factor in China's iron industry, with interests in Hankou and Manchuria.

Hara was succeeded by his finance minister, but this man lacked political skills and lasted only until June 1922. Three nonparty prime ministers followed, two ad-

* Great Britain accounted for 36.7 percent of foreign investment in China, but this was only 5 to 6 percent of all British overseas investments. Three other countries each accounted for more than 5 percent of foreign investment in China: The Soviet Union for 8.4 percent, the United States for 6.1 percent, and France for 5.9 percent.

mirals and one bureaucrat who organized his Cabinet entirely from the House of Peers but resigned when faced by a three-party coalition in control of the Diet. The leader of the strongest of these parties, the Kenseikai (Constitutional Government Association, established 1916), was Katō, who had last served as foreign minister under Ōkuma during the war. He was now called upon to form a new government.

The most momentous event of the years between Hara and Katō was geological, not political: in September 1923 the Tokyo–Yokohama area was devastated by a severe earthquake followed by a conflagration, which came close to leveling the area. The red sky was visible all night from a distance of a hundred miles. Around 100,000 people lost their lives. As so often in a disaster, the earthquake and fires brought out the best and the worst in people. Although some courageously and selflessly helped their fellows, others joined hysterical racist mobs rampaging through the city killing Koreans. The police reacted to the emergency by rounding up socialists, anarchists, and Communists as a "security measure," and there were cases of police torture and killing.

Party Government (1924–1931)

The increase in the power of the parties signified a shift in the balance of power rather than a systemic reordering of power centers. It was the power of the parties that induced Tanaka Giichi, a Chōshū general much favored by Yamagata, to accept the presidency of the Seiyūkai in 1925 when it was out of power. But the party's choice also confirmed the willingness of the parties to work within the existing parameters and highlighted the continued prestige and influence of the army, even during the peaceful 1920s.

The main accomplishments of party government came while Katō was prime minister (1924–1926). Foremost among them was passage of a "universal" suffrage act, which gave the vote to all males twenty-five and older. To still the fears of conservatives apprehensive over the possible spread of radical ideas, a Peace Preservation Law was also passed. This made it a crime to advocate change in the national political structure or to urge the abolition of private property. The Katō government never invoked the law, but it was available to later, less liberal regimes.

Katō also tried to reform the House of Peers (changing its composition and reducing its powers) but succeeded in making only minor changes. His government was more successful in introducing moderate social reforms, including legalizing labor unions, establishing standards for factory conditions, setting up procedures for mediating labor disputes, and provisioning health insurance for workers. There was, however, no similar program to alleviate the problems of the rural poor.

Katō soon became embroiled in difficult political negotiations with other parties and the House of Peers, among others. When Katō died in 1926, he had not transformed Japanese politics, but he did leave a record of accomplishment that might, under different circumstances, have served as a basis for building a strong system of party rule. That this did not happen is partly the result of the kinds of problems Japan had to face during the next five years, but it also reflects the weakness of the parties. Even the increased suffrage was a mixed blessing, because the larger electorate made election campaigns costlier and politicians more open to corruption.

From 1927 to 1929 the government was led by Tanaka. In foreign policy Tanaka departed from Shidehara's conciliatory approach. When, in 1927, Chiang Kai-shek resumed the military expedition to unify China, Tanaka, under political pressure at home, sent an army brigade to Shandong, where clashes with Chinese soldiers ensued. Still more ominous was the assassination, in June 1928, of Zhang Zuolin by a group of Japanese army officers who did not think him sufficiently pliant and hoped their action would pave the way for the seizure of Manchuria. This did not happen—at least not then. Instead, Manchuria was brought under the new Chinese government by Zhang's son, and Tanaka had to recognize the GMD regime in Nanjing as the government of China. Tanaka's government itself collapsed when he incurred the displeasure of the Showa emperor (r. 1925–1989) and court by failing to obtain from the army suitable punishment for Zhang's murderers. This episode was a harbinger of future unilateral army actions, but first, party government had one more chance.

In 1929, Hamaguchi Ōsachi became prime minister, and in 1930 his party, the Minseitō, won the election. Shidehara once again became foreign minister and resumed his policy of reconciliation with China. He cooperated with Britain and the United States in negotiating the London Naval Treaty of 1930, which provided for a 10:10:7 ratio for other than capital ships. The treaty was ratified only after heated debate and the forced resignation of the naval chief of staff. It generated bitterness among the military and members of patriotic societies, such as the young man who shot the prime minister in November 1930. Hamaguchi never recovered from his wound but hung on in office until April 1931. From then until December 1931, the Minseitō Cabinet continued under Wakatsuki Reijirō (1866–1949), who earlier had served as home minister under Katō and as prime minister from January 1926 to April 1927. He was an experienced politician, but during 1931 the government lost control over the army.

The restlessness of the military was not government's only problem. During most of the 1920s, Japan was beset by persistent economic difficulties, including an unfavorable balance of payments, failure of jobs to increase fast enough to keep up with population growth, and a sharp decline in the price of rice, which helped consumers but hurt farmers. The giant *zaibatsu* profited from new technology, the economics of scale, and the failure of weaker companies, but times were hard on small operators. In 1921 a dramatic dockyard strike in Kobe resulted in an eight-hour day, which was extended to other heavy industries, but the union movement progressed only slowly. This was also the case for unions of tenants, many of whom now worked for landlords who had moved to the city. Carol Gluck aptly summed up the situation when she characterized Japan as being in "a hiatus between a traditional agrarian paternalism that was disintegrating and a modern industrial paternalism that was still in its formative stages. The landlords were no longer offering succor to distressed tenants, and the companies were not yet acting in a paternalist role on any significant scale."[9]

To solve the balance-of-payments problem, there were calls for the government to cut expenses and retrench to reduce the cost of Japanese goods and improve their competitive position in international trade. This was the policy followed by Hamaguchi, who also strengthened the yen by returning to the gold standard. Unfortunately, he initiated this program just as the Great Depression was getting under way and persisted in it despite great economic dislocations and suffering. From 1925 to 1930 the real income of farmers declined about a third. The poorest were, as always, the hardest hit. As in earlier periods of famine, there were cases of peasants eating bark and digging for roots or maintaining life by selling daughters into brothels.

The government's economic failure undermined the credibility of the political parties, which even in normal times had little public esteem. No mass movement arose directed against them, but there was also little in their record to inspire people to do battle in their defense. Their enemies included those dissatisfied not only with their policies and politics but also with just about every facet of 1920s liberalism, internationalism, and "modernity."

Popular Culture

During the 1920s a wave of Western influence affected lifestyles, diet, housing, and dress, particularly in Tokyo and other great cities, where there was a boom in bread consumption, Western dress became prevalent in public, and fashionable houses included at least one Western room. On the Ginza, the "modern boy" (*mobo*) and "modern girl" (*moga*), dressed and coiffured in the latest imported styles, might be on their way to listen to jazz or see a movie. Although there was always an audience for films filled with melodrama and swordplay, others dealt with the problems and joys of daily life.

Western sports gained ground, including baseball, although the first professional teams date from the 1930s. People began playing golf and tennis. Friends met in cafes, or a fellow could practice the latest steps with a taxi dancer at The Florida or another of Tokyo's dance halls. The old demimonde dominated by the geisha, a world fondly chronicled by Nagai Kafū (1879–1959), was on the decline, and modern mass culture was in the ascendancy.

Centered in the cities, the new popular culture was steadily diffused as even the remotest village became accessible by train and car, not to speak of the radio, introduced in 1925. Mass circulation magazines, some directed at a general audience and others written especially for women or young people, catered to the unquenchable thirst of the Japanese public for reading matter.

Fine Arts

Internationalism was represented not only in politics but also in the arts. Tokyo was not far behind Paris or London in experimenting with the latest styles and techniques. Indeed, it sometimes led the other capitals, such as when in 1922 Frank Lloyd Wright built the Imperial Hotel in Tokyo, a break with Japan's own version of the European Art Nouveau. The American architect, influenced by the Japanese tradition, was not the only stimulating visitor from abroad during the Taishō and early Showa years. Japanese scientists, for example, could converse with Einstein on his visit to their country in 1919, and music lovers enjoyed concerts by eminent foreign performers: both Kreisler and Heifetz gave concerts in Tokyo in 1923. Bach, Mozart, and Beethoven were becoming as much a part of the musical life of Japan as of any other country, foreshadowing the time when, after World War II, the Japanese pioneered in teaching young children to play the violin and became the world's foremost manufacturers of pianos.

A grand piano dominates the four-panel screen (see Figure 10.4) painted in 1926 by Nakamura Daizaburō (1898–1947), which is representative of the followers of the Okakura school. Conversely, there were Japanese artists who, like Xu Beihong in China, depicted traditional subjects in Western style.

FIGURE 10.4 *At the Piano*, Nakamura Daizaburō. Not only the traditional dress of the young woman playing by the light of an electric lamp but also the technique and aesthetics of the painting recall the earliest Japanese art rather than contemporary Western styles. Fourfold screen, color on silk, 1926, 9.9 feet × 5.4 feet. (© Kyoto Municipal Museum of Art)

A major influence for modernism was the *White Birch* (*Shirakaba*) journal (1910–1923), one of whose editors was Shiga Naoya (1883–1971). In contrast to the school of naturalism and the advocates of proletarian literature, the *White Birch* group was dedicated to the exploration of the inner self, the pursuit of deeper personal understanding and self-expression such as in the "I novel" or in individualistic art. Seeking to become "children of the world," they introduced many European writers and published articles on the work and theories of such artists as van Gogh—whose suicide for art's sake they praised as superior to that of General Nogi.

Much of the art produced during this period was imitative, but one artist who developed his own style was Umehara Ryūzaburō. A disciple of Renoir, Umehara also owes something to his childhood in Kyoto, where he became thoroughly familiar with the styles of Sōtatsu and Kōrin as still practiced in his family's silk kimono business (see Figures 7.2 and 7.3).

European pointillism, cubism, futurism, dadaism, and surrealism all affected the Japanese avant-garde, here represented by a painting dated 1926 (see Figure 10.5). Tōgō Seiji (1897–1978), in Europe at the time, was influenced by French and Italian futurism and dadaism but here shows an inclination toward cubism.

FIGURE 10.5 *Saltimbanques,* Tōgō Seiji. The title of this cheerful, decorative picture is French for "traveling showmen," and it would take a keen eye, not to say considerable imagination, to detect a particularly Japanese element. Oil, 1926, 30 in. × 44.9 in. (© Tōgō Tamami. Courtesy Tōgō Tamami and the National Museum of Modern Art, Tokyo)

Mingei

Many trends converged in the "folk craft" or "folk arts" movement promoted by Yanagi Muneyoshi (or Sōetsu, 1889–1961), who coined the term *mingei* in 1926. His deep belief in the creative genius of the people was in tune with Taishō democracy, while his rejection of machine mass production and his devotion to the strong, honest beauty created by anonymous craftsmen working together to create objects for daily use are reminiscent of John Ruskin (1819–1900) and William Morris (1834–1896), founder of the late Victorian Arts and Crafts Movement. Yanagi, like Morris, championed the dignity of the craftsman and linked the aesthetic beauty of folk art to the ethical qualities under which it was produced. His attempt to establish a commune for *mingei* artists failed, but he succeeded in inspiring a new appreciation for traditional woodcarving, housewares, woven and dyed cloth, and all kinds of articles made of bamboo, straw, handmade paper, wood (including furniture and traditional buildings), metal, and leather. The list goes on to include virtually all the products of traditional workmanship. Such works found a home in the museums, such as the Japan Folk Art Museum in Tokyo (1936), where they continue to be displayed, studied, enjoyed, and celebrated.

Yanagi's interest in folk culture was shared by Yanagida Kunio (1875–1962), Japan's foremost scholar of folklore. The massive survey he directed in the 1930s laid the foundations for a whole field of studies. Beyond preserving and studying the folk craft (his preferred translation of *mingei*) of the past, he strove to further the production of *mingei* as a living force. Foremost among his associates in the *mingei* movement were four potters: Tomimoto Kenkichi (1886–1963), the British potter Bernard Leach (1887–1979), Kawai Kanjirō (1890–1966), and Hamada Shōji (1894–1978). Others worked in textiles and other crafts. Among the woodcut artists influenced by Yanagida was Munakata Shikō (see p. 284).

Literature

Naturalism, symbolism, social realism, neoperceptionism—in literature as in the visual arts, a multitude of agendas had their proponents and special vocabulary, "pushing this or that 'ism,' this or that school and inflicting on the reader who wishes to comprehend the book's argument prior belief in this jargon." These words were written in 1930 by Kobayashi Hideo (1902–1983), Japan's foremost modern critic, who went on to say, "I don't trust the jargon. I believe that not trusting jargon is the mark of the critical spirit."[10]

Kobayashi admired Shiga Naoya, already mentioned as a member of the *White Birch* group, master of the autobiographical short story and "I novel" and of a concise, unaffected (although carefully crafted), sensitive style. Shiga was much admired and imitated, but he also had his detractors. Prominent among those who rejected the autobiographical mode were the advocates of proletarian literature exemplified by such novels as *The Cannery Boat* (1929) by Kobayashi Takiji (1903–1933), in which the workers revolt against a brutal captain. Although much of this literature was propagandistic, it did make the reader and writer more sensitive to social conditions.

A gifted writer who defies classification was Akutagawa Ryūnosuke (1892–1927), author of some 150 short stories between 1917 and 1927, many of them modern psychological reinterpretations of old tales. Because of the famous film of the same name released in 1950 by Kurosawa Akira, he is probably best known in the West for "Rashomon," which presents the story of a murder and rape as told from the viewpoint of three protagonists and a witness. In doing so, it raises questions about all our perceptions of historical truth. Akutagawa's stories are frequently eerie but are saved from being merely macabre by the keenness of his psychological portrayals. Pessimistic, given to self-doubt, and distressed at the changing world about him, he committed suicide in 1927, citing "a vague unease."

In poetry as in art, some dedicated themselves to new experiments and others continued working with the old forms. In the nineteenth century, Masaoka Shiki (1867–1902), known primarily as a haiku poet, contributed toward revitalizing traditional poetry, which continued to be written and published throughout the twentieth century. Others, however, looked to the West, and some even employed the Roman alphabet (*rōmaji*). Foreign influence did not necessarily produce timeless verse; one poet proclaimed, "My sorrow wears the thin garb of one-sided love."[11] The most admired master of free verse was Hagiwara Sakutarō (1886–1942), whose collection *Howling at the Moon* (1917) caused a sensation. Moving from the canine to the feline, he published *Blue Cat* in 1923—using "blue" in the sense of the blues. *Age of Ice* (1934), his last book of new free verse, includes a poem in which he identifies with a caged tiger.

A major prose writer was Tanizaki Junichirō (1886–1965), who began with a fascination with the West but turned increasingly to the Japanese tradition. The protagonist of *Some Prefer Nettles* (1917), unhappily married to a "stridently" modern wife, finds comfort in the arms of a Eurasian prostitute, symbolic of the West, but as the novel unfolds he is increasingly attracted to a traditional Kyoto beauty. Tanizaki himself moved to Kyoto following the great earthquake of 1923. Some of his best work still lay in the future, including his masterpiece, *The Makioka Sisters,* written during World War II. One theme in this long, panoramic novel is the contrast between two of the sisters, one traditional in appearance and mentality, the other modern. Tanizaki's devotion to tradition also led him to translate the *Tale of Genji* into modern Japanese.

A similar trajectory from avant-garde to tradition was followed by Kawabata Yasunari (1899–1972), whose main works and fame were still to come. A very different writer then also at the beginning of her career was Uno Chiyu (1897–1996), whose persona and writings were more in tune with the 1920s and the post-World War I years than with the 1930s, when she published her best-known novel, *Confessions of Love* (*Iro Zange,* 1935), based on the well-known failed love suicide attempted by Tōgō Seiji (see Figure 10.5) in 1929. Uno's interview with Tōgō a month later led that same night to a famous liaison that lasted five years.

Intellectual Trends

Philosophers and political theorists, like artists and writers, were challenged by claims that modern Western ideas possessed universally valid principles and by their need to make sense of and find value in their own tradition. On the left, there was a revival of interest in anarchism and socialism, suppressed in 1911, and Marxism enjoyed new prestige after the Russian Revolution. Some were active in the labor movement, but the labor parties formed after passage of the universal suffrage act suffered from an excess of factionalism and a lack of mass participation. This was also true of the Japanese Communist party, which was dominated by intellectuals, some of great personal status. There was also a fledgling feminist movement, which campaigned for equality and women's rights, particularly the right to vote, because at the time women were legally minors and remained excluded from the political process.

Most widely read among liberal theorists were Minobe Tatsukichi (1873–1948) and Yoshino Sakuzō (1878–1933), both deeply versed in German thought. Minobe was a legal scholar who followed his teacher at Heidelberg, Georg Jellinek, in making a distinction between sovereignty, which belongs to the whole state, and the power to rule, which is supervised by the emperor. In this sense, the emperor becomes the "highest organ" of the state, limited by the other components of the state and by the constitution. The constitution, furthermore, in Japan as elsewhere (according to Minobe), allows, and indeed requires, continuing change in the direction of increasing rationality, responsible government, and popular participation. Minobe's work gained wide currency, and his book was the most frequently assigned text in courses on constitutional law. In 1932 he was appointed to the House of Peers, but his prominence was to cost him dearly later on.

Yoshino did not obtain such Establishment approval, but his many articles were widely read. A Christian populist and a democrat, he was a philosophical idealist who argued for democracy as an absolute rather than on utilitarian or pragmatic grounds. He also held an idealistic view of the nation and rejected any suggestion that democracy was incompatible with the Japanese tradition: "Those who argue that democracy is not compatible with the national spirit believe in the anachronistic and erroneous notion that the Emperor and people are mutually exclusive of each other."[12] Democracy would fulfill, not diminish, the emperor's role.

After World War I, Japanese intellectuals were attracted to Hegel, Kant, and Nietzsche; the phenomenalism of Husserl; the hermeneutics of Heidegger; and the vitalism of Bergson and Eucken. Outstanding among the philosophers who digested Western philosophy and assimilated it into their own original work was Nishida Kitarō (1870–1945), strongly steeped in Buddhism and best known for his philosophy of transcendent nothingness. Other theorists used Western philosophy to differentiate an authentic Japaneseness from the West and what they perceived as the diluted or hybrid culture that they disliked and dismissed. Nishida was not alone in refraining from discussing politics, but others defined Japanism in political terms and demanded political action.

Some ideologues, conscious of the hardships suffered by the countryside, condemned the life and values of the cities and called for a return to virtuous agrarianism. Among the most severe critics of the parties and *zaibatsu* was Kita Ikki (1883–1937), who combined advocacy of imperialistic assertiveness abroad with a call for egalitarianism at home to bring emperor and people together. Unhappy with Japan's political organization and its stance in the world, he did not look to the electorate or a mass popular movement for salvation but placed his faith in change from above enacted by a few dedicated men. Accordingly, his ideas found a friendly reception in small societies of superpatriots and among army officers who saw themselves as continuing in the tradition of the *rōnin,* who had selflessly terrorized Kyoto during the closing days of the Tokugawa. Kita also found more recent exemplars among the ex-samurai who, after Saigō's death, had formed the Genyōsha (Black Ocean Society, 1881) and the Kokuryūkai (Amur River Society, also translated Black Dragon Society, 1901). The former was dedicated to expansion in Korea; the latter concentrated on Manchuria. Both employed intimidation and assassination.

The story of the attempts made by these men to effect a "Showa Restoration" belongs in the 1930s, but Kita's most influential book was written in 1919. The rejection in the 1930s of party government and internationalism that had prevailed in the 1920s revealed that these had as yet shallow roots.

Notes

1. Louise Young, *Japan's Total Empire: Manchuria and the Culture of Wartime Imperialism* (Berkeley: Univ. of California Press, 1998), p. 21.
2. Mark R. Peattie, in Ramon H. Myers and Mark R. Peattie, eds., *The Japanese Colonial Empire, 1895–1945* (Princeton: Princeton Univ. Press, 1984), p. 8. See p. 10 for colonies as "the ultimate status symbol."
3. Quoted in Natsume Soseki, *Ten Nights of Dream–Hearing Things: The Heredity of Taste,* Aiko Ito and Graeme Wilson, trans. (Rutland, Vt., and Tokyo: Charles E. Tuttle, 1974), p. 12.
4. Natsume Soseki, *The Three-Cornered World,* Alan Turney, trans. (Chicago: Henry Regnery, 1965), p. iii.
5. Natsume, *The Three-Cornered World,* p. 181.
6. Shuji Takashina and J. Thomas Rimer, with Gerald D. Bolas, *Paris in Japan: The Japanese Encounter with European Painting* (St. Louis: The Washington Univ. Press, 1987), p. 105.
7. William P. Malm, "The Modern Music of Meiji Japan," in Donald H. Shively, ed., *Tradition and Modernization in Japanese Culture* (Princeton: Princeton Univ. Press, 1971), p. 300.
8. Arthur E. Tiedemann, "Big Business and Politics in Prewar Japan," in James W. Morley, ed., *Dilemmas of Growth in Prewar Japan* (Princeton: Princeton Univ. Press, 1971), pp. 278–79.
9. Carol Gluck, *Japan's Modern Myths: Ideology in the Late Meiji Period* (Princeton: Princeton Univ. Press, 1985), p. 282.
10. Quoted in Paul Anderer, ed. and trans., *Literature of the Lost Home: Kobayashi Hideo—Literary Criticism, 1924–1939* (Stanford: Stanford Univ. Press, 1995), p. 108.
11. Quoted in Donald Keene, ed., *Modern Japanese Literature: An Anthology* (New York: Grove Press, 1956), p. 20.
12. Tetsuo Najita, "Some Reflections on Idealism in the Political Thought of Yoshino Sakuzō," in Bernard Silberman and Harry D. Harootunian, eds., *Japan in Crisis: Essays on Taisho Democracy* (Princeton: Princeton Univ. Press, 1974), p. 40.

11

Militarism and War

The Manchurian Incident and Its Consequences

Japanese Politics and the Road to War

War with China

Expansion of the War into a Pacific War

The Course of the War

Japan at War

Colonial East Asia during the War

The End of the War

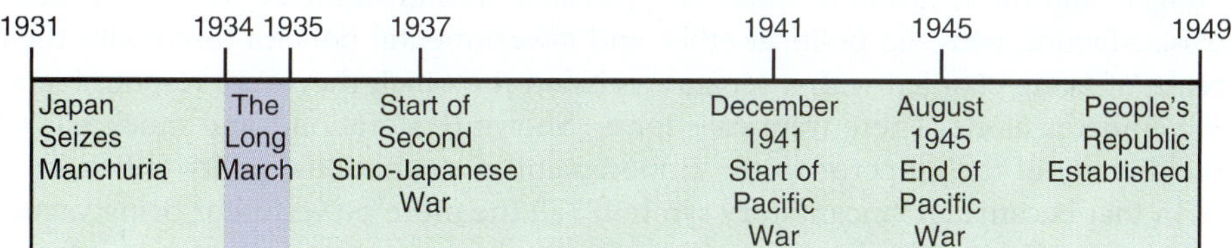

For much of the world, the 1930s were bleak and somber years. In the capitalist nations of the West, the Great Depression ushered in an economic crisis that deepened the rifts in society and threatened existing institutions. In the Soviet Union, struggling to catch up with the West economically, the decade was marred by the brutalities of forced collectivization and Stalin's purge trials. To many people desperate for vigorous action, dictatorship of one kind or another seemed the most effective way of pulling a nation together, and it was not in Italy and Germany alone that fascism was viewed as a non-Communist means to achieve national unity and greatness and regarded as the wave of the future. The crisis of Western democracy was not lost on observers in East Asia, where traditions of liberal constitutionalism were shallow at best.

During most of the decade, those nations that preserved democratic government were preoccupied with domestic problems and the strongest, the United States, was committed to a policy of isolationism. International statesmanship was at a low ebb; national leaders gave only lip service to the principles of collective security embodied in the League of Nations. There was no credible external deterrent to keep Japan from expanding its empire, at China's expense.

The future of Nationalist China and Imperial Japan became fatally intertwined when Japan seized Manchuria in 1931, entering into what in Japan is now called "a dark valley." This not only marked a turning point for those directly involved but also revealed the weakness of the League of Nations, whose condemnation of Japan was not followed by meaningful sanctions. Those throughout the world who had relied on the community of nations to provide collective security had been proved wrong. The League emerged from the episode badly damaged.

The Manchurian Incident and Its Consequences

The Japanese government derived its legitimacy from the emperor, but the ruling political parties confronted charges that they were betraying their sacred trust. In the name of the emperor, the enemies of constitutional government criticized the political manipulations of the Diet leaders, their ties to business, and their policy of accommodating the West and conciliating China, exemplified by the Washington Conference of 1921–1922. Such sentiments animated the members of various patriotic organizations and prevailed in the army, chafing from the cuts made in its budgets and the restrictions imposed by civilian administrations. Military leaders' dissatisfaction with the political ethos and governmental policies fused with their sense of being charged with a separate mission for which they were responsible to the emperor alone. There were calls for a "Showa Restoration," and much talk of the divinity of the emperor as the embodiment of the national polity (*kokutai*), a term that became an "incantatory symbol"[1] all the more powerful for being vague.

Among the most vehement critics of party government were radical egalitarians such as Kita Ikki, who favored nationalizing industry, and radical agrarians like Gondō Seikyo (1868–1937), who would abolish industry and return Japan to rural simplicity. Although their visions of the future differed, they agreed on two things: that the existing government obtruded on the imperial will and must be swept away and that Japan had a divine mission overseas. Such ideas formed the agenda for small societies of extremists given to direct action, such as the Cherry Society, which planned an unsuccessful military coup in Tokyo in March 1931. The membership of this society consisted entirely of army officers, none higher in rank than lieutenant colonel.

The assassination of the Manchurian warlord Zhang Zuolin in 1928 was the work of men such as these. They hoped that Zhang's murder would trigger a war in which this vast, strategic, and potentially wealthy area would be conquered for Japan. This did not happen, but another attempt to start a war appealed to the superpatriots, not only because it might gain Manchuria but also because it would strengthen their support in the army, increase the army's power and popularity at home, and undermine the government they so detested.

Emphasis on Manchuria was also consistent with the thought of more analytical army men, such as Ishiwara Kanji (Ishihara Kanji, 1886–1949), who worked out the plan of attack. He and other students of World War I wanted Japan to control the economic resources of Manchuria as a step toward attaining the economic independence required for waging total war. Many officers, concerned with the possibility of war with the Soviet Union, were also mindful of Manchuria's strategic value.

In the fall of 1931 the time seemed ripe, because China was hampered by floods in the Yangzi River valley and the Western powers were neutralized by the depression. The seizure was masterminded by Ishiwara and other officers serving with the Japanese Army on the Liaodong Peninsula. These officers, none higher than colonel, fabricated a supposed Chinese attempt to sabotage the South Manchuria Railway Company as an excuse for hostilities and then made sure that the fighting continued until the army controlled Manchuria. Although certain high army officials in Tokyo likely knew of the plot, it was carried out without the knowledge, let alone the authorization, of the civilian government in Tokyo, which, once informed, tried to halt the operations but found itself powerless to do so. An attempted military coup in Tokyo in October did not immediately topple the government, but it did intimidate civilian political leaders. The Wakatsuki government, divided and helpless, resigned in December. It was followed by a Seiyūkai government under Inukai Ki (Inukai Tsuyoshi, 1855–1932), which for another half year tried to maintain a semblance of party control.

Events moved swiftly on the continent and at home. In Manchuria, the army consolidated its hold and established a puppet state, which early in 1932 declared its independence from China. Manchukuo, as it was known, was placed under the titular rule of Puyi, who as an infant had been the last emperor of China—but it was actually controlled by the army. Meanwhile, the fighting had spread to China proper; for six strenuous weeks, Japanese and Chinese fought around Shanghai until a truce was arranged. However, Japanese efforts to reach a general settlement with China and obtain recognition of Manchukuo were rebuffed. Japan was condemned by the League of Nations and withdrew in March 1933. The failure of the League to do anything more than talk was not lost on Mussolini and Hitler.

After Japanese troops crossed the Great Wall in the spring of 1933, a truce was concluded in May 1933 that left Japanese troops in control of the area north of the Wall and provided for a demilitarized zone whose boundaries were marked by the railway line running between Beijing, Tianjin, and Tanggu—but it did not prevent the Japanese from setting up a puppet regime in that area or from exerting continuous pressure on North China. In December 1935, Japanese army officers failed in their plans to engineer a North Chinese puppet regime, and full-scale war broke out in the summer of 1937. In the meantime, in Manchuria and Korea, the Japanese concentrated on the development of heavy industry, building an industrial base on the continent under army control.

Japanese Politics and the Road to War

At home, too, 1932 was an eventful year, as members of the patriotic societies continued to further their cause by assassinating prominent men, including the head of the house of Mitsui. On May 15 they raided the Tokyo power station, a bank, Seiyūkai headquarters, and the official residence of the prime minister. They assassinated Inukai in his home.

When the men responsible for the May 15 violence were brought to trial, they were treated with great respect. They were allowed to expound their doctrines for days at a time and were given a national podium from which to proclaim the selflessness of their patriotic motives. In this way they largely succeeded in portraying themselves as martyrs. The light sentences meted out at the conclusion of the lengthy trials further discouraged those who hoped for a return to civilian rule. Instead, power shifted from the political parties into the hands of civilian bureaucrats and especially the military.

In 1936 the leftist Social Mass Party managed to win half a million votes. The following year that party's total climbed to 900,000 votes, and it captured thirty-seven seats in the lower house of the Diet. In that same election, the Seiyūkai and Minseitō together polled some 7 million votes, giving them 354 out of 466 seats. But their showing in the polls was to little avail. The parties were too weak to control the military. Those who wished to preserve constitutional government chose to compromise with the military establishment in the hope of averting a complete overthrow of the existing order.

Efforts to achieve political stabilization through a national union government, in which all the power centers were represented, were fostered by Saionji, the last of the *genrō,* who hoped to protect the throne from involvement in politics. But these efforts met with only partial and temporary success. The next two Cabinets, in office from May 1932 to March 1936, included party men but were headed by admirals, who were considered more moderate than certain potential prime ministers from the army.

Prime sources of continued instability were the divisions within each of the power centers. Within the bureaucracies there was rivalry among ministries and disagreement between conservative officials and technocrats who envisioned radical restructuring of state and society.

The military, too, was divided. The army and navy frequently clashed, and the breakdown in discipline during the actions in Manchuria and the violence at home reflected disunity in the army. The lines of army factionalism were complex: for example, there was a division between those who had studied at the Central War College and those who had attended officers' training school. However, two main groups stood out. The more extreme faction, led by Generals Araki Sadao (1877–1966) and Mazaki Jinzaburō (1876–1956), was known as the Kōdōha, or "Imperial Way faction," because it emphasized the imperial mystique and advocated an ill-defined doctrine of direct imperial rule. Like the radical civilian theorists of the right, it opposed existing political and economic institutions and sought a moral and spiritual transformation that would assure a glorious future for both army and country. In contrast, the Tōseiha, or "Control faction," led by General Nagata Tetsuzan (1884–1935), the leading proponent of total war, and including Ishiwara and General Tōjō Hideki, gave priority to the long-range buildup of the economy and the transformation of Japan into a modern military state.

For a few years the advantage lay with the Imperial Way faction, but it suffered a setback in 1935 when General Mazaki was dismissed from his post as director-general of military education. A lieutenant colonel retaliated by assassinating General Nagata. The Control faction responded by arresting the officer and laying plans for the transfer of other firebrands to Manchuria. The lieutenant colonel's trial was still in progress when, on February 26, 1936, a group of junior Kōdōha officers, commanding more than 1000 men, seized the center of the capital and killed several prominent leaders, although some of their intended victims, including the prime minister, Admiral Okada Keisuke (1868–1952), managed to elude them. The young officers hoped that their action would bring down the old system and that Generals Araki and Mazaki would take the lead in restructuring the state, but these senior generals remained aloof. As in 1928, the emperor intervened, and the navy responded to the crisis with vigor. On the third day of the insurrection, the rebels surrendered. This time the leaders were tried rapidly and in secret. One of those who perished at the hands of a firing squad was Kita Ikki, who had not participated in the mutiny but was too closely associated with the young officers and their movement to escape punishment.

The elimination of the Imperial Way faction actually increased the army's political power because it could now threaten a second mutiny if it did not get its way. The army still had to consider the wishes of other components of the power elite, but it was able to secure a substantial increase in military spending. Japan now withdrew from the naval limitation agreement, opening the possibility that it might have to confront the combined might of the Western powers and the Soviet Union. The army's strategic planners thought primarily in terms of a war with the latter, thus providing a strong inducement for Japan to sign an anti-Comintern pact with Hitler's Germany in December 1936.

Domestically, there ensued an intensification of propaganda and indoctrination with a continuation of repression directed at the radical left and those whose ardor for emperor and *kokutai* was deemed insufficient. The most notorious case took place in 1935 when Minobe Tatsukichi, the distinguished legal theorist, was charged with demeaning the emperor by considering him merely "the highest organ of the state." Minobe defended himself with spirit but was forced to resign from the House of Peers. Even so, in 1936, while living in seclusion, the old man suffered an attempt on his life that left him wounded. By that time, his books had been banned. Censorship became more severe, and expressions of intense national chauvinism filled the media.

The abandonment of the gold standard and the military buildup stimulated the economy and enabled Japan to recover from the depth of the depression, but agriculture remained depressed, and small companies benefited much less than did the *zaibatsu.*

War with China

The international situation was very problematic. The great powers refused to recognize Manchukuo or agree that Japan was entitled to an Asian version of the Monroe Doctrine. Nor was anyone able to devise a formula regarding China acceptable both to the Chinese government and the Japanese army, which, after its conquest of Manchuria, was steadily moving into "autonomous zones" in North China. Until the summer of 1937, the Japanese pressure was primarily economic and political, but there was the danger that an unplanned military incident might escalate into a major war. This became more likely after December 1937 when Chiang Kai-shek was kidnapped in Xián by Manchurian forces who insisted on fighting the Japanese rather than Chinese Communists.

Matters came to a head in July 1937 when there was a clash between Chinese and Japanese soldiers on the Marco Polo Bridge outside of Beijing, and the Chinese refused Japanese demands for further concessions. Thus began the second Sino-Japanese War that, in 1941, merged into World War II, although this is not what Japan intended in 1937.

The conflict rapidly expanded into large-scale fighting. By the end of July, the Japanese were in possession of Beijing and Tianjin, and in August Japanese forces attacked Shanghai, the main source of Nationalist revenue. Here, Chiang used some of his best German-trained troops in three months of heroic and bloody fighting with heavy casualties. After Shanghai fell, the Chinese retreated in disarray and failed to take a stand at Wuxi as planned but poured into Nanjing, which fell in December.

The Nanjing Massacre followed. Japanese soldiers, backed by their superiors, went on a rampage, terrorizing, killing, raping, burning and looting for seven weeks. Sixty years later, the number of people who perished remains a matter of bitter contention—as though sheer numbers can measure the horror. The figure inscribed in the memorial erected in Nanjing (1985) is 300,000, but "whether 200,000 or 240,000 people were killed does not alter the dimension of the horror."[2] How and why it happened, and the lessons to be drawn therefrom, continue to generate intense controversy and stimulate reflection. The Japanese acquired a reputation for terrible cruelty, which stiffened the Chinese determination to resist and continued to cast a pall long after the war.

After Nanjing, the Japanese maintained and continued their offense, taking Canton in October and Wuhan in December; Chiang, refusing to submit, adopted a strategy of "trading space for time." Japan's prime minister at this time was Prince Konoe Fumimaro (1891–1945), a descendant of the Fujiwaras and protégé of Saionji. He held office from June 1937 to January 1939 and again from July 1940 to July 1941. Japanese policy making continued to be a very complicated process. The general staff, for example, did not share the optimism of the armies in the field, yet the government continued to expand the war, encouraged by a string of victories. As the war escalated, so did the Japanese government's aims and rhetoric. What had begun as a search for a pro-Japanese North China turned into a holy crusade against the West and Communism (see Figure 11.1).

In 1938, unable to obtain Chinese recognition of Manchukuo, the Konoe government declared Chiang's regime illegitimate and vowed to destroy it. In November Konoe proclaimed Japan's determination to establish a "new order in East Asia" that would include Japan, Manchukuo, and China in a political, economic, and cultural union, a bastion against (Western) imperialism and against Soviet Communism. Those who did not see the light were to be brought to their senses by force. Originally, in the summer of 1937, Japanese plans had called for a three-month campaign by three divisions, at a cost of 100 million yen, to destroy the main Chinese force and take possession of key areas while waiting for Chiang to ask for peace. But by the following spring they were preparing orders for twenty divisions and had appropriated more than 2.5 billion yen with promise of more to come and no end in sight.

The Nationalist government moved its wartime capital to Chongqing in Sichuan. Many refugees followed the government to the southwest (see Figure 11.2). Not only universities but also hundreds of factories were transported piecemeal to help the war effort in Chongqing, where Chiang held on gamely. Before the Japanese attack on Pearl Harbor (December 1941), China obtained financial assistance from the United States and the Soviet Union, and Stalin sent some pilots to be stationed in Gansu Province. From 1939 to 1941, Chongqing suffered repeated bombings. Not until August 1941 did help come in the form of the

FIGURE 11.1 China, 1930–Spring 1944. Also shown is the route of the Chinese Communist Party's Long March, October 1934–October 1935.

Flying Tigers, volunteer American pilots later incorporated into the Fourteenth U.S. Air Force, commanded by General Claire L. Chennault. However, the West's support remained primarily moral, and the Soviet Union alone sent some official assistance. Meanwhile, from 1939 to 1941, fighting on the ground was limited to skirmishes, with both sides working to consolidate their positions.

In 1940, when it became obvious that the Chinese would not bow to their demands, the Japanese established a puppet regime in Nanjing headed by Wang Jingwei, the erstwhile follower of Sun and leader of the left wing of the GMD. However, like a similar regime established earlier in Beijing, it was clear to the Chinese populace that the Japanese were pulling the strings.

Expansion of the War into a Pacific War

A major Japanese foreign policy concern during the 1930s was relations with the Soviet Union. From 1937 to 1940 there were three military confrontations along the Soviet Union's frontier with Korea and, far more serious, along the Mongolian border with Manchukuo. These operations, which increased in scale, involved the deployment of armor, artillery, and aircraft. The Japanese fought well, but the

FIGURE 11.2 *Refugees Crowding onto Trains Bound for Guilin,* Cai Dizhi. Chinese refugees escaping from Japanese-occupied territory followed the Chinese Nationalist government southwest to its temporary wartime capital in Chongqing. Scenes such as this were common in 1937 and 1938. Woodcut. (From *Woodcuts of Wartime China, 1937–1945,* Yonghua lingxin, ed. [Taiwan: L. Ming Cultural Enterprises, Dist.].)

Soviets proved more than a match. The last and most severe conflict cost Japan 180,000 men and resulted in an armistice.

Japan was caught off guard diplomatically when Germany, without warning, came to terms with the Soviet Union in August 1939. Japan was therefore neutral when World War II began in Europe shortly thereafter. However, the dramatic success of the German blitzkrieg strengthened the hands of those in Tokyo who favored a pro-German policy, and in September 1940, Konoe signed the Tripartite Pact, forming an alliance with Germany and Italy.

The Germans again surprised the Japanese in June 1941 when Hitler invaded the Soviet Union. Some army men wanted Japan to join the attack on the Soviet Union. As Alvin D. Coox pointed out, they saw this as a way out of the China impasse, "apparently convinced that the best way to climb out of a hole was to widen it."[3] However, the navy wanted to advance into the oil- and mineral-rich south. Officially, Japan claimed its mission to be the creation of a "greater East Asian co-prosperity sphere," but the underlying perception was that the resources of Southeast Asia were essential for Japan's economic security.

FIGURE 11.3 General Tōjō. (© The Mainichi Newspapers Co.)

Konoe hoped that, armed with the Tripartite Pact, he would be able to reach his aims without going to war with the United States, but the American government was becoming increasingly alarmed over Japanese expansion. When in the summer of 1941 Japan moved troops into southern Vietnam, the United States, Britain, and Holland (then in control of the East Indies, modern Indonesia) retaliated by applying the economic sanctions they had withheld in 1931. An embargo on scrap iron was serious, but the crucial product cut off from Japan was oil.

America and Japan were on a collision course. Michael A. Barnhart put it as follows:

> The Japanese Empire was determined to retain the rights and privileges it considered necessary for its economic and political security. The United States thought these rights and privileges contrary to its own deeply held principles and to the survival of what were now in effect its allies in the struggle against global aggression.[4]

The United States was determined that Japan should withdraw from China and Indochina. For Japan, this would have meant a reversal of the policy pursued in China since 1931 and the relinquishment of the vision of primacy in East Asia. Dependent on oil and rubber from Southeast Asia, the Japanese were in no position to carry on protracted negotiations. They had to fight or retreat. It is a bitter irony that Japan now prepared to go to war to attain the self-sufficiency that its proponents of total war had once considered a precondition for war.

When it became clear to Konoe that the situation had reached an impasse, he resigned; he was followed by General Tōjō Hideki (1884–1948), prime minister from October 1941 to July 1944 (see Figure 11.3). When last-minute negotiations proved fruitless, the Japanese decided on war as the least unpalatable alternative. It began on December 7, 1941, with a surprise attack on Pearl Harbor, Hawaii, that destroyed seven American battleships and 120 aircraft and left 2400 dead. With the United States and Japan at war, Hitler, too, declared war against the United States, but German–Japanese cooperation during the war remained limited.

The Course of the War

At first the war went spectacularly well for Japan. By the middle of 1942 Japan controlled the Philippines, Malaya, Burma, and the East Indies. Japan was also in charge in Indochina (officially under the jurisdiction of Vichy France) and enjoyed the cooperation of a friendly regime in Thailand. However, contrary to hopes in Tokyo, the United States, far from being ready to negotiate a quick peace, mobilized for full-scale war.

In June 1942 Japan suffered a major defeat when it was checked at the battle of Midway, 1200 miles northwest of Hawaii (see Figure 11.4). The Americans, taking advantage of advance knowledge of Japanese movements obtained from breaking the Japanese secret code, destroyed many Japanese planes and sank four Japanese aircraft carriers, losing only one of their own. Three more years of intense warfare, including bloody hand-to-hand combat, lay ahead, but the American use of aircraft carriers and the extensive deployment of submarines, which took a tremendous toll on vital Japanese shipping, were two factors contributing to Japan's ultimate defeat. Another was the island-hopping strategy, whereby the American forces seized islands selectively for use as bases for further advances, bypassing others with their forces intact but out of action. One consequence of this strategy was that although the Allies wanted Japan to remain bogged down in China, China itself was not a major war theater.

In China, the Japanese patronized puppet armies and even tolerated trade with the Guomindang-controlled areas of China, but the Wang Jingwei regime was too obviously controlled by the Japanese ever to gain credibility. At best, life in occupied China went on as usual, but Japanese arrogance alienated many Chinese. Humane behavior on the part of some individuals was overshadowed by acts of cruelty that evoked Chinese hatred and resistance. An example is the notorious "kill all, burn all, destroy all" campaign carried out in 1941 and 1942 in parts of northern China in retaliation for a Chinese Communist offensive. Implemented literally, the Japanese hurt the Communists badly, but they also helped turn apolitical peasants into determined fighters.

As the war dragged on, the Communists established widespread peasant support in northern China, where they became the effective government in the countryside behind the Japanese lines. The Japanese, concentrated in the cities and guarding their lines of supply, did not have the manpower to patrol the rural areas constantly and effectively.

In the areas nominally under Japanese control, the Communists skillfully pursued policies to fuse national resistance and social revolution. The key to their ultimate success was mass mobilization of the peasantry, but the mix of policies and the pace of change varied according to local conditions. Carefully avoiding pre-

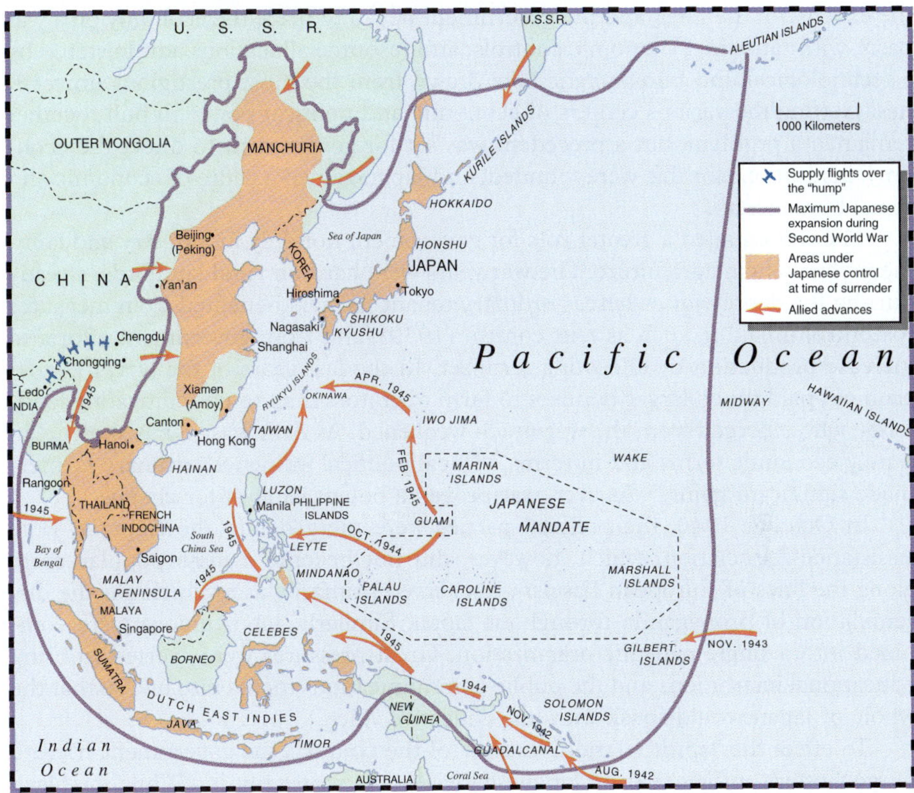

FIGURE 11.4 The Pacific War.

mature class warfare, they frequently began by organizing the peasants to wage guerrilla war, enlisting support from the village elites for the war effort, and manipulating them into going along with rent and interest reduction. Building their military power, they enlisted elite support even as they undermined elite power. The Chinese Communist Party emerged from the war stronger than it had ever been. The outcome of the civil war that followed was not obvious to observers, but it is one of the ironies of the war that the Japanese, who proclaimed that they were combating Communism in China, instead ended by contributing to its victory.

Japan at War

Well before Pearl Harbor, the effects of the continued war in China were felt by the Japanese people as militarization and authoritarianism increased at home. The National General Mobilization Law of 1938 strengthened the prime minister at the expense of the Diet, and the government began to place the economy on a war basis, with rationing, economic controls, and resource allocations administered by a technological and bureaucratic elite drawn from the most prestigious universities. Getting the various centers of economic and political power to pull together remained a problem, but a precedent was set for government to direct the economy; institutions for this were founded, and Japan gained a cadre of economic and social bureaucrats.

The war entailed a greater role for government not only in industry and commerce but also in agriculture. The war years were hard on rural landlords, already hurt by the depression, whereas ordinary tenant farmers benefited from measures to control inflation, such as rent control (1939), and from government efforts to increase production by allocating fertilizer. In the last years of the war, the government paid much larger bonuses to farm operators than to noncultivating landlords, who emerged from the war much weakened. As Ann Waswo has shown, "in purely economic terms and in terms of local political influence, ordinary farmers made significant gains."[5] As ever, war proved a potent catalyst for change.

In October 1940, the political parties were merged into the Imperial Rule Assistance Association, which, however, did not become a mass popular party along the lines of European Fascism but served primarily as a vehicle for the dissemination of propaganda throughout Japan. Similarly, labor unions were combined into a single patriotic organization. Great pressures were exerted to bring educational institutions and the public communications media into line so that the whole of Japan would speak with one collective voice.

To effect the "spiritual mobilization" of the country, the government tried to purge Western influence from Japanese life. As one writer put it, "While the black ships that represent the material might of the West have left, a hundred years later the Black Ships of thought are still threatening us."[6] Prominent intellectuals insisted on Japanese uniqueness and exceptionalism and drew on German concepts of irony and angst, nostalgia for the past, and aesthetics of death, subjectivity, and poetry to attack the "modern" at home and abroad. Not only were foreign radical and liberal ideas banned from theoretical discourse, but popular culture was also purged. Permanent waves and jazz, so popular during the 1920s, were banned. Efforts were made to remove Western loanwords from the language, and the people were bombarded with exhortations to observe traditional values and revere the divine emperor. Heterodox religious sects with no ostensible political agenda were suppressed, and in a "triumph of religious stateism,"[7] all religions were subordinated to the imperial cult. To mobilize the public down to the ward level, the people were formed into small neighborhood organizations.

Colonial East Asia during the War

Japan's attempt to win over the population of the conquered areas by encouraging their native religious traditions, exploiting their resentment against Western imperialism, and teaching them the Japanese language was more than offset by

Japan's own imperialistic exploitation, the harshness of its rule, and the cruelty of its soldiers. The slogan "Asia for the Asians" did not disguise the realities of what Mark R. Peattie has characterized as a "mutant colonialism when the tightening demands on the energies, loyalties, and resources of Japan's colonial peoples by a nation at war with much of Asia and most of the West transmogrified an authoritarian but recognizably 'Western' colonial system into an empire of the lash, a totalitarian imperium, that dragged along its peoples as it staggered toward defeat."[8]

Conditions were particularly harsh in Korea, but in Taiwan, too, there was a campaign to assimilate the population and turn them into people who spoke Japanese, had Japanese names, and even worshiped at Shinto shrines. Although Taiwanese were regimented and controlled at home, Taiwanese entrepreneurs took advantage of new opportunities in Manchuria and elsewhere, and young people responded positively to efforts to recruit them into the Japanese military. The largest contingent served on Hainan island, where many perished. However, on the whole, people in Taiwan, as in Korea, welcomed Japan's defeat. When Chinese Nationalists forces arrived in October 1945, they were welcomed as liberators.

Japanese forces dominated Vietnam, although until the fall of Vichy France in March 1945, they left the Vichy French colonial administration in place. The Japanese conducted a cultural campaign claiming that they had come as liberators from all European colonialism and seeking support especially among Buddhists, in contrast to the French who encouraged and gave new freedoms to Catholics. Resisting both Japanese and French were the Viet Minh (short for Viet Nam Doc Lap Dong Minh, or League for the Independence of Vietnam), established in the northwest by Ho Chi Minh when he returned to Vietnam in 1941. Viet Minh policy was to postpone the Marxist revolutionary agenda to form a broad nationalist coalition and possibly to gain assistance from the Allies. Established in 1941, the policy resulted in Ho's cooperation with the American Office of Strategic Services in 1944. That the United States would support the reimposition of French colonialism was not yet apparent by war's end.

Elsewhere in Japan's bloated empire the colonial authorities were replaced by Japanese-controlled puppet regimes. The history of Southeast Asia is beyond the scope of our text, but we should note that although Japan won no friends, they shattered the myth along with the actuality of Western hegemony and paved the way for the end of colonialism—ultimately throughout the globe.

The End of the War

The closer the American forces came to the Japanese homeland, the easier it was for them to bomb Japan itself. Such raids were aimed not only at military and industrial installations but also at economic targets and population centers. Incendiary bombs were dropped to sap the morale of the people, who by the last years of the war were suffering from scarcities of all kinds, including food and other daily necessities, many of which were available only on the black market.

In July 1944, after the fall of Saipan, largest of the Mariana Islands, General Tōjō was forced out of office, but there was no change either in the fortunes of war or in policy under his successor, General Koiso Kuniaki (1880–1950). General Koiso remained in office until April 1945, when he was succeeded by Admiral Suzuki Kantarō (1867–1948). Some civilian leaders sent out peace feelers to the Allies, but their efforts were hampered by the noncooperation of the Soviet Union, anxious to have the war continue long enough to allow it to participate, and by the demand issued at Potsdam in July 1945, insisting on Japan's unconditional surrender.

This demand reflected the Allied belief that it had been a mistake to allow World War I to end in an armistice rather than in a full capitulation, permitting Hitler to claim that Germany had been "betrayed" into defeat, not beaten on the field of battle. Determined not to commit a similar mistake, the Allies now demanded an unconditional surrender, which stiffened the resistance of Japanese leaders concerned about the fate of the emperor.

The last year of the war was especially terrible; on one night in March 1945, some 100,000 people died as the result of a firebomb raid on Tokyo, and a similar raid in May devastated another large part of Japan's capital city. Meanwhile, bombers created an "iron-storm" over Okinawa, sending local people to seek refuge in caves, where some would perish after Japanese soldiers forced them into "compulsory group suicide."[9] Short of resources, and with its cities in ruins, during the last months of the war Japan was reduced to desperate measures, such as the use of flying bombs directed by suicide pilots, called "kamikaze" after the "divine wind" that once had saved the land from the Mongols.

Tokyo and other major cities had been practically leveled by conventional bombing, but on August 6 the United States dropped an atomic bomb on Hiroshima (see Figure 11.5) in southwestern Honshu, razing more than 80 percent of the buildings and leaving some 200,000 people dead or injured and countless others to continue their lives under the specter of radiation sickness. Two days later, on August 8, the Soviet Union entered the war, and the next day the United States dropped a second atomic bomb, this time on Nagasaki.

Recent scholarship shows that all along the emperor paid careful attention to the war without intervening in actual military operations. But now his throne was at stake, as Edward J. Drea explains:

> In the face of total defeat, he valued the imperial institution more than his people, his army, and his empire. . . . Perhaps more than fire raids, atomic bombs, the Soviet entry into the war against Japan, and the specter of invasion, it was the threat to his imperial ancestors, and therefore the survival of the imperial institution itself, that provided the steel otherwise missing from Hirohito's regal backbone.[10]

In any case, twice during these fateful days a government deadlock was broken by the personal intervention of the emperor, each time in favor of peace. Even after the final decision for peace, diehards tried to continue the war by a last resort to violence in the tradition of the terrorists who had first helped steer Japan toward militarism and war. They set fire to the homes of the prime minister and president of the Privy Council and invaded the imperial palace in search of the recording of the emperor's peace message, but they failed. When all was lost, several leaders, including the war minister, committed ritual suicide.

FIGURE 11.5 *Hiroshima.* Through the vault over the Memorial Cenotaph for the Atomic Bomb Victims can be seen the Atomic Bomb Memorial Dome. The steel skeleton of the dome and the gutted building (formerly the city's Industrial Promotion Hall) have been left standing unaltered, in witness to the tragedy. (© John Van Hasselt/Corbis Sygma)

On August 15, the imperial recording was broadcast over the radio, and throughout Japan the people, for the first time, heard the voice of their emperor. In the formal language appropriate to his elevated status, he informed them that the war was lost. This is how Ōe Kenzaburō, the future winner of the Nobel Prize for literature, ten years old at the time, recollects the effect of the broadcast:

> The adults sat around their radios and cried. The children gathered outside in the dusty road and whispered their bewilderment. We were most confused and disappointed by the fact that the Emperor had spoken in a human voice, no different from any adult's. None of us understood what he was saying, but we had all heard his voice. One of my friends could even imitate it cleverly. Laughing, we surrounded him—a twelve-year-old in grimy shorts who spoke with the Emperor's voice. A minute later we felt afraid. We looked at one another; no one spoke. How could we believe that an august presence of such awful power had become an ordinary human voice on a designated summer day.[11]

Notes

1. The term "incantatory symbol" comes from Masao Maruyama, in Ivan Morris, ed., *Thought and Behavior in Modern Japanese Politics,* expanded edition (New York: Oxford Univ. Press, 1969), p. 376.
2. Joshua A. Fogel, "Introduction," in Joshua A. Fogel, ed., *The Nanjing Massacre in History and Historiography* (Berkeley: Univ. of California Press, 2000), p. 6.
3. Alvin D. Coox, in Peter Duus, ed., *The Cambridge History of Japan, Vol. 6: The Twentieth Century* (Cambridge: Cambridge Univ. Press, 1988), p. 324.
4. Michael A. Barnhart, *Japan Prepares for Total War: The Search for Economic Security, 1919–1941* (Ithaca: Cornell Univ. Press, 1987), p. 234.
5. Ann Waswo, in *The Cambridge History of Japan, Vol. 6*, p. 104.

6. Kamei Katsuichiro, quoted in Kevin Michael Doak, *Dreams of Difference: The Japan Romantic School and the Crisis of Modernity* (Berkeley: Univ. of California Press, 1994), p. 101.
7. Sheldon Garon, *Molding Japanese Minds: The State in Everyday Life* (Princeton: Princeton Univ. Press, 1997), pp. 84–87.
8. Mark R. Peattie, in *The Cambridge History, Vol. 6,* p. 269. For "mutant colonialism," see p. 234.
9. Norma Field, *In the Realm of a Dying Emperor: Japan at Century's End* (New York: Vintage Books, 1993), p. 61.
10. Edward J. Drea, *In the Service of the Emperor: Essays on the Imperial Japanese Army* (Lincoln: Univ. of Nebraska Press, 1998), p. 215.
11. Ōe Kenzaburō, *A Personal Matter,* John Nathan, trans. (New York: Grove Press, 1968), pp. vii–viii.

12

The New Japan

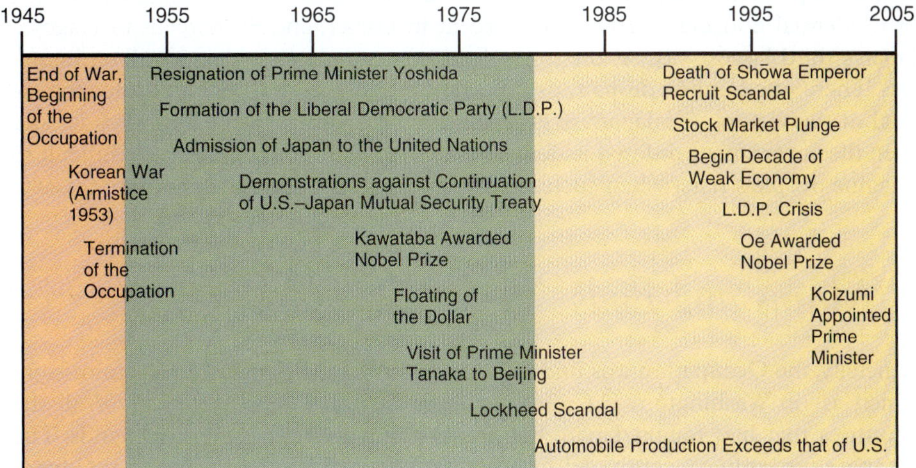

Throughout East Asia, as across the globe, World War II was followed by a period of change unprecedented in its rapidity and scope, affecting the direction of civilization, economic systems and social structure, and the lives of millions of people. The war destroyed the Japanese Empire, confirmed the eclipse of the Western European powers begun by World War I, and hastened the end of the old colonialism. In Asia, the British Empire was dismantled as India and Burma attained independence (1947), and followed by the Malay Peninsula (1957), leaving only Hong Kong as a Crown Colony—and it was scheduled to revert to Chinese rule in 1997. However, the Dutch in Indonesia and, especially, the French in Indochina resorted to military means in a futile attempt to preserve their colonies.

The war left only two superpowers, the United States and the Soviet Union, with the capacity to exercise major influence over events in East Asia. By 1947 they had developed a bitter rivalry and a "cold" war. To quote I. M. Roberts:

> Even if the Cold War stopped short of actual armed conflict between the two principals, subversion, bribery, murder, espionage, propaganda and diplomatic quarrelling long gave fresh colour to the basic premise, that it was impossible for communist and non-communist societies to cooperate and relate to one another in the way civilized societies had once believed to be normal."[1]

An immediate result of the war was that Japan had to relinquish not only Manchuria and other areas seized since 1931, but all lands acquired since 1895, most notably Taiwan and Korea. At home, Imperial Japan was discredited.

I. The Occupation (1945–1952)

The war left Japan in ruins, its cities largely destroyed, the economy wrecked. About 40 percent of Japan's total urban area was wiped out, including 65 percent of residential housing in Tokyo, 57 percent in Osaka, and 89 percent in Nagoya, Japan's third largest city. At the time of the surrender there were 9 million homeless. There was hunger, despair, psychic shock, and fear. In preparation for the arrival of the victors, the Japanese evacuated many women to the countryside, and even the government ordered its female employees out of town. It is not difficult to imagine people's relief when such measures turned out to have been unnecessary.

Means and Ends

Officially, the Occupation was under the authority of the Far Eastern Commission, which sat in Washington, D.C. Its members included representatives of all the countries that had fought Japan, but actual control was in American hands. The Japanese government continued to function, but it did so according to the directives and "suggestions" of the Occupation authorities, headed by General Douglas MacArthur, Supreme Commander for the Allied Powers (SCAP). Despite the "Allied Powers" in the title and the presence of some British and Commonwealth officials, the Occupation was essentially American. In General MacArthur it had a leader who won easy credibility—a commanding figure, a "blue-eyed shogun" convinced of his historic mission, and a military man who commanded respect, exuded confidence, and had a flair for drama. The process of policy formation was complex, involving Washington, the Occupation bureaucracy, and the Japanese and reflecting divisions within and among these groups. But General MacArthur had a strong hand in fashioning, interpreting, and administering policy.

The Occupation's mission to demilitarize Japan and turn the country into a peaceful and democratic state was accepted with enthusiasm by a staff composed partly of New Dealers and by General MacArthur, who regarded the Japanese as an immature people ready for and in need of tutelage. Despite or because of their lack of preparation, the Americans were convinced they had the answers, and their conviction of the righteousness of their values and policies remained firm, even after the onset of the Cold War induced them to change course.

At the outset, the Occupation faced the pressing tasks of disarming the Japanese military and providing enough relief to prevent famine. The widespread destruction of capital goods and industrial plants, a soil starved for lack of fertilizers, the loss of the natural resources from the former empire and of the entire merchant fleet, and the need to feed around 6 million Japanese expatriates and refugees from overseas threatened economic catastrophe. In this situation, suffering was unavoidable. By supplying food and medical supplies, the Occupation authorities helped avert the worst, but the alternative to the black market was starvation. It was not until 1947 that the United States became seriously concerned with rebuilding the Japanese economy. Even in 1948 a magazine editorial complained, "in today's Japan, the only people who are not living illegally are those in jail."[2]

Demilitarization entailed dismantling the military establishment and purging from positions of political and economic leadership those most closely associated with leading the country to war. Outside Japan—and excluding the Soviet Union and parts of China controlled by the C.C.P.—5700 individuals were tried by fifty military tribunals with the result that 984 were sentenced to death, among them 173 Taiwanese and 148 Koreans. Twenty-eight top leaders charged with responsibility for the war were tried in Tokyo by an international tribunal of eleven judges that sat in Tokyo from May 1946 to April 1948 and included a Chinese, a Filipino, and an Indian jurist but no Korean. When the sentences were handed down in November 1948, seven leaders were condemned to die, including Tōjō Hideki, the rather colorless general who had headed Japan's wartime government. His role during the war had been more like a chairman of the board than a dictator, but wartime propaganda had cast him as a Japanese Hitler. The lengthy judicial proceedings produced voluminous records but never attained the legal clarity or the moral authority achieved by the trial of Nazi leaders at Nuremberg.

In the end, around 200,000 persons were purged, about half of them from the military. However, most of these men were later reinstated, and some became prominent. The military elite lost the most, but the decision of the Occupation to operate through, rather than to replace, the existing government made for a high level of continuity within the bureaucracy. This contributed to the continuing importance of the bureaucracy even after a new constitution placed government on a new footing.

Although he had sanctioned a war fought in his name, the emperor was not charged with war crimes, nor was there a judicial inquiry into the part he had played. Instead, SCAP's policy was to use the emperor's authority yet demystify his person and throne. He was pressured to substitute a more open lifestyle (akin to that of the British monarch) for the secluded and ritualized existence traditionally led by Japanese emperors. An example of the demystification process was the emperor's unprecedented visit to General MacArthur at SCAP headquarters. The resulting photograph (see Figure 12.1), showing the stiffly formal emperor standing next to the open-shirted general, caused considerable shock and dismay throughout Japan. In his New Year's message of 1946, the emperor publicly denied his divinity, and under the new constitution he became a symbol of the nation. For the remainder of his life he never acknowledged any responsibility for the war, setting an example not lost on his subjects.

This constitution, which went into effect in May 1947, was drafted and practically dictated by the Occupation. It stipulated that sovereignty belongs to the people, placed the highest political authority in the hands of the Diet (to which the executive was now made responsible), and established an independent judiciary. Another noteworthy set of political changes were those decreasing the power of the central government, particularly the Home Ministry, and fostering local self-government. Accompanying these structural changes were provisions for universal suffrage and human rights, including the equality of women. A unique feature was the renunciation of war. Article IX stipulates, "The Japanese people forever re-

FIGURE 12.1 General Douglas MacArthur, Supreme Commander for the Allied Powers (SCAP) occupation forces, and Emperor Hirohito of Japan, soon to publicly deny his divinity. (© AP/Wide World Photos [APA5163982])

nounce war as a sovereign right of the nation and the threat or use of force as a means of settling international disputes," and it goes on to say, "land, sea, and air forces, as well as other war potential, will never be maintained."[3] In this way, the authors of the constitution sought to incorporate peacefulness into the very framework of the new Japanese state.

Social Policies

The authorities at SCAP headquarters knew that Japan could not be turned into a democracy simply by changing the political system. Consequently, they tried to change Japanese society. Because many American officials lacked previous study or experience in Japan, they tended to rely excessively on American prototypes without taking into sufficient account Japan's own experience and situation. Thus, they restructured the educational system to conform to the American sequence of elementary school, junior high school, high school, and college, and they forced the Japanese to eliminate their old technical schools and special higher schools, which previously covered the eleventh to thirteenth years of education and prepared students for university study. Under the old system, only the student elite had access to a university education, but under the new, all students were to be given equal educational opportunities through high school. In an effort to expand opportunities for higher education, many of the old technical and higher schools were upgraded to become universities. But these new universities were not of a quality comparable to the old, established schools, such as Tokyo University. Competition for admission to this and other prestigious universities remained brutal. Students found themselves embroiled in a veritable "examination hell."

To reform the content of education, the Occupation abolished the old ethics courses and purged textbooks fostering militaristic and authoritarian values. Its attack on these old values was rather successful, especially because they had already been largely discredited by defeat. Similarly, language reform found ready acceptance: the list of standard characters, many of them simplified, issued by the Cabinet in 1946 (1850 *tōyō kanji*) required only minor modifications and additions when revised in 1981 (the current system of 1945 *jōyō kanji*).

The Occupation was less successful in its attempts to create a positive sense of individual civic responsibility and citizenship. Social change entails a transformation of values, and thus naturally takes longer than institutional change, but changes in the legal system can encourage social change. Among the Occupation's notable efforts in this direction were measures to enhance the status of women and to limit the powers and privileges of the family's male head. The new constitution stated explicitly in Article XXIV, "Marriage shall be based upon the mutual consent of both sexes, and it shall be maintained through mutual cooperation, with equal rights of husband and wife as a basis." The presence of thousands of Americans in their country also gave the Japanese an unusual opportunity to observe foreign mores. It may have encouraged them to become somewhat more relaxed toward authority, and it stimulated a measure of cosmopolitanism.

Economic Policy

It was generally recognized that the desired political and social changes demanded an economic foundation, and the authorities set about restructuring the Japanese economy. Most successful in this respect was the program of land reform. This prohibited absentee landlordism and restricted the amount of land a resident landowner could hold to a maximum of seven acres to work himself and another two acres to rent out (except in Hokkaido, where the average farm was twelve acres, because the climate precludes intensive rice cultivation). Anything in excess had to be sold to the government, which resold it to former tenants. There was provision for compensation for the landlords, but inflation made this meaningless. The old inequity in the countryside was eliminated. In terms of productivity, too, the land policy was a success, because the agrarian sector was the first to recover.

In the urban industrial sector, the Occupation began by trying to eliminate, or at least reduce, the concentrations of economic power, which Americans viewed as a major component of Japanese authoritarianism. One policy was to foster labor unions. The constitution guaranteed the right of workers to organize and to bargain and act collectively. As intended, a vigorous union movement developed, but contrary to American wishes, the Japanese unions did not, like the American Federation of Labor and Congress of Industrial Organizations, limit themselves to economic demands. Much like European unions, they were political in orientation, developing into labor arms of the Socialist and Communist parties. In February 1947, the Occupation banned a planned general strike and thereafter was less friendly toward the unions. Laws prohibiting public employees from striking followed.

On the management and ownership side, the Occupation did break up the old holding companies and purged the old *zaibatsu* families from positions of economic leadership. Contrary to initial expectations, however, this did not lead to genuine decentralization. Where old systems were broken up, new and equally pervasive patterns of trade and finance developed, bearing a marked resemblance to the old. Furthermore, a plan to break up operating companies petered out: of 1200 companies initially considered, only 28 were, in the end, split apart. Economic power and decision making remained concentrated. The reasons for this are instructive for understanding the accomplishments and failures of the Occupation as a whole, because they include both a Japanese and an American component.

On the Japanese side, strong support for land reform contrasted with a marked lack of enthusiasm for American-style trust busting. Few shared the American faith in the ultimate benefits of maximum competition. Instead, the feeling was that Japanese companies needed to be large to compete in the international market. Radicals and conservatives disagreed about ownership and control, not about the structure of industry and commerce.

Decentralization of the economy also faltered because it was abandoned with a shift in American policy already signaled by the ban on the 1947 general strike. In an atmosphere of mounting Cold War tension and in line with what is frequently called the "reverse course," economic and strategic considerations prevailed. Increasingly, the United States saw Japan, called by the secretary of state "the workshop of Asia," as a potentially valuable and much-needed ally after the victory of the Chinese Communists in 1949. On the advice of Joseph Dodge, a Detroit banker sent out by Washington in 1949, in April of that year the value of the yen was set at 360 to the dollar—low even then—to encourage exports by making Japanese goods inexpensive abroad and to promote frugality at home. In May, the Ministry of International Trade and Industry (MITI) was formed by merging the Ministry of Commerce and Industry and the Board of Trade, "constituting a greater centralization of economic authority than had been achieved at the peak of Japan's mobilization for war."[4] Meanwhile, the Ministry of Finance exercised paramount sway over budgets and monetary policy. Both would continue playing these roles long after the Occupation ended.

More than labor and economic policies were affected by the policy shift. Communists were purged (1949–1950), and others who had been purged earlier were allowed to reemerge in public life. Because an armed ally, capable at least of self-defense, would be more valuable than an unarmed one, the United States had second thoughts about Japan's renunciation of military force.

Dodge's deflationary policies led to economic decline until the outbreak of the Korean War in June 1950 brought a flood of orders for equipment and supplies, a procurement boom that gave an enormous boost to the faltering economy.

The Korean War

Increasing international tensions between the United States and the Soviet Union and bitter antagonism between the governments of the two Koreas reduced the chances for unification by negotiation. Both the Communist state in the north and the anti-Communist government in the south harbored the ambition to rule the entire country. These ambitions erupted into war in June 1950 when North Korea attacked South Korea.

The period of intense fighting can be divided into three main phases, each with its own subdivisions. First, from June to September 1950, the North Koreans were on the offensive, pushing the South Korean and American forces back until they established a defense perimeter around Pusan from which they could not be dislodged. The second phase began with General MacArthur's amphibious landing at Inchon in September, which led to the recapture of Seoul and then to an offensive intended to unify Korea by force. Then, in November, the Chinese, alarmed by the American advance to the Yalu River and having had their warnings ignored, sent massive "volunteer" armies into Korea. These succeeded in regaining the North but were unable to win control over the South. This became clear in late May 1951, and in July of that year truce talks began. Earlier, in April, President Truman had dismissed General MacArthur, thereby making it clear that America would not extend the war beyond Korea. His dismissal of the eminent and popular general also demonstrated the American system of civil control over the military, a demonstration that had a considerable effect on Japan.

Casualties in this war were heavy on both sides. They included more than 800,000 Koreans (approximately 520,000 North Koreans and 300,000 South Koreans) and probably as many or more Chinese soldiers. The southern forces were sanctioned by the United Nations and fought under a United Nations command, but approximately half of the ground troops and most of the air and naval forces were supplied by the United States, which suffered 142,000 casualties. South Korea supplied two-fifths of the remaining United Nations troops, and thirteen other countries combined to make up the remainder. The truce talks dragged on for two years until an armistice was signed in July 1953. Although marred by incidents, this armistice remains in effect today.

For Japan, the war brought profitable orders for equipment and supplies, a procurement boom that gave substantial boost to a still-faltering economy. Even after the war, orders to supply American troops and bases continued to benefit the Japanese economy. Under American encouragement, Japan also created a paramilitary force of 75,000, a first step toward limited rearmament. A basic pattern of internal economic growth and dependence on the United States for ultimate military protection was set. For decades, Japan continued to take its foreign policy cues from the United States.

The End of the Occupation

The end of the Occupation, a subject broached by General MacArthur as early as 1947, was delayed largely because of Soviet opposition. Although the Occupation continued, by the time General MacArthur took command in Korea in July 1950, its work was practically complete. Dismissed by President Truman, he departed from East Asia for good in April 1951. Although in his subsequent testimony to Congress he spoke glowingly of the Japanese, they were distressed to hear him compare them with children.

Under the Occupation, electoral politics was reintroduced, and political parties representing a broad range of ideas and a variety of interests battled for votes. The Diet again became the central arena for national politics. The leading political personality to emerge during the Occupation was Yoshida Shigeru (1878–1967), a former diplomat who had opposed the military leadership in Japan during the 1930s. Yoshida dominated Japanese politics for the better part of a decade, serving as prime minister in 1946 and 1947 and again from 1948 to 1954. A coalition of conservatives and socialists of various shades of radicalism held power briefly in 1947 and 1948 but was unable to create a viable government, partly because of divisions within its ranks and partly because of Occupation hostility toward socialism. Upon reassuming the prime ministership, Yoshida called a new election. Held in 1949, it provided his Liberal party with an absolute majority.

It was Yoshida who signed the peace treaty in San Francisco in September 1951, which was ratified the following April and accompanied by a defense treaty that provided for American bases in Japan and continued occupation of Okinawa. At the insistence of the U.S. Senate, Japan signed a parallel treaty with the Chinese nationalists on Taiwan and agreed to follow the American policy of nonrecognition and containment of the P.R.C. The Soviet Union was not a party to the San Francisco treaty. Formal diplomatic relations were established in 1956, but Moscow and Tokyo could not agree on the disposition of four small islands and entered the twenty-first century without ever signing a peace treaty to conclude World War II.

Assessments of the Occupation must naturally take into account later history because so many institutions and practices of contemporary Japan are rooted in this period. What came to be known as the Japanese model of bureaucratic capitalism has been dubbed the "SCAPanese model."[5] Some people think the reforms went too fast and too far, and others deplore the "reverse course" taken in response to the Cold War and the persistence of certain traditional institutions and patterns. These include the treatment and retention of the emperor, the role of the bureaucracy, the relationship between government and business, and the failure to adhere strictly to Article IX.

What seems clear is that the Occupation brought about major changes, but it was most successful in areas in which there were Japanese precedents and substantial support. This was true of much of the political program, the land reform, and the advocacy of liberal values. Representative institutions, after all, went back to the nineteenth century, and demands for land reform, calls for equality, and opposition to authoritarianism all predate the rise of militarism. The movement for women's rights had begun in the 1910s. Despite misconceptions and mistakes, and despite the contradiction inherent in a plan to foster democracy by command, much of what the Occupation attempted took hold.

The Occupation also had unplanned side effects, including the influx of foreign culture. Intellectuals who were eager to catch up with the recent Western developments devoured translations of Western books. Many turned to Marxism, but the whole spectrum of ideas found translators and readers. Popular culture was more open than ever to foreign influence. In some respects, the scene resembled that after World War I. It did not take the Occupation to introduce the Japanese to baseball and jazz. However, this time change went deeper, and there was to be no radical turning away such as took place in the 1930s. If anything, the doors and windows opened by defeat and occupation are even more widely open today.

II. The New Japan (1952–1989)

Economic Growth and Political Stability

The Economy

Government and Politics

The 1970s and 1980s

After regaining independence in 1952, Japan went on to achieve such phenomenal economic growth that by the 1970s it had become one of the world's industrial giants. By the 1980s, people in the United States and Britain were turning to Japan for lessons in industrial management. Despite a setback in the last decade of the century, Japan remained an economic power second only to the United States. Japan's economic growth was part of a broader transformation that affected every aspect of life.

Economic Growth and Political Stability

The Economy

In Japan as elsewhere, economic and political history are deeply intertwined. As we have seen, the Japanese economy was greatly stimulated by the Korean War. Thereafter, Japan continued to profit from access to foreign raw materials, technology, and markets, including those of the United States. Because of popular sentiment, constitutional constraints, and the country's reliance on the American "nuclear umbrella," Japan was freed from the burden of supporting a large and costly military establishment, releasing funds and energies for economic development. At the same time, business benefited from a probusiness political system.

Politically, the period began with Yoshida in power and his Liberal party in control of the Diet. He remained in office until 1954, when he was forced to resign in the wake of a scandal involving the shipping industry. In the elections of 1955, the Democratic party, a rival conservative party, won a plurality but not the majority required to govern. It therefore entered into negotiations with the Liberal party that led to the formation of the Liberal Democratic Party (L.D.P.) which dominated Japanese politics until 1993.

By 1953, economic production had practically returned to prewar levels, although the volume of trade was still only half of what it had been previously. After 1954, the economic surge continued, transforming recovery into growth at an average of 10 percent a year from 1955 to 1974 (including more than 11 percent during the 1960s). During the 1950s, with government support, great strides were made in heavy industry—even though Japan lacks raw materials and is poor in energy resources. By building manufacturing plants in port cities, which provided the advantage of low-cost ocean transport, and through the sophisticated application of modern technologies, Japan was able to become the world's leading shipbuilder and the third largest producer of iron and steel (after the United States and the Soviet Union). By 1974 its steel production had reached 89 percent of that of the United States. There were investments in chemicals, textiles, and consumer products. The washing machine, vacuum cleaner, and refrigerator of the 1950s were soon joined by the television set and the air conditioner, with the video recorder, microwave, and computer following in the 1980s. Car production reached 10 million in 1966, dubbed "year one of the My-Car Era" by the media. Cameras, watches, and even pianos—it is difficult to think of a major consumer technology in which Japan failed to excel.

Some of these products were built by new companies, such as Sony or Honda, founded by entrepreneurs who took advantage of the opportunities offered by postwar economic dislocation to build new enterprises from scratch. Other ambitious men (in what remained a man's world) reorganized or rejuvenated older companies, often importing technology by buying rights to foreign patents. In the dominant position in the economy, however, familiar old names reappeared, including Mitsui, the world's oldest major company, as well as Mitsubishi, Sumitomo, and others.

The names were old, but they now designated a new kind of enterprise grouping consisting of affiliated companies (*keiretsu*) rather than the family-centered *zaibatsu* of the prewar period. Each group included a bank, likely an insurance company, a real estate firm, and a cluster of companies engaged in every conceivable line of business, where its main competitor was most frequently a member of a rival group. The activities of the various member firms of each group were coordinated in periodic meetings of their presidents in presidents' clubs. Interlocking directorships, mutual stock holdings, and internal financing further held the organizations together, although more loosely than in the old *zaibatsu*. The *keiretsu* grew in size and strength until in the mid-1970s a study by Japan's Fair Trade Commission found that the six major groupings, composed of 175 core companies, held 21.9 percent of all the capital in Japan and had a controlling interest in another 3095 corporations that held 26.1 percent of the nation's capital. In addition, there were their substantial investments in other companies that they influenced without controlling.

Among the member firms of these enterprise groupings, the most spectacular were trading companies (*shōsha*) that conducted their business not only at home but all over the world. These were exporting and importing, transporting and storing, and financing and organizing a host of multifarious projects—an airport in Kenya, a large commercial farm on Sumatra, a petrochemical industry for Iran, or copper mining in Zaire, linked by communications networks that, for a time, were unparalleled. Furthermore, Mitsui, Mitsubishi, and the others built their own research organizations, analyzing information, charting future trends, and drawing up plans to provide for future project recommendations. Their experts engaged in city planning, energy research, and research into the world's oceans.

Japanese companies provided varied services and facilities for their employees, including company dormitories for the unmarried. There were company athletic teams and a host of recreational activities, such as organized outings to mountain retreats. These were intended not only to foster the health and well-being of the employees but also to strengthen feelings of group solidarity and identification with the sponsoring company, which used them to convey an image of paternalistic solicitude. At Toyota, Japan's leading automobile manufacturer, white-collar men received an entire year of training, including a month in a company camp. Recruitment patterns that centered on certain universities, encouraging ties among men entering a company in the same year; an emphasis on longevity in promotions; the practice of extensive consultation; and a strong preference for decision by consensus all helped foster management solidarity.

Japanese companies, especially the large modern concerns, mostly retained the loyalty of their employees, who were made to feel that what was best for the company was also best for Japan. This business ideology gained credence from management's practice of plowing earnings back into the company so that it could continue to grow and hopefully surpass its rivals. At the same time, the efficacy of persuasion should not be exaggerated, because company extras increasingly became matters not of paternalism but of contractual rights subject to collective bargaining, like fringe benefits in other countries. However, management was able to get workers to agree to moderate wage increases and fringe benefits. The threat of foreign competition was also used effectively, and for years Japanese companies enjoyed a lower labor bill and more labor peace than many of their competitors in Europe and America. The quest for economic growth gave Japan a sense of national purpose even as it promised an improved standard of living for the people.

Japan's concentration on economic development was epitomized in the income-doubling policy of Ikeda Hayato (1899–1965, prime minister 1960–1964), that provided for the doubling of per capita production in ten years. The government fostered growth by establishing a political climate favorable to economic expansion, by investing in infrastructure, by adopting appropriate fiscal and monetary policies, and by setting production targets, assigning priorities, and generally orchestrating the economy. It sponsored the bullet train, which in 1964 reduced what had been a major overnight journey between Kyoto and Tokyo to a trip of three hours and ten minutes. The government built roads and dams, and it financed the reclamation of coastal lands.

Although the Construction Ministry controlled the bulk of infrastructure spending, the Finance Ministry and the Ministry of International Trade and Industry (MITI) coordinated economic growth. The importance of the MITI reflected the crucial role of foreign trade in Japan's economy and the determination of the government to oversee the country's economic and political relations with other countries. By deploying foreign exchange allocations, manipulating quotas, and establishing barriers protecting native capital from foreign competition, the government channeled the flow of investment funds. It could also extend or deny tax privileges. It thus had at its disposal a variety of weapons to bring recalcitrant companies into line if persuasion, pressures, or both failed. Generally, it preferred to rely on discussion and to act as much as possible on the basis of a shared government–business consensus. Businesses competed with each other within a more tightly defined arena than in most other capitalist nations.

Consensus was possible not only because of the shared aims and interests of government and business but also because of ties between the government and the business community. Often these ties were personal, because the men at the top in the private sector and those heading the influential and prestigious government ministries tended to share similar backgrounds (both included a high proportion of Tokyo University graduates). Some ties were ideological, because Japan was ruled during these years by conservatives. And some ties were financial, because elections were costly and business constituted a major source of funds for conservative politicians.

Government and Politics

After 1955, the L.D.P. was opposed by the two Socialist parties (the Japan Socialist Party and the Democratic Socialist Party), by the Clean Government Party (formed in 1964, it first ran candidates for the lower house in 1967), by the Communist party, and by independent politicians. This opposition was too divided to constitute a serious alternative to conservative rule, but it was sufficient to prevent the L.D.P. from gaining the two-thirds majority in the Diet needed for revising the constitution. Some conservatives, concerned about Japan's security, favored the revocation of Article IX to enable Japan to acquire its own military power. In view of a dangerous world and in response to American urgings, the Self-Defense Forces were expanded to include well-equipped naval and air arms, and the defense budget continued to increase. However, Japan persisted in foregoing offensive weapons or capabilities, and total defense expenditures remained limited to 1 percent of GNP until 1987.

About a quarter of L.D.P. Diet members were former bureaucrats, as were Prime Minister Ikeda, his immediate predecessor, Kishi Nobosuke (1957–1960), and his successor, Satō Eisaku (1964–1972). Subsequently, only Nakasone Yasuhiro (1982–1987) occupied that position for more than two years. Throughout the period, the well-educated, capable, and prestigious higher bureaucracy wielded great influence not only on executing government policies but also on policy making.

Dominating the internal dynamics of the L.D.P., and thus determining the composition of Japan's government, was the interplay of political factions. After 1972, all prime ministers came from five factions—formal, recognized political groupings built around a leader, usually a potential prime minister. From his faction a member derived political and financial support in his election campaigns and backing in his attempts to gain high government or party office. In return, he owed his faction leader political support, especially during the complex maneuvering that determined the party presidency and the prime ministership. What counted was skill in assembling political combinations and seniority, not popular appeal.

The L.D.P.'s origin as an association of independently based politicians helps account for the strength of the factions. Another factor was a system of multimember election districts in which there were frequently more conservative candidates than could reasonably expect to win election. Thus, in a five-member district, there might be four L.D.P. candidates with only three likely to win. In such cases, they would be backed by rival factions within the L.D.P.

The power of the factions set limits on the prime minister's authority and weakened the party at the grass-roots level, where each politician cultivated his (or in rare cases her) own local support organization composed of various groups within his constituency. The politician maintained his following by supporting various community activities and offering personal assistance to constituents. He kept his political machine oiled by maintaining a "pipeline to the center" so that he could take credit for obtaining public works and other special-interest legislation. In seeking to fulfill these expectations, politicians depended on the political clout of their faction and a purse kept full by friendly interests. Although the most successful politicians were solidly entrenched, there were enough shifts in political fortunes on both the local and the national levels to provide for political interest. More importantly, the system retained the flexibility to adjust policies to changing circumstances.

For the opposition parties of the left, these were years of frustration. The two Socialist parties were closely associated with labor, each linked to one of the labor confederations. They depended on organized labor for votes, and labor leaders figured prominently in their leadership. Many of their Diet members also came from a labor background. Ideologically, the Socialists ran the gamut from Maoist radicals calling for revolution to moderate reformists. During the 1950s the Communist party was weak, but it picked up strength in the late 1960s after adopting pragmatic policies. However, even had they been able to unite, the three leftist parties lacked the strength to topple the L.D.P. regime.

Domestically, the opposition parties viewed with special alarm L.D.P. measures that looked suspiciously like a retreat from Occupation reforms and a return to the past—for example, measures to recentralize the police and education functions and to give Tokyo greater control over local government. Socialist fears were fortified by the prominence in the conservative leadership of men who had held Cabinet offices in the 1930s and had been purged from politics by the Occupation authorities. The left was adamantly opposed to government moves to recreate a military establishment and did what it could to block or at least delay the expansion of the Self-Defense Forces.

The left also objected to the government's pro-American foreign policy, protested against the continued presence of American bases, and argued against American nuclear weapons and tests. Unrestrained by expectations of forming a government themselves, they engaged in bitter struggles, including boycotts of the Diet and physical disruption, prompting police intervention. The L.D.P. did not refrain from using its majority to ram legislation through the Diet with little regard for the niceties of parliamentary procedure. This is what Prime Minister Kishi did in 1960 to gain renewal of the Security Treaty with the United States, first signed in 1952 together with the peace treaty. The renewal of this treaty prompted demonstrations sufficiently strong to prompt the cancellation of President Dwight Eisenhower's planned visit to Japan.

Political animosity now reached its greatest intensity. Opponents felt that instead of providing for Japanese security, the treaty endangered Japan, threatening to involve it in American wars. The specter of nuclear war was particularly terrifying to a people who had experienced Hiroshima and Nagasaki. The Socialists mustered impressive support for their opposition to the renegotiated treaty. Union workers, housewives, students, professors, and members of diverse organizations took to the streets in mass demonstrations in which millions of people participated. There was also a one-day general strike. All this did not block ratification or enactment of the treaty, but Kishi did resign.

After the 1960 confrontation, politics simmered down to less violent exchanges as the success of Japan's economic development became apparent. Ikeda's ten-year plan to double per capital GNP was achieved in only seven years. Although there were student protests against the Vietnam War, the Security Treaty was renewed in 1970 with little trouble.

In 1964 the political scene was complicated by the appearance of the Clean Government Party, formed by the Sōka Gakkai (Value Creation Society), a religious sect. As implied by its name, the party program opposed corruption, but it was vague on other issues. After obtaining 10.9 percent of the vote in the 1969 election, it declined to 8.5 percent in 1972 but remained a presence for the rest of the century. Meanwhile, the L.D.P. aroused little enthusiasm and was particularly weak in the cities. Before 1967 its candidates had received over half of the vote, but in the election of that year it declined to 48.8 percent and continued slowly downward until it bottomed in 1976 at 41.8 percent. Even then it remained by far the largest vote getter and benefited from an electoral system that favored rural areas.

The 1970s and 1980s

In the 1970s, Japanese resilience was tested by a series of short-term economic and political shocks. The first came in 1971, when the United States, Japan's largest trading partner, placed a 10 percent surcharge on imports and abandoned a fixed rate of exchange. Instead, it was left to the international monetary market to determine the value of the yen, with the result that it rose, making Japanese goods more expensive overseas but also making imports cheaper. Both these American actions were aimed at reducing, if not eliminating, a mounting U.S. trade-and-payment deficit with Japan, but they proved ineffective, and the problem persisted.

A political blow followed these economic acts when, still in the same year, Washington announced the impending visit of President Nixon to China, an act on which Japan was not consulted and one that undercut Prime Minister Satō, who, primarily to please Washington, had been following the unpopular policy of maintaining the fiction that the Nationalist regime on Taiwan was the government of China. In 1972, after Tanaka Kakuei (prime minister, 1972–1974), became the first Japanese prime minister to visit Beijing, Japan recognized the P.R.C.

The next shock came in 1973 when the Arab oil boycott reminded Japan of its dependence on imported energy and was followed by a quadrupling of the price of this vital import. As a result, from 1974 to 1976 Japan suffered a severe recession. However, the system demonstrated remarkable resilience. An outstanding example was the rescue of the Japanese automaker Mazda, saved from collapse through the cooperation of government-backed financial interests, management, workers, dealers, suppliers, and the local community. This "lesson in managing interdependence" led two American experts to conclude, "Relatively low interest rates, MITI bureaucrats, trade barriers, and the like are, no doubt, important factors in a comparative history of economic growth, but only managers and workers build cars and other products. And their capacity to pull together in a crisis is a crucial measure of a society's strength."[6]

In the later 1970s and 1980s, Japan's emphasis on high technology led to a decrease in dependence on imported raw materials. By 1984, Japan had reduced its use of imported raw material per unit of manufacture to 60 percent less than it had been twenty years earlier. This change also positioned Japan to compete with the emerging economies of such neighbors as Korea and Taiwan. Encouragement was given electronics, telecommunications, biochemicals, and machine tools. In these ways, the economy continued to sustain a population that by 1985 had reached 121 million, up from 65 million in 1930 and about four times the number of inhabitants of Japan at the time of the Meiji Restoration.

As elsewhere, the move away from "smoke-stack industries" hurt the labor movement by reducing the number of its members. Furthermore, most people considered themselves middle class. Growth of GNP declined to the level of other fully developed countries, but Japan's trade imbalance, especially with the United States, posed a continuing problem. Expectations to the contrary, it was not solved by the rising value of the yen, which did, however, facilitate Japanese investment in the United States.

One business response to new conditions was the transformation of Japanese companies into multinationals. Increasingly, Japanese concerns, in addition to trading in world markets, became involved in manufacturing overseas. These operations were generally successful on the factory floor, but it proved more difficult to internationalize management or "localize" the "transplants." In many cases, Japanese companies were resented for reserving the best jobs for those at home, for building factories far from the troubled and job-hungry cities, for favoring their *keiretsu* partners, and for generally taking advantage of opportunities abroad denied to foreign companies at home.

In politics as in economics, the system proved vulnerable but resilient. Early in 1976, the Lockheed scandal ("Japan's Watergate") shook the political world when it was revealed that millions of dollars of the American company's funds had been used to corrupt the highest Japanese government officials. Although prosecutors lacked the independence and tools to be truly effective, they were able to indict the former Prime Minister Tanaka Kakuei, who was found guilty in a 1983 decision upheld in 1987.

Predictions that the L.D.P. would decline to the point of losing its ability to form a government proved false. It reached a low of 41.8 percent of the popular vote in 1976 but made a strong comeback in 1980. In 1986 it won 49.6 percent of the vote, entitling it to 300 seats, the highest number of the party's history. Not only the party but also its internal factional structure remained essentially the same. Despite the Lockheed scandal, Tanaka continued to control his faction until he suffered a stroke in 1985.

The leading political figure in the 1980s was Nakasone Yasuhiro (1918–), who, as prime minister from 1982 to 1987, brought an unusually vigorous style of leadership and national assertiveness into the office. Prosperity, self-confidence, and American pressure combined to induce the government in 1986 to exceed the previous 1 percent of GNP cap in the military budget for the next year. Although the increase was modest, it had symbolic significance. At the same time, the Socialist party dropped its long-standing opposition to the Self-Defense Forces based on Article IX of the constitution. It now held that the Self-Defense Forces were "unconstitutional but legal." Ten years earlier the Supreme Court had ruled that the constitutionality of the forces was for the legislature to decide and had left it up to the legislature to rectify an electoral system that was unconstitutional in discriminating against urban voters.

Nakasone cooperated with the United States to reduce the trade surplus by emphasizing domestic spending, cooperating on monetary policy, and trying to open Japanese markets to more imported goods. The last of these, however, was difficult in face of powerful, deeply entrenched domestic interests and business patterns. Farmers and construction companies were just two examples of major domestic constituencies on which many L.D.P. leaders had long depended. For the rest of the 1980s, the trade imbalance was more acute than ever. Japan developed expertise in industrial ceramics, robotics, and biotechnology.

The yen remained strong, propelled by a hot economy that sent the stock market soaring and raised land prices to astronomical levels. Japan became a major exporter of capital—building factories and buying foreign debt, prestigious hotels, and trophy real estate such as New York's Rockefeller Center, acquired by a Mitsui affiliate in 1989. Nevertheless, the balance of payments remained in Japan's favor.

In keeping with a general trend in the capitalist world, Japan divested itself of the government railway in 1987 and sold its shares in the National Telegraph and Telephone Company and in Japan Air Lines. By that time, Nakasone had been succeeded by Takeshita Noboru (1924–2000), who headed the Tanaka faction after 1985 but lasted less than two full years (November 1987–June 1989). He was forced to resign under a cloud arising out of revelations that the head of the Recruit group of companies had attempted to buy influence by giving large amounts in shares and money to leading politicians and bureaucrats. The next prime minister, who lied about giving hush money to a mistress, lasted two months. His successor, too, was a weak leader. The L.D.P.-dominated system was coming unglued, and now the financial bubble burst. Between January and October 1990 the stock market plunged 48 percent, and in 1991 recession set in.

Society, Thought, and the Arts

Social Change and Quality of Life

Economic growth brought unprecedented affluence. The very physiognomy of the Japanese people changed as an improved diet produced a new generation taller and healthier than their parents. By 1990 the Japanese people had the world's highest rate of life expectancy, and this was still the case in 2000, when it reached 74.5 years.

People now ate more fish and meat. Dairy products became daily staples, and wheat consumption rose steadily. Japan became a nation of coffee, as well as tea, drinkers. During the 1970s the arch of McDonald's hamburgers spread from Tokyo's Ginza to the provinces, where it was soon joined by the figure of Colonel Sanders inviting passersby to partake of Kentucky Fried Chicken. Mr. Donut and Dairy Queen did their part to propagate fast-food culture American style.

Changes in dress were equally dramatic. In the 1980s blue jeans became the universal dress of the young, and pants were worn in public by women of all ages. Conversely, the kimono was reserved for special occasions, but wealthy sophisticates now could prance about in the latest fashions by Japan's world-renowned designers.

Consumerism reigned as old crafts declined, and traditional elegance gave way to modern practicality—except that the modern was not always practical; during the 1980s so many realized their dream of owning an automobile that the roads were choked and the savvy driver had to learn how to "diagnose traffic paralysis."[7] Fortunately, public transportation within and between cities was excellent, although in Tokyo's rush hour ("crush hour" would be more appropriate) "pushers" had to cram the people quickly into the overflowing subways.

There was a shift of population from the country into cities. Nevertheless, because mechanization reduced the need for farm labor, agricultural production increased. Thanks to the L.D.P., the government purchased rice at several times the international price. The prewar gulf between urban wealth and rural poverty disappeared, and the spread of television accelerated the process, begun by radio, of diminishing the cultural gap. However, despite the omnipresence of the television set, the Japanese remained the world's most avid consumers of newspapers, magazines, and comic books.

Public transportation, communication, and security were excellent early on, but the environment suffered. Japan's industrial zone, running along the Pacific coast from Tokyo to northern Kyushu, developed into a "polluters' paradise":

> Polluted air choked urban residents with respiratory difficulties, which were fatal in some areas. Water pollution wiped out coastal fishing along the industrial belt. In the cities exhaust from automobiles mixed with pollutants from smokestacks and produced toxic photochemical smog during the day.[8]

Only after Tokyo became enshrouded in a semiperpetual screen of smog did the government take action. In the Mie prefecture, asthma was linked to pollution, and in Toyama a river caused cadmium poisoning. Most notorious was the Minamata disease (1953) caused by people eating fish contaminated by methyl mercury discharged by a fertilizer plant in Kyushu. Because of obstruction by the company and government connivance, the victims had to wait until 1968 for official acknowledgment that mercury was the cause. In 1973 a group of Minamata plaintiffs prevailed in court and won the largest tort award in Japanese history. In 1978 a National Institute for Minamata Disease was established. The name Minamata still conjures up both the deadly threat of environmental pollution and the people's determination to fight back.

Government measures taken in the 1970s ameliorated the problem, but the quality of air and water remained a matter of concern, and excessive dam construction boded ill for the future of Japan's rivers. Visual pollution was all too apparent as Japan's industrial area became one of the ugliest anywhere. Although the Japanese people continued to cherish nature in miniature, lovingly tending tiny gardens on the most unlikely bits of land, Japan's business and political leaders, in their rush to modernize, sacrificed much of the natural beauty that had once been Japan's cherished heritage.

In the 1980s, preserving the environment was widely accepted as a public good, so much so that in 1990 the Ministry of Construction sponsored an International Flower and Greenery Exposition even as it was planning an airport that would kill the last healthy coral reef in Okinawa. By the end of the 1980s, environmentalists not only were expressing concern over the situation at home but also were calling attention to the destruction Japanese companies were inflicting on the tropical forests of Borneo and other lands. If the aims of Japanese environmentalists were similar to those elsewhere, the same was even more true of the power of the forces arrayed against them.

Even before the land boom of the 1980s, the escalating price of land and housing in Japan's large cities forced young married couples to live with their in-laws because they could not afford separate establishments or to crowd into tiny apartments in drab and monotonous buildings made of reinforced concrete. Raising a family in such confined quarters was no easy task. Although the small apartments reduced women's household chores, releasing time for other activities, the residents of such buildings were slow to develop a sense of community because they regarded these quarters as temporary, marking a stage of their lives and careers soon to be surmounted.

The absence of grandparents in the new housing was but one of the factors making for discontinuity between the generations. Such discontinuity was not unique to Japan; in other countries, too, rapid changes during the postwar years created a "generation gap." However, in Japan the gap was particularly severe. Not only did the younger people grow up in a society that had suddenly become very different from that of their parents, but a whole generation of wartime leaders also had been thoroughly discredited and the old values had been blamed for leading the nation to catastrophe. Included were many values that had strengthened the cohesiveness of Japanese society.

New lifestyles and values appeared in the factories as young workers preferred to spend their leisure time manipulating pachinko (vertical pinball) machines, playing video games, or listening to rock music rather than going on company outings. They valued skill more than length of service and tended to regard the factory not as a second home but merely as a place to work. The number of hours they would have to spend there was also decreasing, and a survey conducted in 1990 revealed that workers were more interested in obtaining more leisure than in obtaining higher pay.

Those fortunate enough to survive a brutal entrance examination system gained admission to universities oriented largely to research and graduate work. Ostensibly paternalistic, the universities demonstrated their supposed concern for the youngest members of the academic community by virtually guaranteeing graduation to all matriculants. Neglected after having worked so hard for university entrance, the students expressed their discontent in radical political activities. Their dissatisfaction helped fuel widespread demonstrations and disruptions in the late 1960s, directed against both national and university policies. In this again, Japanese young people were not alone, and, as elsewhere, the pendulum swung back to greater conservatism in the 1970s and 1980s.

The general loosening of traditional patterns and values presented contemporary Japanese with a range of choices but within what remained overall a closely knit society. For example, young people increasingly insisted on making their own selection of a spouse, and they were now always consulted before a marriage was arranged by their parents. Nevertheless, even in love marriages, most young people still asked their employer or teacher to serve as official matchmaker. A surprisingly large number continued to leave the initiative to their parents. Under the postwar legal system, wives and husbands could now initiate divorce proceedings; the divorce rate grew but remained low.

Women now had more options. Many remained content with their traditional roles, which gave them a predominant influence over their children and firmly established the home as their field of authority. Although submissive to their husbands in public, most wives controlled the family budget, ran the household, and often treated their husbands as they would an older, somewhat difficult, and rather special child. They accepted their exclusion from much of their husbands' social lives, which the husbands spent largely in the company of their fellow workers. Such couples, like their Tokugawa predecessors, led separate social lives. These wives did not share in their husband's nightlife. However, as time went on, an increasing number of women chose a career and either a companionate marriage or a single life. They made progress in the professions and, more slowly, in business, where they often had to choose between temporary employment followed by marriage or the more regular male-oriented career path. The passage of the Equal Opportunity Act in 1985, making sex discrimination illegal, reflected a new consciousness, but the law lacked teeth.

As in all periods of social change, there were some who suffered because change was too rapid and others for whom it was too slow. Among the former were old people, bewildered and distressed by the whirl about them. One of the strengths of the old society had been the dignity and security afforded to the aged, but now cramped quarters and new ideas ate away at old values and threatened traditional comforts. These were people who found that the social rules had changed just when their turn came to reap the rewards the system offered those who played by the rules. Although the erosion of respect for the aged diminished the traditional attractions of longevity, forced retirement at an early age (usually fifty-five) and the devaluation of savings because of continual inflation deprived the old of a sense of economic security. Most families managed to take care of the elderly one way or another. Most old people were not shunted off into nursing homes or set up in special retirement communities, but the social arrangements made for the elderly by their children were often grudging and poisoned by resentment.

At the other end of the spectrum were those who felt that change was too slow. They felt stifled rather than supported by a social system that still expected the individual to be subordinate to the group, whether it be family or company. They also balked at conforming to a social hierarchy that had lost much of its theoretical support. The discontented were a disparate group. They included career women frustrated by roadblocks and ceilings, those constrained to maintain and live with parents, and people seeking to fill the vacuum left by the passing of the old values with something more solid than consumerism and the race to elevate the economic standing of their country. Their discontent was frequently shared by students and by radicals impatient for a more egalitarian society. Some young men without prospects for university study joined motorcycle gangs. However, most worked out a modus vivendi for themselves, and many of the young gradually came to terms with society.

Most of the population, however, neither mourned the passing of the old nor were impatient for the arrival of the new. Appreciative of the increase in material wealth, they were nevertheless unsure of the future. Many turned to religion, maintaining home altars, visiting temples and shrines, and going on pilgrimages. Shrines and temples had always offered prayers and amulets protecting against disease, assurance of safe childbirth, and the like. Adjusting to new conditions, many now offered traffic-safety charms; a temple in Tokyo added air safety. Shrines and temples offering examination success were popular with young people. The elderly were serviced by temples offering prayers and amulets to quiet their fears of senility. This had excellent prospects of becoming a growth industry, because, as a byproduct of longevity, Japan counted half a million senile people by 1994, and the average age of the population was on the rise.

New religious sects arose seeking to satisfy the spiritual hunger and alleviate the mental malaise brought on by loss of community. As they moved from traditional village to modern city, people sought "a religious frame of meaning relevant to contemporary life."[4] Attracting the largest membership was Sōka Gakkai, the sponsor of the Clean Government Party. Doctrinally based on Nichiren Buddhism, it denounced all other faiths and insisted that its members proselytize relentlessly and go on a pilgrimage to the head temple at the foot of Mount Fuji, where an average of 10,000 people a day came to pay their homage. By passing a series of examinations, the faithful could rise in an academic-like hierarchy of ranks. For the devoted members, the sect provided not only spiritual community but also a sense of personal worth and of belonging to a large, integrated, purposeful group. Others found it more difficult to find new certainties, however, because the world offered a bewildering range of choices.

Not all the choices were solemn. Everyone, not only the devout, then as now, flocked to temples and shrines on festival days when the lanes leading to their gates were lined with stands offering various trinkets, souvenirs, and good things to eat—everything from octopus snacks to chocolate-covered bananas. This combination of piety and fun also accounts for the continued popularity of roly-poly darumas, popular doll-like figures named after Bodhidharma, the monk who was thought to have brought Zen to China and lost his legs after nine years

FIGURE 12.2 Darumas greet the visitor everywhere in the Hōrinji Temple, Kyoto, founded in 1718 but frequently rebuilt. Commonly known as the Daruma Temple, it houses around 8000 daruma figurines. (© Lore Schirokauer)

uninterrupted wall contemplation. Even the skeptical made sure to paint in an eye and make a silent wish, hoping they would be able to paint in the other eye once their wish was granted. Although ubiquitous, daruma also had his special temples (see Figure 12.2).

Film

If, as is often said, film was the characteristic art form of the twentieth century, then the worldwide acclaim accorded Japanese films is but one more indication of Japan's full participation in that century's culture. By no means were all Japanese films masterpieces: Japanese companies were second to none in turning out ephemeral entertainments—samurai movies that were the artistic equivalents of American westerns, unbearably sentimental tear-jerkers, horror and monster films, and, in the 1970s and 1980s, a wave of erotica with little artistic or social value but plenty of sexual action. Such films, reflecting social stereotypes and people's day-dreams, are of considerable interest to psychologists and social scientists, but it is important to remember that the stereotypes they contain—the self-sacrificing but self-centered mother, the wife finding herself, daughters in various degrees of revolt—are never simple mirror images of society. The more ambitious and truly fine films reflected the times and the society but rose above them. The major films were the creations of fine actors, sensitive cameramen, and, above all, great directors who were able to use the medium to create their own personal styles, conveying their own personal visions. If they had anything in common, it was a superb visual sense employed to create an atmosphere. Some may be said to have used the camera to paint their vision on the screen.

Exercising classic restraint in his insistence on a strict economy of means (empty spaces, simple objects, and minimal plot) and avoiding anything superficial or artificially clever was Ozu Yasujiō (1903–1963), whose traditionalism also extended to his subject matter because he was the filmmaker par excellence of the Japanese family. Other directors, like their Chinese counterparts, were highly critical of their country's traditions and values. For example, in *Harakiri* (*Seppuku,* 1962), directed by Kobayashi Masaki, the hero sets out to avenge his son, who had been forced to commit an unimaginably painful *seppuku* (ritual suicide) using a sword with a bamboo blade, but in the end the whole system is revealed to be founded on hypocrisy. Or there is *Night Drum* (*Yoru no Tsuzumi,* also known as *The Adulteress,* 1958), directed by Imai Tadashi, in which a samurai kills the wife he loves. By doing what society demands, he deprives his own life of meaning. Such vivid and moving historical films were among the triumphs of the postwar cinema, a part of a continuing and sometimes bitter dialogue with a still-living past.

An outstanding director was Kurosawa Akira (1910–1998). His world-famous *Rashomon* (1950) suggests the relativity of all truth through a demonstration of the power of human subjectivity and self-interest. *Ikiru* (1952) takes the viewer through a Faust-like quest for meaning in life. The main character, a petty bureaucrat dying of cancer, in the end finds fulfillment in one meaningful social act: surmounting endless red tape and bureaucratic obstructionism, he gets a small park built. Kurosawa's mastery of large scenes with vast casts and his versatility and creative vigor was apparent in *Ran* (1985), an imaginative metamorphosis of King Lear into sixteenth-century Japan. Like his earlier *Seven Samurai* (1954), it is one of those rare films in which powerful and sensitive acting, beautiful visual composition and realistic detail, story line and structure, friction and harmony, violence and stillness blend into a major artistic statement.

In the 1980s, Japanese studios increasingly churned out films of violence and pornography. Refreshing exceptions were films of Itami Juzo (Ikeuchi Yoshihiro, 1933–1997) who poked fun at the Japanese way of burial in *The Funeral* (1984), noodle mania in *Tampopo* (1986), and tax collection methods in *A Taxing Woman I* and *II* (1987, 1988). His satire on the Japanese mob, *Minbo no Onna—The Gentle Art of Extortion* (1994), provoked the Yakuza (organized crime) to a physical attack on his person. Itami survived this but later committed suicide, leaving a note explaining this act as proving the untruth of rumors that he was having an affair with a much younger woman.

Intellectual Life and Literature

After the war Japan rejoined the international intellectual community, participated in scientific and scholarly meetings at home and abroad, and increasingly contributed to specialized disciplines in important ways. Many scholars became conversant with a foreign language, usually English, and all had access to a broad and steady stream of translations.

Writings addressing broader human or philosophical issues, published in journals of opinion and in books, have attracted less attention abroad than have the works of the filmmaker or novelist. One reason, no doubt, is the language barrier. Another may be that much was derivative. Also, many Japanese intellectuals, like their American counterparts, applied their energies to studying their own society and to addressing their own countrymen. Notably fascinating but problematic has been the literature of exceptionalism (*Nihonjinron*) that burgeoned in the 1970s and continued thereafter to fuel a sense of self-confidence and assertiveness. This literature, which focused on Japanese uniqueness, included the highly respected and stimulating work of such scholars as the psychiatrist Doi Takeo and the sociologist Nakane Chie. Lesser scholars, however, expounded on and frequently took pride in the uniqueness of just about every aspect of Japanese behavior, institutions, and climatic and racial characteristics. Increasing cosmopolitanism did not prevent the persistence of insularity.

What it meant to be Japanese was also one of the themes explored in postwar fiction. After the war, older novelists published manuscripts they could not release during the war, and new writers sounded new themes. An outstanding example of the former is the long novel by Tanizaki translated as *The Makioka Sisters.*

In 1947 Kawabata Yasunari published the last installment of *Snow Country.* Previous segments of the novel had been published in various journals over the preceding twelve years, as though each part were a stanza in a *renga* (linked verse) rather than a building block for a novel. In this and later works, Kawabata explored "the ceaseless attempt of his male heroes to free themselves from their alienation and egotism to achieve a kind of monastic state of grace by a purifying contact with a pure, virginal girl."[9]

Kawabata's novels sacrifice structure and plot for naturalness and poetry. *A Thousand Cranes* (1948) and *The Sound of the Mountain* (1951) followed, each imbued with the author's visual sensibility and with his concern for beauty and sadness, inseparable as ever in Japanese literature and evoking what one critic termed a "vibrant silence."[10] The essential Japaneseness of Kawabata's method and vision was clearly demonstrated in his Nobel Prize acceptance speech (1968). Translated as *Japan, the Beautiful, and Myself,* it is an evocation of the Japanese tradition, a string of poems and images held together by a perception of beauty and truth.

Japan's literary classics were written by women, but most eminent writers during the Tokugawa Period and in the first years of Meiji were men. Women writers reappeared toward the turn of the century but really came into their own after the war. As Donald Keene pointed out, "At no time since the Heian Period had women figured so prominently in the literary world."[11] Appropriately, one of the most distinguished among them, Enchi Fumiko (1905–1986), translated the *Tale of Genji* into modern Japanese (1972–1973). She also wrote realistic novels such as *Waiting Years* (1957) and the subtle and imaginative *Masks* (1958).

A brilliant and versatile but uneven writer was Mishima Yukio (1925–1970), who, in a series of well-constructed novels, developed his ideas on such themes as the nature of beauty and the relationships between art and life and between warrior and poet. One of his most compelling novels is *The Temple of the Golden Pavilion* (1956). Based on an actual act of arson in postwar Kyoto, it includes powerful psychological and philosophical explorations. A dramatist and critic, as well as novelist, Mishima was prolific, self-contradictory, and even self-parodying. He tried to mold his life and his body as he did his art. Wishing to be both athlete and artist, he took up body building and developed a strong torso—but on spindly legs. Seeking to achieve a unity of knowledge and action, as in the philosophy of Wang Yangming, whom he admired, Mishima's culminating act was a dramatic public *seppuku* committed in 1970 after the completion of his final work, a tetralogy titled *The Sea of Fertility.* He was joined in death by a member of his small, private, rightwing army. Mishima exhorted the Self-Defense Forces to rise up before performing his ritual suicide at their headquarters. Regarded by the public as irrelevant and bizarre, Mishima intended this act to be a fulfillment of his life's work.

A productive writer who was well-known abroad was Endō Shūsaku (1923–1996), who, in a series of brilliant novels, grappled with the tensions between his Catholic faith and his Japanese heritage. Just as Endō contributed to both modern Christian and Japanese literature, Abe Kobō (1924–1993) earned an international reputation as an existentialist. He is perhaps best known for his novel *Woman in the Dunes* (1962), subsequently made into a film. In this work and later novels such as *Face of Another* (1964), *The Boxman* (1973), and *The Ark Sakura* (1984), and in such plays as *Friends* (1967), Abe explored themes and predicaments besetting the contemporary human condition, including the search for identity.

The search for identity and roots also infuses the work of Ōe Kenzaburō (1935–), two of whose novels, *A Personal Matter* (1964) and *The Silent Cry* (1967), were widely read in Japanese and in translation. Insight into psychological complexities of modern people—including the sources of violence, a concern for social morality, and a strong personal symbolism—and his grappling with basic problems of existence in the second half of the twentieth century mark him as a major writer who speaks to the central problems of his age.

Working a different vein was Inoue Yasushi (1907–1991), many of whose novels were set in China, including his last, *Confucius* (1989), in which the sage, seen through the eyes of a disciple, is treated with great respect. Less well-known abroad is Maruya Saiichi (1925–), an entertaining writer, serious but funny, whose *Singular Rebellion* (1972) provides a delightful, comic window into the times.

The Visual Arts

Like filmmakers and novelists, Japanese painters, potters, and architects won international recognition. As earlier, some artists found their inspiration in, and took their cues from, the latest trends so that Japan had its practitioners of abstract expressionism, action painting, pop art, and the various other international art

FIGURE 12.3 *Lady in Chinese Costume,* woodcut, Munakata Shikō, 1946, 17.9 in × 12.8 in. There are strong hints of Persia and India in Munakata's work. But in the vigor of his lines, his gentle eroticism, and the decorative qualities of his art, he resembles Matisse, and his coloring is reminiscent of Chagall. (© "Tornado" from the series "In Praise of Shokie" by Munakata Shiko, Munakata Museum in Kamakura)

movements, which, at their best, represented the search for a style appropriate to a bewildering age and, at their worst, degenerated into fads.

More traditional was the work of artists who strove to create beauty without attempting to convey a symbolic message. Japanese potters, innovators and traditionalists, continued to blend shapes, textures, and colors to create works worthy of the tradition.

An old genre in new form was the woodcut. Unlike the earlier *ukiyo-e* artists, their twentieth-century successors took responsibility for the entire process of printmaking. They did their own cutting and printing, although they might have students assist them in the more routine aspects of the process. Among the finest was Munakata Shikō (1903–1975), also a gifted painter, whose style was influenced by traditional Japanese folk art but who also developed new techniques. One was to apply color on the back of the print and let it seep through the paper to create gentle, diffused coloring. This helped Munakata create a general decorative effect, as in his rendition of the clothing in *Lady in Chinese Costume* (see Figure 12.3). In subject matter his work ranged from the religious to the sensuous and the whimsical (for example, a nude with the artist's eyeglasses resting on her belly). In tone his art is positive—there is no echo here of the agony of the century.

Perhaps no art is as revealing of society as architecture. Although many opportunities were missed in the rush of postwar reconstruction, and Japan's industrial centers are among the ugliest cities in the world, there were also buildings of great distinction. The achievements of Tange Kenzo (1913–2005), designer of the

Hall Dedicated to Peace at Hiroshima, were recognized internationally when he received the Pritzker Prize in 1987. The swimming pool and sports center he designed for the 1964 Tokyo Olympics won wide acclaim. Thirty years later, he designed the Tokyo City Hall Complex (1995). His buildings can also be seen in Singapore, Europe, North Africa, the Middle East, and Minnesota (the arts complex in Minneapolis, 1970–1974). In addition to designing superb buildings, Tange involved himself deeply in urban planning.

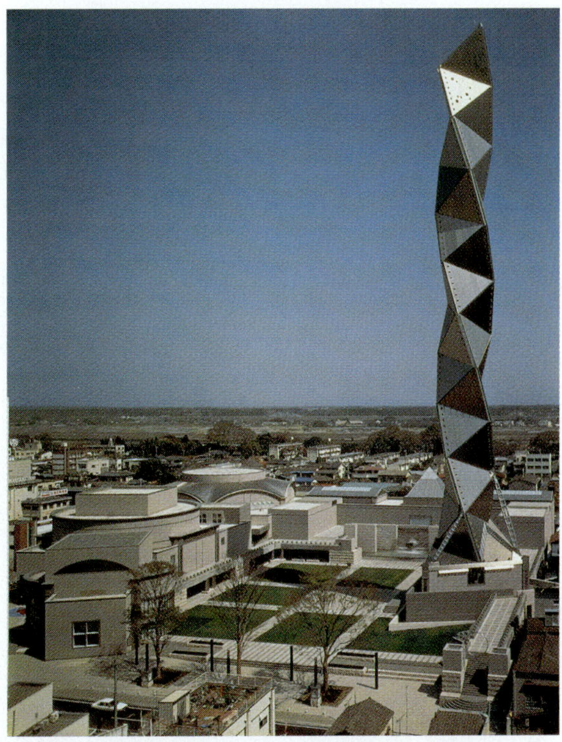

FIGURE 12.4 Art Tower Mito, 328 feet high. Mito Ibaraki, 1986–1990. Although as a postmodernist Isozaki delights in playing with references to buildings of the past, he also likes to give his imagination free play, as in this tower. (© Mita Arts Foundation)

One of Tange's most creative students was Isozaki Arata (1931–). Postmodernist in seeking a "shifting, revolving, flickering style" rather than a "lucid, coherent institutional style" for his Tsukuba Science Center, Isozaki is also an internationalist who could write, "the Katsura Palace, the Parthenon, the Capitoline piazza, and so on all live in a time and place equidistant from us. Anything occurring in the history of architecture even the history of the world—is open to quotation."[12] Such quotation yields new and complex meaning. But often Isozaki does not quote, and some of his most successful buildings employ solid geometric forms, as in his Museum of Contemporary Art in Los Angeles. Illustrated here (see Figure 12.4) is the tower for his arts center in Mito, which, although located in a place once famous for historiography, does not refer to anything except itself.

The diversity of modern Japanese architecture is far too great for any single building possibly to be representative, but architecture can, among other things, be fun. The example of Japanese "pop architecture" in Figure 12.5 was built to house an exhibit on coffee for an exposition celebrating the completion of an artificial island in Kobe. Later, it was turned into a permanent coffee museum and given a more dignified but conventional exterior. Perhaps the cup ranneth over

FIGURE 12.5 Coffee Pavilion, 82 feet high, c. 72 feet in diameter. Port-pia Exposition, Kobe, 1981. Takenaka Construction Firm. Although the era of pop architecture has passed and the coffee museum has changed the face it shows the world, coffee has found a permanent home in Japan. (© Arata Isozaki & Associates, Photo by Yasuhiro Ishimoto)

and the joke wore off—humor may be as ephemeral as beauty. Still, it is a splendid museum, housing exhibits on the history, the preparation, and the consumption of coffee and providing facilities for study and a "training room" for coffee makers. It is a striking reminder that Japan, which had perfected the tea ceremony, became a world leader in coffee appreciation, famed for its many and varied coffee houses serving the choicest South American beans. A serious beverage befitting hard workers and diligent students, coffee had found a home in Japan.

III. From 1989 into the New Century

The absence of the drastic shifts in direction like those that punctuated Chinese history enables us to discuss the new Japan in a single chapter—but it makes it difficult to periodize. We have chosen to break our story at 1989, when a new emperor ascended the throne, primarily because the end of the cold war coincided with the end of the economic exuberance of the 1980s.

The death of the emperor in January 1989 had little immediate political effect. Most Japanese were happy with the personality of the new, more accessible emperor, the first to have married a commoner. However, the performance of Shinto funeral and enthronement rites as official ceremonies troubled those committed to a secular state. And the focus on the monarchy drew renewed attention to the past role of the throne in leading Japan into the dark valley of authoritarianism and war. The tendency of high government officials to minimize wartime atrocities, government reluctance to compensate Korean "comfort women" forced into sexual slavery during the war, claims that the Pacific War had been righteous, and the widespread view of the Japanese exclusively as history's innocent victims combined to disturb people, at home and abroad, who knew otherwise.

For progressives, Japan had paid far too high a price for development. They saw the system as "a kind of state capitalism brokered by the elites that held the masses in thrall and precluded the emergence of a genuine democratic polity . . . a capitalism brokered by conservative elites in order to achieve nationalist goals."[13] A strong voice for a more positive appraisal was that of Murakami Yasusuke (1931–1993), professor of economics at Tokyo University and author of *An Anticlassical Political–Economic Analysis* (1992). Murakami blamed Japanese imperialism on the West and historical circumstances, and he emphasized the positive achievements of Japanese-style developmentalism. A nuanced thinker, he was not uncritical and sharply warned against Japanese particularism, but, convinced that there was more than one road to success, he maintained that Japan, with its "capacity to nurture a community of cultural systems,"[14] had achieved a viable way that could serve as a model for late developing nations and enable Japan to be a leader in the post–Cold War world.

The message that there is more than one road to development was a timely one for a world in which only one superpower remained and triumphalism was in the air, but it seemed increasingly less likely that Japan would serve as an economic, let alone political, exemplar. Essentially, the country muddled through the decade but did not shine.

As already noted, recession took hold in earnest in 1991. That same year Japan contributed $13 billion to the war effort in the Persian Gulf but did not send troops. Two years later, however, despite Article IX of the constitution, it sent a token noncombatant force to support United Nations peacekeeping in Cambodia.

Yet talk of Japanese membership in an expanded Security Council remained talk, and a new, more prominent international role eluded the nation with the world's second-largest economy. If the Persian Gulf War again highlighted Japan's dependence on foreign oil, the conference on global warming held in Kyoto in 1997 was a reminder that we all live on the same planet.

During the 1990s the economy sputtered along, each small spurt followed by a stall so that it neither advanced into sustained recovery nor sank into the depths of depression. The excesses of spending abroad were liquidated—Rockefeller Center went bankrupt in 1995. Japan was not as badly hit by the Asian Crisis of 1998 as Korea but nevertheless suffered serious losses. At the end of the decade there was an uptick, but all too soon it was clear that the banking system remained unsound and that Japan had not yet found a way back to economic health.

Although earlier the Japanese economic system had been widely admired, the pressures now were toward opening its markets to American-style entrepreneurs and to foreign companies and goods. By the end of the decade, the *keiretsu* were dissolving as banks sold stocks and companies became more dependent on equity financing. American financial institutions became a major presence. Among the companies taken over by international firms based elsewhere was Mazda, the erstwhile survivor of the oil shock, which became a Ford subsidiary. Movement toward more efficient marketing and even discounting accelerated. In 2004 Wal-Mart opened its first supercenter in Japan.

Several factors kept the economy afloat. A vital one was Japan's sheer wealth. This enabled the government to finance substantial deficit spending on public works, to underwrite housing projects and small business loans, and to prime the economy in general. In 1994 it completed the scintillating Kansai Airport. Designed by the Italian architect Renzo Piano (Pritzker, 1999), it was built offshore in fifty-nine feet of water on soft foundations that keep subsiding, running the cost up to the enormous figure of roughly 5 trillion yen with no end yet in sight. In addition to stimulating the economy with construction money, this project gave easy international access to the Osaka area.

There were numerous smaller projects nourishing the politically and economically important construction industry. In 1995 these included 400 dams either under construction or planned. By that time, postwar Japan had already built 1000 dams, many of which were already clogged by more than 1 billion tons of silt. Writing in 1996, Gavan McCormack described the situation as "an ecological nightmare to which Japan is only beginning to wake."[15] Economic recovery remained Japan's top priority, and the national debts continued to mount until it reached 130 percent of gross domestic product in 2002.

Another way the government sought to stimulate the economy was by lowering interest rates, which at one point reached zero. Even so, the yen did not sink precipitously. The balance of payments with the United States remained in Japan's favor, although by 2000 China had replaced Japan as the country with the largest U.S. trade deficit. Trade with a booming China was a major factor in revitalizing the Japanese economy during 2003 and 2004, creating a mood of optimism despite the possibility that this could be one more false start.

An element of strength was Japan's continued technological excellence. People everywhere eagerly bought Japanese cars, laptop computers, and electronics. Robotics not only led to triumphs in manufacturing but also gave birth to toys that delighted children throughout the world. It is too early to know whether robotic cats and dogs will eventually catch on. Somewhere between a tool and a toy were the cellular email telephones ubiquitous among Japanese teenagers, who found a space of their own in cyberspace.

Companies cut back but tried to limit layoffs. People did not prosper, but most continued to work. The authorities worried less about present or future unemployment than about the aging of the population and a declining birthrate that reached 1.34 per 1000 in 1999. An increase to 1.35 per 1000 in 2000 was thought to be temporary, a product of a belief that this was an especially propitious year ("the millennial factor"). Further decline was expected as women sought more fulfilling roles than that of the traditional mother. At home, as abroad, the spending boom was over. Although there was an increase in poverty, most people were able to maintain a satisfactory lifestyle.

People had little faith in government, but there was not a sense of urgency sufficiently strong to stir up an effective public demand for a radical change in political direction or leadership. That all was not well with government was dramatically revealed by its failure to prepare for or deal adequately with the earthquake that shook the Kobe area in 1995, officially designated not earthquake-prone. More than 6000 people died, and the heart of one of Japan's most modern and international cities was destroyed, along with a brand new highway, revealing shoddy construction made possible by corruption. Government failure to assure adequate standards was matched by the slowness and inadequacy of its response. In contrast, organized crime stepped in to provide help and relief. The government was effective in suppressing the apocalyptic Aun Shinrikyō sect after it used sarin in 1995 in a subway attack that shocked people in Tokyo and, even before the September 11, 2001, attack in the United States, demonstrated just how menacing modern terrorism could be. In 2003, after a lengthy trial, the leader of the sect was condemned to death. However, faced with a nuclear mishap in 1999, the government's response was again slow and inept.

On the political stage, the L.D.P. finally came apart in 1993 when there was a major factional exodus, but the first non-L.D.P. prime minister, Hosokawa Morihito, lasted less than a year (August 1993–April 1994) before he was undone by involvement in yet another scandal. In 1989, under the leadership of Doi Takako (1928–), the first woman to become a major force in Japanese politics, it looked as if the Socialists might grow into a viable second party, but this did not happen. Instead, badly divided and compromised by ill-advised political alliances, they declined. Although the women's vote was important and two women served in the Cabinet for a short time, at century's end more than 95 percent of the Diet members were men. With men also in control of the bureaucracy, government and politics remained male domains.

Coalition governments between 1993 and 1996 were hampered by internal rivalry and conflict. One thing accomplished in 1994 was a major change in the electoral system, abolishing multimember districts and providing a total of 500 seats, 300 from small, single-member districts and 200 filled by proportional representation. In 1996 the first election under the new law was held, with the result that a weakened and divided L.D.P. regained power.

Prime Minister Hashimoto Ryutarō (1996–1998) was succeeded by Obuchi Keizo (1937–2000), who died suddenly and unexpectedly in May 2000. His successor, Mori Yoshirō (1937–), lost no time causing widespread consternation by calling Japan "a divine nation with the emperor at its core," saying out loud what more circumspect rightist politicians kept to themselves. New elections were held in June with the result that the opposition gained strength, but Mori managed to remain in office until April 2001, when he was succeeded by Koizumi Junichirō (1942–), who owed his position to a landslide victory in provincial party elections rather than through the usual political horse trading by faction leaders.

Koizumi, an unconventional politician noted for an outspoken and frank manner, with an easy sense of humor and something of a bad-boy image, came in with a broad but vague program of financial reforms, which he warned would cause short-term economic pain but long-term recovery. He also called for constitutional change to legalize the military and pleased nationalists by visiting the Yasukuni Shrine paying homage to Japan's fallen soldiers, including those condemned as war criminals. Koizumi took a bold step in appointing an outspoken woman as Japan's first female foreign minister. She was Tanaka Makiko (1944–), the eldest daughter of former Prime Minister Tanaka Kakuei.

In July, Koizumi, Japan's most popular prime minister since World War II, was able to lead the L.D.P. to an electoral victory. This was a personal triumph, but there was much opposition, especially in his own party, to his plans to remake the banking system, halt public works projects, and get the L.D.P. to change its ways. Many were disillusioned after he gave in to Foreign Ministry pressure and forced Tanaka out of the Cabinet at the end of January 2002.

Lower house elections in 2003, followed by those for the upper house in 2004, left both Koizumi and his L.D.P.–led coalition weakened but still in charge. At home, progress was made in restructuring the banking system; abroad, the Koizumi government supported the United States in its war on terrorism and sent a small contingent of troops to help rebuild Iraq. At home and abroad, the government showed little inclination for the kind of bold innovation once associated with Koizumi's name.

An ardent critic of Establishment thinking was Ōe Kenzaburō, who in 1994 became only the second Japanese—or, for that matter, East Asian—to receive the Nobel Prize for literature. In conscious contrast to Kawabata, he titled his acceptance speech "Japan, the Ambiguous and Myself" and not long after shocked the public by refusing the Imperial Order of Culture. In 1995 he completed his trilogy *The Burning Green Tree* (*Moegaru midori no ki,* 1992–1995), its title derived from "Vacillation," a poem by William Butler Yeats (1865–1939). *Burning Green Tree* remains untranslated but not so *Somersault* (1999), which revisits many of the themes that animate Ōe's earlier novels but does so in a post-Aun Shinrikyō age. This long, complex novel is not his most accessible, but it moved Fredric Jameson to praise Oe as an author who does honor to the Noble Prize rather than being honored by it.[16] Ōe's trilogy, like Mishima's tetralogy, ends with a death, but, to quote Susan J. Napier:

> Unlike Mishima whose dead protagonists leave the living with only a feeling of betrayal and emptiness, or Abe whose characters survive in misery, and above all unlike Murakami whose protagonists commit a sort of suicide to the outside world, Ōe gives us a vision of the outside world revitalized by the sacrifice of a body.[17]

As we have seen, Mishima and Abe belonged to the recent past, but Murakami Haruki (1949–), a prominent writer of the 1980s and 1990s, represented a generational shift that Ōe deplored:

> In contrast to much postwar writing which fictionalized the actual experience of writers and readers, who, as twenty- and thirty-year-olds, had known war, Murakami and Yoshimoto convey the experience of a youth politically uninvolved or disaffected content to exist within a late adolescent or postadolescent subculture.[18]

Yoshimoto is Yoshimoto Banana (Yochimoto Mahoko, 1964–) who had adopted "banana" as her pen name. Both writers are easy to read and prolific. Both were attuned to the market, enjoyed sensational sales, and were found lacking in gravitas by their elders. Bananas are, after all, delicious but not taken that seriously. Both were steeped in popular culture, probably read too many comic books, and have been taken to represent a postmodern comodification of literature. Especially Yoshimoto, beginning with *Kitchen* (1987), is treated as much a cultural as a literary phenomenon. Her novels often depict alternate lifestyles in deadpan, commonplace language. They signal the disintegration of the traditional family but are bright and cheerful. Murakami, who once ran a jazz bar, wrote long novels filled with the music of his youth, interesting situations, and characters not given to reflection. Pico Iyer had this to say about *The Wind-up Bird* (*Nejimaki-dori kuronikuru,* 1994–1995):

> It does not require much reflection that almost every image in the book's 600 pages—a dry well, a haunted house, a faceless man, a dead-end street—stands in some way for a hollowed out Japan, whose motto might be, "I don't think, therefore I am." Again and again, characters say, "I was like a walking corpse" or "I was now in a vacant house" or "I felt as if I had turned into a bowl of cold porridge." Murakami's storytelling ease and the pellucid, uncluttered backdrop he lays down allow moments to flare up memorably. Yet the overall effect of his grand but somewhat abstract novel is to give us X ray after X ray into the benumbed soul of a wannabe Prozac Nation.[19]

In the 1990s, the director Kurosawa, then in his eighties, drew on his earlier films to produce works new in content and technique. An example of the latter, described by Stephen Prince, is his use of axial cutting, and the dreams in *Dreams*

(1990) represent an old theme given new meaning. Once he had seen dreams as being in tension with social commitment, but now Kurosawa cherished them as "the fruit of pure and human desire" and went on to say, "A human is a genius while dreaming."[20] Be that as it may, it takes a great artist to convey a dream to others. One who was able to do so was Miyazaki Hayao (1941–), who, in a series of works, raised film animation to new heights. His *Princess Mononoke* (1997) won widespread popular and critical acclaim. Similarly, *Spirited Away* (2001) broke all box-office records in Japan.

Japanese architects, too, continued to dream. One who did so with great imagination was Ando Tadao (1941–; Pritzker, 1995), a self-taught master who, early in his career, built a lovely, small Christian church in Osaka. Among his most notable subsequent works were an underground temple entered though stairs in a lotus pond (1991) and, on Naoshima, an island in the Inland Sea, a museum/hotel for contemporary art (1992). The art, mostly non-Japanese, is not confined to the inside but continues outdoors and includes an enormous pumpkin and a Chinese stone garden. In 1997 I. M. Pei completed his masterpiece, the Miho Museum at Shigaraki. Like Ando's temple and museum/hotel, it is mostly underground, and it blends in with and makes the most of the natural beauty of the landscape.

In the Pulitzer Foundation for the Arts in St. Louis (2001) and Modern Art Museum in Fort Worth (2002), Ando brought his feeling for the possibilities of concrete to the United States. Meanwhile, as earlier, Japanese artists participated in all the international styles and movements of the day. Some of them spent considerable time overseas. Performance and installations remained popular, conveying the sense that art, like all things, was not forever. A sculptor obsessed with time was Miyajima Tatsuo (1957–), whose *Running Time* (1994) consisted of battery-powered "U-cars," each with a colored, single-number light emitting diode counter on its roof and with sensors front and back so that the cars changed direction as they randomly bumped each other. The effect has been likened to "glowing numerical fireflies," and the artist explained that the "U" refers to the "uncertainty principle," as in the physics of Heisenberg.[21]

Running Time, like the writings of Yoshimoto and Murakami, is a work in a modern idiom with it own aesthetic appeal. It says something in a new way without reference to what others in the long tradition have said on the subject. Like traditional works of art, it leaves interpretation to the viewer, but, unlike them, it does not demand the cultivation of connoisseurship to unlock the message.

Notes

1. I. M. Roberts, *Twentieth Century: The History of the World, 1901–2000* (New York: Viking, 1999), p. 462.
2. Quoted in John W. Dower, *Embracing Defeat: Japan in the Wake of World War II* (New York: W. W. Norton, 1999), p. 97.
3. Article IX of the constitution. A convenient source is David John Lu, *Sources of Japanese History, Vol. 2* (New York: McGraw-Hill, 1975), pp. 193–97.
4. Dower, *Embracing Defeat,* p. 544.
5. Dower, *Embracing Defeat,* p. 558.
6. Richard Pascale and Thomas P. Roblen, "The Mazda Turnaround," *Journal of Japanese Studies* 9.2 (Dec. 1983): 263.
7. David Plath, "My-Car-isma: Motorizing the Showa Self," in Carol Gluck and Stephen R. Graubard, eds., *Showa: The Japan of Hirohito* (New York: W. W. Norton, 1992), p. 239.
8. Koji Taira, "Dialectics of Economic Growth, National Power, and Distributive Struggles," in Andrew Gordon, ed., *Postwar Japan as History* (Berkeley: Univ. of California Press), p. 171.
9. Roy Starrs, *Soundings in Time: The Fictive Art of Kawabata Yasunari* (London: Curzon Press, 1998), p. 218.
10. Masao Miyoshi, *Accomplices of Silence: The Modern Japanese Novel* (Berkeley: Univ. of California Press, 1974), p. 120.
11. Donald Keene, *Dawn to the West: Japanese Literature in the Modern Era* (New York: Holt, Rinehart, and Winston, 1984).
12. Isozaki Arata, in Masao Miyoshi and Harry D. Harootunian, eds., *Postmodernism and Japan* (Durham: Duke Univ. Press, 1989), pp. 57 and 59.
13. Kenneth B. Pyle, "The World Historical Significance of Japan," in Kozo Yamamura, ed., *A Vision of a New Liberalism? Critical Essays on Murakami's Anticlassical Analysis* (Stanford: Stanford Univ. Press, 1997), pp. 233 and 237.
14. Pyle, in Kozo Yamamura, ed., *A Vision of a New Liberalism?* p. 127.
15. Gavan McCormack, *The Emptiness of Japanese Affluence* (Armonk, N.Y.: M. E. Sharpe, 1996), p. 46.
16. Fredric Jameson, "Pseudo-Couples," *The London Review of Books* (20 November 2003): 21.
17. Susan J. Napier, "Oe Kenzaburo and the Search for the Sublime at the End of the Twentieth Century," in Stephen Snyder and Philip Gabriel, eds., *Oe and Beyond: Fiction in Contemporary Japan* (Honolulu: Univ. of Hawaii Press, 1999), pp. 32–33.
18. Quoted in Snyder and Gabriel, *Oe and Beyond,* p. 2 of introduction.
19. Pico Iyer, "Tales of the Living Dead," *Time* 150.8 (Nov. 3, 1997), available at http://www.time.com/time/archive/preview/0,10987,987303,00.html.
20. Kurosawa Akira, as quoted in Stephen Prince, *The Warrior's Camera: The Cinema of Akira Kurosawa,* revised and enlarged edition (Princeton: Princeton Univ. Press, 1999), p. 303.
21. Michael Auping, org., *Tatsuo Miyajima (1957) BIG TIME,* exhibition catalog (Fort Worth: Modern Art Museum of Fort Worth and Hayward Gallery London, June 19–Aug. 17, 1997), pp. 25–26.

Afterword

A major theme of modern history is the interaction of regional civilizations and cultures, each with its own dynamic, in an accelerating process that links us all, in varying degrees, and, for better or worse, in a multitude of ways—some obvious, others less apparent. The roots of contemporary globalization extend deeply into the past, but the process has reached new dimensions in our time as history becomes increasingly world history and not Japan alone but no country, no matter how large or how powerful, has the luxury of withdrawal.

Around the globe, the modern era saw the growth in power of the nation-state to a degree unprecedented by any institution in human history, even as economic links were formed that became the precursor of the contemporary global economy. At the start of the twenty-first century, in Japan as elsewhere, the state's role in managing the economy was diminishing in the face of a global economic and financial system grown beyond the power of even the strongest state to control. Nevertheless, the nation-state remained the dominant military and political institution, in many cases reinforced after 2001 by participation in a campaign against non-state terrorist enemies with radical religious and antiglobalization agendas.

Both globalization and nationalism held promise of a brighter future, but both also entailed dangers. It remains to be seen whether sovereign states can solve global problems while focusing on local issues and while national rivalries continue to generate international dangers.

Economic Globalization

The Japanese economy remains deeply imbedded in the global system even as it remains the world's second largest economy. However, a momentous development emerged in 2004 when the growth of the Chinese economy reached the point that it too became a major player in global trade and finance. As a result, China has become Japan's major customer and the country with which the United States has the largest trade deficit. Chinese demand for crucial commodities such as oil and iron became a decisive factor in setting world prices. China became more dependent on the global economy, but the global economy and Japan depend more on China.

Globalization has benefited some but harmed others. It has created new customers abroad and reduced the prices of imports at home. Small mom-and-pop shops struggle to survive competition by chains, which benefit from more effective and ruthless distribution.

As elsewhere, cities are the nodes of the global system, and Tokyo continues to glitter, enlivened by buildings of startling architecture, designed by leading foreign and Japanese architects, and as up to date as any city in the world. Earthquake danger precludes Tokyo from entering the competition for the world's tallest building, but no other city can boast of anything equal in dimensions and ambitions to the huge Roppongi Hills complex that opened in 2003, boasting some 700 shops and boutiques, a Grand Hyatt Hotel, elegant apartments, Tokyo's largest movie hall, some 68,000 plants and trees, and a museum as global in the provenance of its displays as it is indiscriminate in its tastes. Setting the tone for the architecture is Louise Bourgeois's giant spider, which spent the 2001 season at Rockefeller Center but has reportedly found a permanent home—although real-life spiders, after staying still for a long period, are prone to sudden, unexpected moves (see Figure A.1). Roppongi Hills is, among other things, an expression of optimism in the future, when the chal-

FIGURE A.1 Spider by Louise Bourgeois (1911–). A spider by a Franco-American sculptor has found a fitting home in a global Tokyo, where people go about their business underneath with only an occasional passerby taking note. (© Photograph by Lore Schirokauer.)

lenges to Japan's technological edge and economic well-being are sure to increase. Meanwhile, internationally Japan's situation seemed stable but not without peril.

International Tensions

Although it was on good terms with its neighbors, Japan and its people remained aware of the dangers posed by tensions between the two Koreas, as well as those between the People's Republic of China and Taiwan—indeed, only the elderly could recall when it had been otherwise. Similarly, despite their own military buildup, the Japanese continue to rely on American diplomacy and military might, depending, in the final analysis, on the goodwill and good sense of the world's only superpower.

In the long run, the growth of the Chinese economy not only provides a splendid market for Japanese companies, but also a challenge to avoid overdependence on that potentially unstable market. Strong and strengthening economic ties and a common interest in the stability of the region—particularly the Korean Peninsula—continue to foster friendly relations between Japan and China, but they do so in the face of strong anti-Japanese sentiment among the Chinese populace unconvinced of the depth and sincerity of Japanese contrition, their misgivings confirmed by Koizumi's annual visits to the Yasukuni Shrine.

Anti-Japanese nationalism is particularly strong among China's youth and is particularly dangerous now that China's government's credibility depends on its performance in the economic and nationalist arenas. Japan is only indirectly involved in the future of Taiwan, but potentially dangerous points of friction are the tiny Senkaku/Diaoyu (or Diaoyu/Senkaku) Islands in the China Sea claimed by Japan as well as China and Taiwan.

Contending Trends

Contending trends can be found in almost every dimension of human life, including the political, the economic, and the relationship between politics and economics. On the one hand, globalization has entailed a strengthening of markets and has asserted pressure for financial and commercial restructuring; on the other, the establishment continues to hold great power in the L.D.P. and Koizumi's reform movement have lost much of their dynamism. Consciousness of the larger world, political and economic, is strong, but people are groping for a new definition of the role Japan should play in what some conjecture may end up as "China's Century." They may or may not be on the mark, but there is little prospect of the century being Japan's. For Japanese, unlike Germans and their neighbors, there is no East Asian political or cultural identity comparable in depth and strength to the one that has broadened the vision of many Europeans.

In the absence of a broader regional identity, some Japanese affirm their Japaneseness, others are determined internationalists, but most try to combine the two. This strategy is made considerably easier by the strong presence of Japanese designs, products, and a hybrid, transnational culture at home all over the globe, and, conversely, the presence in Japan of works by leading transnational, non-Japanese artists—represented here by an artist who was born French but became American.

For those in the know and those who listen to her words, Louise Bourgeois's signature spider represents motherliness, but, as with all effective contemporary sculpture, everyone is invited to let their imagination roam. Is she a symbol of creativity, persistence, and (although shown here without a web) interconnectedness, a symbol of female strength with a hint of potential menace? What is she doing there standing in front of Roppongi Hills as people go about their business underneath, with only an occasional passerby taking note? And what is she doing here at the conclusion of our book?

Appendix: Suggestions for Further Study

The literature in English on the history and civilization of Japan is so extensive that careful selection is imperative for student and researcher alike. The effort here has been to suggest books that are broad enough in scope to serve as introductions to their topics, that incorporate sound and recent scholarship, that make for good reading, and that in their totality reflect a variety of approaches. This listing gives special attention to sources with well-researched bibliographies. When such sources are up-to-date and readily available, additional readings are generally not given. Please also note that the length of individual subsections depends in part on the availability of a good recent source for further readings—not on the intrinsic importance of a topic nor on the current state of research. Therefore, there may be fewer items given for a well-researched topic on which there is a recent bibliographical essay or other source of readings than for a topic on which less work has been done but for which there exists no good bibliography. Textbooks and collections of classroom readings are not included. Years given are dates of first publication. For the most part, we have not listed here books already cited in the individual chapters.

General

"The Bibliography of Japanese History to 1912" at http://www.oriental.cam.ac.uk/jbib/ bibtitle.html covers a range of subjects. Less up to date but still valuable is John W. Dower and Timothy George, *Japanese History and Culture from Ancient to Modern Times: Seven Basic Bibliographies* (revised 2nd ed., 1995). Gary D. Allinson, *The Columbia Guide to Modern Japanese History* (1999), includes a resource guide. Helen Hardacre, *The Postwar Development of Japanese Studies in the United States* (1998), provides assessments, with bibliography, of the current state of American-Japanese studies on history, foreign relations, art, religion, literature, anthropology, political analysis, and law that prove excellent points of departure for further study. *The Cambridge History of Japan* is a major resource. Although outdated in varying degrees, the essays in these volumes offer reliable accounts of the field and provide bibliography for further study. However, inevitably there is some unevenness. The *Journal for Japanese Studies* is interdisciplinary and well edited, and *Monumenta Nipponica* includes articles on history, culture, and religion of consistently high quality. The *Kodansha Encyclopedia of Japan,* online or in its more extensive although less up-to-date print version, is a useful reference work. For a readable historical survey with edifying maps and extensive illustrations, see Martin Collcutt, Marius Jansen, and Isao Kumakura, *Cultural Atlas of Japan* (Facts on File, 1988).

Considering the explosion of knowledge, the age of monumental, all-inclusive syntheses seems past (and only teachers of survey courses and textbook writers are left to dare a general overview). It therefore seems unlikely that anyone soon will emulate George Sansom's *A History of Japan,* three vols. (1958–1963). Although out of date, it can still be read with profit and pleasure.

Sherman E. Lee, *A History of Far Eastern Art,* 5th ed. (1994), includes a consideration of Indian art that is helpful for understanding the Buddhist art of East Asia. It is a well-written, insightful perceptive but also a demanding book. European knowledge of Asia in early modern times and European reactions to Asian cultures and peoples is the subject of a detailed study: Donald Lach, *Asia in the Making of Europe,* 3 vols (Chicago, 1965). Surveys of early East Asian history and archeology are provided by Charles Holcombe, *The Genesis of East Asia 221 B.C.–A.D. 907* (2001), and Gina L. Barnes, *The Rise of Civilization in East Asia: The Archaeology of China, Korea, and Japan* (1999). Bruce Batten, *To the Ends of Japan: Premodern Frontiers, Boundaries, and Interactions* (2003), is an ambitious examination of Japan's premodern history viewed in terms of its borders.

A number of books concern intellectual and religion developments common to China and Japan. *East Asian Civilizations: A Dialogue in Five Stages* (1988), by Wm.Theodore de Bary, is a masterful brief interpretative overview of the mainstream of Chinese and Japanese intellectual history. For more recent perspectives, see *Rethinking Confucianism: Past and Present in China, Japan, Korea, and Vietnam,* edited by Benjamin A. Elman, John B. Duncan, and Herman Ooms (2002). Gilbert Rozman, ed., *The East Asian Region: Confucian Heritage and Its Modern Adaptation* (1991), contains stimulating essays treating Japanese Confucian tradition in comparative perspective. Also recommended is *Women and Confucian Cultures in Premodern China, Korea, and Japan,* edited by Dorothy Ko, JaHyun Kim Haboush, and Joan R. Piggott (2003).

The literature on Buddhism in English is rich and varied. Heinz Bechert and Richard Gombrich, *The World of Buddhism: Monks and Nuns in Society and Culture* (1984), is a well-illustrated introduction. Donald S. Lopez, Jr., *The Story of Buddhism: A Concise Guide to Its History and Teachings* (2001), is a more recent introduction. Two well-regarded books on Buddhist thought are Paul Williams, *Mahayana Buddhism: The Doctrinal Foundations* (1989), and Roger J. Corless, *The Vision of Buddhism: The Space Under the Tree* (1989). Donald W. Mitchell, *Buddhism: Introducing the Buddhist Experience* (2002), focuses on the history of Buddhist ideas and religious practice. There are good entries on many topics in Mircea Eliade, ed., *The Encyclopedia of Religion,* 16 vols. (1987, 2nd ed. forthcoming).

General Works on Culture, Literature, the Arts, Thought, and Religion

On the visual arts, see Penelope Mason, *History of Japanese Art* (2005). A still-valuable survey is Robert Treat Paine and Alexander Soper, *The Art and Architecture of Japan* (1955). Other fine books on art include the volumes in the *Heibonsha Survey of Japanese Art* (1972–1975) and *The Japanese Arts Library* (1976–). For the visual arts, see "Studies of Japanese Art by Period" at http://www.asiasociety.org/arts/japan_guide/index.html. William Howard Coaldrake, *Architecture and Authority in Japan* (1996), is a readable and wide-ranging survey.

For an introduction to literature, see J. Thomas Rimer, *A Reader's Guide to Japanese Literature* (1988). Donald Keene, *The Pleasures of Japanese Literature* (1988), is itself a pleasure, as are his collections, *Anthology of Japanese Literature* (1955) and *Modern Japanese Literature* (1956). Other important anthologies include Helen Craig McCullough, *Classical Japanese Prose: An Anthology* (1990); Steven Carter, *Traditional Japanese Poetry: An Anthology* (1991), Haruo Shirane, *Early Modern Japanese Literature: An Anthology, 1600–1900* (2002), and Theodore W. Goossen, *The Oxford Book of Japanese Short Stories* (1997). For an extensive and readable literary history, see Donald Keene's four volumes: *Seeds in the Heart: Japanese Literature from Earliest Times to the Late Sixteenth Century* (1993), *World within Walls: Japanese Literature of the Pre-Modern Era 1600–1867* (1976), and *Dawn to the West: Japanese Literature of the Modern Era* (two vols., 1984). A large and up-to-date listing of translations of premodern works can be found at "Classical Japanese Texts and Translations," http://www.meijigakuin.ac.jp/~pmjs/trans/trans.html.

On drama, see Karen Brazell, *Traditional Japanese Theater: An Anthology of Plays* (1998), and Benito Ortolani, *The Japanese Theater: From Shamanistic Ritual to Contemporary Pluralism* (1990).

H. Byron Earhart, *Japanese Religion: Unity and Diversity* (1974), is an excellent introduction, and Joseph M. Kitagawa, *Religion in Japanese History* (1966), is more extensive. See also George Tanabe, *Religions of Japan in Practice* (1999), and John Breen and Mark Teeuwen, eds., *Shinto in History: Ways of the Kami* (2000). Hitomi Tonomura et al., *Women and Class in Japanese History* (1999), includes essays covering all periods of Japanese history. Roy Andrew Miller, *The Japanese Language* (1967), is still of great interest, although a more recent survey is provided by Masayoshi Shibatani, *The Languages of Japan* (1990). Finally, fascinating accounts of two important areas of cultural and intellectual history can be found in Masayoshi Sugimoto and David Swain, *Science and Culture in Traditional Japan* (1989), and Peter Kornicki, *The Book in Japan: A Cultural History from the Beginning to the Nineteenth Century* (1998).

Beginnings and Foundations

The best introduction to prehistory can be found in Keiji Imamura, *Prehistoric Japan: New Perspectives on Insular East Asia* (1996). Richard Pearson, *Ancient Japan* (1992), is a lavishly illustrated and clearly written exhibition catalog. Junko Habu, *Ancient Jōmon* of Japan (2004), is demanding but up to date and informative, and Mark Hudson, *Ruins of Identity: Ethnogenesis in the Japanese Islands* (1999), is a clear survey of the onset of the Yayoi Period and subsequent developments. William Wayne Farris, *Sacred Texts and Buried Treasures: Issues in the Historical Archaeology of Ancient Japan* (1998), is thorough and accessible. For a groundbreaking account of the early state, see Joan Piggott, *The Emergence of Japanese Kingship* (1997). The eighth-century histories are available as Donald L. Philippi, *Kojiki* (1968), and William G. Aston, *Nihongi: Chronicles of Japan from the Earliest Times to A.D. 697* (1896, with multiple reprints). For translations of poems from these texts, the *Man'yōshū*, and other early sources, see Edwin Cranston, *A Waka Anthology, Vol. 1: The Gem-Glistening Cup* (1993).

Aristocrats, Monks, and Samurai

Institutional history from the Heian Period to the mid-sixteenth century is well represented in *The Cambridge History of Japan, Vol. 3,* edited by Kozo Yamamura (1990). It can be supplemented by the numerous books written and edited by John W. Hall and Jeffrey P. Mass. On politics, also see G. Cameron Hurst, III, *Insei: Abdicated Sovereigns in the Politics of Early Heian Japan* (1976). William Wayne Farris, *Population, Disease and Land in Early Japan, 645–900* (1985), presents findings and ideas that merit the attention of all students of early Japan. Robert Borgen, *Sugawara no Michizane and the Early Heian Court* (1986), is important for both political and cultural history. A recent treatment of Late Heian and early medieval history is Mikael Adolphson, *The Gates of Power: Monks, Courtiers and Warriors in Premodern Japan* (2000).

For more on the religion of the Heian Period, see Paul Groner, *Saichō: The Establishment of the Japanese Tendai School* (1984); Ryūichi Abé, *The Weaving of Mantra: Kūkai and the Construction of Esoteric Buddhist Discourse* (1999); and Allan G. Grapard, *The Protocol of the Gods: A Study of the Kasuga Cult in Japanese History* (1992).

Heian literature is well represented in translation (see the "Classical Japanese Texts and Translations" website), and there is a growing literature on the *Tale of Genji* in English. A useful introduction to Japan's greatest novel is Richard Bowring, *Murasaki Shikibu: The Tale of Genji* (1988). Critical studies include Norma Field, *Splendor of Longing in the Tale of Genji* (1987), and Haruo Shirane, *Bridge of Dreams: A Poetics of the Tale of Genji* (1987). A delightful although outdated description of Heian elite lifestyles is Ivan Morris, *The World of the Shining Prince: Court Life in Ancient Japan* (1964). In addition to the general anthologies cited previously, Joshua Mostow, *At the House of Gathered Leaves: Shorter Biographical and Autobiographical Narratives from Japanese Court Literature* (2004), provides a new perspective on Heian narrative. For an introduction to traditional poetry, see Koji Kawamoto, *The Poetics of Japanese Verse: Imagery, Structure, Meter* (2000).

An engaging survey of history from the Late Heian Period through the mid-sixteenth century is Pierre François Souyri, *The World Turned Upside Down: Medieval Japanese Society* (2001). The leading Western authority on Kamakura institutional history was Jeffrey P. Mass, who wrote and edited several books. Good places to start are *The Bakufu in Japanese History* (1985), edited with William B. Hauser and concerning later periods, and *Yoritomo and the Founding of the First Bakufu: The Origins of Dual Government in Japan* (1999). Also see Karl F. Friday, *Samurai, Warfare, and the State in Early Medieval Japan* (2004). Andrew Goble, *Kenmu: Go-Daigo's Revolution* (1997), is a superb study of the attempt at imperial restoration during the Kamakura–Ashikaga transition. Two books by H. Paul Varley are recommended for the political history of the fourteenth and fifteenth centuries: *Imperial Restoration in Medieval Japan* (1971) and *The Onin War* (1967).

Suzanne Gay, *The Moneylenders of Late Medieval Kyoto* (2001), shows how things actually worked. The history of Kyoto is further explored in Mary Elizabeth Berry, *The Culture of Civil War in Kyoto* (1994), already cited in our text. We also recommend Thomas Conlan, *State of War: The Violent Order of Fourteenth Century Japan* (2003).

William R. LaFleur, *The Karma of Words: Buddhism and the Literary Arts in Medieval Japan* (1983), includes an excellent description of Buddhism, literary analysis, and a provocative thesis. Daigan and Alicia Matsunaga, *Foundations of Japanese Buddhism* (two vols., 1976), provides a detailed account of Japanese Buddhism. James Dobbins, *Jodo Shinshu: Shin Buddhism in Medieval Japan* (1989), deals with a subject central to Kamakura religious history.

There is a vast literature on Zen. The standard work on its history remains Heinrich Dumoulin, *Zen Buddhism: A History: Japan,* 2nd ed. (1989). For an excellent philosophical study, see T. P. Kasulis, *Zen Action–Zen Person* (1981). On the monasteries and their role in society, see Martin Collcutt, *Five Mountains: The Rinzai Zen Monastic Institution in Medieval Japan* (1981). Recommended with enthusiasm is Jan Fontein and Money L. Hickman, *Zen Painting and Calligraphy* (1970), a catalog of an exhibition of both Chinese and Japanese works. For other works on the arts, see the appropriate volumes in *The Japanese Arts Library* (1976–) and *Heibonsha Survey of Japanese Art* (1972–1975) series. Paul Varley and Kumakura Isao, eds., *Tea in Japan: Essays on the History of Chanoyu* (1989), is recommended on this subject.

The heroes of an age reveal much about its values: See Helen Craig McCullough, trans., *Yoshitsune: A Fifteenth-Century Japanese Chronicle* (1971). Among McCullough's numerous contributions to our understanding of traditional Japanese literature is her translation of *The Tale of the Heike* (1988), which includes a description of this work as literature. Other aspects of the period's literature are apparent in Donald Keene's translation of the *Essays in Idleness* (1967), and Thomas B. Hare, *Zeami's Style: The Noh Plays of Zeami Motokiyo* (1986). *Japan in the Muromachi Age* (1977), John W. Hall and Toyoda Takeshi, eds., includes essays on cultural and social–political topics.

Modern General

James L. McClain, *Japan: A Modern History* (2002), a masterful survey begins with the Tokugawa Period. The following recent surveys are also worthy of consideration: Andrew Gordon, *A Modern History of Japan from Tokugawa to the Present* (2003), and Elise K. Tipton, *Modern Japan: A Social and Political History* (2003). Also see *The Making of Modern Japan* (2000) by Marius Jansen, author of many thoughtful and well-researched books. Conrad Totman, *Early Modern Japan* (1993), is particularly strong on the history of the environment. Helen Hardacre, *The Postwar Development of Japanese Studies in the United States* (1998), mentioned previously, provides assessments with bibliography of the current state of American-Japanese studies on history, foreign relations, art, religion, literature, anthropology, political analysis, and law that prove excellent points of departure for further study.

Volumes 5 and 6 of the *Cambridge History of Japan,* edited by Marius Jansen and Peter Duus, respectively, deal with the nineteenth and twentieth centuries. Akira Iriye, *Japan and the Wider World: From the Mid-Nineteenth Century to the Present* (1997), is a survey by a senior authority. Andrew Gordon, ed., *Postwar Japan as History* (1993), contains essays on social, cultural, political, and economic history by the foremost contemporary scholars.

Tessa Morris-Suzuki, *A History of Japanese Economic Thought* (1989), provides a clear and balanced brief survey of its topic from the Tokugawa to the present. Also see the same author's *The Technological Transformation of Japan: From the Seventeenth to the Twenty-First Century* (1994). Similarly broad in scope are the essays of Thomas C. Smith collected under the title, *Japanese Industrialization, 1750–1920* (1988). For a more recent masterly and geographically informed study of the same period, see Karen Wigen, *The Making of a Japanese Periphery, 1750–1920* (1995).

A. J. H. Lathan and Heira Kawakatsu, *Japanese Industrialization and the Asian Economy* (1994), is an important, and in places somewhat technical, contribution to economic history. Albert Craig and Donald H. Shively, eds., *Personality in Japanese History* (1971), spans the last two centuries.

Donald Keene, *Dawn to the West: Japanese Literature of the Modern Era* (two vols., 1998–1999), is a comprehensive and authoritative account of modern Japanese literature from the Meiji Period until the present with an extensive bibliography. A fine book that approaches modern Japanese literature through its historical roots is J. Thomas Rimer, *Modern Japanese Fiction and its Traditions: An*

Introduction (1978). On poetry, see Makoto Ueda, *Modern Japanese Poets and the Nature of Literature* (1983). William Howard Coaldrake, *Architecture and Authority in Japan* (1996), begins with the Ise Shrine and ends with contemporary Japan. Donald Richie, *A Hundred Years of Japanese Film* (2001), is highly recommended as the work of a distinguished, perceptive, and erudite critic.

Tokugawa and Its Immediate Background

For the Tokugawa political system and its background, see Harold Bolitho, *Treasures among Men: The Fudai Daimyo in Tokugawa Japan* (1974). Many aspects of the Tokugawa system go back to Hideyoshi; see Mary Elizabeth Berry, *Hideyoshi* (1984). Hideyoshi also appears as a major player in George Elison, *Deus Destroyed: The Image of Christianity in Early Modern Japan* (1973). Another well-written, informative account is C. R. Boxer, *The Christian Century in Japan* (1951). Also see Michael Cooper, *They Came to Japan: An Anthology of European Reports on Japan, 1543–1640* (1965, 1974).

For foreign relations under the Tokugawa, see Ronald P. Toby, *State and Diplomacy in Early Modern Japan: Asia in the Development of the Tokugawa Bakufu* (1984). Tokugawa was the age of the samurai; see *The Taming of the Samurai: Honorific Individualism and the Making of Modern Japan* by Eiko Ikegami (1995). For insight into what it meant to be a woman in a late Tokugawa samurai family, see Edwin McClellan, *Woman in the Crested Kimono: The Life of Shibue Io and Her Family Drawn from Mori Ogai's "Shibue Chusai"* (1985), and *Women of the Mito Domain: Recollections of Samurai Family Life* by Yamakawa Kikue, Kate Wildman Nakai, trans. (2001). *Tokugawa Japan: The Social and Economic Antecedents of Modern Japan,* edited by Chie Nakane and Shinzaburō Ōishi and translated by Conrad Totman (1990), presents the views of Japanese scholars, including those of the influential Chie Nakane.

The variety of Tokugawa thought and of scholars' approach to it is illustrated by Herman Ooms, *Tokugawa Ideology: Early Constructs, 1570–1680* (1985), and Mary Evelyn Tucker, *Moral and Spiritual Cultivation in Japanese Neo-Confucianism: The Life and Thought of Kaibara Ekken (1630–1714)* (1989). For the intellectual history of the merchant class, see the important book by Tetsuo Najita, *Visions of Virtue in Tokugawa Japan: The Kaitokudo Merchant Academy of Osaka* (1987). Najita's *Readings in Tokugawa Thought* (1998) provides translations of twenty-four Japanese articles. James McMullen, *Idealism, Protest, and the Tale of Genji: The Confucianism of Kumazawa Banzan (1619–1691)* (1999), is highly recommended. A good place to begin studying nativism is Peter Nosco, *Remembering Paradise: Nativism and Nostalgia in Eighteenth-Century Japan* (1990). A delightful book on Dutch Learning is Donald Keene, *The Japanese Discovery of Europe, 1720–1830* (1969). Keene is also author of the masterful survey *World within Walls: Japanese Literature of the Pre-Modern Era, 1600–1867* (1976). Benito Ortolani, *The Japanese Theatre: From Shamanistic Ritual to Contemporary Pluralism,* revised ed. (1995), is a valuable resource. Ronald P. Dore, *Education in Tokugawa Japan* (1965), is a major study of a major topic.

The lively culture of the Tokugawa is depicted in several books. Howard Hibbett, *The Floating World in Japanese Fiction* (1959), remains a good place to begin, as does Richard Lane, *Images from The Floating World: The Japanese Print* (1978). On Japan's master of haiku, see Haruo Shirane, *Traces of Dreams: Landscape, Culture, Memory, and the Poetry of Basho* (1997). For individual artists, see the volumes in the *Masterworks of Ukiyo-e* series published by Kodansha (1968–). Other worthy books on Tokugawa art include *Hokusai: One Hundred Views of Mt. Fuji,* introduction and commentaries by Henry D. Smith, II (1988), and the same author's *Ando Hiroshige 1797–1858: One Hundred Famous Views of Edo* (1999, 1981). Elise Grilli's superb *The Art of the Japanese Screen* (1970) is a beautiful book, a feast for mind and eye.

Local history has proved a particular fertile field of research with far-reaching implications. Notable recent studies include Philip C. Brown, *Central Authority and Local Autonomy in the Formation of Early Modern Japan: The Case of Kaga Domain* (1993); Herman Ooms, *Tokugawa Village Practice: Class, Status, Power, Law* (1996); and Luke S. Roberts, *Mercantilism in a Japanese Domain: The Merchant Origins of Economic Nationalism in 18th-Century Tosa* (1998). Two studies that include solid research on the Tokugawa Period, even as they take the story beyond the Meiji Restoration, are Karen Wigen, *The Making of a Japanese Periphery, 1750–1920* (1995), and David L. Howell, *Capitalism from Within: Economy, Society, and the State in a Japanese Fishery* (1995). The rewards of comparative urban studies are illustrated by *Edo and Paris: Urban Life and the State in the Early Modern Era,* edited by James L. McClain, John M. Merriman, and Kaoru Ugawa (1994). Also see Nishiyama Matsunosuke and Gerald Groemer, trans., *Edo Culture: Daily Life in Urban Japan, 1600–1868* (1997), and Susan B. Hanley, *Everyday Things in Premodern Japan: The Hidden Legacy of Material Culture* (1997).

The investigation of traditionally neglected topics continues to enliven the study of Tokugawa history. Although different in all but the solidity of their scholarship, the following three books are essential reading in major aspects of Tokugawa history: Ann B. Jannetta, *Epidemics and Mortality in Early Modern Japan* (1987); Gregory M. Pflugfelder, *The Cartography of Desire: Male–Male Sexuality in Japanese Discourse, 1600–1950* (1999); and Conrad Totman, *The Origins of Japan's Modern Forests* (1985), which analyzes and documents a case of successful reforestation and poses a basic question: "What level of human disaster must overtake a society before it is moved to confront its problems?" (p. 58).

Meiji

Meiji was the formative period of modern capitalism. For underlying ideas and attitudes, see Byron K. Marshall, *Capitalism and Nationalism in Prewar Japan: The Ideology of the Business Elite, 1868–1941* (1967), and Earl Kinmonth, *The Self-Made*

Man in Meiji Japanese Thought (1981). Mikiso Hane, *Peasants, Rebels, and Outcastes: The Underside of Modern Japan* (1982), calls attention to those who did not benefit from "modernization." See also E. Patricia Tsurumi, *Factory Girls: Women in the Thread Mills of Meiji Japan* (1990); Andrew Gordon, *The Evolution of Labor Relations in Japanese Heavy Industry, 1853–1955* (1985); the same author's *Labor and Imperial Democracy in Prewar Japan* (1991); and Sheldon Garon, *The State and Labor in Modern Japan* (1987). On agriculture, see Penelope Francks, *Technology and Agriculture Development in Pre-War Japan* (1984) and *Agriculture and Economic Development in East Asia: From Growth to Protectionism in Japan, Korea, and Taiwan* (1999). Michael A. Barnhart, *Japan and the World since 1868* (1995), provides a concise account.

Donald Keene, *Emperor of Japan: Meiji and His World, 1885–1912* (2002), is a masterful account of the Meiji Emperor. For Meiji political history, the following are still useful: George Akita, *Foundations of Constitutional Government in Modern Japan* (1967); Nobutaka Ike, *The Beginnings of Political Democracy in Japan* (1950); and Joseph Pittau, *Political Thought in Early Meiji Japan, 1868–1889* (1967). A study of a major Meiji statesman is provided in Roger F. Hackett, *Yamagata Aritomo in the Rise of Modern Japan, 1838–1922* (1971). An important institutional development is examined in Robert M. Spaulding, Jr., *Imperial Japan's Higher Civil Service Examinations* (1967). Also see Mark E. Lincicome, *Principle, Praxis, and the Politics of Educational Reform in Meiji Japan* (1997).

A good way to begin studying Meiji intellectual history is by examining the life and ideas of Fukuzawa Yukichi. His *An Encouragement of Learning,* David A. Dilworth and Umeyo Hirano, trans. (1969), is a collection of essays written in the 1870s. Also worth reading is *The Autobiography of Fukuzawa Yukichi,* Eiichi Kiyooka, trans. (1934). Important secondary studies are Carmen Blacker, *The Japanese Enlightenment: A Study of the Writings of Fukuzawa Yukichi* (1964), and an article by Albert Craig in *Political Development in Modern Japan,* Robert E. Ward, ed. (1973, 1968). Also see James L. Huffmann, *Creating a Public: People and Press in Meiji Japan* (1998), and William R. Braisted, trans. and ed., *Meiroku Zasshi: Journal of the Japanese Enlightenment* (1976). Two other valuable books on intellectual history are Kenneth B. Pyle, *The New Generation in Meiji Japan: Problems of Cultural Identity, 1885–1895* (1969), and Irwin Scheiner, *Christian Converts and Social Protest in Meiji Japan* (1970). For intellectual and social history from a different perspective, see Sharon Sievers, *Flowers in Salt: The Beginnings of Feminism in Modern Japan* (1983). This might be read with Gail L. Bernstein, ed., *Recreating Japanese Women, 1600–1945* (1991).

For Meiji art, see Frederick Baekeland's *Imperial Japan: The Art of the Meiji Era, 1868–1912* (1980) and Julia Meech-Pekarik, *The World of the Meiji Print: Impressions of a New Civilization* (1986). For literature, see Donald Keene's *Dawn to the West: Japanese Literature of the Modern Era* (two vols., 1998–1999). A good selection of the period's foremost poet is contained in *Masaoka Shiki: Selected Poems,* Burton Watson, trans. (1998); Robert A. Rosenstone, *Mirror in the Shrine: American Encounters with Meiji Japan* (1988), is subtle and sensitive.

Late Meiji and Imperial Japan

Late Meiji saw the beginnings of imperial Japan. Carol Gluck, *Japan's Modern Myths: Ideology in the Late Meiji Period* (1985), is a brilliant, nuanced study that considers a range of sources. *Japan's Competing Modernities: Issues in Culture and Democracy,* Sharon A. Minichiello, ed. (1998), is a collection of essays on important issues.

L. W. G. Beasley, *Japanese Imperialism, 1894–1945* (1987), is a thoughtful synthesis. For a major recent study, see Louise Young, *Japan's Total Empire: Manchuria and the Culture of Wartime Imperialism* (1998). *The Japanese Empire, 1895–1945,* Ramon H. Myers and Mark R. Peattie, ed. (1984); *Japan's Informal Empire in China, 1895–1937,* Peter Duus, Myers, and Peattie, ed. (1989); and *The Japanese Wartime Empire,* Duus, Myers, Peattie, and Zhou Wanyao, ed. (1996), all published by Princeton University Press, are all recommended.

Late Meiji politics are analyzed by Tetsuo Najita in *Hara Kei in the Politics of Compromise, 1905–1915* (1967). For the political system as it developed during the next decade, see Peter Duus, *Party Rivalry and Political Change in Taishō Japan* (1968). For the 1930s, see Gordon M. Berger, *Parties out of Power in Japan: 1931–1941* (1977), and Michael A. Barnhart, *Japan Prepares for Total War: The Search for Economic Security, 1919–1941* (1987).

The increasing reach of the state is the topic of Sheldon Garon, *Molding Japanese Minds: The State in Everyday Life* (1997). Also see Helen Hardacre, *Shinto and the State. 1868–1988* (1989). J. Thomas Rimer, ed., *Culture and Identity: Japanese Intellectuals during the Interwar Years* (1990), is wide ranging. Gail L. Bernstein, *Japanese Marxist: A Portrait of Kawakami Hajime (1879–1946)* (1976, 1990), is indispensable for the study of Japanese Marxism. Kevin Michael Doak, *Dreams of Difference: The Japan Romantic School and the Crisis of Modernity* (1994), is a closely argued study that excels in placing 1930s Japanese discourse in an international perspective. *Overcome by Modernity: History, Culture, and Community in Interwar Japan* by Harry D. Harootunian (2000) is brilliant and difficult. Also see Harootunian, *History's Disquiet: Modernity, Cultural Practice, and the Question of Everyday Life* (2000).

Most major writers are available in excellent translations too numerous to list here, and there is a growing corpus of secondary studies. See http://library.kcc.hawaii.edu/asdp/biblio/lit/easian/japan/jplitbib.htm. For Japan's own critics, we suggest two books by Paul Anderer, *Arishima Takeo and the Bounds of Modern Fiction* (1983) and *Literature of the Lost Home: Kobayashi Hideo—Literary Criticism, 1924–1939* (1995). Also see Karatani Kōjin, *Origins of Modern Japanese Literature,* Brett de Bary, trans. (1993), and Maeda Ai, *Text and the City: Essays on Japanese Modernity,* edited with an introduction by James A. Fujii (2004).

On a different facet of cultural history see J. Victor Koschmann, Keibo Oiwa, and Shinji Yamashita, *International Perspectives on Yanagita Kunio and Japanese Folklore Studies* (1985).

A great deal has been written about the Pacific War. Barbara J. Brooks, *Japan's Imperial Diplomacy: Consuls, Treaty Ports, and War in China 1895–1938* (2000), provides a fresh look at the Foreign Ministry officials involved in China policy. Edward J. Drea, *In the Service of the Emperor: Essays on the Imperial Japanese Army* (1998), is a good place to begin reading on the Japanese army. For the navy, see Paul S. Dull, *A Battle History of the Japanese Navy* (1978). Additional perspectives are provided by Akira Iriye, *Power and Culture: The Japanese–American War, 1941–1945* (1981), and John W. Dower, *War without Mercy: Race and Power in the Pacific War* (1986). Saburo Ienaga, *The Pacific War 1931–1945: A Critical Perspective on Japan's Role in World War II* (1978), is an unflinching account of the "dark valley."

The Pacific War began with Pearl Harbor and ended with the atomic bomb. Both events have been written about extensively and remain controversial. On Pearl Harbor, see Gordon Prange, *Pearl Harbor: The Verdict of History* (1985), and *Pearl Harbor Reexamined: Prologue to the Pacific War,* Hilary Conroy and Harry Wray, ed. (1990). The emperor's role before and during the war is examined in depth in *Hirohito and the Making of Modern Japan* by Herbert Bix (2000). For a bibliography on the atomic bomb, see http://www.doug-long.com/bibliog.htm. For a study of how the war is remembered in different places and by different peoples, see *Perilous Memories: The Asia–Pacific War,* T. Fujitani, Geoffrey M. White, and Lisa Yoneyama, eds. (2001).

Postwar and Contemporary

The basic book on the occupation of Japan is John W. Dower, *Embracing Defeat: Japan in the Wake of World War II* (1999). Also see Dower's *Japan in War and Peace: Selected Essays* (1993).

Nathan Thayer, *How the Conservatives Rule Japan* (1969), is a cogent analysis of the system of local support organizations. Also see Gerald L. Curtis, *The Japanese Way of Politics* (1988). For a blow-by-blow analysis of the L.D.P.'s response to various challenges until the 1980s, see Kent E. Calder, *Crisis and Compensation: Public Policy and Political Stability in Japan, 1949–1986* (1988). One of the more interesting and informative analyses of Japanese politics remains Karel Van Wolferen, *The Enigma of Japanese Power* (1989).

The end of the Showa Period (1926–1989) with the death of the emperor drew new attention to his role during the war and stimulated some to look at the Showa Period as a whole. One happy result was the publication of *Showa: The Japan of Hirohito* edited by Carol Gluck and Stephen R. Graubard (1992). Norma Field, *In the Realm of the Dying Emperor: Japan at Century's End* (1991), is eloquent and vivid.

Theodore C. Bestor, *Neighborhood Tokyo* (1989), is a worthy sequel to Ronald P. Dore's fascinating and thoughtful *City Life in Japan: A Study of a Tokyo Ward* (1958). A book with implications beyond Japan is David Plath, *Long Engagements: Maturity in Modern Japan* (1980). Plath is also the editor of *Work and Life Course in Japan* (1983).

Studies of the changing role of women include Jane Hunter, ed., *Japanese Women Working* (1993); Mary C. Brinton, *Women and the Economic Miracle: Gender and Work in Postwar Japan* (1993); and Anne E. Imamura, *Re-Imagining Japanese Women* (1996). Also see Vera C. Mackle, *Fighting Women: A History of Feminism in Modern Japan* (1997).

A great deal has been written on the postwar Japanese economy. Ezra Vogel's influential *Japan as Number One: Lessons for America* (1985) exemplifies the views of its time. A valuable perspective is provided by Hugh T. Patrick in his *The Development of Studies of the Japanese Economy in the United States: A Personal Odyssey* (1988). His many other works are recommended, including *Crisis and Change in the Japanese Financial System* (2000). Gavan McCormack, *The Emptiness of Japanese Affluence* (1996), is a trenchant indictment of environmental abuse, political irresponsibility, and unmitigated developmentalism. See William J. Holstein, *The Japanese Power Game: What it Means for America* (1990), for a picture of the business–bureaucrats–politician nexus in the 1980s.

Shunsuke Tsurumi, *A Cultural History of Postwar Japan 1945–1980* (1987), is unsystematic but contains worthwhile information on popular culture. Also see Ross Mover and Yoshio Sugimoto, *Images of Japanese Society: A Study of the Structure of Social Reality* (1986), and John Whittier Treat, ed., *Contemporary Japan and Popular Culture* (1996). Peter N. Dale, *The Myth of Japanese Uniqueness* (1986), pulls no punches.

A Hundred Years of Japanese Film is by Donald Richie (2001), the foremost foreign critic and student of Japanese film. The serious student of films will also want to consult Beverly B. Bueher, *Japanese Films: A Filmography and Commentary, 1921–1990* (1990). Fortunately for those interested in fiction, the works of the writers described in the text are available in good translations, and the number of works available in English continues to increase. The Japanese enthusiasm for reading extends also to comic books; see Sharon Kinsella, *Adult Manga: Culture and Power in Contemporary Japanese Society* (1998). D. P. Martinez, *The Worlds of Japanese Popular Culture: Gender, Shifting Boundaries and Global Cultures* (1998), includes descriptions of sumo, soccer, and other sports; karaoke and soap operas; woman's magazines and morning television dramas.

Ian Reader, *Religion in Contemporary Japan* (1991), is based on intimate knowledge gained from fieldwork and from reading. The same holds for the book he coauthored with George J. Tanabe, *Practically Religious: World Benefits and the Common History of Japan* (1998). Another outstanding book on Japanese religion is Karen A. Smyers, *The Fox and the Jewel: Symbolizing Shared and Private Meaning in Japanese Inari Worship* (1998).

Botond Bogner, *The New Japanese Architecture* (1990), is a valuable study. Katsukiyo Matsuba, *Ando, Architect* (1998), examines a leading contemporary Japanese architect (and a Schirokauer favorite). The Japanese tradition of woodworking is evoked by the American master craftsman George Nakashima in his *The Soul of a Tree: A Woodworker's Reflections* (1988).

Photo Credits

This page constitutes an extension of the copyright page. We have made every effort to trace the ownership of all copyrighted material and to secure permission from copyright holders. In the event of any question arising as to the use of any material, we will be pleased to make the necessary corrections in future printings. Thanks are due to the following authors, publishers, and agents for permission to use the material indicated.

A.1: Photograph Lore Schirokauer **PO.1:** © TNM Image Archives, http://TNMArchives.jp **PO.2:** © Tokyo National Museum **PO.3:** © Tokyo National Museum **PO.4:** © Schirokauer Collection

Chapter 1. 1.02: © The Cleveland Museum of Art, John L. Severance Fund, 1984.68 **1.03:** © Scala/Art Resource, NY **1.04:** © Tohoku University Archeology Laboratory stored **1.05:** © Tomb of Emperor Nintoku, Mozu, Sakai City Osaka

Chapter 2. 2.02: © Archivo Iconografico, S.A./CORBIS **2.03:** © Askaen **2.04:** © Chris Lisle/CORBIS **2.05:** © Chris Lisle/CORBIS **2.06:** © Lore Schirokauer **2.07:** © Askaen **2.07:** © Askaen **2.08:** © Askaen **2.09a:** © Lore Schirokauer **2.09b:** From Robert Treat Paine & Alexander Soper, *The Art and Architecture of Japan: Pelican History of Art,* 2nd revised ed. (Penguin Books, 1974), p. 186. Reprinted with permission. **2.10:** © Schirokauer Collection

Chapter 3. 3.01: © Lore Schirokauer **3.02:** Calligraphy by Dr. Léon L.Y. Chang **3.03:** © Lore Schirokauer **3.04:** © Muroji Publishers **3.05:** © Sakamoto Photo Research Laboratory/CORBIS **3.06:** © *Red Fudo,* Myooin, Koyasan, Wakayama **3.07:** © The Tokugawa Art Museum **3.08:** © Kozanji, Kyoto **3.09:** © Sakamoto Research Laboratory/CORBIS **3.10:** © Lore Schirokauer

Chapter 4. 4.02: © Rokuhara Mutsuji, Kyoto/M. Asanuma **4.03:** © Michael S. Yamashita/CORBIS **4.04:** Photo by Mark Schumacher, www.onmarkproductions.com **4.05:** © Royalty-Free/CORBIS **4.06a:** © Lore Schirokauer **4.06b:** © Lore Schirokauer **4.07a and b:** From Robert Treat Paine and Alexander Soper, *The Art and Architecture of Japan* (Pelican History of Art, 2nd rev. ed., 1974). Reprinted with permission of Penguin Books Ltd.

Chapter 5. 5.01: © "Six Persimmons" by Muqi, Daitokuji, Kyoto **5.02:** © "Patriarchs of the Three Creeds" by Josetsu, Ryosokuin, Kyoto **5.03:** © Tokyo National Museum **5.04:** © Lore Schirokauer **5.05:** © Lore Schirokauer **5.06:** © 1988 Kyoto National Museum

Chapter 6. 6.01: © Lore Schirokauer **6.02:** © Sakamoto Photo Research Laboratory/CORBIS **6.03:** © Sakamoto Photo Research Laboratory/CORBIS **6.04:** © Tokyo National Museum **6.06:** © Freer Gallery of Art, Smithsonian Institution, Washington, D.C.: Purchase, F1965.22 **6.07:** © Rijksmuseum voor Volkenkunde Leiden

Chapter 7. 7.02: © Kyoto National Museum **7.03:** © Sakamoto Photo Research Laboratory/CORBIS **7.04:** © Allen Memorial Art Museum, Oberlin College, Ohio. Mary A. Ainsworth Bequest, 1950.202 **7.05:** © Fine Arts Museum of San Francisco, Achenbach Foundation for Graphic Arts Purchase (A057901 1970.25.14) **7.06:** Museum Purchase made possible by the Margaret Watson Parker Art Collection Fund 1968/2.22 **7.07:** © Mr. & Mrs. John D. Rockefeller, 3rd Collection of Asian Art 1979.219. Asia Society, New York: Photograph by Lynton Gardiner **7.08:** © Spencer Collection (SOR579:Hokusai), New York Public Library, Astor, Lennox, and Tilden Foundations

Chapter 8. 8.02: Courtesy of the Peabody Essex Museum **8.03:** Courtesy of the Peabody Essex Museum **8.04:** "The Ginza" Taisei Corporation

Chapter 9. 9.01: © Imperial Household, Tokyo, Japan **9.02:** © Arthur M. Sackler Gallery, Smithsonian Institution, Washington, D.C.: Robert O. Muller Collection, S2003.8.1179 **9.03:** © "Morning Toilet" by Kuroda Seiki

Chapter 10. 10.01: © Arthur M. Sackler Gallery of Art, Smithsonian Institution, Washington, D.C.: Gift of Gregory and Patricia Kruglak, S1999.131. **10.02:** © TNM Image Archives, http://TnmArchives.jp/ **10.03:** © Nagasaki Prefectural Art Museum **10.04:** © Kyoto Municipal Museum of Art **10.05:** Collection of The National Museum of Modern Art, Tokyo. © Togo Tamami. Used by permission

Chapter 11. 11.02: From *Woodcuts of Wartime China, 1937–1945,* Yonghua lingxin, ed. (Taiwan: Li Ming Cultural Enterprises, Dist.) **11.03:** © The Mainichi Newspapers Co. **11.05:** © John Van Hasselt/CORBIS SYGMA

Chapter 12. 12.01: © AP/Wide World Photos (APA5163982) **12.02:** © Lore Schirokauer **12.03:** "Tornado" from the series "In Praise of Shokei" by Munakata Shiko, Munakata Museum in Kamakura **12.04:** Arata Isozaki & Associates, Photo by Yasuhiro Ishimoto **12.05:** © Lore Schirokauer

Text Credits

This page constitutes an extension of the copyright page. We have made every effort to trace the ownership of all copyrighted material and to secure permission from copyright holders. In the event of any question arising as to the use of any material, we will be pleased to make the necessary corrections in future printings. Thanks are due to the following authors, publishers, and agents for permission to use the material indicated.

Chapter 2. 25: From *Sources of Korean Tradition,* ed. by Peter H. Lee and Wm. Theodore de Bary. New York: Columbia University Press, 1997, p. 54. **33:** From Ryusaku Tsunoda and L. Carrington Goodrich. *Japan in the Chinese Dynastic Histories,* 2ed. (Kyoto: Perkins Oriental Books, 1968), pp. 40–41. **39–40:** From Edwin Cranston, *A Waka Anthology Volume I: The Gem-Glistening Cup* (Stanford: Stanford University Press, 1993), p. 205. Copyright © 1993 by the Board of Trustees of the Leland Stanford Jr. University. All rights reserved. Used with permission of Stanford University Press, www.sup.org. **40:** From Edwin Cranston, *A Waka Anthology Volume I: The Gem-Glistening Cup* (Stanford: Stanford University Press, 1993), p. 362–363. Copyright © 1993 by the Board of Trustees of the Leland Stanford Jr. University. All rights reserved. Used with permission of Stanford University Press, www.sup.org.

Chapter 3. 62: From Burton Watson, trans., *Japanese Literature in Chinese, Volume I* (New York: Columbia University Press, 1975), pp. 122. **63:** From Steven Carter, *Traditional Japanese Poetry: An Anthology* (Stanford University Press, 1991), pp. 106–107. Copyright © 1991 by the Board of Trustees of the Leland Stanford Jr. University. All rights reserved. Used with permission of Stanford University Press, www.sup.org. **63:** From Steven Carter, *Traditional Japanese Poetry: An Anthology* (Stanford University Press, 1991), p. 84. **64:** From Helen McCullough, *Classical Japanese Prose: An Anthology.* Copyright © 1990 by the Board of Trustees of the Leland Stanford Jr. University. All rights reserved. Used with permission of Stanford University Press, www.sup.org.

Chapter 4. 96–97: From Steven Carter, *Traditional Japanese Poetry: An Anthology* (Stanford University Press, 1991), p. 161. Copyright © 1991 by the Board of Trustees of the Leland Stanford Jr. University. All rights reserved. Used with permission of Stanford University Press, www.sup.org. **97:** From Earl Miner, *An Introduction to Japanese Court Poetry.* Copyright © 1968 by the Board of Trustees of the Leland Stanford Jr. University. All rights reserved. Used with permission of

Stanford University Press, www.sup.org. **97:** From Steven Carter, *Traditional Japanese Poetry: An Anthology* (Stanford University Press, 1991), p. 197. Copyright © 1991 by the Board of Trustees of the Leland Stanford Jr. University. All rights reserved. Used with permission of Stanford University Press, www.sup.org. **97:** Steven Carter, *Traditional Japanese Poetry: An Anthology* (Stanford University Press, 1991), p. 133.

Chapter 7. 156: From Ryusaku Tsunoda, W. Theodore de Bary, and Donald Keene, comps., *Sources of Japanese Tradition* (New York: Columbia University Press, 1958), p. 454. **157:** From Clavin French, *The Poet-Painters: Buson and His Follower,* exhibition catalog (Ann Arbor: University of Michigan Museum of Art, 1974), p. 132. Used with permission.

Index